Also by Al Gore

Earth in the Balance:
Ecology and the Human Spirit

Also by Tipper Gore

Picture This:
A Visual Diary

Raising PG Kids in an X-Rated Society

JOINED
at the
HEART

To Al & Molly,

Al Doe Blggington

JOINED

at the

HEART

———————

THE TRANSFORMATION

OF THE

AMERICAN FAMILY

AL *and* **TIPPER GORE**

HENRY HOLT AND COMPANY | NEW YORK

Henry Holt and Company, LLC
Publishers since 1866
115 West 18th Street
New York, New York 10011

Henry Holt® is a registered trademark of
Henry Holt and Company, LLC.

Library of Congress Cataloging-in-Publication Data

Gore, Albert, 1948–
   Joined at the heart : the transformation of the American family /
Al and Tipper Gore.
     p.   cm.
   Includes bibliographical references and index.
   ISBN 0-8050-6893-7 (hb)
    1. Family—United States.   I. Gore, Tipper, 1948–   II. Title.

HQ536 .G666   2002
306.85'0973—dc21

                             2002027252

Henry Holt books are available for special promotions and
premiums. For details contact: Director, Special Markets.

First Edition 2002

DESIGNED BY KELLY S. TOO

PHOTOGRAPHS BY TIPPER GORE

Printed in the United States of America
1 3 5 7 9 10 8 6 4 2

To our parents and our children,
with love and gratitude for teaching us about family;
to our grandparents and grandchildren,
with happiness and a joyful prayer
that the circle be unbroken.

Set me as a seal upon thine heart.

—SOLOMON

Make use of what I leave in love.

—ANNE BRADSTREET

.

Contents

JOINED
at the
HEART

INTRODUCTION

We started dreaming of having a family soon after we met, thirty-seven years ago. We were just teenagers then, and unlike most high school sweethearts these days, we somehow grew together instead of apart. Now, four children, two grandchildren, and thirty-two years of marriage later, we are looking beyond the family we have created together to write a book about the rapidly changing American family.

This work has taken on a deeper meaning for us over the two years we have devoted to it. In the months that have passed since the attacks of September 11, 2001, a lot of people have told us that they have been thinking long and hard about what is most important to them in life—and have concluded, as we have, that a big part of the answer is family. But where do you go from there? It's not enough to mouth clichés like "quality time." Most people have been reflecting deeply on *why* family is so important to them, and they want to make changes in their lives that truly reflect the commitments they feel in their hearts.

They are asking, as we have, what comes next? After making a decision to genuinely rededicate ourselves to our families, what can we do, in today's busy world, to follow through in good conscience? How do we deal with all of the extraordinary changes that American families have been going through in the last few decades? What does it mean to be a family today?

That is what this book is all about. We have written it because of our unshakable belief that a strong and successful family can bring new meaning and fulfillment to *everyone's* life. We want to help dispel a lot of the mythology about family that is sometimes promoted as part of some ideological agenda. There are all kinds of families—and no one has the right to tell you that your family isn't the right kind. The American family has been going through a lot of changes—some good, some bad, some just different—but individual families are responding to their problems with creative new solutions.

In many ways, the beginning of the twenty-first century is a disorienting, confusing time for American families. The ways we work, commute, communicate, and learn have all been revolutionized over the past few generations. And the rate of change is increasing all the time. The chaotic fragmentation and subsequent re-forming of every organization, tradition, habit, custom, and institution familiar to our great-grandparents a hundred years ago has left a new emotional landscape with few of the guideposts and landmarks by which families used to get their bearings.

Some families have had a tough time adjusting to those changes—sometimes with tragic consequences. But even as many families are feeling stressed and strained to their limits they persevere, and somehow, in the process, most are finding remarkable dignity and courage under pressure.

If we really care about families, we need to change our thinking about what they need, and how we as individuals, as communities, and as a society can help meet those needs. Valuing families means recognizing that families—in all their shapes and sizes—really *are* trying hard to do right by one another. Valuing families also means finding ways to nurture and support and strengthen families so that they can realize their best aspirations and provide a better future for their children.

Without strong families, we are all much more vulnerable to stress, despair, and unhappiness and their consequences. And worse still, families that malfunction and turn negatively inward can generate nearly unbearable emotional anguish. How we love, how we live, how we relate to other people, how we see ourselves—all this and so much more comes from the foundation of the families in which we grow up and the families we form ourselves. Families give our destiny its first momentum. In creating and shaping our families, each of us forms our own future. We must not take families for granted: instead, we need to realize that for families to be able to nurture us, we need to nurture families.

We are all in this together. We are all feeling our way toward the future in an uncharted world. But new problems require new solutions. And the American family—in all its forms—is rising to that challenge in ways that no one could have predicted. We believe the real values that all American families aspire to are very simple: love, respect, honor, caring, nurturing, and doing everything in one's power to give our children a better world.

For the two of us, studying the American family and writing this book has been as much a personal journey as a professional one. As we have faced challenges in our own family life, we have thought deeply about what it is that makes families strong, what makes families fragile, and what makes families triumph. We have tried to understand the many complex challenges facing families and how families can best navigate those challenges.

We don't claim to be any more expert than millions of other

Americans who have also worked hard to fit all of the moving pieces of family together. We do feel blessed in our own family life, and our good fortune began with parents—and grandparents— who cared for us very deeply. It continues with four wonderful children: Karenna, who is now twenty-nine, Kristin, twenty-five, Sarah, twenty-three, and Albert, twenty. And we are thrilled to be the grandparents of Wyatt Gore Schiff, who is three, and Anna Hunger Schiff, who is one—the children of Karenna and her husband, Drew.

We have also been fortunate to meet and talk with a number of knowledgeable men and women who have helped us learn a lot about how families do and don't function. Though we have always talked between ourselves and with friends about the endlessly compelling topic of family, we first began talking with experts in family issues eleven years ago, when our passion for the subject led us to organize a gathering of people who shared our interest. We invited family studies experts, psychologists, education experts, and many other academics and practitioners who had been studying family issues, and who had especially focused on how American families were coping with the new pressures of life in the late twentieth century.

That turned into our first national conference on family issues, which we called Family Re-Union. In addition to the scholars and experts, we also invited a number of families to join our gathering to tell us about the stresses and strains they were experiencing in their daily lives. The magic of having so many different perspectives on the daily struggles of family life helped us all understand even more deeply the challenges we face. The first gathering was the beginning of an ongoing, collaborative effort to find out what we can do as individuals, as families, as communities, and as a nation to strengthen and empower families.

We ended up deciding to make this conference an annual event. In many ways it has become a touchstone for us. It has been a great privilege each year to have the opportunity to meet with and learn from experts and from grassroots activists, as well as from average families about how to handle the wide array of new challenges and hurdles facing families today. Over the years, we have had Family Re-Unions that focused on the family as it relates to balancing work and family, the media, learning, health, intergenerational relationships, and how families fit into communities.

We will hold the eleventh Family Re-Union in the fall of 2002—this one on teenagers and youth development—and we are looking forward to continuing this tradition in the years to come. The inspiring families we have met and the insights we have gained through Family Re-Union have been an amazing gift to us, one for which we are extremely grateful.

We are also very grateful to the families who have shared their stories with us in detail and allowed us to share them with you. The families you will meet in this book are all real, as are their names, and the quotes included here come from our many conversations with them. We also share a few of our personal experiences—not because we think of our family as having achieved any kind of ideal, but simply because family is a topic we all experience first and foremost in a personal way. In those cases where we have had separate experiences or points of view, we refer to ourselves in the third person as "Al" or "Tipper" to avoid the confusion of both of us using the first person singular. Whatever the pronoun, we have shared in all the writing here. The photographs of the families that appear at the beginning of each chapter were taken by Tipper.

In the words that follow, you will find a four-beat rhythm that's repeated with variations in each chapter: the story of a real family whose life illustrates the subject matter of the chapter; the insights of the leading experts in the particular field; the latest research; and, finally, personal stories. The families we interviewed for the book were not chosen randomly. Rather, we looked for families whose stories would breathe life into each topic. Over time, they told us about emotions and experiences they do not normally share with others. In the process, we learned anew that there really is no such thing as an "ordinary family." If you go deeply enough below the surface, *all* families are uniquely and incredibly complex.

As it happens, we believe that pictures can convey many important truths about family on another level. And so, in an effort to communicate some of them, we have also compiled a collection of photographs, called *The Spirit of Family*, which is being published simultaneously with *Joined at the Heart*. In preparing this second book, we reviewed more than 15,000 pictures taken by many of America's leading photographers, and carefully selected 256 images of contemporary American families.

Ultimately, what we hope to communicate in both words and pictures is that the American family has been undergoing a profound transformation over the past two generations, and that the dramatic changes we describe have led to new feelings, new relationships, new patterns, new understandings, and a radically new experience within families. If we can fully appreciate the nature and extent of these changes—and the myriad ways families are adapting to them—we will be better able to support and celebrate the central role of family in American life.

THE FADLEYS

Claire Fadley, Maggie Fadley, Katie Fadley, Susan Fadley, Joseph Fadley (on
Susan's lap), *Jacob Fadley, Dick Fadley, and Emily Fadley*

Chapter 1

FAMILY REDEFINED

Life belongs to the living, and he who lives
must be prepared for changes.
—JOHANN WOLFGANG VON GOETHE

THE FADLEY FAMILY

As Susan Fadley was walking down the aisle to say "I do," she knew she was making a big mistake. Her brother, who was giving her away because their father had died when they were young, also knew the marriage was a mistake. When the music signaled the entrance of the bride, the three hundred wedding guests who filled the church stood up and turned around to get a good view—but of course they couldn't hear what Susan and her brother were saying to each other as they started walking slowly from the back of the church toward the preacher and the groom.

"He looked at me right when the church doors opened to walk down the aisle," she recalled. "And he goes, 'Susan, it's not too late.' And I looked at him and I said, 'Yeah, it is.' And he goes, 'No, it isn't. It is not too late.' "

Now, eleven years later, Susan says she went through with the wedding because "I couldn't see what I should have done. If I was the age I am now I wouldn't have done it. I was young—well, I wasn't *that* young. Shoot, I was twenty-nine years old! But I wanted to have kids. I wanted to have a family. I wanted to *be* a family."

The one benefit that came from knowing that she'd made a mistake was that she reconsidered her intention to have kids right away. Susan's new husband agreed that they weren't ready for children, so they decided that even though they were legally joined in matrimony, they didn't want to start their own family until they felt a stronger emotional connection. Shortly after the wedding, Susan came to a sad conclusion: she liked her husband, but she really didn't love him. And so, predictably—at least these days it's predictable—two years and three months after getting married, Susan and her husband divorced.

Susan is a resilient and loving woman: she bounced back from her mistake and is now happily remarried, to Dick Fadley. Together, she and Dick have created a beautiful and happy family. They live with their children in a house with a big backyard and a jungle gym for the kids in a middle-class suburb of Columbus, Ohio, that was a cornfield until just a few years ago. Like most parents today, they both work. He sells flooring for a successful building subcontractor, and she is a kindergarten teacher with expertise in special education. He's a hockey fan; she likes to read. They love each other and spend most of their free time with the children. They have a friendly dog named Buttons. You could say they're an all-American family.

End of story? Well, no. Not in today's world. After all, they are a 2002 model of the American family, not a 1960 model. Dick, too, was married before, and now he and Susan have two children—or four, or five, or six, depending on how you redefine family. Theirs, you see, is a so-called blended family, and they are fully or partly responsible for six children from four different couples.

This is all still something of a surprise to Susan, who told us that when she was growing up, she thought she would someday have her own version of the classic American family. "I guess I figured—like everyone did at that time in America's life—that you would grow up, get married, have children, and stay married. That was just the expectation I had—and it didn't happen. And that's okay."

The story of how Dick and Susan's six children came into their lives says a lot about how different Susan's reality is from her original expectation. But first a warning: as so often happens with the new and often complicated families that populate our country today, you may need a scorecard to keep all the family members straight.

Although Susan had no children from her first marriage, Dick's first wife, Dee, had already had a child, Jacob, before she met Dick. After they married, Dick legally adopted Jacob, then three years old, having obtained the written consent of Jacob's father. Then Dee and Dick had two daughters, Katie and Maggie, who now both live with Dick and Susan. Jacob, now eighteen, lived with his mother and has just enlisted in the U.S. Navy.

After his divorce from Dee, Dick fell in love with another woman, Caitlin. They were together for three years and had a child, Emily, who is now eleven and lives with her mother. Emily is a frequent visitor in the Fadley household, and surprisingly—if there's anything left that is surprising in the new kinds of families Americans are now creating—Caitlin and Susan are also close. They talk on the phone and visit regularly to coordinate child care and baby-sitting for Emily, as well as for Dick and Susan's own children—Claire, who is five, and Joseph, who is one and a half. "Caitlin and I have been pretty good about helping each other out when we need it," Susan told us. "It's very complicated, and at times it can be crazy trying to figure out schedules and who is coming when and all that, but for the most part it works really well."

For Susan, one of the hardest challenges in making her new blended family work came four years ago, when she had to figure out how her relationship to Maggie changed when Maggie moved in with them. "I am not her mom. I told her—and we have had many discussions about this—I am her stepmother. And I want to be her friend. Yet I am in charge of this house." It all runs pretty smoothly now, she said, but at first it was really tough: "We have our moments, but we were having our *months* before."

One of the keys to resolving the conflict was to reach beyond the relationship between stepmother and stepdaughter and reexamine the role Dick was playing in the family as father and husband. "He was going through a transition of being a weekend parent to having to be a full-time parent. That was hard for him. He had to step up and be a full-time parent. And he did. And once he stepped in and took the lead—because he had to—everything started falling into place."

Three years later, when Katie followed her younger sister to join the Fadley household, once again there was another major adjustment to be made. This time, Susan recalled, "It was quite a bit easier. I think a lot of that is age. Also experience, having been through it once already. And also the fact that Katie was a little older when she came, and could understand the family dynamic." Now everyone "pretty much" gets along, especially Susan and the girls, because, as Susan says, "Through our struggles we just bonded." What conflict there is now seems to be mostly between the two full sisters, now sixteen and fourteen years old. Maggie acknowledges, "Me and Katie sometimes go at it, but it's because of our age."

Looking back, Susan says that her childhood imaginings of the ideal family were based in part on her "biggest family influence," the marriage modeled for her by her paternal grandparents. "They had the one and only loving married relationship that my siblings and I saw on a consistent basis, and it was an awesome one. You could tell how much they really loved each other. And it was a lot of fun to go there. It was a really safe place to go."

Susan's parents divorced, and then, when she was fourteen, her father died in a car accident. For a few years, her grandparents played an even bigger role in providing stability for her and her siblings and giving them an example of how wonderful and warm it felt to live in a happy, fun, and safe household.

By contrast, the relationship between her grandparents on her mother's side was not the best. Susan told us that her mom "didn't have any role models for a happy marriage and had some insecurities as a result, but Mom tried her best to make sure we didn't feel any of that. My mom has been—for me—the most awesome mom in the whole world. I'm sure history has a way of repeating itself in some form, so I'm sure we had some impact from it, but you do the best you can." Susan added that despite their marital difficulties, her grandparents were very loving to all the grandchildren.

One of Dick and Susan's biggest challenges in their own marriage stems from not always having enough time and energy left over for each other after working and taking care of the children and managing all of the relationships in their complex family. A lot of the time, Susan says, "We're doing the parent thing and not the couple thing. I think that neither one of us are very good about planning a time for us to get away together, just us, even if it's out for dinner. I know that is a part of marriage we have to work on, and we have talked about that."

The one thing that is absolutely certain about their marriage, they both agree, is that it *is* going to last. "The two of us have flat out decided that we are sticking it out. We're both so determined that we're not giving up because we've both been through relationships that haven't lasted. We are going to stay together and we are going to figure it out. We do have a lot of stresses in our lives. It's not an easy family relationship we have built here. It's very, very stressful."

Finding harmony in a blended family can be—to say the least—challenging. "This family is definitely a crazy, mixed-up family," Susan says. "But we've figured out a way to make it work. It would have been real nice to have a family with two parents and children from those parents, but life's choices didn't have it happen that way, unfortunately—or fortunately, because then we wouldn't have who we have now."

THE TRANSFORMATION OF THE
AMERICAN FAMILY SINCE 1960

The Fadleys' story offers a vivid illustration of how much the American family has changed over the past two generations. Both Dick and Susan were born in the early 1960s—he in 1961, she in 1962—which proved to be the fault line of an era. America in the period right after World War II for the most part seemed conservative, traditional, and homogeneous. In fact, many changes were afoot. Turmoil in the South was sparked when African-American servicemen returned from World War II to rightfully claim full and equal rights, eventually leading to the Supreme Court's reversal of officially sanctioned school segregation. Contrary to popular impression, the rate of teenage pregnancies peaked in 1957. Still, the 1950s were certainly placid compared to what came in the 1960s: the full-blown civil rights movement, the sexual revolution, feminism, distrust of government, the beginnings of the modern environmental movement, and many other trends that still affect our lives. It was a remarkable decade in our culture, when everything, including families, began to change dramatically.

If the Fadleys provide one snapshot of how much has changed in the past forty years, the U.S. Census Bureau and other government statistics provide another. When the reams of data gathered by the Census Bureau and other government sources are reduced to their essence, what emerges is a kind of family portrait of America. We decided to compare the statistical portrait taken in 2000 with the one taken in 1960, and then isolate the ten trends we think are the most important. When you place these snapshots side by side, some of the differences are truly startling; families today are as different as Ozzie Nelson, of *Ozzie and Harriet* fame, and Ozzy Osbourne of *The Osbournes,* a "reality" television show that's surprisingly popular at the moment.

Here's our top ten list:

1. **Americans are creating fewer married-with-children families.** Married couples with children under age eighteen now represent only 35 percent of all families; they made up over half of all families in 1960.

2. **The divorce rate has doubled.** For every four marriages in 1960, there was one divorce. There is now a divorce for every two marriages.

3. **Single parents head more families.** Single-parent families with children under age eighteen—only 5 percent of all families in 1960—now account for 13 percent. Those families now raise almost one in three children under age eighteen, a steep increase from the one in ten just two generations ago.

4. **More children are being born to unmarried mothers.** In 1960, only 5 percent of American children were born to unmarried mothers. In 2000, only two generations later, the comparable figure was 33 percent—a sixfold increase.

5. **More mothers are working outside the home.** By 2000, more than 60 percent of married mothers with children under six worked outside the home, three times as many as in 1960.

6. **Fewer people are married.** In 1960, almost 70 percent of the entire marriageable population was married. In 2000, just over 55 percent were married. The number of cohabiting unmarried couples as a proportion of all households increased fivefold from 1960 to 2000.

7. **Families are forming later.** Forty years ago, women married at about age twenty and men at about age twenty-three. Now,

women are about twenty-five and men about twenty-seven at their first marriage. Children are coming much later as well: today, a quarter of all women have not yet had a child before they turn thirty-five, almost double the rate in 1960.

8. **Families are having fewer children.** The average family had 2.3 children in 1960 and only 1.9 in 2000. (And yes, we know that's impossible, but these are statistics after all!)

9. **More grandparents are playing an active role in raising children.** The average life span today is approaching eighty years old, nearly ten years longer than it was in 1960. More than 5.5 million grandparents now share a home with one or more grandchildren. The proportion of children being cared for by grandparents has gone up, particularly for families where the middle generation is a single parent or not present.

10. **Families are becoming more diverse.** In 1960, America was about 90 percent white, and there were fewer than 200,000 interracial couples, accounting for less than half a percent of all married couples. Now, America is 75 percent white, and there are almost 1.5 million interracial couples, representing almost 3 percent of all married couples. If marriages between Hispanics and non-Hispanics are included, the proportion of diverse marriages is much higher still.

There are, of course, a lot of other statistics we could cite, but the main point ought to be clear. In the last two generations, the American family has undergone a profound transformation, one that will forever change the way we think of ourselves as individuals, family members, and citizens. The classic nuclear family of our childhood—the breadwinning dad, the homemaker mom, two or three kids—is not gone, but it's very much a minority of families now. Alongside it today are two-income families, single-parent families, and a host of other types. When you compare the snapshot taken in 1960 with the one taken in 2000, the face of the

American family—like the face of the country as a whole—looks entirely different.

If we were to choose just one trend that has caused the greatest change in the day-to-day lives of families, it would be the dramatic increase in the number of mothers of young children who now work outside the home. (If men had compensated by picking up more of the burden of care, the changes for children would perhaps have been less tumultuous. Studies show that even though men have been playing an increasing role at home, women still do about two-thirds of the housework and four-fifths of the child care.) The factors contributing to the trend of more women in the workforce are complex, but it's not difficult to single out a few obvious ones. First, women are better educated today; they are going to colleges and graduate schools in far greater numbers than they did in the past. So much so, in fact, that the majority of college degrees awarded today are to women. Second, their opportunity to make a significant income has improved dramatically. Though women still don't make as much money as men employed in an equivalent position, the gap has narrowed. Women are also making great advances into industries and professions that used to be dominated by men. Third, women are often delaying the decision to have children because they want to pursue their careers, and when they do finally have kids, they're less likely to be full-time, stay-at-home moms. Fourth, the average earning power of working-class men actually declined in the 1970s, and in the 1980s that trend of falling average earnings extended across the board, adding to the pressure on women to join the workforce.

The effect of this change is profound, and touches on everything from family finances to child care, from decisions about where to live to the balance of power in a marital relationship. And the change seems permanent—it's hard to imagine that the majority of women will ever want to give up at least the opportunity to pursue both a stimulating career and a satisfying family life. Moreover, for many families it's not a choice, since one wage earner alone often can't support a family anymore.

Of course, women have always worked, and contrary to the prevailing myth, many worked outside the home well before the modern era. Family historian and sociologist Donald Hernandez of the State University of New York, Albany, notes, "For almost all of human history, both fathers and mothers had to work to sustain their families, on farms and later in factories or offices." Tamara Hareven, a professor of history at the University of Delaware and founder of the *Journal of Family History: Studies in Family, Kinship, and Demography*, emphasizes that the post–World War II era was unusual in that "for about twenty-five years it was a golden era, when most middle-income families could afford for women not to work. And their productivity was in the home." Nevertheless, the participation of mothers in the labor force continued to increase steadily after 1945. "Although there were some increases in the previous fifty years, largely in urban areas, the real changes began after World War II," Hernandez said.

The increasing number of mothers in the workplace is just one change. On so many fronts, today's families are finding themselves presented with new choices and challenges. Some of them are exciting, others daunting, still others exhausting. But American families are finding surprising and often inspiring ways to meet these new challenges. Ever more diverse, today's families are coming up with many creative ways to fulfill the most important functions of family: furnishing the essentials and providing love and nurturing.

Hareven summed it up eloquently when she told us, "The American family is not breaking down . . . it's undergoing major changes, and pluralism has become a very important aspect of it, and acceptance of pluralism in the U.S. has become very important."

THE HISTORY OF FAMILY: A (VERY!) BRIEF OVERVIEW

Experts on family issues, the Family Re-Union conferences, and the many conversations we've had with families like the Fadleys have taught us a great deal about the rapid changes that are affecting every American family. They've also taught us about the importance of context. Yes, families have changed—but compared to what?

It often seems that every mother and father feels that their newborn baby is the first baby in recorded history. Likewise, every couple feels that the challenges they face as they begin the journey of becoming a family must be unique. But human beings have been forming families of a sort for many tens of thousands of years, so the journey is in fact a very old one. Perhaps a good way to begin an investigation of the family, then, is by asking two questions: Why *do* we form families anyway? And have families always been pretty much the same, or have they evolved over time? The answers could easily take up the rest of this book; instead, we'll present a very short version of what we discovered in the course of our research.

Creating a strong family—and it *is* a very creative undertaking—is difficult enough that sometimes it seems remarkable that we have such a continual and optimistic desire to do so. We form families because our evolutionary and cultural heritage has led us to. Anthropologists argue about exactly why the precursor of marriage, or what they refer to as "pair-bonding," began in the earliest days of the human race, but some of the basic facts are agreed upon. Virtually unique among all living species, we humans have a very long period of helplessness during infancy. Our species was endowed with high intelligence, requiring a large brain inside a large skull. The extent to which our brains can grow in utero is limited by the size of the birth canal.

The evolutionary compromise we developed was a lengthening of the time for brain growth by extending the brain's formation and development for several years after it passes through the birth canal. (As any mother can tell you, a newborn baby's head has a soft spot and "plates" that begin to pull apart right after he or she is born so that the head can get bigger.) This allows for much larger brains once the growth has finally taken place—but all that growth delays the time when the brain can start coordinating the arms and legs, so it comes with the cost of constant, attentive care during our extended infancy, particularly for the first three years. Such intense care for such a long time is difficult, if not impossible, for a mother to provide without reliable help from others. It's therefore in our biological heritage to live in families and communities. It's one of the ways our ancestors survived.

The drive to form families is as essential today as it was 130,000 years ago on the African savannah. We do not know much about the precise nature of those early families, but we do know that our earliest histories speak of men, women, and children in families. It ought to be reassuring to anyone concerned with the durability of marriage as an institution that marriage was well established—in some form—in all of the major ancient civilizations, from the Mesopotamians to the Egyptians, from the Chinese to the people of the Indus Valley, from the Aztecs, Incas, and Mayans to the Greeks and Romans.

For much of history, however, what we now call the extended family was more important than what we call the immediate or nuclear family. For decades, family scholars argued about the origins of the nuclear family (a phrase coined during the 1950s when atomic bombs gave rise to numerous metaphors) and whether it had much significance at all until the Enlightenment. Recent scholarship by Harvard University historian Steven Ozment and others has established compelling evidence that the nuclear family was the basic economic unit of society more than five hundred years ago, and arguably much earlier. In fact, Ozment told us, "there has never been a time when people haven't formed nuclear families. At times they have certainly been in the minority, but throughout history you can find people who come together, stay together, and have children."

Historians, incidentally, draw a distinction between "families" and "households." Hareven told us that what historians observe in earlier centuries is a "nuclear household instead of the nuclear family." University of Michigan historian Maris Vinovskis adds, "The distinction between family and household is worth making because in the past many families had servants, boarders, and lodgers, or sometimes even slaves as part of their household. In the more distant past the distinction between household members and family members was not as sharp as it became in later years."

Although the nuclear family has existed in some form throughout history, it began to appear in its modern form in Europe during the Middle Ages. Brigitte Berger, professor emerita of sociology at Boston University, argues that its emergence was a key factor in the modernization of Western civilization that began early in the second millennium and accelerated during the Renaissance and Enlightenment. "The inner dynamics of the nuclear family," she told us, "produce behavioral attitudes that are very conducive to democracy and a market economy." Steven Ozment told us that after analyzing family archives and church documents, he concluded that in the twelfth and thirteenth centuries, "it was difficult for couples of ordinary means to establish an independent household and pursue the married life they desired. Thus, lots of illegitimate births, some infanticide, officially sanctioned houses of prostitution in the cities, and other signs of a society with a large population of single men and women were present. One of the reasons the Church intervened in family creation at this time was to bring needed discipline to the perceived moral disintegration of the secular single life."

Ozment also offered a fascinating comparison between then and now: "From this point of view, today's family 'disintegration' seems rather more like an updated version of a singles-style Middle Ages than some brave new phenomenon. More importantly, as their behavior attests, most people then, as now, wanted a real marriage, not a chaotic single life. The ideal of a 'nuclear family,' committed and loyal, was then the new form or phenomenon being sought."

Not until the early thirteenth century did the Roman Catholic Church establish its rule of celibacy and marriage regulations for laity. Ozment told us that one of the main effects of the Church's decision to codify the legal institution of marriage was to decisively tip the balance toward the nuclear family. Interestingly, he also told us that many women worked outside the home during the Middle Ages. In fact, Ozment said, "feminist scholars today describe the late Middle Ages as a 'golden age' for women wanting to work outside the home." Ozment called the late thirteenth and fourteenth centuries "working women's best centuries before the twentieth," and said there is evidence of power-sharing between couples. At the time, Martin Luther even criticized men who refused to change diapers and help out in the home, Ozment explained.

According to Ozment, married couples who formed the basis of nuclear families probably did not become the majority until some time after the recovery from the epochal Black Death, which is estimated to have killed one-third of the population in Europe between 1347 and 1351. Then, in the sixteenth century, the Reformation accelerated the trend toward the nuclear family. And by the time European settlers first came to America, the nuclear family was clearly their dominant form of social organization. As Vinovskis told us, the family was "the most important economic and governance unit in our society—from the very beginning." Vinovskis points out, however, that while much of the historical emphasis has been placed on New England families, "the situation in the colonial South was quite different because sex ratios there made it much harder for males to marry." That's because single males made up a far larger percentage of the immigrants to the colonial South. It's also important to note that there were very different patterns of family life among different ethnic and racial groups, especially among slaves, who were subjected to unspeakable cruelties, including the total destruction of families.

During the colonial era, the family was largely self-sufficient and able to perform a wide variety of functions. According to Uni-

versity of Houston historians Steven Mintz and Susan Kellogg, the
family was thought of as a "little commonwealth" that reflected the
governing principles of hierarchy and deference to the larger society. Over time, the family changed to become a more private and
more democratic social structure.

As the structure of the American family changed, so too did the
perception of marriage. Toward the end of the eighteenth century,
"marriage was increasingly conceived not as a property arrangement but as an emotional bond involving mutual esteem, mutual
friendship, and mutual confidence," explains Mintz. "Spouses displayed affection more openly, calling each other 'honey' or 'dear.' "

The profound economic changes that came with the Commercial and, later, Industrial Revolutions during the eighteenth and
nineteenth centuries brought sweeping modifications to the American family. Some families went to work in industry, but many
more took part in developing commercial activities. Both these
new kinds of work began to pull more and more fathers away
from home, which caused a growing separation of work from the
household and the increasing specialization of skills. As this trend
strengthened, children were no longer seen as primarily economic assets, but instead more as dependents requiring education
and nurturing. According to Mintz, "The family's social and economic significance declined, and institutions such as almshouses,
schools, and businesses assumed many traditional family functions." Vinovskis reminded us, however, that although the Industrial Revolution is often treated as a single process, "there was great
regional variation in the extent of industrialization and the numbers of families affected."

The new wealth created by the Industrial Revolution and the
new emphasis on education, including the education of women,
were among the factors that led to a sharp reduction in the average
size of families. (Interestingly, in both the United States and
France, the decline in family size actually began in the late eighteenth century—prior to industrialization and around the time of

the American and French Revolutions.) Moreover, improvements in public health—notably in nutrition and the water supply—reduced the chances that a child would die. Parents began to feel more confident that most of their children would survive to adulthood and then take care of them when they got old, so they no longer felt the need to have lots of children as an insurance policy. In turn, the smaller number of children in each home led parents to invest more resources and emotions in each child. Longer life spans (the average American's life span has actually doubled since the beginning of the Industrial Revolution) created the relatively new family experiences of extended grandparenthood and middle-aged couples living without children in the home.

Meanwhile, as women developed greater independence, in large part through financial security gained from their participation in the workforce, they began to expect much more than economic security from marriage. A more extended education became increasingly important to both sexes, causing many young people to delay marriage so that they could complete schooling. As they became better educated, more women took jobs outside the home. Then both world wars, particularly the second, brought a new, even larger wave of women into the workforce.

One of the most significant changes in the American family came with the establishment of the Social Security Administration during the interwar period in the 1930s. Prior to that time, families took it for granted that they would need to try to save enough to help take care of their parents when their parents got too old to provide for themselves. Not long after being relieved of that perceived obligation by Social Security, families began to shift that extra money to more consumption and began to feel more comfortable with higher levels of personal debt.

The period immediately after World War II brought a brief but significant increase in the number of divorces, as the returning GIs sorted out their lives and the status of relationships that had been interrupted for three to four years. But then at the end of the 1940s, the American family entered a period of unusual stability—a period that ended with the upheavals of the 1960s.

THE CONSEQUENCES OF DIVORCE

Now let's slow the story down again and look at a crucial trend that began to emerge into public view during the 1960s: the rising incidence of divorce. As usual, the various statistics available can be interpreted in different ways, but it's probably accurate to say that the divorce rate is now about twice as high as it was forty years ago. Contrary to conventional wisdom, however, the divorce rate didn't begin rising in the 1960s: in fact, the rate began rising slowly but steadily in the second half of the nineteenth century, and continued through the first half of the twentieth century. It then stabilized in the 1950s. Then, in the early 1960s, the rates began accelerating. Hernandez dates the acceleration to 1964, when the baby boom ended: "Once the baby boom was over, people no longer felt that they had to stay at home with the children. [That's when] we see this increase in divorces." As women entered the labor force in even greater numbers, their increasing economic freedom gave them more options, including leaving the marriage if they wanted to. Women working also increased the independence of men, who began treating their incomes as their own and came to believe they could leave without destroying the family financially, Hernandez observed.

In 1960, there were about twenty-six divorces for every one hundred marriages. The divorce rate rose steadily for the next twenty years and peaked around 1980, when there were about fifty divorces for every hundred marriages; since then, it has dropped to forty-eight per hundred. Currently, according to the Centers for Disease Control and Prevention, one in three first marriages ends in separation or divorce within ten years, and 43 percent end within fifteen years. Each year an estimated one million children are involved in a divorce. According to Hernandez, however, divorce has now reached a kind of saturation point. "The fundamental reason is that for the past twenty years or so it's been necessary to have two incomes in order to support a middle-class style of living."

Susan Fadley, of course, knows divorce firsthand: her parents divorced, she has been divorced once herself, and now she's raising stepchildren who have been through the breakup of a marriage. She feels that it's hard to judge someone else's decision on divorce, because it all depends on the situation. Her mother's parents, for instance, stayed in an unhappy marriage for years. As she put it, "They stuck it out but didn't pursue any ideal. They didn't work at it." She feels they definitely should have gotten a divorce, in part because of the harmful effect of their constant and bitter conflict on their children.

But Susan acknowledged that for a younger generation—hers—which considered divorce much more acceptable, the effects were turning out to be harder to deal with than they'd expected. Indeed, many of the single-parent households that were created found a great deal of economic hardship.

For all of the problems and difficulties associated with divorce, it is worth noting that in some cases those who divorce feel that it was their best course of action. E. Mavis Hetherington, a professor emerita of psychology at the University of Virginia in her three-decade-long study of fourteen hundred American families and their experiences with divorce, found that one out of every four women who divorced "were really enhanced after divorce and they developed competencies they never would have found staying in an unhappy, or demeaning, or abusive marriage." She told us, "They went back to school; they got better jobs; they were wonderful mothers. They were involved in community activities, often religious groups. They were just remarkable. And they were good parents with it all."

As divorce rates have risen, many people have expressed great concern about the state of marriage in our country. But it's important to consider that, as demographers Lynne Casper and Suzanne Bianchi explain, "[I]ncreased life expectancy translates into extended length of family relationships. Married couples today have many more years to spend together." If couples are in unhappy marriages, they are more likely to eventually divorce as they face so much of their lifetimes together after their child-rearing years are over. But, Casper told us, "family is still something very much on people's agendas and marriage is still very much part of people's lives. Regardless of the fact that divorce as well as single parenthood increased, people are still very positive about the institution of marriage."

Indeed, most people still do marry, even if more of them wait longer before doing so, and a great many of those who divorce usually go right back out to marry again. For example, half of women who were divorced in the 1980s were remarried within five years, many of them creating new blended families in the process. By contrast, in the past, people were more likely to remarry only after a husband or wife had died.

Before they marry—or remarry—many couples are now testing out the seriousness of their commitment by living together. Fueling the trend is the revolution in attitudes about sex and the desire by many young people to complete their education or job training prior to marriage. In fact, in the United States, the number of unmarried couples living together increased by 72 percent in the last decade alone; yet rates of cohabitation among American couples are still lower than those in many European countries, particularly the Netherlands and Sweden. According to one study, more than half of all American women are now living with a partner before getting married—and an even higher percentage are living with partners before getting remarried. Many argue that this practice enables couples to avoid making a mistake in their choice of a spouse, and that the marriages that do result are likely to be stronger as a result of the trial run. The evidence, however, is mixed; others believe that couples who live together before marriage are less likely to have a marriage that lasts.

Despite high divorce rates, couples today appear to be more satisfied with their relationships than did those of two generations ago. When asked in a poll in 1997 whether they would still marry the same person if they had the opportunity to do things over again, 90 percent of married people polled said they either "probably would" or "certainly would," as compared to only 77 percent of those surveyed in 1948. Only 6 percent said they "might not," whereas earlier the figure was 10 percent.

Meanwhile, blended American families, like the Fadleys, have increased dramatically in the past two generations. Three out of four families are still headed by married couples but more of them are blended families. Today nearly one-third of all children will spend time in a blended family at some point in their lives. Research collected by the Stepfamily Association of America estimates that—accounting for both remarriages and cohabitation—more than half of all Americans and two-thirds of all women will spend some time in a stepfamily.

That there has been an increase in divorce over the past two generations is beyond dispute. What is less clear, however, is how divorce affects parents and children. There is a continuing debate among family experts about the impact of divorce, and they disagree vigorously about the nature and extent to which it affects such wide-ranging characteristics as aggressiveness, ability to create and maintain loving relationships, and performance in school.

When Tipper was two years old, her parents separated. They divorced when she was four. Her mother, Margaret Ann, never remarried, but when Tipper was five, her father, Jack, married a woman with three of her own children.

Tipper points out that those were the days before the movie *Kramer vs. Kramer* and the increased awareness of the father's rights after a divorce. Her mother was awarded custody of her, while her father was granted "visitation" rights one day a week. In practice, that meant Sunday visits and a week together during the summer. As a result, she lived in a blended family one day a week, and was in a three-generation family the rest of the time, living with her mother and her grandparents.

Tipper remembers some of the complicated emotions of being a stepchild. When she went to visit her stepsisters in her father's new home, she felt envious that they could spend more time with him. But over time, she developed a close bond with one of her stepsisters in particular. She also began to notice that often, when the three girls wanted something from her father, the stepsisters would say, "You go ask him. You're his real daughter."

Despite the then-unusual arrangement, Tipper—and both of her families—survived just fine. Experiences like hers form the basis for the view of experts like Mavis Hetherington, who believes divorce has negative effects on families and their children in the short term, but that most children of divorced families turn out to be no different than those who grew up in married families.

Another school of thought, however, maintains that divorce is catastrophic for kids, arguing that as many as half of them will not ever be able to fully recover from its impact. This conclusion has led some people to insist that divorce should be formally discouraged in our values and culture, through new laws that would restrict the availability of divorce or require premarital counseling or other conditions for marriage. We believe that couples should be supported and encouraged as they try to make their marriages work, and especially when children are involved, we tend to view divorce as one of the least desirable outcomes of marital conflict. Nevertheless, we do not support restricting the legal availability of divorce as an option because the husband and wife are ultimately in the best position to make that judgment.

Judith Wallerstein, founder of the Center for the Family in Transition, is one of the best-known adherents of the theory that divorce has dramatic and pervasive consequences for children, the effects of which persist into adulthood. In her study, which consists of twenty-five years of personal interviews with sixty divorcing families in Marin County, California, she presents a troubling picture of the various types of psychological scars that divorce can leave in some people. According to her study, which she presents in her book *The Unexpected Legacy of Divorce*, children of divorce may struggle with the fear of betrayal, which in turn impairs their ability to develop and maintain romantic relationships. Lacking role models for healthy relationships, they often have difficulty creating successful families of their own.

Hetherington also found problems among some children of divorce, but found that serious problems were far less common than the evidence in Wallerstein's study suggests. In some ways, however, given that they reach such different conclusions, the data presented by researchers on both sides of the argument appear surprisingly similar. Our own view of the issue is that, generally speaking, kids are definitely better off in a two-parent family in which the parents' relationship is harmonious. When parents have conflict, children are *still* better off with the parents staying married if they can manage their conflict and avoid inflicting emotional or physical harm. However, most researchers agree there is clearly a point at which the children and parents are both definitely better off with a divorce. Moreover, divorce should not be seen only as a single event. It is also the start of an ongoing process, particularly where children are involved. Hetherington said she found in her study that the effect on children depended largely on the quality of the family relationship before the divorce. "If kids think that their family is very happy, then they will respond adversely to divorce, and over the first few years, you'll see them get worse. If kids were in a family that they felt was full of conflict, they improve after the divorce."

Overall, both Wallerstein and Hetherington agree that the majority of children will survive the impact of their parents getting divorced and will go on to enjoy successful relationships. However, some evidence suggests that even these children may carry deep psychological bruises that can make them more vulnerable to self-doubt where relationships are concerned. Said Wallerstein, "It's self-doubt about 'Will I have a loving relationship? Will I find [someone] who loves me?' Now, everyone at twenty-five worries about that, but [children of divorce] worry about it with much more intense anxiety and with greater fear of failing." But that does not mean they will fail. Hetherington told us, "If a person from a divorced family marries a stable, supportive spouse from a nondivorced family, their divorce rate drops down to the divorce rate from nondivorced families . . . So choice of spouse becomes really important, but one of the problems is that people who have problems tend to pick other people who have problems."

What does seem clear is that whenever divorce takes place, the impact on children will be greater or smaller depending on the quality of the postdivorce relationships and the presence or absence of protective factors that foster resilience in the children themselves. These factors can include the presence of adult mentors, a supportive work or school environment, and social maturity. Children are generally more resilient than they are given credit for, and a child who has been raised by loving parents and has learned from their example to express their feelings openly is likely to be in a much better position to understand that his parents' divorce is a reflection only of their own relationship with each other, and not an indication that the child is the reason his mother and father were unhappy. Conversely, a child whose parents have not reinforced his self-worth and who does not have strong cognitive and communication skills may have a diminished capacity to make this distinction and may be less likely to rebound from setbacks. It is especially harmful for parents to use their children as pawns in the conflict that led to the divorce in the first place.

The involvement of the extended family and the availability of appropriate community supports can also have a big impact. Having others to turn to for emotional support, and being willing and able to seek it or receive it, can provide another source of strength for children during a divorce. The role of stepparents is important, too. Let's face it: at the beginning, many children may resent a new stepparent. But a child can grow to love a stepparent, whether they live together part-time or full-time. Hetherington observed that "certain kids have characteristics that make them able to elicit support from other people. They may have a sense of humor, they may have an open personality, they may be more physically attractive, they may be more sensitive to other people's feelings. . . . [T]his ability to elicit social support was very important. . . . [These kids] have a sense of self-efficacy, a feeling that they can deal with things, that they're in control of things rather than their fate is in the hands of outside forces."

If this is true, resiliency skills could turn out to be a key to limiting the impact of divorce on children. Even Wallerstein, who is identified with a much more pessimistic view of the impact of divorce, told us that the harmful impact on children "doesn't necessarily last, because a lot of these young people in their twenties teach themselves what they weren't able to learn at home. They learn it the hard way, but many by their early thirties are able to learn it and regain a sense of hope."

THE EMERGENCE OF NEW TYPES OF FAMILIES

Divorce, the declining prevalence of the "traditional family," the growing numbers of single mothers, the lower rate of marriage, the sextupling of births out of wedlock—all these trends and others could lead a reasonable person to conclude that the American family is in a state of collapse. Is that what's happening?

Some of these developments are alarming and demand a thoughtful response. But sometimes what seems to be disintegration is really the chaotic start of a new form or phenomenon, and that's what we think is occurring in America today. Yes, a lot of families are breaking up and traditional families are no longer the norm, but families are also finding ways to come together again in novel and more resilient forms that can reweave and strengthen the vital family ties that provide the love and support and nurturing we all need.

Our optimism about the future of the American family is based on our belief that many of the ways in which families are coping with the realities of modern life will result in new strategies to preserve the essence of what family is all about. What is that essence? Some people still say that family requires a "blood relationship." But three-quarters of Americans agree with the definition of a family as a "group of people who love and care about each other, regardless of blood relation or marital status." We think family is all that and more, that its true essence lies in the love and support given to you by people who are always there for you, no matter what.

We also think family is, by definition, a work in progress. Whoever you are, however wise and experienced you might be, you have to keep working at it. Successful families work every day, in ways large and small, to strengthen the foundations and shore up the walls. Though we are deeply concerned about persistent warning signs of domestic violence, abuse, and behavioral disorders undermining too many families, we don't accept the gloomy prophecies for the American family, because we're optimistic that Americans will do the necessary work to preserve the essence of family even as its outward form changes.

As the country becomes ever more diverse, so too will its families. How surprising is it, for instance, that interracial marriages—once viewed as unusual and even shocking—have become so much more common? There are now 700,000 Asian-white couples and 400,000 black-white couples. The number of marriages between people of different ethnicities is much greater than the number of interracial marriages. There are nearly 2 million couples in which one partner is Hispanic and one is not. Changed attitudes are especially prevalent among the young: in a 1997 *USA Today*/Gallup poll, 57 percent of teenagers queried said they already had dated interracially and another 30 percent had no objection to doing so. Interracial marriages are much more acceptable now than in the past.

When we talked to Todd Alexander, who is black, and his wife of five years, Pat Letke-Alexander, who is white, about their courtship and marriage, we asked whether they had discussed the racial differences as a potential challenge or obstacle when they'd first started dating. They were almost baffled by the question, because it really hadn't been a major issue for them. Both Pat and Todd had dated interracially before. Todd's younger sister had married a white man, and his younger brother recently married a white woman he had been dating since graduating high school. For Pat and Todd, what really mattered was that they felt a sense of commonality on so many other levels. "Culturally we come from a similar background. So the skin colors are different—but our upbringing and culture are so similar that it hasn't been that big of a deal," Pat said.

As often happens with new couples, Pat and Todd each chose a major family holiday—Thanksgiving for one and Christmas for the other—to introduce their mate to their families. Had those dinners taken place forty years ago, they might have unfolded much like variations on the classic movie *Guess Who's Coming to Dinner?* In that film, a white woman brings a black man home to meet her parents, causing major worry, consternation, and conflict. His parents come for dinner as well, and all four parents openly express their concerns about the marriage and their fears for their children due to the societal censure and difficulties they would surely face. There was certainly some awkwardness at both Pat's and Todd's homes—especially since neither had thought it necessary to tell their parents that they were bringing home someone of a different race. Pat's father, in particular, initially harbored some strong reservations about his daughter's new boyfriend, but never said anything explicitly. His concerns eventually receded. These days Pat's father spends many a loving hour playing with his grandsons, and he and Todd have developed a good relationship. Todd told us his parents, meanwhile, also found that it required a serious adjustment on their part when three of their four children married white spouses. "But they respected our decisions as adults," said Todd, adding that they very much love Pat, their son-in-law, and their other daughter-in-law.

Pat and Todd represent just one kind of new American family, just as the blended family of Susan and Dick Fadley represents another. Meanwhile, many other new family constellations are also emerging. Adoptions of all kinds are much more widely accepted. Interracial adoptions, for instance, are becoming more common, as are so-called open adoptions, where the child can maintain a relationship with his or her biological parents. Also on the rise is the multigenerational family, in which grandparents adopt an especially close caretaking responsibility for grandchildren—sometimes in conjunction with the middle generation and sometimes in the absence of that generation. While grandparents have always played an important role in the nurturing of the extended family, in recent years there has been a sharp increase in the number of children being raised primarily by grandparents, and over 5.5 million grandparents are now living in homes with a grandchild. In many cases one or both of the parents are also present. For many families, grandparents are the single most frequently relied upon relatives in providing care for preschoolers. But in an increasing number of cases, grandparents are solely responsible for the upbringing of their grandchildren. Since 1970, the number of children under age eighteen living in a household headed by a grandparent has risen 74 percent.

Tipper vividly remembers the role played by her grandparents in her upbringing. As a young child, she lived with her maternal grandparents following her parents' divorce. Her father was always there for her, but was occupied with work and his new family. Her mother was present in the home most of the time, but she was sometimes ill for extended periods, and on those occasions Tipper's grandparents mostly raised her themselves. Tipper's grandparents—like many grandparents who end up being the primary caretakers for their grandchildren—didn't choose this arrangement, but because their daughter suffered from a mental illness, they found themselves in the position of being Tipper's caretaker and they simply adjusted. When Tipper was older, she could see that they had had to make changes and concessions in their own lives to adapt to the responsibility just as they were getting ready to retire themselves. But as a child, Tipper had never felt it. To her it was just a wonderful, stable home life for her. Her grandfather was a banker and her grandmother a homemaker. Her grandmother, whom she called Maw-Maw, was the stabilizing element in the household. She was always home for Tipper, able to take care of her while her mother was at work or when she was ill. Maw-Maw showed Tipper how to cook, how to bake an apple pie from scratch, and, through her storytelling about life in Kentucky, where she had been raised as a little girl, shared her values with Tipper.

Some of Tipper's fondest memories of childhood were from when she was just seven or eight years old and her grandfather, whom she called Papa, would take her to work with him at the bank. They would walk down to the corner and catch the bus to downtown Washington, and in his office she would play with the typewriter and see what he did all day long. This was long before anyone thought about "Take Your Daughter to Work" days. Though she never considered it at the time, Tipper realizes now that perhaps the reason she went to work with him was because her grandmother may have had appointments and that was the only child care for her they could improvise. Sometimes she would stay with her father's parents. Other times she would stay with her aunt, if her grandparents needed to go on a trip. Whenever there was a child-care gap, it was always one of the extended family members who stepped in. Her father also took her to work with him on

many occasions. He had a wholesale plumbing and heating supplies company, and Tipper loved to play in the warehouse.

When Tipper was a senior in high school and wanted to go to
Cambridge, Massachusetts, to visit Al, who was a freshman in college, her grandmother would chaperone her on the trip, because
she insisted on proper, old-fashioned values. We recently found Al's
handwritten letter to Tipper when he found out that Maw-Maw
was coming along with Tipper for her visit: "I don't know how in
the hell I can entertain both you and your grandmother for a week.
It'll be awfully awkward. . . . I hope this isn't making you mad, but
I don't care about spending a week with your grandmother. I want
a week with you. . . . [Of course] I would rather see you and your
grandmother than not see you at all. As I think more about it, . . . I
don't like it worth a damn."

Demographer Lynne Casper told us, "We still find a lot of intergenerational influences that support the family as a very strong
institution." In unfortunate situations where young parents have
difficulties raising their kids, grandparents have been playing a vital
role as a backup, taking charge in raising the kids on their own,
Casper said. It's often a difficult task because they don't necessarily
receive the same legal or financial benefits that parents or even foster parents might get in a similar situation.

The overall relationship between grandparents and their families has been changed dramatically by the unprecedented increase
in our average life span. The amazing thirty-year increase in our life
expectancy over the course of just the last century has caused
major structural changes. Among other things, it means that grandparents can play an important, and more extended, nuturing role
in families. It also means that children and grandchildren face the
responsibility of caring for more of their elders for longer periods
of time.

The elderly are often in need of special care. And with the cost
of that care—and of housing for seniors—increasing faster than the

rate of inflation, many of their children and grandchildren are finding that they must either pay for nursing-home care out of their own funds or take their aging parents or grandparents into their own homes.

Another major trend involves significant changes in the overall relationship between fathers and families, with the number of children in father-only families quadrupling in the past forty years. Further, there's evidence of a shift toward shared custody by fathers and mothers after divorce. Although the vast majority of children in single-parent homes still live with their mothers, fathers—regardless of marital status—are more involved and spending more time with their children than in the past. "[I]t's become more expected for fathers to be involved in their children's lives, not just from an economic standpoint. Both women and men are starting to change their views about the involvement of fathers in their children's lives, and I think that is very positive," Casper said. The importance of men in children's lives was brought home to us by our third Family Re-Union, which led to a number of initiatives to strengthen men's involvement with their children.

In yet another emerging family configuration, nearly 1.2 million people in the United States say they are part of gay or lesbian couples, according to the 2000 census. (Demographers and gay activists point out that accurate counts are difficult to obtain and that the census figures do not account for gay and lesbian couples who may not be comfortable identifying themselves in a federal study.) This is not just a big-city phenomenon. Same-sex couples live together in all but 255 of all 3,141 American counties, according to Urban Institute demographer Gary Gates. Further, in an estimated 800,000 families, children are being raised by gay or lesbian couples, and according to the American Civil Liberties Union, researchers estimate that the total number of children nationwide living with at least one gay parent ranges from 6 million to 14 million.

Families are being redefined in many other ways as well. The traditional notion that you should only date and marry someone of the same faith is simply ignored by many modern families. (In a recent poll, only 42 percent of single young adults said they believe that it is important to find a spouse who shares their religion.) As well, single people are choosing to adopt or have a child. Many other people remain single and, in addition to their birth family, become a part of community families.

All of these increasingly diverse family forms and configurations suggest just how profoundly the American family has changed. But this transformation goes well beyond statistical snapshots and current trends. Ultimately, what's really emerging is a new definition of the family as an institution.

THE SPIRITUAL DIMENSION OF FAMILY

It is impossible to tell the story of the American family, much less trace its evolution and transformation, without placing it in the context of faith. That is not to say that religion is a necessary part of every family. The choice of whether or not to embrace a religious faith is one each family and each individual makes independently in America. Yet it is undeniably true that the history of family and the history of our various faith traditions have long been intertwined.

In America, faith finds its expression through many different religious traditions. Indeed, tolerance of religious diversity has been strong and growing in America since our country's inception. We take pride as a nation in being a home for all religions and in respecting the rights of those who choose not to believe in God. And the large majority of us believe in the importance of maintaining a clear separation between the government and religion.

As a result of our unique religious history, most American families have passed down to each successive generation a blend of devotion and tolerance, deep commitment to one faith tradition and respect for other faith traditions. That mixture is what both of us received from our parents, and we have tried to pass it on to our children. Like most Americans, we know that plenty of families are happy, successful, and deeply committed to strong morals, even if they do not ascribe to any religion at all. We also know that it's not hard to find examples of families that profess strong faith but appear to behave in a highly unethical and immoral manner. Still, in our experience, the odds for achieving stability, success, and happiness seem to be very much in favor of families that invest their children with a strong, moral, and tolerant faith tradition.

A shared commitment to faith has always been a central element in the life of our own family. Our deeply held beliefs form the very core of the values we hold in common, and the rituals of our faith tradition have always provided a reassuring and stabilizing rhythm to family life. Grace before meals, especially the evening meal, came to seem as necessary as the food itself. Bedtime stories were sometimes expendable, but bedtime prayers were *always* said. Going to church on Sunday morning—especially as our children were growing up—was the central and most important family activity every week.

For both of us, the process by which we made a commitment to try to live our lives according to the spiritual principles of Christianity began when we were young children ourselves. Our parents taught us all the rituals we later passed on to our children. We were married in the church, and we always assumed that we would raise our children in the church. Along the way, like many others, we have often felt the presence of God and the power of prayer, so although we have grown up in the church, we are believers not by habit but by decision.

For our family, as for so many others, the most important contributions of faith have been its presumptions that life has meaning, that the universe has a purpose, and that God is love. Accepting these propositions as true means recognizing a duty to choose right over wrong, kindness over cruelty, good over evil, and justice over selfishness. We also believe that since family is the beginning of civilization, these choices matter a great deal.

Of course, nothing about faith remains simple for very long. Organized religions seem to carry the same vulnerability to abuse and excess that can flourish in any group that inspires passion and confers a distinctive identity. But luckily for America's families, that lesson was fresh in the minds of our founders after all the religious wars and persecutions that swept Europe before and during the time of our colonization, thus motivating many of the first European settlers to sail for our shores.

When the settlers traveled to America, they came—especially in the northern colonies—in families, and they brought with them strong religious traditions. The New England Puritans, for instance, placed great importance on the family as a spiritual institution and believed it was the responsibility of the head of the household to provide religious education to all who lived under his roof and to make certain that they could all read the Bible. In fact, in the seventeenth century, there were actually a few recorded instances of children being removed from families because the head of the household failed in his responsibilities for religious instruction. Over time, these early settlers were followed by members of numerous religious minorities—including Irish, Italian, and other European Catholics; European Jews; and, later, Muslims, Hindus, Buddhists, and Sikhs—all of whom came to America in search of freedom and usually found it.

From the Colonial era onward, cyclical periods of deep concern for the morality of families have triggered huge religious revival movements, the largest of them known as the "Great Awakenings." Each of these movements, in turn, has had a profound impact on the behavior of families for an extended period thereafter.

Interestingly, the high level of religious activity in America compared to most other nations has been attributed by many experts to the high degree of separation between church and state, and the consistent emphasis on religious freedom. The choice of faith is not coerced; it is made by individuals and families. Families therefore feel a greater responsibility to step forward and offer the faith leadership they believe is needed.

For our part, we have joined millions of other families in inheriting and trying to pass on to our children a family legacy of "faith in action," teaching our children to volunteer to help the poor and the homeless and to fight for justice. We believe in the African proverb quoted often by Congressman John Lewis: "When you pray, move your feet."

FAMILY REDEFINED

As we think about the profound shift in the role played by family in our culture, we find ourselves again asking a simple question: what do we expect of family?

Three or four generations ago, men and women would have answered that question very differently. Most men would have said that they expected a wife to take charge of the home, raise their children, and nurture the family. Most women would have said they expected a husband to be a good provider, work hard, make a decent income, and protect and lead the family.

Today, some families still enter marriage with similar expectations, but they are unusual. More typically, the vast majority of couples are acutely aware of a new emotional bargain at the core of family. Most women expect to be fully capable of providing for themselves, and when they begin to think about getting married they seek a husband who will be a soul mate, who will be capable not only of communicating his deepest feelings but also of understanding hers. (In fact, a recent public-opinion survey of young American women asked them to choose between a husband who could make a good living to provide for the family and a husband who could "communicate about his deepest feelings"; 80 percent chose the one who could talk about feelings.) Most men, meanwhile, are also looking for a soul mate. In most cases, neither husband nor wife will expect—as many used to—that their wedding night will be an initiation for either of them into the mysteries and joys of sexuality, since both are likely to have been sexually active for about eight years before marriage.

Most couples are also aware of the high divorce rate, and one source of stress for families today is that their expectations for their marriage have not really changed quite as much as the new realities. Even thoroughly modern couples usually hope and dream of a lasting, stable, happy marriage—just as they uphold such nuptial traditions as a long, white wedding dress and a multilayered cake with a miniature bride and groom on top.

We're glad they hold on to their dreams so tightly. Because even though the mismatch between their hopes and their odds can lead to painful disappointments, we find *their* hope to be a source of *our* hope. In fact, one of the reasons we are optimistic is that most young people getting married today firmly believe they will beat the odds and are determined to do so. Furthermore, according to a recent study, 86 percent of them agree that "marriage is hard work and is a full-time job." They're right about that, but what's still especially difficult for too many people is letting go of the idea that the primary purpose of marriage is personal fulfillment.

As Americans, we tend to define ourselves first and almost exclusively as individuals. Even though we live our lives primarily in the emotional embrace of family, we still reflexively deal with most of our challenges and opportunities in terms of how they affect us singly. Yet healthy families have a life and integrity of their own that transcends the individuals in the family.

Susan Fadley offered some wise words on this dilemma. She believes that most people became much more "me-oriented" in the 1970s, and much less concerned with the needs of the family. She thinks that attitude continues: "People believe that they have to be totally gratified the whole time, and I think there are times you're just not. Life works in cycles, and I think relationships work in cycles, and you have to just keep plugging along." This is why she told her husband it was time to "step up" and become a "full-time father" when children from his first marriage came to live in their home. She believes women's expectations have become particularly unrealistic, in part because society encourages them to think they can have it all. But she sees signs of positive change, too: "Now a lot more women are seeing that yes, you *can* have it all, but not all at one time. Somebody does need to take the helm and take care of these children. They can't be in day care all the time. You can't work twelve hours a day and expect that you're going to be the biggest influence in your child's life."

Susan has it right: the life of the family *is* larger than the life of any one member. For those who understand that, family is a living reality in their lives and their way of being in the world. That internal family reality is reproduced in their own families and in following generations, with each new generation adding to or subtracting from or transforming what "family" means. The emotional terrain of family is the real space in which people live their lives, and the inner topography of that emotional sphere shapes each of us and teaches us our first and most basic lessons—not only about relationships but also about the most essential truths at the core of our lives: How do we relate to everyone and everything? Who are we? How do we affect the world around us? How do we experience love? How do we express our emotions? How do we make decisions about our lives? How do we work together? How do we then shape the families we start?

The lessons we learn as we try to answer these questions are the enduring structures upon which the rest of our lives is forged and tempered. They remain at the center of our lives, and they give form to even the outermost layer. How could they not? After all, our most important relationships, by far, are those we have within our families. It is with family that we share in our celebrations. It is

THE NALLEYS AND THE PHILPOTTS

Cindy Nalley, Lee Nalley, Mitch Philpott, and Brett Philpott

THE LOGANS

Noah Logan, John Coon, Josh Tuerk, and Marcus Logan

Chapter 2

LOVE

I love you,
Not only for what you are,
But for what I am
When I am with you.

I love you,
Not only for what
You have made of yourself,
But for what
You are making of me.

I love you
For the part of me
That you bring out.

—ROY CROFT

THE PHILPOTT AND NALLEY FAMILIES

Brett Philpott, fourteen, seems to inspire a feeling of love in everyone around him. Part of it has to do with the way he smiles. He just beams joy. And when he laughs, it's impossible not to laugh with him.

"Brett is pure love," says his father, Mitch Philpott, and then adds with utmost sincerity, "Brett has made me a better person. He's the best thing that ever happened to me. He brings us so much joy. He gives us so much more than we ever give him."

That is saying a lot. Brett's father, mother, and stepfather have built their lives around caring for him, because Brett is severely disabled and cannot walk, talk, or see. Despite the love that Brett radiates and draws forth from people, the work and dedication involved in taking care of him and nurturing him is enormous. Since he was born, his parents have been responsible for bathing him, changing his diapers, lifting him in and out of his wheelchair, taking him to school, and being available at a moment's notice in case he has a seizure and needs to be rushed to the emergency room. They also tend lovingly to his emotional needs, inventing games that Brett can control himself with the limited mobility he has in one hand, singing to him, playing with him, laughing with him, talking to him, and simply reveling in his company. "When we get home at six P.M., till eight-thirty, it's a hundred percent Brett. Mixing his medicines, feeding him, bathing him. We worry about our dinner later on," says Lee Nalley, Brett's stepfather, who is an equal partner in his care. "At first it seemed a little overwhelming. Now it's like clockwork."

Brett is at the center of a unique and loving family—that lives in two separate homes. One is the home of his father, Mitch Philpott. The other is the home of his mother, Cindy Nalley, and her new husband of seven and a half years, Lee. "We've got a close-knit, two-home family," says Lee, who feels that in getting married to Cindy he got a "new best friend" in her ex-husband, Mitch. Likewise, instead of feeling jealous of his ex-wife's new husband, Mitch has taken to calling Lee his "husband-in-law." "I couldn't have gone out and picked someone better to be Brett's stepfather," Mitch said. "I don't guess Cindy could either," he joked.

Mitch and Cindy divorced when Brett was four because their relationship could not survive the constant stress associated with Brett's condition. Mitch told us the divorce was all his fault. In retrospect, he realizes that he was suffering from depression, but undiagnosed and untreated, he just totally withdrew and didn't communicate with Cindy at all, let alone work at strengthening the marriage. "I was just a jerk," he admits. But when the Philpotts divorced, they worked out an unusual agreement for sharing custody of Brett. Originally, Cindy wanted primary custody of Brett with Mitch having weekend visitation, but Mitch wanted to share custody. To break the impasse, their lawyers recommended that they try alternating custody a week at a time. But Mitch and Cindy told us that neither one of them could bear to be away from Brett for that long. As one of them said, speaking for both, "We would miss him too much."

So over the lawyers' objections, they settled on an idea Mitch came up with to switch custody of Brett every other day and every other weekend. The sheer logistics of this arrangement would seem daunting to most people, but to Mitch and Cindy, it's the only arrangement they could imagine. Every night that Brett stays in Mitch's home, Cindy and Lee call to say good night. In turn, Mitch calls every night Brett is at Cindy and Lee's house to tell his son good night.

The Philpotts and Nalleys, in their own creative way, have discovered an arrangement for their three-parent, two-home family that enables them to maximize the love and the energy they can devote to their son, and yet still restore and renew themselves as individuals so that they can continue to meet the challenges to do right by their unique family.

While to most of us this might seem like an exhausting and overwhelming responsibility, for Mitch, Cindy, and Lee, it is all part of a normal day filled with love and joy. Cindy told us that before having Brett, she used to see a disabled person and think, "Oh, that poor person." But now that she's had Brett, and knows how rich and full of love his life is, she has a completely different perspective. Mitch agrees, saying that he used to avoid people with disabilities. "But now I see handicapped kids and I go to them. You're drawn to them. You know how much love there is."

And it is not only from his parents that Brett draws love and affection. Recently, Brett came home with an apology card signed by forty of his classmates. Mitch worried that it meant that something bad had happened to Brett at school. But it turns out that the other children had misbehaved and, as a punishment, the teacher had told them they couldn't sing in music class. That made them feel terrible, because they like to make Brett laugh and smile and they all know that one of Brett's favorite things during the school day is when he can listen to them sing. So when they realized that their misbehavior was going to deprive Brett of that joy—and deprive them of his laughter—all forty of them signed the apology card.

During her pregnancy with Brett, Cindy Philpott was the ideal expectant mother. She had wanted a child so badly, and was thrilled that after nine years of marriage, she was finally about to give birth. The whole time she was pregnant she was careful about her diet. "No alcohol, no coffee, no tea. I wouldn't even eat chocolate," she told us. Throughout her pregnancy, Cindy was healthy and the doctors did not expect that the twenty-eight-year-old or her baby would have any problems. When her son was born, however, it was clear that something was gravely wrong. An older pediatrician who was in the hospital was the one to diagnose that the baby boy was suffering from an extremely rare birth defect called Sturge-Weber syndrome.

As the doctors started examining him, a flurry of medical jargon overwhelmed her. She was told that there was a 40 percent chance the baby would suffer seizures, a 70 percent chance he'd be blind and suffer glaucoma, and a high chance of brain damage. "There were all these words," Cindy said. "There would be a whole sentence and not one word I could understand." Over the course of the next several days, as scores of doctors performed batteries of tests on the newborn, Cindy and Mitch remained in a state of shock. Recalled Cindy, "I loved him, but I was just in shock. I didn't know how he could be my child." It was several days before she could even speak.

Over the course of the next months, Mitch and Cindy endured a roller coaster of medical crises as doctors attempted to find the right form of treatment for Brett. Along the way, they became experts in the details of Sturge-Weber. In this congenital birth defect, a malformation of a nerve leading to the brain causes a proliferation of blood vessels and the appearance of a distinctive port-wine stain that, tragically—unlike most birthmarks—is accompanied by serious problems affecting the organs in the area of the birth-mark. In Brett's case, the large stain over the upper half of his face was accompanied by vision problems, breathing problems, and an excess of blood vessels on and near his brain.

"As an infant, Brett cried all the time because he was in so much pain," Cindy told us. He was never able to sleep for more than two hours at a time. And then Brett did in fact develop the seizures that the doctors feared he might, and began experiencing up to 150 of them a day.

When he reached twenty-one months, the doctors recommended a radical intervention that they hoped would help: a hemispherectomy, which consists of the removal of an entire hemisphere of the brain. The surgery had been performed successfully a number of times at Johns Hopkins on young children. Because of the resilience and regenerative qualities of the brain in children that young, the remaining hemisphere will often simply take over all brain functions of the removed tissue. "It was supposed to make him a normal kid," Cindy said.

Unfortunately, the operation did not succeed and, worse still, Brett suffered a stroke during the procedure, leaving him in a coma for several days. He ultimately lost his ability to walk and talk because of those complications. To this day, Mitch is racked with guilt that perhaps it had not been the right decision to have the operation. "We'd pray every night that Brett would be well. Two or three weeks before the surgery, he hardly had any seizures at all, and I've always wondered whether maybe our prayers had been answered, and I just didn't listen. He might still be having seizures, but maybe he'd be running around and playing," Mitch said. Before the operation, Brett was just beginning to be able to walk if his mother or father held his hand, and Mitch told us that he had said his first word, "Daddy."

We met Cindy, Mitch, and Brett thirteen years ago when they

were back in the intensive care unit of Johns Hopkins several months later for a second surgery to try to remedy some of the complications of the first. We were there with our son, Albert, who had suffered a near-fatal accident. Following a Baltimore Orioles game, the three of us were leaving the stadium when Albert pulled free of Al's hand and chased a friend across the street, where he was hit by a car. As we and the Philpotts logged round-the-clock hours by our sons' bedsides, we had the chance to talk and share our experiences. We grew to know Mitch, Cindy, and Brett well during that time, and have stayed in touch ever since.

Thirteen years later, Mitch and Cindy have been through divorce and remarriage to others—in Mitch's case, three times. (Mitch had two children in his first marriage before he met and married Cindy, and is on excellent terms with both those children—Christie, now thirty-three, and Josh, now twenty-five.) And yet, in spite of—or perhaps in part because of—everything they have gone through and learned along the way, they are today part of one of the strongest families we have ever met.

Mitch, Cindy, and Lee all recognize that they have each changed tremendously as a result of their commitment to Brett and their long, determined search to find just the right combination of care and support that he needs—and that they can sustain. Perhaps one reason Mitch says Brett is the best thing in his life is because he realizes that he himself has been transformed because of Brett. "I've changed since Brett came into my life," he says. "I'm a better person. I don't worry about myself. Instead of me looking at myself, I am more worried about taking care of Brett."

It took quite a while for Mitch to bounce back to where he is today. In the months immediately following Brett's unsuccessful brain operation, Mitch was anything but a supportive, responsive father and husband. Each night he'd come home from work and sit in the car and cry. Once inside the house, he would hold Brett and cry some more, but would not talk to Cindy at all about how he was feeling, or how they could manage the situation together.

By contrast, today Mitch, Cindy, and Lee talk to each other every single day, usually several times a day. The extraordinary resilience they have developed stems from their enhanced ability to communicate openly with one another and find solutions together. They consult frequently on Brett's education, medical care, and any important decision concerning him—and they make decisions together.

Lee, Cindy, Mitch, and Brett are very much a family bound together by love. Despite the fact that Lee's title is "stepfather," he says, "I feel more the daddy." Indeed, from the very first time Lee met Brett, Cindy sensed the potential of a very unique bond between them. "Lee just went up to him and sat next to him and held his hand," recalled Cindy, noting that no one else she'd dated after her divorce from Mitch had ever responded so warmly and so immediately to her son, whose appearance often unnerves people.

But there is one other way this family is not traditional. It's not just that Brett has both a loving stepfather and a father; Cindy is the only one with a biological connection to Brett. Mitch, who is twelve years older than Cindy, had a vasectomy after fathering two children in his first marriage before he met Cindy. Because Cindy so badly wanted a child with Mitch, they went to a sperm bank, which is how they conceived Brett. The fact that Brett is not Mitch's biological son, however, clearly does not matter. He and Brett are joined at the heart, and through Brett's heart he is joined to Cindy and Lee.

The circles of love that radiate out from Brett have even embraced the extended family. Mitch told us, "My dad never said 'I love you' till the day he died. He just couldn't say it. He loved Brett, but he never could bring himself to do a lot with him." But when Mitch's father was dying, his father told him that he loved him. Then he said, "One day, you and Brett and I will run together and everything will be okay."

JOINED AT THE HEART

In order for us to feel "okay" here on earth, we have to love and be loved—just as we have to breathe in and breathe out. Neither is an option. In fact, scientists have proven that an absence of love causes emotional withering, increases susceptibility to disease, and shortens lives. During the 1940s, the renowned psychiatrist René Spitz studied the developmental fate of American and Canadian orphans and found that, despite adequate food and cleanliness, about one-third of the infants in the orphanages died before their first birthdays and many others suffered from severe developmental problems. Spitz concluded that the infants withered away from lack of physical and emotional affection, which most children enjoy in the arms of loving, caring parents. Love is not simply a feeling; it is a powerful elemental force that molds our lives and binds our families from the moment we are born. It is invisible, much like gravity. But just as you know gravity is present when you feel the ground beneath your feet, you feel love's presence when your beloved walks into the room, or when you touch the tiny fingers of your grandchild reaching out for your hand. The lovesickness of a young lover is not the same as the joy of a grandparent. But having experienced both, we believe they have one important element in common: both engender a feeling of commitment to and responsibility for another person. That is the essence of love. A sense of commitment is central to the urge to form families in the first place.

In the past, however, families have been connected in other ways as well. They not only lived but also worked together—hunting, planting, harvesting and preparing the food, sewing and weaving, cutting wood and tending the hearth, singing, telling stories, entertaining one another, praying, discussing religious values, playing, and much more. They depended on one another and each made his or her own contribution to the well-being of the family as a whole. Your "self-esteem" didn't depend solely on the nature of your relationship with your parents; larger families meant that many more relationships were available. And if one relationship wasn't emotionally fulfilling, there were always others to fall back on. Love was, of course, always a big part of what bonded the family together. Love is not, after all, some social invention. But in the past, love was only one of the factors.

That slowly started to change as the modern world emerged and people began to believe that love should play a bigger role in families. Around the same time, people started to think differently about a lot of things—like Galileo's evidence that the earth was actually orbiting the sun instead of the other way around, and that men and women ought to have some say about who they married instead of letting somebody else make that decision for them.

Historian Steven Ozment told us that even though occasionally there were forced marriages, "particularly among royalty and other self-interested elites," average families at the beginning of the modern era felt that emotional bonding was very important to a marriage. "Contrary to the fate of Romeo and Juliet, most parents have wanted their children to be happy in marriage—both for their own sake and because a happy marriage also better serves the self-interested, material purposes of a marital union," he said.

Gradually, the importance of emotional bonding came to eclipse the other factors that bound families together. And eventually, according to the late Talcott Parsons, one of the first scholars to study the impact of this trend, what has resulted is "the transfer of a variety of functions from the nuclear family to other structures of the society," the transformation of the American family, and a narrowing of its focus. "This means that the family has become a more specialized agency than before," he continued, adding that it is now probably "more specialized than it has been in any previously known society."

So what is left as the clear domain of the family? It's where we go for the love, nurturing, support, and emotional intimacy we need. We look to family as both a refuge and a reservoir. When we talked to

Graham Spanier, the eminent family sociologist who now serves as president of Pennsylvania State University, he put it this way: "One hundred to one hundred fifty years ago, families were the center of everything. But the most distinctive thing about the American family today is that it is based primarily on love. It is the locus of intimacy and emotional support."

This transformation of the family has had a big effect on both the parent-child relationship and the relationship between partners. To begin with, since emotional intimacy has grown in its importance within families today, the strength of family connections depends on the perceived quality of these relationships. That means there is a lot of pressure because more seems to be at risk if the relationship is damaged. So, as family members focus more attention inward, on the quality of family relationships, "the bonds between nuclear family members grow more intense, far more emotional," in the words of Jan Dizard and Howard Gadlin, the authors of *The Minimal Family*.

As the enormous demographic and societal shifts of the last forty years result in an increasing diversity of family types, the emotional connection that makes people consider each other family, and therefore define themselves as a family, is increasingly important. For the first time, "family" is now determined for many people not by structure but by subjective experience.

Martha Minow of Harvard Law School has worked extensively on family cases that have revolved around the question of who constitutes a family and what ties (legal, biological, emotional, societal) need to be present for people to consider themselves and be considered a family. In one pivotal case, two women had a child together through artificial insemination. They lived and raised the child together but two years later separated. For a time, the birth mother let her ex-partner have visitation rights. But when she tried to cut them off, the other woman sued. Minow's task was to argue why that woman, who had helped raise the child, loved the child, but had no biological relationship or traditionally recognized claim on the child, was nevertheless entitled to be considered as a parent. She and the other lawyers on the case argued that what was important was not whether a group of individuals adhered to a formal legal definition of a family created by marriage or adoption, but rather "whether the group of people function as a family: do they share affection and resources, think of one another as family members, and present themselves as such to neighbors and others?"

Minow argues that what really matters in deciding who should be treated like family is "getting behind words, legal formalities, and even blood ties to see how people really live and who cares for whom." In essence, whether a group of people are intimately connected emotionally—regardless of their background, blood ties, or legal relations—and whether they create through their thoughts, deeds, words, and emotions the closeness and joy that creates family. At the time, the court ultimately ruled against that definition of family and denied the woman visitation rights. Nonetheless, for countless "families" that have untraditional ties that bind them together, Minow's definition of family is the one that best describes their daily lives together. It is interesting to note that in recent months, New York City and New York State have moved to provide compensation to domestic partners of victims of the September 11 attacks, arguing that the determination of family benefits eligibility should consider the "totality of circumstances," including "emotional and financial commitment" and "exclusivity and longevity."

Spanier says family life survives for two fundamental reasons. First, because it is the "most efficient means of satisfying several of society's most basic requisites, including replacement of dying members, socialization of the young, and most notably, the provision of emotional support, intimacy and love." Second, a person who is accustomed to the intimacy and support in a family develops deep attachments to those family members and so becomes deeply invested in perpetuating the family. As demographic and societal changes lead to the emergence of alternatives to the traditional nuclear family, these vital emotional functions can continue to be fulfilled "by building on individual and interpersonal strengths," Spanier says. "We are not likely to change the configuration of contemporary families," he adds, referring to the increase in blended families, single-parent families, and same-sex families, "but we can alter how we adapt to the challenges they present."

To put it another way—the way we like to think about it—family is quite simply the people about whom you care the most in the world, regardless of their legal or biological relationship to you. A family is a group of two or more individuals who are joined at the heart.

A lot of the people we have met and talked with live in what we know as families, though they are not necessarily recognized by their religious institutions or the law. They may not fit a traditional mold, yet they are very much families and they are truly joined together. When we think about "family values," for us that includes thinking about how we value families in all shapes and sizes and what we can do to help those families—as well as traditional families—survive and be stronger.

ATTRACTION AND COMMITMENT

Just as love is at the heart of families, it is also at the start of families. Indeed, when most people think of love, they think first of the seemingly magical magnetic force that brings a couple together and forms the potential for a new family, with or without children. For the two of us, it happened on one of our first dates. We had been intrigued by each other when we first met at Al's high school prom party. (We had both come with other dates.) Al called the next morning and asked Tipper out for the following Saturday night. We know it seems unbelievable, but on that next date, there was a moment that neither of us will ever forget: while dancing and talking, our eyes met and everyone else melted away. A deep connection was made—and remains to this day.

When Sarah, our third child and youngest daughter, asked us

once, "Was it love at first sight?" we described that moment to her. But as everyone who has had a similar experience knows, it's never that simple. During our courtship, certainly there were times when, emotionally, we could have gone separate ways. And during thirty-two years of marriage, there have been plenty of disagreements, arguments, stresses, and fights; plenty of struggles to try to change each other to more closely conform to the ideal we each held; frustrations when the demands of marriage, children, work, and pursuing our other interests created the unavoidable tensions; and times of testing that every long-term relationship goes through.

Luckily, we have also had plenty of joy, happiness, play, and pleasure, and we have learned to deeply appreciate those wonderful qualities we see clearly in each other, while accepting what cannot change. It has helped us a lot to laugh at ourselves and at each other. It seems to us that the most important aspect of our journey together has been our willingness to work through our differences and to value and respect the fact that we share such similar goals and values in life.

We were raised by parents who grew up in a vastly different world than the one we currently inhabit. Al's mother and father met when they were both in law school; at that time it was an unusual path for a woman. But Al's mother, who grew up in rural western Tennessee, figured she would become educated and be prepared to support herself. Pauline Gore got her law degree in 1936, but she subsequently sacrificed her own career to help her husband, and to rear her children. They shared a political life.

Tipper's mother, though much younger than Pauline, also grew up in an era when women were expected to get their education but marry a "breadwinner." Ironically, because of divorce, she ended up working as a single mother most of her life. We made our own choices, which were right for us in our marriage. But today's young men and women are preparing for a life where they expect to juggle both careers and parenting demands. Our eldest daughter, Karenna, and her husband, Drew Schiff, are examples of the new paradigm. Drew is a doctor who has now moved into business and she is a lawyer who works three days a week. They try to share parenting responsibilities for their two children, and they work hard to balance the demands of work and family.

In the hope of improving their chances of choosing the right lifelong partner, many couples in today's America decide to live together before (or instead of) marrying. That was the choice made by Gabrielle and Chris Wagener, who are both in their late twenties. A few months after they began dating, they decided to share an apartment in Washington, D.C. Privately, they'd both begun thinking about the possibility of marriage early in their relationship, and living together was a way to "test things out beforehand," as Gabrielle put it. But the experience of waking up every morning next to your new love can be a big adjustment. As Chris recalled, "We wanted to spend as much time as we could together, but we weren't ready to get married. The next thing I knew there was a hair dryer and all this stuff."

Happily for Gabrielle and Chris, the trial run was successful, and after two and a half years of living together they got married in May 2001. Then came the really big changes. Chris finished medical school and the couple moved to Birmingham, Alabama, so he could complete his medical residency. Gabrielle got a new job as an event planner; they bought a house, and then began the endless struggle to balance long hours at work with time at home and together.

What Gabrielle and Chris also began to understand was that they were becoming a family. Chris also feels a new sense of responsibility: "Not that I didn't feel responsible before for Gabrielle, but there's obviously something deeper there now." They planned to wait to have kids until they were financially more secure, but even without children they felt they'd crossed a threshold and become something more than a couple. As Gabrielle told us, "It felt different right away. Like now we were our own little family, and there was a security in that. It gave me more confidence, like I can take the world on now, because I have this person who is behind me."

Gabrielle will need her confidence, because marriage is in some respects more difficult today than it was in the past. Now most people want a partner who will simultaneously be best friend, passionate lover, and economic partner. These extraordinarily high expectations make it ever more difficult for couples to satisfy each other over the long term—and partly explain the reluctance of more singles to marry. If marriage is so difficult, why marry at all?

The answer we've come to is that marriage represents commitment, and that commitment is a large part of love. Marriage is an outward sign that two people are asking the community to honor and support their commitment to each other. Implicit in this commitment is the couple's determination to give their children (should they choose to have them) a strong foundation of trust and support that will serve them throughout their lives. Recent studies of children's needs show convincingly that, all other things being equal, the sustained attention of two loving adults is the most important factor in improving the chances for emotional and physical good health and avoiding poverty, crime, and other social dysfunctions. It is important to note that studies show that those loving adults do not need to be birth parents or even parents at all—as long as there is someone to whom a child can consistently turn for unconditional love and support. That is the most critical asset for a child to be able to beat the odds. If a child has rough circumstances but there is even just one person who is crazy about him or her and the child knows it, that is the life preserver that the child can hang on to. However, when a child does not have that caring adult but, rather, a revolving door of caretakers, that child is at a greater risk of not making it.

We can't say it enough: marriage takes hard work. It takes work to resolve conflicts, to maintain open lines of communication, to keep commitments and discharge obligations even when it may not be convenient. It can feel like work just to make time with family a priority over all the other competing demands in a busy, modern life. Love alone is not enough. Or, as Susan Fadley told us, "Love is more of an action than it is a feeling."

The way love is shared between two people depends upon the complex interplay between the commitments each has made to the other, the social and cultural environment in which the marriage exists, and the inescapable biological facts of life. There is infinite variety in the ways couples approach this challenge. But there are clearly recognizable patterns, and knowledge of these patterns can help prepare couples, and the families they create, for success in meeting their goals. And the goal of most is to share a strong bond of love that endures and sustains the health and well-being of their family.

Even though Gabrielle and Chris are still relatively early in their relationship, it is clear that they envision a bond that will grow and deepen over the years. "He's my best friend," Gabrielle told us. And more than that, "he's the person that when I think about being sixty-five and having grandkids, I see myself still cracking up, sitting there with him on the couch and laughing at his jokes."

While various biological and biochemical factors certainly play some part in our first, instinctive responses toward other people, one of the deepest and most wonderful mysteries about love is when it moves beyond and transcends those basic instincts. In our own experience, we were initially drawn together by attraction and the fun we had together. But as our relationship matured, we came to love each other much more because we shared the same values and the same aspirations. Spending the last three decades together and raising our four children together has been our single greatest joy. The love we feel for each other today is a thousand times deeper and richer than when we first met and fell in love.

Growing up, Al had a powerful example in his own parents of what love for a lifetime means. His father respected his mother as an equal, if not more; he was proud of her. And it went way beyond

that. When Al was a young boy growing up, it never once occurred
to him that the foundation upon which his security depended—his
family—would ever shake. From his parents he learned the value
of a true, loving partnership that lasts for life.

The families we interviewed in the course of writing this book
have shown us so powerfully, time and time again, that one of the
most important aspects of love comes after the infatuation and
romance has left center stage. It comes in the daily struggles to
understand each other, to work through problems, and to find the
way to honor common values together. It pleases us to see that
many young people we know are reflecting quite deliberately on
what they are looking for in a mate. Although they are certainly
drawn together by attraction, they are also searching for someone
who is compatible with them not just physically but also emotionally, intellectually, and spiritually.

THE LOGAN FAMILY

For the millions of American families that include children, the
bond between parent and child remains central to the definition of
family. But this relationship too has changed over the past two
generations. For one thing, the sharp reduction in family size has
meant that each child is much more likely to receive a lot of emotional attention from the parents. As Judith Wallerstein puts it,
children "have grown in importance because there are fewer of
them, and they're reliable relationships." Wallerstein adds that,
especially with the increase of divorce, children are really "the relationship that you can count on the most."

Now, for so many couples, children are the most important thing
in their lives. That is certainly the case with John Coon and Josh
Tuerk, two young professionals who as children in Maryland lived
only ten blocks away from each other but didn't meet until years
later, and who finally found in each other a partner who is compatible in every way. They have a committed caring relationship. They

are building a family together. They adore their two children, take great joy in playing with them, and worry about their future. As they build their life together, what is in some ways most striking about their relationship is how absolutely "normal" it is. But the luxury of being ordinary—if two gay men raising two adopted children can now be called ordinary—has been born from years of searing emotional trauma and struggle that each has turned into remarkable strength of character.

As young boys, they both struggled with the reality that they were "different"—and that they might be gay. Though they both sensed it when they were children, they still had to deal with not only accepting themselves for who they were but also with having their families accept them as well.

Josh recounts how in elementary school his parents sent him to therapy four days a week in order to try to "fight" his homosexuality. As a little boy, he wondered, "What is wrong with me?" And he tried, along with his parents, to "fix it." In fact, he said, he tried desperately, because "I was really struggling, trying to be straight, wondering why I would rather be playing with flowers than with girls, or football. It was really awful."

Four years after Josh and John fell in love and made a commitment to become life partners, they decided to create a family, even though they knew the odds were against them. Now that they are approaching their eight-year anniversary together, they have no doubt that the adoption of their two little boys was the turning point that transformed them and defined them as a family.

John was the one who always knew he wanted to adopt. "Even before I knew whether it would be with a woman or a man," he told us, "I knew that I would adopt a child." One big reason for his determination is that John and his sister were both adopted, and his parents were very open with them about it. John had been looking all along for the right person and the right time to begin a family.

Josh, on the other hand, had never dreamed of having a child. "It never occurred to me it would be a possibility," he told us. "I was envious of my girlfriends who were going to marry and have children, because I knew that was never going to be an option for me." John really had to work on Josh to convince him to adopt a child. He increased the pressure when he informed Josh, four years into their relationship, that he was ready to begin the adoption process. After a lot of discussion and negotiation, Josh finally agreed.

The decision made, Josh and John began to talk seriously with the local child and family services agency. Fortunately they were financially successful. (Josh runs a pet-care-services business; John runs a paint contracting company, and together they run a property management company.) Even though Josh thought their chances were slim, they signed up for the required course, which covered caring for a foster child, racial sensitivity in the case of interracial adoptions, and discipline issues. "Two white gay men?" he said. "Not a chance." But they were determined. Their next challenge came when they had to fill out the paperwork. Should they lie about the nature of their relationship—which they feared would jeopardize their chances—or should they be forthcoming? Actually, that choice turned out to be easy for them. Josh recounted how, on that day, "We started filling out the forms and the questions were right there and I remember just thinking, I don't want to start my family off based on lies." After going through the process, they have nothing but praise for the people at Family Services, Josh said. "They were inclusive, supportive people. Their mission is to find families for babies, not babies for families."

Nevertheless, Josh and John were still apprehensive about whether or not they would be deemed suitable parents. They were painfully aware of the fears and prejudices aimed at gay men. They really did not believe it would happen for them, in part to avoid getting their hopes up too high—lest they be crushed. John remembers saying to Josh, "There is no way they are going to choose us over the other people."

But the call came, there was a baby, and they had to make a quick decision. They were overcome with feelings of joy and anticipation, "nerves," and an urge to shop at Babies "R" Us. They had only forty-eight hours to decide whether or not to take the newly born boy out of the hospital. Technically, they were foster parents at first; later on they were allowed to adopt Noah.

Josh still vividly remembers going to the hospital. "The nurse had told me that our baby was in the nursery. So I go in there, and I didn't know which one of the five infants was ours." When Josh saw their baby, he felt a rush of emotion. "I swear, I fell in love with him immediately. Immediately. And all my fears were completely dispelled." As a white person, he had been worried about whether he'd "be able to relate to a little black baby." After one look at Noah, those concerns were gone.

As for John, this was the first time he had ever held a newborn baby in his life. Though he wasn't worried about raising a child of another race, he wanted to make sure his family of origin could handle it. Earlier, he had talked with his father about it and asked if it bothered him. John's father gave him a simple answer. "No, I don't mind at all," said the future grandfather.

Josh and John also knew in advance that the baby most likely would come from an addicted, possibly HIV-positive mother, both of which turned out to be the case. (This information was given to them by the agency; Josh and John never actually met Noah's mother.) Josh and John knew that there would be a lot of risks involved, but they felt ready. John says, "If he is HIV-positive, we will handle that. If he has birth defects, we'll just do what you do and take care of him."

But they were both unprepared for the fear they felt while they were waiting for Noah's first HIV test. They could see both sets of possibilities for his life, and were so relieved when he turned out to be healthy. (Since the doctors knew the birth mother was HIV-positive, they had given her the drug AZT before she gave birth.

Noah was lucky, because, unfortunately, one of his mother's previous children was indeed HIV-positive.)

When we asked them how long after Noah's arrival they began discussing the possibility of adopting a second child, John gave a quite unexpected reply. "Oh, Marcus was an accident. We didn't plan to adopt." Al's response was, "What—you got the pills wrong?"

What actually happened is an interesting example of how family has been redefined. Like some two-career families with a new baby, Josh and John decided to hire a nanny. After a few weeks of working for them, the young woman they hired asked if she could bring her own baby to work with her, since she was having childcare difficulties of her own. When they said yes, her three-month-old son Marcus entered their life. Seeing what a beautiful and caring home John and Josh were providing for Noah, she felt that they would be able to give her son a better home than she was able to. As a single mother who already had one child, she didn't feel that she could provide well for her son. She soon asked them if they would adopt Marcus. John and Josh thought long and hard about whether to adopt another child. In many ways, it was not unlike the talks many couples have when they differ over when they think it's the right time to have a second child, with one important difference—once they decided, there was no nine-month waiting period; they added their new family member in a record nine days. Marcus's birth mother is still a part of his life, periodically coming over to visit and share a meal with the whole family.

Just when we thought it was safe to conclude that they had told us about every unusual characteristic, John told us about their family name. Josh wanted them all to have the same last name—not just the two new brothers, but all of them. They might have considered hyphenating their two last names for the whole family, but John didn't think that his last name, Coon, was appropriate for the children, since Noah is African-American and Marcus is African-American and Latino. Meanwhile, each set of grand-parents was rooting for the new grandchildren to carry on their family names.

After reflection—and fending off the lobbying efforts of their parents—John and Josh came up with a novel solution: an entirely new family name for all of the members of this newly formed family. They decided to become the Logans. The couple loves the name Logan—Josh's grandmother's maiden name was Logan, plus they live in the Logan Circle neighborhood of Washington, D.C. So when they adopted Noah, and then Marcus, they gave each of them Logan as their family name, keeping their birth names as their middle names. And John and Josh plan to legally change their names in the same way so they will become John Coon Logan and Josh Tuerk Logan. "That's right—we'll be four Mr. Logans living in the house," Josh said proudly. (With their permission, and because they will eventually all be Mr. Logans, we call them the Logan family throughout the book.)

Meanwhile, both sets of grandparents seem to have accepted the decision. All four are active, supportive, loving grandparents to Noah and Marcus, who adore their grandparents in return.

The way they see it, theirs is a hometown story, really. They each married the guy around the corner. They point out that the really unusual thing is that both sets of their parents are still together!

Adopting the boys changed them profoundly. Josh puts it well: "We were not even thinking about the possibilities of having children, my fears were that I was not going to be able to love a child. . . . And it's been such a wonderful experience to know that I can love them as much as I do. I just didn't realize I had that capacity, which has really been incredible for me."

When asked how they define family, Josh and John sum it up in four entirely apt words: "Love. Sharing. Responsibility. Contentment."

A FATHER'S LOVE

Noah and Marcus Logan are lucky: they are being raised by not one, but two caring, committed fathers. But many children are growing up without any father at all. Indeed, one of the great challenges facing American families is that too many fathers are absent from the lives of their children. We believe that most single mothers do an excellent job of raising their kids, but it must be acknowledged that families are almost always better off with two loving parents present in the home, sharing both the work and the joy.

It's distressing how many obstacles still make it difficult for fathers to play a full and constructive role in the family. As is often the case, the first hurdle is an obsolete way of thinking—in this case about fatherhood. In the early editions of his famous book on child-rearing, *Baby and Child Care*, Dr. Benjamin Spock actually cautioned, "Of course, there are some fathers who would get goose flesh at the very idea of helping to take care of a baby, and there's no good to be gained by trying to force them. Most of them come around to enjoying their children later 'when they're more like real people.' " And Ernest Hemingway once said that the key to being a successful father was as follows: "when you have a kid, don't look at it for the first two years." Although many American men now take a far more enlightened view of the father's role, vestiges of these outdated attitudes remain surprisingly strong.

Many family researchers used to focus almost exclusively on studying the mother-child bond, as if the father had been cropped out of the family photograph. Two generations ago, experts would often say that the best thing a father can do for his children is to love their mother. Although that is indeed one of the father's primary responsibilities, more recent research—a flood of it in the past few years—has confirmed the older, commonsense view that fathers have a unique role to play in raising children. Fathers are not just male mothers—in fact, new studies suggest that infants recognize very early the emotional differences between the father's and the mother's styles of relating and interacting. Even so, a surprising number of people still resist the idea that a father's love has special meaning to a child.

Outdated thinking about fatherhood also continues to pervade too much of both the public and private sectors. For instance, many social policies that address families typically still assume the absence of fathers. At one of several policy forums that we have held on the role of fathers, a housing official in Connecticut told us about a meeting with tenants in a housing project in Hartford that was interrupted when a man entered the room and a small boy rushed up to him, saying, "Daddy! Daddy!" Instantly, the child's mother admonished him to "Hush!" And then, more quietly but still with alarm, she added, "How many times do I have to tell you not to call him Daddy when people are around!" The mother, this official realized, was afraid that if she acknowledged a relationship with the father of her child, she might lose her housing.

Businesses, too, can make it more difficult than it should be for middle-class married fathers to be committed parents. Taking paternity leave or leaving work in the middle of the day to drive a child to a doctor's appointment is still not acceptable to numerous employers. Many companies develop a work culture that does not respect a father's desire to leave the office in time to be home for dinner. Subtly and not so subtly, corporate America demonstrates a stubborn resistance to the idea that fathers have an important role in the family beyond simply earning a paycheck.

It is true, however, that the positive impact of that paycheck is considerable. Several of the nation's leading scholars have documented the economic consequences of absent fathers. For example, studies show that compared to children whose fathers live with them, children in homes without fathers are five times more likely to be poor, twice as likely to drop out of high school, twice as likely to get pregnant when they are teenagers, and one and a half times as likely to be out of school and out of work in their late teens.

One leading scholar in the field, David Ellwood of Harvard, sums up the data related to this issue with a jolting starkness: "The vast majority of children who are raised entirely in a two-parent home will never be poor during childhood. By contrast, the vast majority of children who spend time in a single-parent home will experience poverty."

Of course, the consequences of involved fatherhood reach well beyond the economic effects. Dads mean a lot more to children and families than dollars. Not long ago, we met a young student from a low-income family who told us that her father picked her up after school every day in his taxi. She said that because many of her friends could say, "My father is a doctor" or "My father is a lawyer," she used to be embarrassed to say "My father is a taxi driver." But as she got older, she said she came to realize that she could say something many of her friends felt they could not say: "I could say, 'My father loves me.'"

In the same vein, we read a series of essays about the meaning of fathers written by young people. One eleventh grader wrote: "I don't know what it is to have a father. I see people that have one and wish I had mine. Sometimes my days are bad and I cry because I need someone there to talk to, to share my troubles, my fears, and most of all, my dreams. . . . I feel empty inside. I just wish that parents who have kids don't forget that they . . . have brought something beautiful into this world. And they must take care of that beautiful person that they created."

Many of the other essays were from children who described what it meant to *have* their fathers. "Without my father," one sixth grader wrote, "it would be like a ball without any air inside. And you can't play without any air inside." A fifth grader recounted a single exchange: "The other night my Dad came up to me and said, 'Goodnight Carrie. I love you.' 'Goodnight,' I said. 'I love you too.' Then out of the blue he said, 'Best friends forever?' And I said, 'Yes.'" And a third grader wrote about how, "My Dad 'God blesses' us before we leave for school. Mom says he watches us walk to the school out the window until he can't see us anymore. She says he gets tears in his eyes almost every time."

Grassroots organizations working to strengthen families have recently come to appreciate the unique transformational power of a father's emotional connection to his child—for both the child and the father. Joe Jones Jr., who founded and runs an organization on the streets of Baltimore that reconnects fathers with their children, told us of numerous men who resisted every effort to help them turn away from drugs, alcohol, and crime until the experience of bonding with their child and respecting their child's mother brought about a profound transformation in their behavior and attitude toward life.

By the same token, society often overlooks the devastating emotional impact on fathers who lose their children in divorce proceedings. As one close friend of ours who went through a divorce put it, "Typically, the divorce courts remove men from the family; the wife gets custody, and he is left in an emotional gulag, void of the close bonds of family. There is a certain loss of identity that can often lead to the loss of emotional equilibrium or depression." We don't question the ways courts are handling custody disputes; that is and should be handled carefully on a case-by-case basis. But the loving relationship between a father and his children has a power that should never be overlooked or underestimated.

Fortunately, many fathers across America are becoming more involved with their children. Richard Louv, author of *FatherLove*, documents the steady increase in father involvement, and has studied the extent to which involved fathers are more satisfied with their own lives. They're more likely to help out with tasks that were traditionally regarded as mother's responsibilities: "more than 40 percent of America's dads are intimately involved with everything from childbirth to diaper changing to running the kids to play dates in the family station wagon," Louv observes. But they also rediscover aspects of fatherhood more common before the Industrial Revolution, and more traditionally associated with masculinity, including community-building—for example, working with other parents, often other fathers, to make their neighborhoods safer for children and families. It is also important to note that all of the research demonstrates that a male father figure—whether an uncle or grandfather or close family friend—who is appropriately and deeply involved in the life of a child *as if* he were the father, can provide most of the emotional and spiritual benefits of a father.

We held our third annual Family Re-Union forum on "The Role of Men in Children's Lives" back in 1994, and the following year announced the creation of the "Father-to-Father" program, a national grassroots effort designed to enhance existing community-based initiatives by forming networks for men to assist one another in the tasks of fatherhood. Like others, we were pleased to find that many American fathers want to become far more involved in their families and especially in the lives of their children.

We were also deeply moved to learn of the efforts by numerous men to reach out to children who have no father in their home. The impact of this involvement on the psychological health of a child can be enormous, and the child will often acknowledge it by offering the highest possible praise, saying, "He was just like a father to me" or "He was the father I never had." Men who find the time and energy to give to a community program or a lonely child are not just meeting an immediate need, they are building the fathers of the future.

We believe it is critical to instill in every generation of fathers the belief that fatherhood is a sacred trust, and that it is a father's nonnegotiable responsibility to support his children both financially *and* emotionally. We believe that children need and deserve a father's love—and that all men have a responsibility to all children. Shakespeare once wrote, "It is a wise father that knows his own child." And, we would add, it is a wise society that knows how important that is—for both father and child.

THE CRUMPTON FAMILY

The power of love to transform our lives and our families can be seen in all the relationships found in families. For example, despite all the jokes about mothers-in-law, and notwithstanding the fact that many in-law relationships are strained, it is nevertheless true that a strong feeling of love often grows across the in-law divide.

Our brother-in-law, Frank Hunger, has formed the closest relationship to our children of anyone outside the immediate family. Or to put it another way, he *is* part of our immediate family. Frank, who was married to Al's sister, Nancy, became a widower eighteen years ago, when Nancy died of lung cancer at the age of forty-six. But he and Nancy, who did not have children, met Karenna the week she was born, and over the years they grew very close to her and then to her sisters and brother. After Nancy's death, the relationship between Frank and our children deepened. Frank loves games and practical jokes; whenever he appeared, he became the male equivalent of the character Auntie Mame, and our kids knew there would be lots of laughing and action and fun. He would invite the children to fly with him on his plane, and take them on bicycle and skiing trips. Equally important, our children know they can always count on Frank to help them with a problem or serve as a confidant. To put it simply, he adores them and they him.

One of our children's favorite stories about Frank involves a culinary mystery. It's our family's tradition to spend the holidays in Tennessee and feast on roast duck the day after Christmas. One year, Uncle Whit, Al's uncle on his mother's side, brought the ducks to cook, as he usually does. But the birds had already been plucked by the man who hunted them, and someone noticed that along with the many ducks was one unidentifiable body. Frank and the kids had a great time determining whether the mystery animal was a goose, a large frog, a rabbit, or a strange duck. For some reason, Frank's technique for making the determination involved chasing Sarah around the kitchen with the carcass. The kitchen was filled with screams and laughter, and there's no question that Frank laughed hardest of all. Eventually, we roasted the ducks and the mystery animal with a great sauce, and we all decided that the hunter had indeed bagged a rabbit.

Frank's unique role in our family was acknowledged in a very special way in 2001 when Karenna and her husband, Drew Schiff, named their baby daughter, Anna Hunger Schiff. Anna's middle name honors both Frank and Nancy, and Frank says that it's the nicest thing anyone has ever done for him. Now Frank is deeply involved in our family's newest generation: he's the most doting uncle imaginable to Anna and her three-year-old brother, Wyatt, and it's more obvious than ever that Frank is less an in-law than a brother, uncle, and much-loved family member.

Grandparents, too, can play a transformative role in family life. For the two of us, Anna and Wyatt have been our instructors in the joys of grandparenting. But we have been especially inspired by two fellow grandparents we interviewed, Rodney and Melissa (Missy) Crumpton.

For the love of his young grandson, Caleb, who was born in 1998, Rodney Crumpton quit driving his truck; then he and Missy took out loans, scrimped and saved, and went back to college in their mid-forties so they could set an example for Caleb and their whole family. Rodney and Missy of Murfreesboro, Tennessee, are a loving couple who have been married for twenty-eight years. They actually married secretly, because Missy was only seventeen at the time and didn't think her parents would approve of her marrying so young. Missy and Rodney knew each other as children, but Rodney, three years older, never paid much attention to her, according to Missy. But time passed, and one day Rodney came by to visit her older brother and started noticing. Soon their relationship turned romantic.

Over the years, their love grew and deepened, and they weathered many challenges together—including the fear that their first son, Zach, who was born premature, wouldn't survive. Then especially after the birth of their second son, Shane, several bouts of unemployment made it difficult to make ends meet.

They also survived one of the toughest of all challenges to a marital relationship, when Rodney had an affair with an old girlfriend. When Missy found out, she was shattered. She said, "We had always had total trust in each other. I was upset that I was so naïve and so blind." The fight that ensued lasted two to three days, Missy told us, and it took far longer to restore the trust between them. But they eventually were able to "get back together emotionally," Missy said.

Today, eleven years later, Rodney and Missy say they are deeply in love and say they are each other's best friends. "Very few people have been loved like I have by a wife," Rodney said. "She is the best person."

They also have a nontraditional member in their immediate family. Both Rodney and Melissa regard Michael Kennedy as their "third son," even though there is no blood relation. Michael entered their life sixteen years ago through a mutual friend. "He was a rejected orphan, transplanted from Connecticut," Rodney says. They all liked each other enormously and "became like family." Michael, now thirty-seven, became a big brother to Zach and Shane. "Sometimes he's more like a brother to me than my real one," says Zach.

Rodney and Missy say that when they reach old age, it will be Michael—not Zach or Shane—to whom they look for security and caregiving. Missy explained that their sons Zach and Shane will both probably have their hands full taking care of their own families and children. (Shane's first marriage ended in divorce, and his son, Joshua, lives with his ex-wife in Montana; Shane recently remarried.) But Michael is "more the caretaking kind," Missy says. And Michael, who now rents an apartment directly below the Crumptons', is fully prepared for the role he is expected to play, Missy told us. "He wouldn't let anyone else do it," Rodney said. Just like Zach and Shane, Michael is named as one of Rodney and Missy's beneficiaries on their life insurance policies. And he in turn has named Missy and Caleb on his. "He *is* family," Rodney says simply.

But as much as Missy's and Rodney's love for each other and "all three of their sons" is special, it has actually been their love for their grandson, Caleb, that profoundly transformed their lives. Rodney was a good father to his two sons, but somehow fatherhood never affected Rodney the way grandfatherhood did. "I just didn't have that wave of love come over me and the maturity I needed to parent my own kids," Rodney says regretfully. "If only I had loved my kids the way I loved Caleb. I was too demanding with them." But he is proud that his going to college is also setting an example for his sons, and he talks constantly about hoping his success will help open doors for them as well.

"When Caleb came along, I just couldn't take my eyes off him," Rodney says. The changes started with small things, like the Super Bowl. Missy marveled at the way Rodney, a big football fan, held Caleb in his arms during the game and "never once looked at the TV." Then they even changed pets. Even though they're "dog people," as soon as they realized that "Caleb's a cat person," they switched and now have a cat named Didi.

Caleb lives with Rodney (whom Caleb refers to as "Oompa") and Missy every weekend from Friday night to late Sunday night, because Zach and his wife, Christy, work on weekends at different fast-food restaurants. While Caleb is with them, Rodney and Missy (whom Caleb calls "Missy" because she feels too young to be "Grandma") do everything they can to help him learn and explore the world. Oompa makes flash cards for his grandson to increase his vocabulary. Instead of what Rodney calls "old words" like "cat" and "dog," he has made cards with words like "start" and "play" that are helpful to Caleb in working with the computer they have installed in their living room. Zach says, "Caleb never would have learned the computer without coming here to Oompa and Missy's. He knows more than I do about the computer."

The biggest change in Rodney and Missy's life brought about by their love for Caleb has been their decision to go to college. "I want him to have that example. I want Caleb to grow up to be something," Rodney said. Both Rodney and Missy took out federal student loans and went back to college together. A few times, Rodney was tempted to quit school and return to truck driving so they would have more money to live on. But he has stayed at it, motivated by the determination to leave "a record that Caleb will grow up with." Now that he and Missy are close to graduating (Rodney this year and Missy the next), Rodney hopes desperately to get a good job, to prove to Caleb that the hard work of college is worth it.

The transformation in Rodney has also brought him closer to his own sons. They view him with a new sense of admiration—and a feeling of competition to finish college soon after he does. While both Zach and Shane completed high school, neither of them had been serious about college. But now that both their parents are on the brink of completing their degrees, both boys—as well as Michael Kennedy—are eager to get their degrees as well.

Rodney grins like a Cheshire cat when he talks about how the whole family is racing to catch up with the legacy that he is building by being the first one in the family to graduate from college. And he knows instantly who deserves the credit: Caleb. "Tell the world how much my love for Caleb has changed my life for the better," he told us. "That love is a powerful medicine, and most of all we pray and wish and hope that our actions will result in a better chance at life for Caleb when we are long gone."

Rodney credits one other source of love for the dramatic transformation in his life: Missy. "I talk about Caleb so much, but it is because of the love that Missy and I have always had that we can love Caleb so much together. I have won the lottery twice with Missy and Caleb. I will never know why God loved me that much." Together they just hope that they can provide enough love and support to help him through life. And along the way they are all teaching each other something about love. Rodney told us about an incident recently when another young child was mean to Caleb. Rodney and Missy asked Caleb why he thought the boy was mean. Caleb said, " 'Cause nobody loves him, Oompa."

Rodney and Missy's love for their grandson goes far beyond the fact that they share the responsibility of primary caretaking with their son and his wife. They rent one of three apartments in a meager house near campus, and though they wish they could do more for Zach and Christy, they don't have extra money themselves— and Zach and Christy understand that. They have no financial assets to speak of, other than the life-insurance policies they have taken out on themselves so that they can leave an inheritance of several thousand dollars to their grandsons Caleb and Joshua. They are heartbroken that Joshua is "lost to them" because his mother has taken him away to Montana and they are not able to see him or spend time with him. But the inner life of the family has been utterly transformed because of their love for Caleb. Each Sunday night when Caleb is getting ready to go back to his parents after having spent the weekend with them, they all sing a little song together, called "Clint Eastwood" by Gorillaz. The way Rodney sings it, the chorus goes, "I'm happy, I'm feeling glad, I've got sunshine in a bag. I'm useless, but not for long, the future is coming on, is coming on, is coming on."

Love is commitment. And a loving family is one whose members are committed to one another.

THE LETKE-ALEXANDERS

Noah Alexander, Pat Letke-Alexander, Nathan Alexander, and Todd Alexander

Chapter 3

COMMUNICATION

There's no vocabulary
For love within a family, love that's lived in
But not looked at, love within the light of which
All else is seen, the love within which
All other love finds speech.
This love is silent.

—T. S. ELIOT

A SMALL COMMUNITY OF SPEECH

Strong families are not born—they are built, shaped, and strengthened, moment by moment, through thousands of thoughts and deeds and words. But words, when used in families, are not just words; with all of the emotional connections and personal histories that surround every exchange in families, a rose is a rose is . . . not necessarily a rose.

All families have a language of their own, in which many of the words have long footnotes written in invisible ink. In some families, just making it safely through a simple conversation can seem like driving a car backward while using one of those mirrors that's labeled, "Caution. Objects may be closer than they appear."

According to Deborah Tannen, a well-known linguist and author who studies family communications, the family is "a small community of speech, an organic unit that shapes and maintains itself linguistically." What makes communication in families so tricky, Tannen says, is that "[e]verthing we say to each other echoes with meanings left over from our past experience. . . . This is especially true in the family—and our history of family talk is like a prism through which all other conversations (and relationships) are refracted." As a result, what we're trying to say often gets lost in a tangle of powerful feelings inadvertently summoned by words that on their surface do not seem to justify such feelings. And the extra layer of embedded meaning can be either positive or negative. For example, most families enjoy talking about shared past experiences that were fun or funny. As Tannen told us, "You can say 'It's like the time . . . ' and then one word and suddenly, everybody's laughing because they remember the whole story. So that's the positive side. But the negative part of it is that you can step on these land mines without meaning to."

Many people—ourselves included—often make the common mistake of assuming that the logical meaning of the words we choose will accurately convey the message that is received by the person to whom we are talking. Our culture teaches us to exalt the rational and to ignore the irrational or nonliteral. This approach to communication may work in a scientific conference, but in families, the nature and quality of the emotional connection is almost always more important than the logical content of the words. Or to put it another way, the heart will trump the head every time if the head has no idea what's going on in the realm of the heart. Scientists have made remarkable discoveries about the human brain that illuminate the huge differences in the way it interprets emotions and rational thought.

Actually, two completely different parts of the brain are brought into play. Emotions are handled by the so-called mammalian brain (or "limbic brain"). Logic is handled by the neocortex, which was the last part of the brain to evolve. The distinction between them is exactly what we mean when we talk about the difference between the heart and the head.

Listening with the heart as well as the head requires *not* interrupting or leaping ahead to finish the speaker's sentence and react to it in the same breath. You need to be mindful not only of the words themselves but also of facial expressions and other body language so you can sense feelings as well—and to encourage the person to speak more about those feelings. It also means noticing times when a family member needs you just to listen.

The art of listening effectively is more complicated than it may seem; for most people it's a lot easier to talk than to listen. That's why it's usually so important to create appropriate emotional space for a family conversation. Timing can make all the difference. In our marriage, and in our relationships with our children, we learned early that we couldn't talk about really important things on the fly. There has to be enough time set aside for adequate discussion. We also learned that when particularly difficult information has to be imparted, it is best to wait patiently for the right time, the right setting, and the right mood so that the information will be received in the right frame of mind. In other words, timing is everything when you are trying to deliver an important message.

The two of us have found that communication in our family always seems to be much easier and less subject to stress and misinterpretation when we're doing something together and our talk has a clear purpose. Likewise, we almost always agree on words describing our grandchildren and how much we love them. But when either of us uses words that describe what the other is doing or has done, we are more likely to need an interpreter to sort out all the meanings received from the ones conveyed.

So if time is of the essence for successful communication, how do families find time? The evening meal used to be the best time for many family members to talk and listen to one another, to build and maintain family relationships, and to exchange ideas and opinions in ways that reinforced the values considered important within the family. However, due to increased work hours, split-shift schedules, easy access to takeout food and microwaved dinners, and ringing telephones, many families no longer share this routine. William Doherty, director of the Marriage and Family Therapy Program in the Department of Family Social Science at the University of Minnesota, Twin Cities, cited a national survey that shows that two-thirds of American families no longer eat dinner together regularly. And of the third that do, half of them no longer talk—because they are all watching television while they eat.

Whatever the cause, many family scholars agree that the decline of the family dinner as a daily ritual has had a huge, far-reaching impact on family communication. Studies show that the minority of families that do still maintain the family dinner ritual and guard it from outside intrusions are healthier and stronger by almost every measure. The National Longitudinal Study of Adolescent Health, for example, found that the presence of the parent or parents at home during family dinners is one of the most important factors in making teenagers feel highly connected to them. Moreover, the presence of parents during family dinners was correlated with a delay in teen sexual activity and a reduction in virtually all risk behaviors. The National Center of Addiction and Substance Abuse (CASA) at Columbia University has found that the more parents have family dinners with their children, the less likely the children are to drink or smoke or use drugs. (Of course it may be that families who share dinner share more time together overall, and that is what strengthens the family.) In fact, CASA has begun a national campaign to encourage states to emphasize the importance of family dinners by adopting a "family day," when parents and children share a family meal.

Whether around the dinner table or elsewhere, the sheer volume of communication within a family is important, because it reinforces the natural connections. Quality matters, too, of course, but within a family, quantity matters as much or more. All the minutes and hours and days spent together, communicating verbally and nonverbally without a lot of emotional tension, just being together and talking—that is the coin of the family's realm.

THE LETKE-ALEXANDER FAMILY

Pat Letke-Alexander and her husband of five years, Todd Alexander, already know how important good communication is to a relationship. Like many couples, they trace the beginning of their relationship back to their initial "great conversation," when they felt that they first connected. Pat and Todd met when he was working at Crossing Place, a halfway house that provided crisis housing and other services for homeless people in Washington, D.C. Pat worked at a center that provided medical services for homeless people and Todd often referred clients there and would sometimes come with them.

A few months after they first met, Todd suggested they get together at a St. Patrick's Day parade. But at the last moment he changed his mind and didn't show up. As he explained to us, he suddenly got a bad case of the jitters. "The way she was looking at me and the way I felt about her, even though I didn't know her that well, I knew that my bachelor days would probably be over, and I was scared. I didn't know if I could make that commitment, and so I sort of bagged that."

As it turned out, Todd's intuition that he and Pat would make a powerful connection once they got to know each other was right. When they finally did go out to dinner, Pat recalled, "We were sitting there having drinks and Todd started talking about himself, just sort of nonstop." This was unusual, because he was normally on the quiet side. Over the course of the evening, they both really opened up to each other and felt a real connection through the stories and experiences they shared with each other.

After that first great discussion, their relationship developed very quickly on a day-by-day basis. The day after their first date, Pat asked Todd if he could drive her (in *her* car) to the airport, as she was leaving for a trip the following day. When they arrived at the airport, Todd recalls, right before she got out of the car to get on the plane, "She says, 'Here, why don't you hold on to the car and use it while I'm gone,' and then she tells me she loves me!"

Their immediate ability to communicate so well set them on their way toward becoming a couple and eventually forming a family. Of course, they didn't always communicate perfectly; they even had a few fairly spectacular miscommunications. But in spite of that, Pat and Todd work hard at making sure that a daily regimen of open and trusting communications continues to feed their relationship—both as a couple and as parents.

Pat is thirty-seven and white; Todd is thirty-nine and black. A generation or two ago, their marriage would have raised eyebrows. Now, though, they are a typical, modern American family: they live in a nice suburban development north of Baltimore, Maryland, with two cars, two young children, and a cat named Indy. They love each other and worry about how to provide the best child care, education, and other opportunities for their children.

Pat juggles a full-time job with caring for their toddlers, Nathan and Noah. Even though that leaves virtually no free time during a typical day, she makes a point of using little gestures every day to strengthen her bond with Todd. "I call him at least once a day at work just to say hello," Pat told us. "Often I don't have anything to say, but that doesn't stop me."

Instinctively, Pat knows that often the most important kind of family communication isn't necessarily about having something to say but just keeping the connection alive and warm. On occasion Pat even leaves little notes for Todd. In fact, one of the days we talked with them, Pat told Todd with a sweet smile, "There's a note on the front door for you now. It says, 'Patty loves Todd.'"

But as Pat and Todd can attest, all the sweet notes in the world don't make life a storybook. They argue about money, work, chores, child care, and all the rest. They never seem to have enough time in the day to fulfill all their responsibilities and get enough sleep—let alone have enough meaningful conversation. Like most couples, they haven't found a magic way to work through all the problems. But they are active in searching for ways to keep their connection alive and vibrant. Last Christmas, Todd's surprise gift to Pat was that he would arrange twelve outings during the year when he would get a sitter and the two of them would go out—just the two of them.

Communicating well with each other is challenging enough, but navigating the sometimes complicated terrain of their two extended families can get very tricky. Although Pat and Todd live just a few hours away from Todd's family in New Jersey, Todd chose for a time to limit contact with his father because of unresolved feelings left over from childhood. Todd feels that his father never really appreciated or understood him, so he's more comfortable maintaining only sporadic communication with his dad. In fact, Pat talks to Todd's parents more than Todd does. He continues to work at his relationship with his father, though, and says, "We're closer than we've ever been, but it's still not where I'd like to be."

Meanwhile, Pat has issues with her own parents. When she and Todd moved to a suburb of Baltimore three years ago, they were suddenly quite close to the home where Pat was raised. Her parents, two brothers, and extended family all live nearby. Although Pat enjoys being close to her family, she also finds it difficult to communicate with them at times. "Todd can deal with my mother long after I can," Pat observed. "It's funny, what drives him nuts about his mom drives me nuts about my mom. . . . But I can tolerate it in his mother. It's the exact same thing, but it's not my mother."

On the whole, though, she has a good relationship with her mother. Her relationship with her father, by contrast, is more difficult. For many years, it was strained and distant because they never really communicated well when she was growing up.

"My father was an alcoholic," Pat said. "He drank away from

home, so it was, in a lot of ways, like being raised by a single parent. He's been sober now for about twenty-five years, but I was a teenager. I had written off communicating with him." She added, "Dad's never been a part of any big decisions in my life." The way she looked at it, if he wasn't involved in the small decisions that made up her life as a child, he didn't have any right to be a part of the big decisions later on. When she decided in her early twenties to go work in Papua New Guinea, she recalled, "I never told him. Mom did. I never even asked him what he thought about my going."

Together, Pat and Todd have been discovering how the legacy of communication in their own families when they were growing up still affects their communication patterns today. Thanks to Todd, Pat realized that she was sometimes adopting one of the conversational traits that she finds frustrating in her mother. Pat explained that when her mother says quietly, "Well, it's okay," what she really means is the exact opposite. Pat told us, "She says, 'Well, it's okay.' But it's not okay. That's the way I was taught to communicate. You're left with 'It's not okay'—and you're not sure *why* it's not okay." In the first years of her relationship with Todd, Pat did the same thing, "because that's what I was taught."

Todd was able to point this trait out to Pat and help her change it. "I kept calling her on it. I would say, 'You don't really like it. It's okay if you say you don't like it. Your voice is saying it's okay, but everything else is telling me it's not okay.'" This has now evolved into a running joke between them; whenever Pat claims in an unconvincing manner that she is in favor of something, Todd looks down in mock dejection and says, "Well, it's okay."

While some might assume that this interracial couple must have lots of differences to bridge, Pat and Todd feel that they have a lot in common emotionally. "The situations we grew up in were very similar and sort of molded our values about how we feel about family, relationships, and rearing children," Todd explains. That common set of values helps them communicate well, they think.

Todd also points out the potential danger of assuming too much. "Sometimes you can get into this trap where you think you know the other person better than they know themselves, and you end up making the kind of assumptions that can lead to hard feelings, or feeling like someone's taking you for granted." So occasionally, they ask the other person to clarify his or her feelings, just to make sure they understand each other.

That helps prevent a lot of conflicts, but certainly it doesn't always work. When they do get into an especially heated argument, they usually bring it to a halt pretty quickly. Then, Todd says, "We come back and revisit it; maybe in a couple hours, maybe in a couple days." Todd says he uses that time to think about the problem, brainstorm some solutions, and then present them to Pat as options: "We can do A, B, or C. What do you think about that?"

While they don't view this as necessarily an ideal process, what is important, Pat explains, is that over the years, "We have come to a new kind of acceptance of each other, so that we can work things through from a fairly positive place. We don't always agree, but we work it out somehow." Todd adds, "We talk about it. We get mad. But then we talk about it some more. I try to think about it from Pat's perspective. She tries thinking about it from my perspective. Because we love each other, we want to make each other happy as well."

Asked whether they're still as in love today as when they married, Pat startled Todd by saying, "no." After pausing for just the right amount of time, she added with a smile, "I love you more now." They know the things about each other that they may like or not like. Pat feels comfortable wearing what Todd calls "her granny pajamas." Todd says, "She's seen me sick. I've seen her insides." Pat adds, "Our love now is more real. We know we're in it for the long haul together. I'm not trying to change him anymore. I don't want him to change for the sake of my changing him."

COMMUNICATION BETWEEN PARTNERS

For lots of couples, like Pat and Todd, the demands of work and family often mean that other things get short shrift. Rushing out the door in the morning, many of us have time to exchange only a few quick words about practical things—who's taking the kids to practice after school, what's for breakfast, who's calling the plumber to fix the leaky sink, how did you sleep, who's picking up the takeout food for dinner tonight, and by the way, how are you doing? These conversations are necessary to hold home and hearth together in the most literal of ways—but they don't do much to feed the emotional relationships in the family.

Or do they?

Experts who study marriage and long-term relationships have found that the countless brief interactions we have with one another each day are actually critical in building a deep level of understanding, connection, and trust. The thousands of routine exchanges that occur every day—interactions that may seem too trivial to affect the relationship—play a crucial role in maintaining a strong bond. In one sense, humans are a bit like whales: every comment we make carries with it a faint emotional signal that "pings" off the other person, and determines whether the distance between us is widening or closing. But what's different in our case is that the "ping" bouncing back is the other person's response, and what allows us to measure distance is the emotional content of the reply.

University of Washington psychology professor John Gottman calls this process "bidding," and he notes that a bid can be something as simple as "How was your day?" According to Gottman, any response to a "bid" inevitably conveys one of three basic things: a caring "turning toward" response, a rejecting "turning against" response, or a distant "turning away" response that is really no response at all. Every bid—whether as subtle as a look or a gesture or as direct as a question or a statement—has an effect on a couple's ability to feel connected to each other and to keep their relationship strong and healthy. And since these kinds of small interactions make up the bulk of most relationships, they accumulate over the months and years and powerfully affect the emotional tone of the relationship.

Gottman believes that every communication—whether it is a quick, friendly word or a brusque dismissal—nourishes or weakens the inner life of the couple. After studying videotapes of thousands of conversations between partners in his "apartment laboratory," Gottman concluded that for all who want to improve their relationships with their partners, "the secret appears to be to really change the way [you] connect in everyday moments that are unemotional. And if you can change that, you sort of build an emotional bank account."

Couples who consistently respond positively to, or "turn toward," each other's bids for emotional closeness end up being far more resilient in times of trouble. Even during arguments, they are more likely to use humor or affection and to engage each other's statements in a productive way by drawing on their reservoir of goodwill.

However, couples who "turn against" each other deplete this goodwill, and those who simply fail to respond to their partner's bids for attention and emotional connection experience an increasing emotional distance. Couples who frequently ignore each other tend to divorce quickly—in fact, even more quickly than couples who lash out against each other.

In most relationships, people move gradually from small bids— for humor or entertainment or companionship—to larger and more meaningful bids—for love, support, or intimacy. But in Pat and Todd's case, Pat decided early on to skip a lot of that process. Having sensed that she and Todd were actually really connecting on that first date, she made a direct bid for love when she told him that day at the airport how she felt about him. Although Todd was surprised by how quickly he and Pat connected, he returned that bid for love. Just six months after they started dating, he gave her a ring and asked her to marry him.

However, despite their ability to connect with each other, when Todd proposed, Pat misunderstood his intentions and brushed him off. "I didn't realize he was for real," Pat admitted. "I thought he was just joking around or something! We hadn't been dating that long, and I guess I just wasn't expecting it." Hurt by her noncommittal response, Todd let it drop. "There's a big difference between asking someone for a date and asking someone to spend your life with them," Todd told us. When Pat didn't take his proposal seriously, it felt like a rejection to Todd. It wasn't until months later, when Pat was pregnant with Nathan, that they revisited the topic and decided to act on the marriage proposal that Todd had made (and Pat had missed) months earlier.

As this story suggests, we are all very sensitive to rejection—even when we know that the underlying relationship is strong. Gottman found that even people in stable marriages were easily discouraged: if their initial bid for attention was rebuffed, they tried again only 20 percent of the time. And couples that later divorced barely ever rebid in such situations. Gottman told us, "When you watch somebody in the videotape and they make a bid for their partner's attention and their partner ignores them, they kind of crumple a little bit, and try to do some face-saving things, and then go on to something else. [There's] a gradual erosion of intimacy." That is because they feel ignored, disconnected, and unacknowledged.

Here, too, quantity matters at least as much as quality. Gottman found that happily married couples interacted as many as one hundred times in ten minutes over the course of a typical dinner hour. But couples headed for divorce interacted only two-thirds as much. The quality of the communication also grows deeper and richer the more it takes place.

Understandably, couples often find it difficult to deal with all the emotional baggage carried by every effort to communicate.

When relationships reach a threshold of too much accumulated emotional tension, the two people involved begin searching for relief. One strategy commonly used by couples in such situations is to form a "triangle" by looping in someone else as a kind of intermediary. Although this is sometimes a conscious choice, it is more often an unconscious effort to stabilize the relationship by "triangling in" the third person. Creating these triangles can become an ingrained habit for some couples, and they can make direct substantive exchanges very difficult. Moreover, the third person in the triangle sometimes ends up taking on the stress of the conflict of the other two, as the intermediary tries to shepherd or mend the couple's relationship. And unfortunately, the third person is frequently a child who is placed in that role by the parents.

Still other communication challenges can arise when couples try to avoid any potentially difficult topics. Pat and Todd, for instance, know that money can be a difficult topic to talk about because Pat makes more than Todd does.

"That's just one of those sore subjects. He knows it. I know it. We don't go there," Pat explains. When they have a discussion about family finances, such as child care and whether one of them should perhaps go to a part-time work schedule in order to save on child-care expenses, the difference in their earnings is "the elephant in the room," says Pat.

Sometimes when topics are painful, couples will use other topics as substitutes or proxies that enable them to shadowbox around the sensitive topic. Sometimes the choice of a proxy subject matter may take place subconsciously, with neither party fully realizing why they begin to feel strong emotions in connection with a seemingly benign—even trivial—subject. A small purchase by one spouse might trigger a heated argument because of an underlying conflict over the family's finances. Or a seemingly trivial question involving which partner will choose the movie they go to that night may be a substitute for deep underlying conflict over the balance of power in the relationship.

As men and women have formed more egalitarian relationships both financially and emotionally, the ability to communicate effectively has become even more important. It's therefore especially important to understand some of the gender differences that can play a role in open communication. In her landmark 1982 work, *In a Different Voice: Psychological Theory and Women's Development*, New York University School of Law professor Carol Gilligan discussed how men and women think and speak differently when facing difficult situations. Women tend to focus on caring for others, seeking to prevent or alleviate pain felt by others; men, meanwhile, focus on issues of justice and whether they have done something right or wrong. Gilligan believes that women have a greater need for relationships, leading them to be more motivated by interpersonal loyalty, responsibility toward others, and peacemaking. When asked to describe themselves, women frequently respond in terms of relationships: they define themselves as mothers, wives, daughters, sisters, or friends. Men, however, tend to define themselves by their individual accomplishments.

This finding of Gilligan's meshes with observations from studies of group dynamics that show men tend to be more task-oriented, while women tend to be more concerned with holding the group together. For example, Pat Letke-Alexander takes on the responsibility of maintaining frequent contact not only with her family but with Todd's as well. This is typical of many couples; according to Harvard University professor Robert Putnam, "[W]omen make 10–20 percent more long-distance calls to family and friends than men, are responsible for nearly three times as many greeting cards and gifts, and write two to four times as many personal letters as men."

Recent research has also found differences in the way men and women communicate as they age, because aging affects both their hearing and how their brains process sound in different ways. For both men and women, aging can lead to a reduced ability to hear and interpret subtle cues, such as tone of voice, pitch, and intona-

tion. It can also make it harder to hear speech in a noisy environment. Researchers at Northwestern University and the University
of South Dakota found that men begin experiencing these difficulties as early as age thirty-five or forty—about twenty years before
women do. According to audiologist Teri James Bellis of the University of South Dakota, "The findings may help us to understand
some of the stereotypical male versus female communication differences. For example, women can listen to several things at once—
the kids, the television news, the salesperson on the phone—whereas
men often need to listen to one thing at a time. Women often complain that their husbands 'just don't listen anymore' when they hit
their early forties, while men complain that their postmenopausal
wives 'take everything the wrong way.' This study suggests that
there are real, biological—rather than merely cultural—bases for
some of these gender differences." In fact, a recent study found that
women could have a greater capacity for remembering emotional
events than men because their brains may be better suited to integrate the processes of experiencing emotion and coding those feelings into memories.

Other researchers have found evidence that the structural differences between male and female brains begin to produce diver-
gent patterns of communication during adolescence. Michael
Gurian, author of *Boys and Girls Learn Differently: A Guide for
Teachers and Parents*, believes that boys may have a harder time
processing emotions and, as a result, may find it more difficult to
quickly change gears after a stressful or highly emotional situation.
Girls, by contrast, may have an easier time coordinating both sides
of the brain when processing information and therefore would be
better able to engage in several activities at once, switching rapidly
between them. Similarly, women can carry on several conversations at one time, which can be useful—especially when you're trying to keep up with all the busy members of your family!

For couples, the process of communication is a blend of messages and meanings that are not so much exchanged as commonly

experienced. At its best, it becomes something more than communication. When two hearts are truly joined, a couple achieves what might be called a deep communion.

COMMUNICATION WITH CHILDREN

Our first experience with this deep connection or communion occurs in the womb. A baby's mother feels it intensely as well— Tipper, for instance, still vividly remembers the first time she felt that connection with the new life within her. She was in the dining room with her mother and grandmother when she felt the baby move the first time, and she was amazed at the sensation of a force within her that she obviously didn't control. Another being! She loved the feeling and savored it. The old-fashioned word for this event is *quickening*. Tipper described it for Al this way: "It feels like when you hold a small tree frog in your closed hand and it repeatedly hops against the inside of your hand trying to get out."

In our earliest days and months of life, all of us experience an intense communion with our primary caretaker. During the period of prolonged helplessness in infancy, as we slowly begin to learn about our bodies and our feelings, we rely totally on our mothers (or whomever the primary caregiver is) to take care of us, respond to us, and meet our needs. Long before we can use words, we begin to try to communicate about our wants and needs—through crying or smiling or cooing—and we need our mothers to respond.

The late Canadian psychiatrist Dr. William Line, a former president of the World Federation for Mental Health, said "the importance of communion" in families begins early. "Communion is made possible and necessary by the birth event, wherein two individuals (mother and child) still enjoy and appreciate a oneness despite difference. . . . The principle of communion is basic, without reference to any age, race, or other differential."

Another approach to describing the powerful bond between

parent and child is called <u>attachment theo</u>ry, which is based on years of extensive research into the nature of the parent-child relationship and the kinds of interactions that lead to the healthiest forms of communication, both during infancy and later in life.

Just as Gottman observed three different patterns of communication in couples, child psychologists have identified several different patterns in the earliest child-parent communication. Most of the specialists in this field now believe that infants learn a very basic and powerful lesson about their relationship to the world around them from the way their early signals of desire or distress are interpreted and responded to by the caregiver. If the primary caregiver responds to a baby's signals appropriately, consistently, and reliably, the infant learns that he or she has the ability to affect the rest of the world. On the other hand, if rebuffed or rebuked, the infant can learn a profound sense of powerlessness. Worst of all, if the signals are met with no response, the infant may withdraw to inhabit a bleak and lonely inner world. One vivid and tragic example of the phenomenon was when Romanian orphans were found abandoned after the upheavals there in the late 1980s. Their blank faces and seemingly empty hearts became symbols of devastating neglect for the world.

Though much remains to be determined about the role of attachment in human development, available studies tell us a lot about the significance of that first sense of understanding between babies and their parents. And there is clearly a strong relationship between the quality of that communication and the prospects for that child later in life, as demonstrated by the results of a twenty-seven-year study by Drs. Byron Egeland, Alan Sroufe, and Martha Farrell Erickson at the University of Minnesota. They found that children who felt secure in their attachment to the primary caregiver when they were infants were more confident, more independent, better at solving problems, and emotionally healthier in later years than children who were not securely attached in infancy. In this groundbreaking study these researchers have followed these children since 1975 and are now studying how they relate to their own children. They are finding that those children who had healthy attachments to their parents are indeed replicating that same loving relationship with their own children now.

As children grow, one of the greatest challenges for a parent is learning how to communicate well enough to adapt to the child's changing needs. Over the years, we found that it's helpful to be an "emotion coach"; rather than telling our children what to feel, we tried to teach them how to learn about and understand what they were feeling. Describing emotion coaches, Gottman says, "Much like athletic coaches, they teach their children strategies to deal with life's ups and downs. . . . [T]hey accept negative emotions as a fact of life and they use emotional moments as opportunities for teaching their kids important life lessons and building closer relationships with them." In our family, we learned that it is important to first identify the emotion, and then understand why it's there. (Even if some of the reasons may only be imagined, you still need to acknowledge them as well.) Then you can begin to offer an explanation, and help lead the child to an answer that seems to work. Sometimes very young children may need to be prompted a bit to figure out the solution. As they get older, the parent's role is not so much to teach or guide the child to the right solution, but rather to be supportive and listen—no matter what the problem is.

One thing that's often hard, but important, for parents to accept is that their children often *can* solve their problems on their own. It requires trust to let children come to their own solutions, but giving children that space can help build the trust on both sides of the relationship. When we were talking about family communication, for example, our children told us they appreciate the fact that, as our son Albert said, "Mom doesn't always offer a solution. You don't always have to have one. Sometimes you don't want a solution, you just want to talk." If parents can guide children to learn how to make good decisions on their own, the children will be better prepared to handle tough or even dangerous situations when a parent is not around.

Our children have also told us that they have two other requirements with regard to communicating with us. First, any grievances must be aired immediately, since holding back a complaint can have an adverse effect on the tone of the relationship. Second, we have to recognize and acknowledge our own mistakes instead of trying to justify or rationalize them. Of course, we have no idea what they're talking about.

COMMUNICATION WITH TEENS

Communicating with teenagers has always been difficult. These days it doesn't seem to be getting any easier; the list of parental worries has grown much longer as life has gotten much more unpredictable and new challenges have arisen. Parents are no longer concerned just about school bullies but about school shootings. And many now worry not only about young people having sex before they are ready but about AIDS and other sexually transmitted diseases. They worry not just about explicit music but about a whole range of cultural influences that introduce children to violence and explicit sexuality earlier and earlier. And just when parents start to worry the most, teenagers usually become the hardest to talk to. That's when they experience the "parents as lepers" syndrome, said Dominic Cappello, a communications specialist and author who has been working on the national "Can We Talk?" family communications project. Cappello stresses the importance of parents talking with kids, even about the tough topics, as much as possible in the preteen years. Up through the preteen years, "parents have all this opportunity to infuse and infuse all the good stuff—the information and values." Then during adolescence, teens will often seek out other adult mentors in their lives to check out the values their parents have been giving them. At that time, a supportive community is critical.

As teens start asserting their independence and separating from their family, the close and intimate bonds that comforted them when they were young may suddenly start to feel stifling. For years, Tipper would kiss Albert good-bye on the cheek when she dropped him at a friend's house, until one day he just abruptly said, "Bye, Mom," and was out the car door. Soon she learned to just punch him in the arm and grunt—and he'd laugh and be gone.

As the slow process of asserting their individuality and independence continues, and as friends and peers begin to occupy most of their free hours, teens may seem to resent the kind of instruction and guidance that they accepted unconditionally as young children. So, pressured by the demands of work, many parents succumb to the temptation of leaving well enough alone and sharply reduce their efforts to communicate with their teens. We've felt that. We call it "giving in to the path of least resistance." After all, when the children are old enough to put cereal in a bowl and grab cold cuts from the refrigerator, they're not in danger of starving, and since they didn't seem to want to talk to you anyway, why push your luck and run the risk of an unpleasant confrontation?

Tipper describes communicating with teens as a "taffy pull." With everyone in the family pulling in different directions, the strands holding us together can be stretched thinner and thinner, until sometimes only the most slender of connections remains. But it's important to keep even the thinnest line of connection between parent and child; as long as that connection isn't broken, it can be restored and ultimately become stronger and more resilient. Parents need to be creative about how to respond to the challenges posed by teens. When Karenna was a teenager, for instance, she started spending more time away from the family with her "posse" of friends. We began what can only be called a "solidarity group" with the parents of those friends. Together, we decided to put a stop to the game of "Well, so-and-so can stay out until twelve-thirty . . . why do *I* have to be in at eleven?" We would meet occasionally and share information, discuss the different rules we had given our children, and even coordinate curfew hours. Karenna was slightly horrified to discover that her parents had formed their own "posse" mirroring hers. In the end, though, we believe she and her friends secretly liked what we did, because it showed that we cared about them. One of the most important findings from research into family communication during this tense period is that teens actually want and benefit from parents' continued involvement in their lives—even if all the signals they send are directly to the contrary.

One of the most important benefits of open communication with teens is that when they do hit a trouble spot, they know they can talk to their parents about it. Professor Jose Szapocznik, director of the Center for Family Studies at the University of Miami, told us that one of the critical findings from his research is that those parents who have a history of talking to their children about a variety of topics are able to have much more open and effective conversations when their teens encounter tough decisions about temptations like alcohol, sex, and drugs. Teens, he explained, are much more likely to accept advice and counsel from a parent who has patiently forged a strong and healthy bond by means of countless small but fulfilling exchanges over the years. If honesty and directness are not practiced in the relationship when the child is younger, it will be far more difficult to get through to a teen during the times when communication is crucial. There are no guarantees, of course, but the chances of being heard or being given the opportunity to listen improve dramatically when the foundation has been laid.

As all parents know, talking to teens about tough topics can be tricky, even under the best of circumstances. And sometimes, even when parents think they've done an admirable job, they aren't actually heard by their children. Indeed, a recent survey by Nickelodeon, the Henry J. Kaiser Family Foundation, and Children

Now found that there is a huge disparity between the percentage of parents who *think* they're talking to their children about tough issues like drugs, guns, alcohol, sex, and AIDS and the percentage of children who say they *remember* having had any such conversation. Specifically, 91 percent of parents of children aged eight to eleven said they had talked to their children about alcohol and drugs, but 30 percent of the children of those parents say they don't remember any such conversation. Nearly 40 percent of these children didn't remember the talks their parents say they had with them about sex, and nearly 60 percent of children didn't remember the conversations their parents said they had with them about HIV and AIDS.

One reason for this large disparity may be that parents are often too embarrassed to be direct during these difficult conversations, and sometimes they gloss over some of the facts that kids most want and need to know. When parents can give teens accurate and comprehensive information, however, kids are much more likely to make the right decisions. Szapocznik found that effective parent-adolescent communication is clearly associated with delayed onset of sexual activity and safer sexual practices. And two researchers at the Centers for Disease Control found that mothers who talk with their teenage children meaningfully about safe sex and sexuality in general clearly have an impact in reducing high-risk behavior.

In some ways, parental communication about sex is more valuable than any other kind of communication, especially if the conversations go beyond the clinical facts and include a discussion of their attitudes, beliefs, and values about sex, sexuality, love, and relationships, including such questions as: What makes for a healthy relationship? How does intimacy affect emotions? How can your dreams be dramatically affected by an unwanted pregnancy or by a sexually transmitted disease? These kinds of conversations are tremendously important in helping young people test out their own ideas and explore how their actions could affect their goals in life. Receiving full and accurate information from parents is particularly important because the evidence is clear that if teens don't get adequate information and guidance from their parents, they will turn to their peers—where they are more likely to get the wrong information.

Pepper Schwartz, who coauthored the book *Ten Talks Parents Must Have with Children about Sex and Character,* told us, "Parents need to realize that if they don't give their children their own values about sexuality and relationships, their kids will find them elsewhere. Who do you want to inform your children about ethics and sexuality? You or their schoolmates or the media? If you don't tell them what you believe and what you want them to think, they won't know what you think." The National Campaign to Prevent Teen Pregnancy surveyed young people from across the country to find out what advice teens would give their parents about helping teens avoid pregnancy. The teens responded, "We hate The Talk as much as you do." But they also said "We really care what you think," and urged, "Talk to us honestly."

A professor of human development at Penn State, Anthony D'Augelli, studied one of the most difficult teen-parent conversations of all: those that take place when gay and lesbian teenagers "come out" to their parents. He concluded that "The more positive the relationship was between youths and parents, the more positive parents were about youths' sexual orientations." Yet D'Augelli and others found that although these children on average experienced their first awareness of sexual orientation at age ten, labeled themselves at age fourteen, and first disclosed their sexual orientation to someone else at age sixteen, more than one-third waited until they were eighteen or older to tell their parents. In most cases, the first person a gay or lesbian teen tells is not a parent, but a friend (most often a female friend). Teens' fears about their parents' reactions may play a part; for those teens who did tell their parents, "Only one-half of mothers and siblings and one-quarter of fathers were described as fully accepting; one-quarter of fathers and 10 percent of mothers were actively rejecting. And, in some cases, disclosure to family members was associated with a backlash of verbal abuse, threats, and physical attack."

Professor Ritch Savin-Williams of Cornell University says what gay children most need and what helps them most is being able to communicate. Savin-Williams advises parents who are unsure how to handle the news to keep the lines of communication open and to control their own emotions enough to maintain the ability to talk openly and offer their unconditional love.

Before coming out, Josh Logan struggled silently for years. Although his parents suspected that he was gay and, when he was eight years old, put him into a regime of intensive psychoanalysis to try to "prevent" him from becoming a homosexual, they never really discussed it openly. Yet he knew he was not making his parents happy or proud of him—and that made him miserable. "All it did was just eat away at my self-esteem," he said. He fought his true sexual orientation all through high school and the first half of college. After he admitted it to himself and discovered that doing so finally made him feel comfortable for the first time in his life, he decided he needed to tell his parents. During one of his visits home, he told them—the night before he returned to college.

Josh said, "I told them that I had been struggling over this for years and years and years, which they knew, but that I was gay, and that I was in a relationship, and that I was happy. I knew this was going to be hard for them, but I needed to be able to share it with them. And they were in shock! They were really in shock. They didn't say very much, which was very unusual for my parents. And I think my mother cried, and then we went to bed.

"And I remember my father walking in my room the next morning, and he was crying, and he gave me a hug. And I remember my mom told me how she listened to me take a shower in the morning, and how I used to always play the radio, and she was surprised that it was the same as it was the day before, that I was really the same person, and then I left for school, and they dealt with it without me."

At first they didn't want anyone else in the family to know. "They were afraid that I was going to live my life alone, that I wouldn't have children, and that I wouldn't be in a loving relationship," Josh explained. But they themselves began trying to understand and to be understanding. They started reading all about being gay and within about two years, "really started embracing me and it," Josh said. Josh's mother joined and even became the president of a chapter of PFLAG (Parents and Friends of Lesbians and Gays). "It was very difficult, but they really did an about-face," Josh told us.

By contrast, Josh's partner, John, had an easy conversation with his parents. John remembers that when he was about fourteen or fifteen, his mother came to him and "in a roundabout kind of way asked me if I was gay, without really asking me. At that point I didn't really know. I think I said no. But she said, 'Well, you know, if this is an issue for you, don't worry about it. We're cool.' "

Telling his sister, with whom John was very close growing up, was equally easy. One time John returned from shopping with his dad and put on a new layered set of a turtleneck, a shirt, and a sweater. "And my sister said to me, 'You look gay in that outfit,' " John recalled. Then he just made an expression that conveyed the message "Well, yeah." "She went, 'Oh, I thought so,' and we just kind of went on," John said.

The openness and support of his family members made this transition a relatively easy one for John. And the fact that the family was so accepting, so clear in their unchanging love for him, and so ready to discuss it—on any terms John wanted—helped make their relationships ever closer.

For the more everyday kinds of communication, we know many families who have regular "family meetings." Family meetings can be formal or informal, structured or free-flowing, focused on a single issue or wide-ranging. The one requirement, though, is that every member of the family should feel he or she is invited to fully participate. The family-meeting approach worked for us when our children were young and they all had their own activities. It was a good way to get everyone together. We talked about whatever was important to someone, from soccer games and school plays to when one of us would be out of town on travel. We especially remember a family meeting in 1987 about whether Al should run for the Democratic nomination for president. From oldest to youngest, each child discussed his or her thoughts about the race. We still have a list compiled by Kristin, who was then ten. One of the cons was "We would have Social Security around us all the time." She meant the Secret Service.

If family meetings don't work—or even if they do—involving a teen in an activity can also be a good way of keeping the lines of communication open. Enjoying a sport together, playing cards, catch, or a board game, even going for a walk after dinner—anything that provides some unpressured time can open up space for a conversation. Walks are good because you don't need to worry about eye contact. One of these activities is usually Al's approach when he gets the feeling that one of our children has something to say but isn't saying it. More times than not, after a period of silence, the child opens up.

It's also important to resist the assumption that teens are tough to talk to. Many are, and some are not. Yet we sometimes take it for granted that all teens will be surly, sullen, and absorbed in a culture of their own—assumptions most cultures of the world do not share.

COMMUNICATION AND NEW TECHNOLOGIES

Like many parents, we get at least as much out of a good conversation with our kids as they do. But we also recognize that finding the time and space for meaningful conversations is much harder today than when we were children—often because of the intrusive competition we all face from television and other mass media. These new media have had a deep and profound impact on the nature, frequency, and strength of communication in families.

Unfortunately, one of the most common group activities for many families is sitting in front of the television set, watching the screen, and exchanging comments intermittently—with the subject matter discussed usually limited to the content of the program they're watching or more often, the commercials, when the trance weakens slightly. And let's face it: how are you going to build up layers of emotional warmth, trust, and understanding by sharing sporadic opinions about the latest beer commercials?

Many parents who feel stressed after a hard day routinely succumb to the temptation to use television as an "electronic babysitter," knowing that they can usually rely on TV's hypnotic effect to keep children quiet and motionless while they rest or prepare the evening meal. Pat Letke-Alexander, for example, acknowledges that sometimes she puts her sons in front of the TV to keep them occupied, "especially during the week, when Todd's not home from work yet, I've got to get dinner rolling, the baby's hungry, and Nathan wants a snack." It's not an ideal situation, she says, but sometimes she has few alternatives.

Pat is by no means alone. The average child over age eight in America watches almost three and a half hours of television a day, according to a 1999 study by the Kaiser Family Foundation. The nonprofit TV-Turnoff Network reports that the average young person spends considerably more time in front of a television screen than in school each year. And, according to a 2000 Annenberg Public Policy Center study, the average time a child spent with any type of screen media—television, video games, computers— increased by twenty-one minutes per day just in the previous year. Counting all those different kinds of media, the average child is consuming some form of mass media four and a half hours each day. Disturbingly, the Kaiser study found that one in six children between the ages of eight and eighteen spent more than *ten and a half hours per day* using media. Furthermore, it found that children who used more media than their peers were less likely to report being happy at school, and more likely to get into trouble a lot, and feel bored, sad, or unhappy. In the same study, 65 percent of all children age eight and older reported that in their families the television is usually turned on during mealtime.

Moreover, the increasing prominence of television in the lives of American families has led to a proliferation of television sets in the home. An incredible 65 percent of children age eight and older have a TV set in their own bedrooms. The TV-Turnoff Network found that although 73 percent of parents would like to limit their children's TV watching, 61 percent of children say they have no rules whatsoever about watching television.

Don't get us wrong: we enjoy watching television for limited periods of time and, like most Americans, we consume plenty of mass media every day. But we feel strongly that everyone should think seriously about the role of television in their family and set limits for their kids. Jose Szapocznik told us he believes we've reached the point where families are now watching so much television that "the art of chatting" is beginning to disappear. Some speech pathologists actually believe they are seeing a higher number of speech problems in young children because of the sharp reduction in the amount of conversation they engage in with their parents. Dr. Penney Brooks, the speech pathologist in the Columbus School District in Ohio, for example, told us she is convinced that one of the reasons she is seeing more children in her schools with difficulties in language skills is because children today take in so much information through a passive visual medium—television—rather than listening to and participating in conversations. The problem is not limited to children. As Robert Putnam says, "too many adults *watch* 'Friends' instead of *having* friends."

It's important for parents to engage children in activities other than watching television, but it's also important that parents know what children are seeing and hearing when the TV is on, and what messages they are receiving. Especially when children are younger, they should have guidance from parents on how to interpret these messages, many of which may not be appropriate for their age. And a lot of what's on television seems inappropriate for children of *any* age. For instance, the American Psychiatric Association notes that by the time children reach eighteen, they will have seen sixteen thousand simulated murders and 200,000 acts of violence in TV shows, movies, and video and computer games.

In the late 1970s, Tipper helped form and lead a group to draw attention to the levels of violence in children's television. A few years later, concerned about the increasingly graphic violent images on television and in the movies, she decided she had to begin monitoring how much violence our children were exposed to. Until then, we had been letting them watch MTV, and buy and listen to any music they wanted. One day when Karenna was eleven, she bought an album (yes—back then albums were still the way music came) that had some explicit lyrics on it, and then she and her girlfriend asked Tipper about several of the words. A short while later, our two younger girls, then six and eight, asked Tipper to watch a video on MTV that featured strippers and women in chains. That was how Tipper discovered that "good old rock and roll," which of course had always been about sex and relationships, had ratcheted up the quotient of explicit sex and sexual violence and that it was being marketed directly to kids. It's now been proven that there's a direct link between the violence that young people see and hear and the violent behavior some of them display. A 1992 report by a task force of the American Psychological Association, for instance, reviewed decades of research on the subject and concluded that watching violence on television can lead to more aggressive behavior, particularly among children.

Tipper was angry that the kids were being exploited, and angry that she now had to protect our children from yet another danger. But Tipper believes in the power of the individual to make a difference—especially acting in coalition with others who share the same values and beliefs. She cofounded the Parents' Music Resource Center and led a national effort to ask the recording industry to voluntarily place warning labels on those products the companies themselves determined had explicit lyrics that parents might feel were unsuitable for young children. She saw this as a useful consumer tool for parents, as well as a means of combating the marketing of inappropriate material to kids on television and in movies. She also wrote a book about the issue, *Raising PG Kids in an X-Rated Society*. Her activity did not go unnoticed by the public, but the worst part of it all was that, for a while, our daughter Karenna had to defend Tipper to her teenaged friends. That daughter is now a lawyer. She'd gotten a lot of practice making arguments.

At some point, every parent has to think hard about how to handle inappropriate material that a child will inevitably see or hear. Family communications expert Dominic Cappello told us, "A parent has to decide, 'I am going to take charge of the messages. I can't control them all, but I will help my child filter them.' If the parent creates a strong sense of values attached to rules, that becomes the processing mechanism by which the family and the child can make sense of thousands and thousands of messages."

More recently, the tragic events of September 11, 2001, brought home the difficulty of communicating with children about terrible tragedies they see through the mass media. The American Counseling Association advises parents to remember that after any catastrophe, children are apt to fear that it will happen again and that next time it will hurt them or separate them from someone they love. Experts suggest that because children may be confused by seeing video footage of the terrorist attacks repeatedly and may think that each replay is another occurrence, parents should limit their exposure to such coverage. At the same time, giving children a full opportunity to express what they are feeling is crucial. Providing reassurance while honestly describing exactly what has happened is also important. Returning to a normal routine as soon as possible can also make children feel more secure. But parents should also spend extra time with their children and remember the healing power of touching and hugging.

We aren't able to shield our children from the risks or dangers of the outside world as often as we might wish we could—whether it's graphic content in the media, crime and violence, or traumatic world events that shake all of our foundations. Instead, it seems that we are needing to talk to our children at ever younger ages about tough topics that we wish we could avoid. With our busy work schedules, it's often harder to find the time and energy for these conversations. But it's never been more critical to shoring up and nurturing our families.

The ubiquitous presence of new communications technologies like pagers, e-mail, and cell phones, which would seem to enhance communication, can make it even more challenging for families to communicate effectively. On the one hand, these new technologies extend our ability to communicate over time and space and can serve to strengthen family bonds. For example, when adult children move away from home, these devices make it far easier to maintain the emotional ties and continue strengthening and renewing their connection. Similarly, families trying to balance work and home usually find it convenient to maintain communication through the use of telephones and e-mail. And parents often give cell phones or pagers to their kids for safety reasons, as well as to be able to instantly plan and communicate about pickup times, daily errands, and the like.

However, none of these technologies can replace face-to-face conversation. Moreover, cell phones, instant messaging, and pagers make it much easier for other relationships—with friends and, especially, coworkers—to intrude and interfere at any moment. The simple act of talking to your family in the home has now become a new form of multitasking, with the telephone ringing, pagers (both one-way and two-way) beeping, and e-mail beckoning. Some of these new technologies can become almost addictive. Some people have described cell phones as "the new cigarettes," and it's certainly true that some people immediately reach for their phones and start dialing someone—anyone—whenever they experience a lull in activity.

As heavy users of two-way pagers, we have had to institute a new rule of common courtesy in our own relationship: no reading or typing on the pager while involved in conversation with each other. Even with that rule, the temptation to look at a message is sometimes irresistible, especially if one of us has been waiting for a response to an urgent question. At one point, when Tipper was reading several e-mails during a conversation, Al finally sent her an e-mail of his own, even though they were only a few feet apart: "Will you please stop using your pager and talk to me?" It worked—at least temporarily. But other new seductive technologies are on the way. It is almost as if we are undergoing a technological "enclosure" movement in which there is even less territory for just plain conversation.

Many parents find that the hours spent taking children to and from school or after-school activities are an ideal time to communicate—if, that is, the children aren't wearing headsets. A few years ago, we realized that we looked forward to the long drives from Tennessee to Washington and back because the children were trapped with us for ten to twelve hours, isolated from their friends. They *had* to talk to us. We had many of our best, sustained family conversations hurtling down Interstate 40. But that was before the country was wired for cell-phone coverage; these days, many parents and children like to spend a lot of their time in the car talking on the phone.

COMMUNICATION AND DIVERSITY

Perhaps one of the greatest new challenges for families in America today is learning how to communicate well about issues involving diversity, whether the concern is interracial or interfaith diversity within a family, the rise of same-sex partnerships, or the increasing racial, ethnic, and cultural differences in society at large.

As these trends become more common, Americans are showing an increasing acceptance of these new kinds of families. According to a national survey conducted by the *Washington Post*, the Henry J. Kaiser Family Foundation, and Harvard University, biracial couples now say they experience "widespread tolerance and even acceptance of their relationships." The *Washington Post* reported, "The overwhelming majority of interracial couples said they have introduced their partners to accepting parents and family members, and felt comfortable speaking openly about their relationships." Many said they believe their children are actually better off having parents of different races, and about two-thirds of interracial couples said that different racial backgrounds don't make marriage any harder. Nonetheless, most of the remaining couples said it makes marriage more difficult. Nearly half of black-white couples—a significantly higher proportion than among Latino-Anglo or Asian-white couples—say they believe marrying someone of a different race makes marriage harder. White Americans are more likely than any other group to say that it is better for people to marry someone of their own race.

Open communications about such matters within a family can lead to especially strong bonds. Todd Alexander, for instance, notes that one of the things he loves most about his mother-in-law is how immediately accepting she was of his relationship with Pat. She focused on Todd as a person—not on the fact that her daughter was entering an interracial relationship. "I love my mother-in-law and that's why," Todd said. "We're in the twenty-first century. And interracial relationships are just a fact. It's about getting beyond race and looking at people for who they are inside. When I was young I remember listening to Martin Luther King Jr. saying that it's about the content of your character. That's what it's all about." Pat and Todd do say that they've encountered occasional problems as an interracial couple; a former neighbor, for example, refused to talk to them, and Pat and Todd guessed it was because of their marriage.

Of far greater concern to them is how their children will fare. "I know what it is like to be a black man in America. Patty knows what it's like to be a white woman in America. But neither of us knows what it is like to be biracial," Todd said. "When the kids come to me one day and say, 'You don't understand,' I won't be able to understand. But hopefully when they're older, things will be different. That is a concern I have for their future—that they don't get hurt or feel that they have to choose what race they are."

Despite increasing acceptance, strangers are sometimes remarkably insensitive. A woman once came up to Pat, looked at her child, and announced, "You know he's going to get darker." Pat was flabbergasted. "Where do you go with that? 'Thank you'? 'Have a good day'? It caught me so by surprise, to be honest I kind of laughed about it. I thought, 'Okay, what's your point, lady?' "

Pat and Todd know they will need to have frank conversations with both Nathan and Noah as time goes on. Pat said Nathan recently asked her, "What color is my skin?" She replied, "It's skin color." But he persisted: "No, Mom, what color is it?" Eventually she asked him what color *he* saw when he looked at his skin, but his answer trailed off. Looking back on it, she said, "My feeling is that it's up to him to decide what color his skin is. I just want him to be confident in himself as just 'Nathan,' as opposed to as 'someone who is biracial.' He can be who he perceives himself to be."

John and Josh Logan feel similarly about the challenges their sons may face. On the one hand, like Pat and Todd, John and Josh hope that their boys will be accepted as who they are, without their identity as adoptive sons of two gay men being an issue. "Our lives are so normal. I swear, there is no difference between our lives and heterosexuals' lives. If someone just came to see our lives for twenty-four hours, they would be amazed at how normal and boring it is. Refreshing and wonderfully boring," Josh said. "We are normal. We are happy. We can have a house together and a family."

But they know that sooner or later there will be issues. They talk a lot about how to prepare the children for when they go to school and have to explain that they have two fathers. Currently, they have the boys in play groups where there are children of heterosexual parents as well as children of same-sex parents, and they hope this will help Marcus and Noah adjust to being different from other children but not viewed as an oddity. Ultimately, John and Josh have faith that with the support of loving parents and an increasingly diverse community, their sons will be fine.

Meanwhile, many more people are also addressing the issue of how to forge a set of common beliefs when family members do not share the same faith tradition. Gabrielle and Chris Wagener, for instance, are not strongly religious, but her Jewish background and his Catholic upbringing caused some concerns within the extended family. Chris's family never said anything explicitly, but Chris said, "I think they were concerned. If anything, they'd say, 'How is it going to work?'" Gabrielle told us her family "was a little bit more vocal." They expressed concerns about breaking with tradition, but ultimately didn't object to the marriage because they like Chris so much and saw how happy Gabrielle was with Chris.

Gabrielle and Chris don't plan to renounce their Jewish or Catholic heritage. Gabrielle said, "I'm going to start my own tradition, and it may be different from my parents', but that's okay." Chris told us that when they have children, they will try to forge a common "family belief system." Gabrielle says it will borrow "from Judaism, from Christianity, and from other religions as well."

And if their children grow up and decide to be Jewish or Christian or practice another faith, he says he won't mind. "I hope my kids will make that decision themselves."

THE MEANING OF COMMUNION

The late Dr. Murray Bowen was one of the first to describe a family as an "emotional system," within which family members so profoundly affect one another's thoughts, feelings, and actions that it often seems as if they share the same "emotional skin." When families communicate well, this shared connection makes it possible to forge what we think of as a communion of minds and hearts. This communion embodies a depth of understanding that includes good communication but also goes far beyond it to encompass caring, cooperation, and commitment. True communion helps families share values, tackle problems together, and accept and cherish one another—just as they are. The prospect of a lasting communion motivates family members to continually search for ways to live together in harmony with those we love most.

Communion within a family can be renewed in a number of ways, but storytelling plays a special role. Reminiscing together and passing down family stories from generation to generation help form important bonds. The stories themselves contribute to each individual's sense of his or her own identity and the role family legacy plays in his or her own life. In one sense, what endures in families is their collection of stories.

In our own family, Tipper remembers her grandmother's stories of *her* grandmother enduring the occupation of Yankee soldiers in her Kentucky farmhouse during the Civil War. Al's father always told lots of stories; one of his favorites was about the night he started playing the fiddle in his first congressional race—and how the crowd loved it.

And of course we both love telling stories about our children and, now, grandchildren. One of our recent favorites is about the time our daughter Karenna told her son, Wyatt, it was bedtime and started putting away the ice cream he had eaten for dessert. "Let's say good night to the ice cream, Wyatt," she prompted. "No, Mama. Let's say 'good morning' to the ice cream," he replied. Telling this story reminds us of how wonderful we feel when we are with him and his sister and how special that love is. That is a precious communion, as is the experience of watching the person we married thirty-two years ago light up with pride over our grandchildren.

The daily exchanges that take place in our families may seem routine and insignificant, but these millions of small acts can either build or erode the connection that binds us together. A strong and

THE HANCOCKS

Steve Hancock, Dawn Hancock, and their son, Chase

THE CRUMPTONS

Shane Crumpton, Celine Crumpton, Melissa (Missy) Crumpton, Michael Kennedy (behind Missy), Caleb Crumpton, Zach Crumpton, and Rodney Crumpton

Chapter 4

FOR RICHER,
FOR POORER

Want is a growing giant whom the coat of
Have was never large enough to cover.
—RALPH WALDO EMERSON

THE HANCOCK FAMILY

For as long as she lives, Dawn Hancock will remember November 16, 1993, as the worst day of her life. That day, her husband of almost two years told her to get in the car, drove her twelve miles down the road, and dropped her off at her grandmother's house with their eight-month-old son, Chase, a box of clothes, a bag of diapers, and a ten-dollar bill. Then he drove away and didn't look back.

At the time, Dawn was just nineteen years old. The ten dollars she clutched in her hand was the sum total of all the money she had on earth. With no savings and no professional skills, she had just been turned out of her own home. To make matters worse, when her husband left her and her baby that day, he also took away her only means of getting to her job at Wal-Mart every morning: the family car. So by the time he'd turned the corner and disappeared, she had effectively become a single teenage mother with no money, no car, no job, and no place to call her own.

During their brief marriage, her husband had sometimes been abusive, she said; even so, she called him several times after he left her, begging him to come get her and try to work things out. "I had no idea why he was hitting me, and I had no idea why I wanted him back," she told us. But she did know that she was afraid that she wouldn't be able to make it on her own, as a single mom.

Dawn was no stranger to hard times. Her parents were teenagers themselves when they married and had Dawn; her mother was eighteen, her father seventeen. Her father was periodically laid off from his work, so the family often had to get by entirely on the wages her mother made at an auto-parts factory, where she would work for twenty-four years, until she was laid off last year. It wasn't easy for Dawn and her two younger sisters. Still, they had always been able to manage somehow.

But this was different. She now found herself thrust into a situation where her first and only goal had to be providing the barest of essentials for herself and her son, Chase. She scrambled to get any work she could find, and before long she held down two jobs— as a day-care worker and as a food-service worker. At one point she worked three different jobs simultaneously. Fortunately, she was able to stay on at her grandmother's house for several months after her husband left her, because her minimum-wage jobs would never have covered the rent on a place for herself and Chase.

After several months, however, one of her grandmother's children needed a place to stay and Dawn had to move out. Still unable to afford a place of her own, she called her younger sister, Chastity, and offered her a deal: Dawn would do the cooking and cleaning and take care of her sister's child alongside Chase in exchange for being able to live with her sister in her trailer. Chastity agreed, so Dawn and Chase moved in. It was a real squeeze, since Chastity and her child already had a roommate.

Now, with the addition of Dawn and Chase, five people crowded into a single trailer.

Meanwhile, Dawn had to save up enough money to file for a divorce. She wasn't receiving any financial help from her husband, and it took her more than six months after he abandoned them for her to put aside the $575 in legal fees required to file for the divorce, have him served with papers, and have the divorce finalized. On the day the divorce papers were signed, Dawn's ex-husband argued with her at the courthouse for more than two and a half hours over visitation rights to Chase. Yet in the months and years that followed, he never once came to visit Chase, nor did he pay the child support he owed. In fact, Dawn told us, only once did she ever receive any money from him—other than that ten-dollar bill. He called one day out of the blue and left a message on her answering machine, saying that he was going to marry someone else and wanted to surrender his parental rights to Chase. He was required to catch up on all his back payments—$2,000 at that point, Dawn told us.

Ultimately, Dawn found herself forced to go on welfare. She said she was ashamed of it and hated to let anyone know she was "in the system." And the $142 per month she received didn't begin to cover the costs of supporting herself and her son. Nevertheless, being on welfare was the only way she could qualify to get subsidized day care for Chase so that she could work and save enough money to improve their situation.

It's been a long, hard journey since that awful day in 1993, but over the past few years, Dawn has made enormous progress. She not only found steady work and got off welfare, she also put herself through college and is now getting an advanced degree. She also met and married a man who loves her as much as she loves him. Dawn met Steve Hancock eight years ago on a New Year's Eve blind date arranged by her uncle, who worked with Steve. Dawn's uncle kept Dawn's senior class picture at work, and one day Steve asked about the pretty girl in the picture, and whether he could meet her. They hit it off, became a couple, eventually got engaged, and were married last winter. Fortunately, Steve is a great father to Chase, who calls Steve "Daddy." In fact, Steve wants to adopt Chase, but they can't afford it just yet. Dawn said she has been told it would probably cost at least $500, or maybe even more if Chase's father contested the adoption. Meanwhile, even with their incomes combined, Dawn and Steve still have trouble paying all the bills. But they have the basics more or less covered.

Dawn still has to scramble to balance work and motherhood, though it's easier now. She currently cobbles together a patchwork family arrangement for Chase's care. Her new work hours are 8:00 A.M. to 4:00 P.M., so although Chase gets home at 4:10, she is not home until 4:30. To cover this small gap of time, she has worked out an arrangement with her youngest sister, Felicia, thirteen, who stops by Dawn's house after school every day and watches Chase until Dawn comes home.

She is also still having car problems—but at least she *has* a car, an '89 Sentra. As often as not, though, the car is an expensive hassle. In February 2002 it overheated as she was driving to the church to get some forms for Chase's summer camp. "I thought it was the transmission. I just knew it was the transmission because I knew how our luck was running," said Dawn. Standing there in the church parking lot, she was already trying to figure out how they could afford the repair bill. "I thought, it's the motor, it's the transmission. Everything ran through my mind."

Fortunately, it turned out to be just the thermostat, and Steve was able to fix it himself with just thirty-nine dollars' worth of parts. But the emotional tension the whole family felt over what a more serious repair might have cost suggests how difficult their situation remains. Even little Chase had felt the potential gravity of the situation. As they stood in the parking lot, Dawn remembers hearing him say quietly, "Please, dear God, get us home."

The biggest bills they have, though, are related to their house. In

January, Dawn recalls, "I opened up the electric bill, and it was two hundred and fifty-four dollars, and I about had a heart attack." It was more than twice the highest bill she had ever previously had for the house. She hoped it was a broken meter giving an incorrect reading, but when the utility company sent someone out to look at it, they discovered that there was a hole in the outside coil of the water heater. The electric company gave Dawn and Steve an extra two weeks to pay, but now there's a $12 late fee, and they owe $266 dollars—not counting the bill to repair the heater.

And then there's the mortgage. That's hard to talk about because Dawn is still a little put out with her mother, from whom she bought the house where they now live. Her mother was facing foreclosure, so Dawn offered to buy the house from her, with the understanding that her mother would live with them and pay rent to help cover the mortgage. Her mother agreed, and for a while everything worked just fine—until her mother got remarried and moved out. Dawn found another renter for a while, but then he moved out too. Now, even with Steve's help, the mortgage payments are much tougher to make.

Shortly after the September 11 terrorist attacks, Steve was laid off from his job as a truck driver for a car-hauling company. Meanwhile, Dawn had just finished a temporary job working for her university and hadn't yet found a new job, so they were both out of work for several weeks. As a result, they fell behind on a number of their bills—including some credit cards with such high interest rates that it will be difficult for them to catch up. For several months, neither Dawn nor Steve could afford health care for themselves. Only Chase had coverage because he was eligible for subsidized health care through the state program.

Steve and Dawn, who never used to argue much, have had a number of big arguments lately—primarily about money and whose decision it was to make some of their recent purchases. "We're both feeling the pressure," Dawn said. "He's not an argumentative person but he's starting to feel the pressure now too."

THE EFFECT OF POVERTY ON FAMILIES

Dawn Hancock learned firsthand that the principal task of any family is to meet all of the basic needs of its members: safety, food, clothing, shelter, and health care. Failure to provide one or more of these essentials can quickly drive even the most loving family onto the shoals of hardship, disappointment, and regret.

It is a blessing that most American families today have never known sustained hunger or serious deprivation. But it's a tragedy that many families still face the harsh reality of poverty despite the fact that we live in such a rich nation. When we think of poor families, we usually conjure up the image, made famous in photographs, of people in ragged clothes on the front porch of their shack. Well, when you think of homeless families now—the poorest of the poor—erase the shack from your image. There isn't one. There is no home at all. The impact of the degradation they experience is difficult for the rest of us to imagine. An estimated 800,000—and perhaps more—men, women, and children are homeless on our streets each and every night. One out of every four are children. (It should be noted, however, that it's very difficult to count the number of Americans who are homeless, and some advocates warn that estimates may understate the scope of the problem.) And many more people are at risk of becoming homeless. They are one paycheck—or one domestic crisis—away from that deplorable and wretched state.

To many Americans, homelessness is a problem, and not one they want to think about. But every homeless person is an individual with particular wants and needs. The homeless are young children who should be dreaming about toys and playing games instead of worrying about where they will sleep and what they will eat. They are men and women who work all day and go to school at night to build a better life for themselves and their families but still cannot afford to put a roof over their heads. They are veterans who served their country to defend our democracy only to return home isolated from their communities, stranded on the streets and in the parks, and often in need of health care. And they are people with mental illness who cannot get the treatment and services they need to live full and productive lives. They are on the streets in large part because of the trend of deinstitutionalization without community treatment centers in place. The lack of treatment services for people with mental illnesses and the lack of adequate insurance coverage have only exacerbated the problem.

One reason we have so many homeless families is so basic that it's often overlooked: we have a shortage of homes that low-income families can afford. The average two-bedroom rental unit is now so expensive that it's beyond the reach of two full-time workers earning the federal minimum wage, according to a 2001 report by the National Low Income Housing Coalition. Data from that same report also revealed that there is now not a single state, county, or metropolitan area in the entire United States where one breadwinner earning the prevailing minimum wage can afford the fair-market rent for a two-bedroom unit. That's a huge change. Given the current cost of housing, it's little wonder that approximately 170,000 Americans, according to the Census Bureau's most recent numbers, now live in emergency or transitional housing. (Of course, that estimate only reflects those people who were able to find such housing on a given night; we suffer from a lack of shelters and alternative options for homeless families. As a result, many homeless families don't find emergency or transitional shelter but are forced to live on the streets.) And there are 44,000 children in such emergency housing—some of them, no doubt, the children of eighteen-year-old girls whose husbands or boyfriends left and who, unlike Dawn Hancock, didn't have a grandmother to take them in. These children have numerous problems: compared to children from stable homes, they have not only an increased risk of hunger, but also twice the health problems and a higher rate of delayed development.

Pat Letke-Alexander, who works with homeless families, spoke eloquently about a child's emotional experience of poverty. "A lot of what kids in poverty don't have is hope. Hope for the future. Hope that they can do something with themselves. Hope that they can become what they want to become. Sometimes they suffer from the lack of nurturing for whatever reason—because the parents are working three jobs just to pay the rent, because of addictions, because of mental illness, because of just deplorable conditions around them. People in poverty are trying. There are a lot of people in poverty who are trying who are just stuck."

We understand the impulse to turn away from someone who is homeless and to ignore a tragedy that can sometimes seem overwhelming. After all, that's how we reacted when homelessness resurfaced in the public consciousness as a major social issue in the 1970s. But our response changed when we began seeing homeless people through the eyes of our children. When they saw homeless people, they asked hard questions; they wanted to bring them home with us and take care of them. Soon we began, with our kids, volunteering at local shelters and soup kitchens. Al began working on this issue in the Senate and went on to cosponsor what would become the Stewart B. McKinney Homeless Assistance Act, considered to be the first major federal legislative initiative to combat homelessness. The act became law and included many services for homeless people, including transitional and some permanent housing, emergency shelter provisions, primary health care, education, and job training.

Tipper founded an organization called Families for the Homeless and began volunteering with local organizations in Washington. We became committed to spreading the word that to end homelessness, we must combine housing and equal opportunity with support and security. Put plainly, people need decent wages, job training, child care, health care that covers mental ailments, and, for those who need them, substance-abuse services. We also became convinced that only a creative partnership between the government, local neighborhoods, nonprofits, and the faith community can create a call to action whereby person by person and family by family, we can break the cycle of poverty and put an end to the tragedy of homelessness in America.

In the course of our advocacy for the homeless, we have met and befriended many homeless individuals and families whose stories and resilience have inspired and motivated us. One day, for instance, Tipper was out in Lafayette Park directly across from the White House and came across a woman who was obviously suffering from a mental illness. Tipper asked the woman how she could help, and the woman told her she needed to "get her reality back." She said her name was Mary Tudor (who was one of Henry VIII's daughters). Tipper, whose given name is Mary Elizabeth, let her know that they shared the same first name and that therefore they were meant to be friends. Asked if she would come with Tipper to get some help, Mary Tudor explained that she was waiting for her husband, and that if she left he wouldn't know where to find her. She said her husband was the president. Tipper told her she knew how to get a message to the president, and they walked across the street to the guard posted at the entrance of the White House. The officer on duty recognized Tipper (Mary Tudor did not), and Tipper asked if he would please give the president a note from his wife when he returned. The guard took the note, and Mary Tudor went with Tipper to a shelter. Her real name is Olga, and today, after receiving proper treatment, she is living independently and has a home and a full-time job.

In addition to America's homeless families, there are millions more who have a place to live but are dealing every day with the terrible problems created by poverty. Even amid our general prosperity, providing for essential needs every day is a constant struggle for more families than most Americans realize. Although the poverty rate went down during the 1990s, 11 percent of Americans still live in poverty today.

Even when they have a place to live, poor families often have to stretch to the limit to cover the cost of housing. One of the harsh new realities is that housing in today's America consumes

rent

an enormous proportion of the average family's budget. It is now the largest single expenditure for most families, eating up a third of a typical family's budget. Though home-ownership rates are at historically high levels and housing has been a bright spot in America's economy in the last few years, the average sale price for a new home in the United States is currently over $200,000, far beyond the means of poor families. Meanwhile, rent has been increasing more rapidly than inflation. Because housing now consumes so much of a family budget, many poor families have to choose between scrimping on every expense except rent or living in substandard housing.

Even if they are able to cover housing expenses, many families live so close to their break-even point that a single large, unexpected expenditure—such as health care costs for those with no or poor insurance, major home repairs, or funeral costs after the death of a family member—can quickly throw them into a financial crisis. The breakdown of an automobile, for example, can simultaneously cause missed days at work (increasing the risk of a layoff) and a repair bill that often requires yet more borrowing.

According to the Census Bureau, 6.2 million families live below the official poverty line. But this figure grossly undercounts the number of families who are actually experiencing poverty, because the government formula for measuring poverty is hopelessly out-of-date. Since the early 1960s, the formula has been based on the amount of money it takes to feed a family, multiplied by three. That's because food costs represented the single largest expense for the average family, accounting for a third of the average family budget. Today, food costs are less than 15 percent of the family budget, and they are often dwarfed by other costs, such as housing and day care. As of 2002, to qualify for federal poverty assistance a family of four's income must be below the official poverty line of $18,100. But many families would find it impossible to get by on an annual income of considerably more than that amount, because the government's figure has not kept pace with the rapidly rising costs of housing and other essentials.

One in six American children are growing up in poverty.
According to the National Center for Children in Poverty at
Columbia University, nearly 40 percent of all children grow up in
what is called "near poverty"—a broader measure that also
includes families that are technically above the official poverty line
but are still not making enough to provide adequately for the basic
needs of the family. And the vast majority of children in both
groups are living in families where one or both parents work.

One of America's most respected family scholars, Graham
Spanier, put it very simply when he told us, "Nothing undermines
a family more than poverty." For parents, the burden of not being
able to provide adequately for one's family can be crushing. Many
parents feel guilty or ashamed that they cannot provide a better
life for their children. The stress that accompanies the constant
worry about not having enough money to make ends meet—let
alone give one's children the extras that one would like to—can
contribute to low self-esteem and even depression. That, in turn,
can make all of the relationships in the family far more difficult.

In addition, poverty imposes a heavy toll of very tangible costs
and risks. As numerous studies have shown, poor families are less
likely to have health insurance, and therefore less likely to seek and
receive primary health care when they need it. Poor families tend
to have worse nutrition, both because they may not be able to
afford healthful food and because the food available near where
they live tends to be high in fat, sugar, and calories. Poor neighborhoods often lack grocery stores, so residents have a difficult time
getting fresh produce and healthful foods at affordable prices. And
without a car, going to a good grocery in another area is not feasi-
ble for many poor families. Still others may lack the facilities to
prepare food at home, so they have to rely on prepared foods. Poor
mothers are more likely to have low-birth-weight babies, and poor
babies have higher rates of infant mortality. Public schools in poor
neighborhoods tend to have fewer resources and are less able to
provide a quality education—meaning that poor children are less

likely to succeed academically. Poor families are more likely to be victimized by crime.

Research by Hyun Joo Oh from the University of Michigan's Institute for Social Research indicates that two types of experience with poverty are the most difficult for families. The first is the initial plunge into poverty—especially if it comes suddenly and unexpectedly. This plunge causes unusually high damage to a family presumably by introducing insecurity and instability into everyday life. The second is an extended period or repeated bouts of poverty, which can be a wearing, exhausting experience. Both experiences translate into higher mortality rates for poor families.

Chronic unemployment is often devastating to families. But in addition to the physical hardship and the constant tensions that accompany deprivation and idleness, the various income-support programs, including welfare, still have features that discourage work and make the escape from unemployment more difficult than it should be. Many such programs also unintentionally discourage marriage and family cohesion because when a husband's and a wife's incomes are added together, the total can push the family beyond the threshold of eligibility for public assistance. Some families who have gone through this experience refer to that threshold as "the cliff," because even as they earn more money on their own, they experience a sudden and sometimes catastrophic drop in their total income.

For example, Dawn Hancock told us that one reason that she and Steve delayed getting married—they were engaged for several years—is that Steve's earnings would have pushed their household income over the threshold that would qualify Chase for subsidized health-care coverage. But last winter, tired of always putting off marriage, they finally decided to worry about insurance later. Now, although Dawn reported promptly to the agency so they could change her insurance premiums as necessary, she wonders if she made the right decision to get married. "Honestly, I wish I had worried about the insurance before, because I can't pay," she said. Since she is now married to Steve, she has to pay $150 a month for the same insurance to cover Chase that used to cost her just $30 a month.

Understandably, Dawn doesn't want to risk not having any insurance, because medical emergencies—especially for the millions of low-income families with no or inadequate health insurance—can be especially devastating, particularly when illness causes a loss of income. Because of the rising cost of medical care and prescriptions, health problems that require long-term care put enormous strain on many family budgets, especially when one member of the family who was earning money must instead become the primary caregiver.

Beyond all those families who are unquestionably poor, millions more live in near poverty. They live with an enormous pressure to avoid falling into poverty. If family members have low-wage or casual jobs and are not guaranteed stable amounts of work from week to week, the uncertainty causes further stress in the family. Theirs is an exhausting daily struggle just to continue getting by, and one reason this financial crunch is so disorienting is that many of them are working at jobs similar to their parents'—jobs that used to be enough to retire on. Yet somehow, the old formula of hard work equals a decent living doesn't hold true anymore.

Rodney Crumpton, for example, told us that his father drove a truck for thirty years. He got good union wages for all that time, and when he retired, he received a pension of $26,000 after taxes. Yet when Rodney followed in his father's footsteps and drove a truck for twenty years, he was never able to get a steady union job like his father's. Instead, he always had to scramble to get different hauling jobs on a temporary basis, and he often experienced periods of unemployment between jobs. When, after twenty years, he stopped driving, unlike his father, he had no pension whatsoever to show for it. Meanwhile, Rodney and Missy have not been able to put away any savings, so, other than Social Security, they will have no resources to draw upon when they enter old age. "Unlike our parents, who had good retirements after their careers in good union jobs, we've always known we'd work till we die. We can't retire. We're trapped," Rodney told us.

But at least retirement is in the future. For now—and as they've done their whole lives—Rodney and Missy struggle to make ends meet, especially since they help provide for their grandson Caleb. The rental property where they live is modest, with makeshift furnishings. To cut down on bills, they share a phone line with their informally adopted son Michael, who lives downstairs from them. Although Rodney aims to get a white-collar job after graduating from college, he doesn't currently own dress shoes or a suit. Two pairs of jeans, sneakers, and some shirts make up his current wardrobe. And certainly, they have more than their fair share of anxiety about money. The only money they plan to leave to their grandchildren is in their life-insurance policy. "We will go homeless before we don't pay our life-insurance payments," Rodney said.

Rodney's experience as a working man illustrates how the increasing competitiveness of the global economy has had a particularly heavy impact on lower-skill jobs. In Rodney's case, the trend was manifested in deregulation of the trucking industry, the aftermath of the oil crisis, and the shift away from manufacturing and toward services. In a variety of ways, globalization has put an increased premium on education and made it harder and harder for a wage earner with only a high school education to support a family.

Manufacturing jobs, for instance, have been hit especially hard. When the economy turned down in 2001, the layoffs of high-tech workers got most of the press attention; in fact, however, one publication noted that by February 2002 "blue-collar workers accounted for nearly 60 percent of the 2.3 million jobs lost since the recession began." As the economy has shifted underneath them, Americans have had to find new ways to adapt.

And many of them have adapted. Rodney and Missy, for example, despite the financial challenges they face, are at the center of a strong and resilient family. They have been married (for the most part very happily) for twenty-eight years. They help out their children and care for their grandson; they are role models to the younger generations; and they are hopeful for the future. They know they probably won't significantly improve their financial situation anytime soon, but they find creative ways to make the most of what they have. They don't spend money on movies, but they did splurge on a $50 annual grandparents' pass to the zoo, where they take their grandson Caleb at least once a month so they can visit all his favorite animals. The flash cards Rodney made for Caleb aren't fancy. They're just written with felt-tip pens on some typing paper, but they do the job. Rodney and Missy had to invest in a computer when they both went back to school, so they use it often as an educational toy for Caleb. Perhaps most important, they are committed to leaving behind a legacy of hope and opportunity for their grandchildren. "I wish I could do for my family even half of what my daddy did for us," Rodney said. He told us he'll be happy if his efforts and his example of scrimping to get through school make life "even one inch better" for the generations that follow. As Rodney and Missy demonstrate, the burden of poverty can be crushing, but many families poor in money are rich in spirit and still have dignity and hope, and still dream of a better future for their children.

THE FAMILY AS AN ECONOMIC UNIT

Traditional wedding vows include a promise to remain together "for richer, for poorer," and this familiar phrase reminds us that money plays a major role in the life of every family. When a family has trouble providing the essentials for its members, the stresses can become so great that the family can be torn apart. But affluence brings its own set of challenges, and in today's America conflicts over money in middle-class and higher-income families are often the source of stress and even serious family problems. Whatever a family's income, it's crucially important that the family think of itself as an economic unit and make choices about how to spend money in ways that are in alignment with its true values.

It helps to remember that the family has not only been the key social unit of Western civilization, but also the principal economic unit, at least until recently. For example, Greek poems of the eighth century B.C. portray the nuclear family as the main economic unit of ancient Greek society; in fact, the Greek word for household management gave us the word economics. Aristotle noted that the "family is the association established by nature for the supply of men's everyday wants." The central economic role of the nuclear family was also thoroughly documented during Roman times. It's also true, however, that in some societies, the larger, extended family—or kinship group—played a more important economic role. In India, the multigenerational family still prevails today, much as it did in China up until the 1949 revolution.

Throughout the evolution of the nuclear family, the dominant means of economic production has always had an impact on how the family functioned. In agricultural societies, for example, inheritance laws and customs were typically designed to keep the family's land holdings intact through such devices as conveying title to the eldest son. Historian David Popenoe argues that this practice created an incentive for younger siblings to go out into the world on their own and create independent nuclear families. Similarly, in the seventeenth and eighteenth centuries, largely self-sufficient families would divide labor efforts, with the father and sons working the fields and the wife and daughters spinning and weaving, or tending to the livestock, according to Steven Mintz and Susan Kellogg. The expansion of capitalism further reinforced the model of the family as a "cooperative economic enterprise," as households supplemented their income by pairing with merchants or shopkeepers to produce finished goods, such as spinning yarn from wool, sewing piecework, or dipping candles.

But with the Commercial and Industrial Revolutions, as more

and more families left the farms, the nuclear family itself acquired a new identity, one that was *not* primarily economic in nature. Instead of being a "little commonwealth," the family began to be considered a "haven in a heartless world," a place of emotional refuge.

In the early twentieth century, the impact of industrialization, urbanization, and the changing role of the family led to the social reforms of the Progressive Era. By the 1930s, rapid urbanization and prolonged damage to the country's social fabric were crystallized in the mass suffering of the Great Depression. In response, Franklin Roosevelt launched the New Deal, a massive program of social interventions and family supports intended to help those who had fallen through the cracks during the nation's rapid transition into the modern age. To address the social and economic problems that families and communities seemed no longer able to handle, FDR introduced government programs like Social Security for the elderly, aid for widows and orphans, and the Civilian Conservation Corps, which put many of the unemployed back to work. The New Deal programs and their progeny—like Truman's Fair Deal and Lyndon Johnson's Great Society—alleviated an enormous amount of human suffering and saved many lives. But these federal programs also ignited a debate that still rages today over the appropriate economic role for families on the one hand and government on the other.

We've now reached a point where traditional family roles have been redefined and available resources stretched so thin that more and more basic family functions, such as child care and food preparation, are being performed by non–family members for a fee or packaged into goods that people can purchase (or "outsourced," as business executives would say). New dynamics have emerged within the family, too. Working women now have their own sources of income, and women as a group make more purchases in the economy than do men. Moreover, children have emerged as a significant new force in the economy, actually controlling or influencing the expenditure of billions of dollars of disposable income.

Two and a quarter centuries after our founding, the economic role of the American family has undergone a complete transformation. Within the sphere of the family, family members are now considered to "produce" a great amount of nurturing, parenting, and care. Sharon Hays, in her book *The Cultural Contradictions of Motherhood*, describes a trend of "intensive mothering" in which mothers put increasing amounts of work into providing mothering services to their children. But in terms of the family's role in the economy at large, instead of serving as the primary unit of economic *production*, the family is now the primary unit of *consumption*. Instead of the "little commonwealth" of colonial America, the family has become what could be called the "little purchasing co-op."

WHEN WANT BECOMES NEED

Like Rodney and Missy Crumpton, millions of Americans dream of a better future for their children and grandchildren. And like Dawn Hancock, millions more have worked their way up from poverty to a place of relative security and increased comfort. Americans have a right to be proud that we have continuously raised our sights and redefined what we consider to be essential. And it's a mark of our stunning economic success that each generation has turned goods and services once considered luxuries into what are now widely accepted as necessities.

Only about seventy-five years ago, for instance, cars were considered luxuries. Now cars are utterly integral to the way most of us live. Indeed, without access to a car, many people in America today could not find or keep a job. Dawn, for example, lost her job when her husband left her and she lost access to the family car. A study by the University of Wisconsin at Milwaukee Employment and Training Institute provided a stark illustration of this point: 42 percent of single women with young children in the Milwaukee area who had a car were employed full-time, according to the study, compared with only 12 percent of single mothers without access to a car.

Each decade, it seems, at least one new technology becomes a necessity to millions of Americans. For instance, for many years most people with telephones shared "party lines"; today it would be unthinkable for most not to have single-line service. Most recently, the Internet has become an invaluable tool for those who have access to it. In the future, most users will become impatient with dialing up the Internet using a narrow-band modem; inevitably, broadband access to the Internet will be added to the list of essentials.

We've become so accustomed to these kinds of technological advances that we tend to think of all progress as technological. But some former luxuries that we now consider necessities are actually changes in the way we prepare ourselves for the new requirements of the modern economy. One of the most significant is higher education, which over the past two generations has become a necessity for millions of Americans. When our economy was driven primarily by industrial and manufacturing production, a high school education was sufficient for the large majority of workers. Now, as our economy becomes increasingly knowledge-driven, higher levels of training and education are indispensable. As parents recognize that a college education is essential for their children, they struggle mightily to meet ever rising tuition bills. And that's one reason why federal Stafford college loan commitments have increased from $13.5 billion in 1993 to $23 billion in 2000.

Dawn Hancock certainly came to feel that education was a necessity for her and her family. She knew that if she were able to finish college and maybe even get a graduate degree, she could develop skills that would vastly improve her chances to enhance her family's long-term well-being. Having seen how much her own parents struggled to make ends meet, Dawn told us she was determined to "go to college and make something of myself." She remembered that when she was growing up, her dad, a high school dropout, was "always the first one let go" when his employer's company fell on tough times. "That's why I knew from a very young age that I was going to college no matter what. I remember being in second grade and thinking, 'I'm going to college.'" What she didn't expect was that she would be a divorced single mother by the time she got to college—but when that came to pass, she never wavered for a second in her conviction to pursue her dream.

In the past few years, the benefit of Dawn's college education has become ever more apparent. Once she finished college, Dawn got a steady job at the Tennessee Department of Human Services—and it was that new salary that made it possible for her to buy her mother's house. Encouraged by her progress, Dawn is committed to getting still more education, so she continues to take postgraduate classes even as she works full-time. Both she and Steve believe that, of the two of them, she will ultimately have the higher earning potential and that this will be the key to making it possible for their family to permanently achieve a better standard of living.

The odds are excellent that Dawn and Steve are right, and that Dawn's desire to get the best education possible will continue to pay off handsomely for her family. The premium earned in the marketplace by those who finish their college education has grown steadily larger as our economy has become increasingly global. Between 1979 and 2000, for instance, men who had completed a bachelor's degree or more saw their median real weekly wages rise by about 17 percent, while those with only a high school diploma saw theirs *fall* almost 13 percent. And those without a high school diploma saw their wages plunge by more than 26 percent. For women, the gains from higher education have been even greater. Between 1979 and 2000, female college graduates increased their median weekly wages by about 30 percent. Those with only high school diplomas saw their wages rise only 3 percent, and those without high school diplomas lost about 10 percent in wages. And it's important to note that this penalty for lower levels of education is paid by tens of millions of people. Taken together, 43 percent of all American workers—men and women—have only a high school diploma or less. Some are surprised that even now, only 27 percent of American workers have a bachelor's degree or higher.

If higher education is one example of a luxury becoming a necessity, child care is another. Until generations ago, when women began entering the workplace in great numbers, only well-to-do mothers hired nannies and daytime baby-sitters. Now, with the sharp increases in both single-parent families and families where both parents work, child care has become an absolute necessity for the majority of families with young children. But even for two-parent families and for parents with higher incomes, affording child care often presents a significant challenge. According to the Children's Defense Fund, child care costs $4,000 to $10,000 per child per year for full-day care. The Fund points out that this is at least as much as a year's tuition at a public university—and this at a time when one out of four families with young children earns less than $25,000 a year.

Given what child care costs, it's one of the most expensive new additions to the traditional list of basic needs that most families must address. In some cities, child care can cost more than housing. In addition, it's often very difficult to find child care that is both affordable and high quality. In one poll, over half of all parents say they have trouble finding affordable child care, and the National Center for Early Development and Learning found that only 8 percent of infant care centers and 24 percent of preschool classrooms can be rated as "good" or "excellent." Edward Zigler, head of the psychology section of Yale University's Child Study Center, told us, "There is good quality care, but no one can afford it." Zigler, who is widely regarded as the father of Head Start, added this devastating analysis of the state of child care in America: "The quality of care on average is mediocre, and it is no better today than thirty years ago. This is a non-system and a disgrace to this country."

Usually, quality and availability tend to go up as customer demand increases gradually, but that hasn't happened with child care. In 1980, only 47 percent of women with children under six worked; now 65 percent do. Similarly, the proportion of women with children over six who work has jumped from 64 percent to nearly 80 percent. Although there have been increases in the supply of child care, demand has grown more rapidly—and yet there has been no improvement in quality. "The link between quality of care and children's outcomes is absolutely nailed down," Zigler said. The concern shared by many parents about getting good child care may be one reason why an increasing number of two-career parents adopt split shifts so that one of the parents can always be with the children.

Single parents, however, don't have that option, and the combination of women's lower average earnings, inadequate public assistance, and lack of child support from nonresidential fathers means that providing quality child care is a huge challenge for most single mothers. On average, a low-income single parent spends close to 20 percent of total earnings on child care—nearly double what a low-income two-parent family spends and triple what the average two-parent family spends. In a study of Minnesota's Family Investment Program, lack of affordable child care proved to be the most common reason women were not able to move from welfare to work, and also the most common reason they left jobs and returned to the welfare rolls. The National Academy of Sciences Institute of Medicine notes that "affordable child care is a decisive factor in promoting work among low-income mothers."

You might reasonably conclude that paying for all these new necessities—advanced technologies, higher education, child care, and the like—would be just about impossible for most American families. But remarkably, many of us still have money left over when our needs—including these new needs—are met. Indeed, we are such a wealthy country that most Americans can still afford things we want but arguably don't need. This raises a dilemma now faced by so many American families: How do we distinguish what we need from what we merely want? What is necessity and what is a luxury? Does it make a difference? And assuming it does, what do we teach our children about those distinctions?

Dawn Hancock and her husband, Steve, now wrestle with exactly this dilemma. After battling their way out of poverty, they're confronted with a whole new set of choices, some of them surprisingly difficult. Decisions about what nonessentials to buy most often involve her son. Eight-year-old Chase's list of both needs and wants is growing rapidly. In just the past few months, the list of things Chase has asked his mom to buy him would choke a pony: a dirt bike, a four-wheeler, a Game Boy Advance, a Nintendo GameCube, a gecko, a rabbit, a falcon, a hawk, and more Pokémon cards. To most of these requests, Dawn has simply said no. But sometimes she splurges and gets him what he wants (generally by increasing her credit card debt), especially when she feels guilty denying him something he really, really wants.

If heavily marketed toys are a primary example of the needs-versus-wants dilemma, another interesting example is provided by food. As late as 1918, the average family spent 40 percent of their entire household budget just on obtaining the food they ate, which at that time was fairly basic. But over the course of the twentieth century, the variety and quality of foods increased exponentially, even as prices have fallen dramatically. Thanks to a range of new technologies and extremely efficient distribution, it's now possible to get almost every manner of fruit, vegetable, dairy product, or meat at just about any time of the year, albeit along with new concerns about pesticides, hormones, and genetic modifications.

But with abundant and inexpensive food comes a problem. Providing sufficient food is an essential function for every family, but even as we can take care of our need for food better than ever before, we can also satisfy our desire for it more easily than ever. Unfortunately, some of the food we want isn't good for us at all, at least not in excessive quantities. Our bodies were designed for a world of nutritional scarcity, not excess. For example, sugar helped our ancestors identify fruit as a healthy source of energy—and that may help explain why most of us experience pleasure when we consume it, and why we haven't developed internal safeguards against consuming too much of it. Our diet has changed radically from that of our ancestors, and our bodies were simply not designed to handle the regular abundance of calories, concentrated sugar, and harmful varieties of fat now common in what we eat.

Little wonder, then, that obesity among adults has doubled in the last twenty years; the number of overweight adolescents has tripled. Well over half of all adult Americans are now considered to be overweight—and approximately half of those overweight are considered obese. Even though some quarrel with the definition of "obese," according to former surgeon general David Satcher, the nation's obesity epidemic has gotten so bad that it may soon overtake tobacco as the leading cause of preventable deaths. Currently, some 300,000 deaths per year are attributed to illnesses directly caused or worsened by being overweight.

Which brings us back to the necessary question: when it comes to food, how do we distinguish between our wants and our needs? Even among those who are eager to improve their nutrition and eating habits, changes in family life have made it more challenging to do so. With both parents working in more families and more single parents working long days to make ends meet, many people don't want to come home and cook. Partly as a result of this, restaurant meals and other meals prepared away from the home now account for almost 40 percent of an average family's total food budget.

Schools often contribute to the problem too, since many of them now have vending machines selling candy, chips, and soda in their hallways and in some cases right in their lunchrooms. Indeed, many cash-strapped schools now rely on that money to bolster their budgets. Faced with crowded cafeterias and long lines, many students buy their lunch from the machines, and it's usually not healthy. On a hopeful note, some schools have started removing these junk-food machines; perhaps more will follow.

Many food companies haven't hesitated to cater to our desires and cravings. One striking phenomenon is the trend in recent years toward larger and larger portion sizes, both in restaurants and in packaged foods. The typical portion for many foods in a restaurant today is actually two to seven times larger than the amount recommended by nutritionists, and this problem—sometimes called "portion distortion"—has been getting worse for some time as restaurants and food processors compete to more than satisfy our rising expectations. One advocacy group notes that even the plates themselves have increased in size, from ten and a half inches in diameter to today's twelve inches.

If providing food and other essentials is a useful measure of a family's success, American families are without question among the most successful in human history. But if we can take considerable pride in this accomplishment, many of us must also think seriously about whether we are too often confusing wants with needs.

CONSUMERISM AND COMMODIFICATION

In the never-ending effort to bring our wants and needs into balance, families play a crucial role. It is in our families that we first learn how to ask for what we need, and it's in our families that we also learn that the fulfillment of some desires must be delayed or even denied.

But some families develop patterns of spending that teach a distorted lesson about the relationship between need and desire. In those families, the act of consumption can itself take on emotional significance. University of Florida professor of English and advertising James Twitchell says Americans "live through things." He observes, "We create ourselves through things. And we change ourselves by changing our things." Some people may also use the purchase of something as a way to express love or as a substitute for time spent together. Soon, a pattern of consuming can become associated with a feeling of emotional satisfaction. And then, as can happen with any behavior routinely used to relieve anxiety, consuming for its own sake can start to become a habit.

According to economist Juliet Schor, shopping "has become an important leisure activity, and there's a lot of impulsive buying that goes on." Schor told us that a sizable portion of the population, especially among families with above-average incomes, displays fairly high levels of compulsive purchasing, "buying stuff they didn't intend to, stuff that doesn't have a lot of value to them, stuff they can't afford . . . and that then brings with it a whole set of issues around which you get conflicts, because in terms of the values, [compulsive purchasing is] a hedonistic kind of thing." Schor also told us that a hundred years ago there were many more constraints on purchasing. Those constraints were practical, cultural, and religious. "There was a stronger religious orientation which gives the counterweight [that] says, 'Affluence is bad. Money is bad. Materialism is bad.' "

Another factor responsible for the confusion of needs and wants is a new twist on the old cliché about "keeping up with the Joneses." In his *New York Times* column, economist Paul Krugman observed that "human beings are hard-wired to judge themselves not by their absolute standard of living, but in comparison to others. It may be true that in material terms today's borderline poor live as well as the upper middle class did a few decades back, but that does not stop them from feeling poor. And consumer spending ultimately disappoints because of habituation: once you have become accustomed to a given standard of living, the thrill is gone."

This basic principle is not new. In 1776, Adam Smith wrote in *The Wealth of Nations*, "By necessaries I understand, not only the commodities which are indispensably necessary for the support of life, but whatever the custom of the country renders it indecent for creditable people, even of the lowest order, to be without." But today there's a new twist. Schor believes that the weakening of community bonds ended the practice of comparing one's economic well-being to the neighbors ("the Joneses") and that the mass media's regular portrayal of wealthier families changed the "target of aspiration." Further, Schor told us, a shift in the distribution of income toward the top 20 percent of the population stimulated conspicuous consumption on their part and made them not only a "lifestyle target" for the middle class, but a moving target. As a result, the middle class is "having a very hard time keeping up, because [recently] it's only that top 20 percent who's getting any real gains in income and wealth."

To stay even, middle-class families go into debt and work longer hours. Schor believes that families have gone from "comparing themselves to people with a similar level of income—the old 'keeping up with the Joneses' idea—to comparing themselves to people much higher up in the income distribution. I think a lot of the middle-class anxiety has to do with the fact that the consumption standards for being middle class and upper middle class have been escalating so rapidly, and it's very hard for people to keep up with them," Schor said.

Modern advertising also plays a role in encouraging families to buy a lot of things they may or may not actually need. Moreover, many ads are now aimed at encouraging children to nag their parents to buy particular products. Many of us know what it's like to have one of our children race in from the other room pleading to be taken straightaway to the mall to purchase some new product that he or she has just seen portrayed in a television commercial. With so many influences encouraging children to acquire more toys and more gadgets, many families are finding that values like moderation, thrift, self-sufficiency, and the appreciation of simple things are much more difficult to teach and to maintain.

Over the last century, the boundary between desire and necessity has also been blurred by changes in the consumer-goods markets. As mass production improved the quality, variety, and affordability of consumer goods, many items such as well-designed furniture and fancy clothes—once available only to the well-to-do—were no longer beyond the reach of average families. And as these products became available to much larger numbers of buyers, the advent of mass marketing began to change the relationship between *people* and *things*. Marketing experts began developing sophisticated campaigns to persuade consumers that they should purchase particular goods and services—not by making a logical case that they *needed* them, but instead by stirring an impulse to *want* what was being advertised.

The difference may seem subtle and slight to us, but according to some historians of culture, our inability to see the distinction clearly is itself part of the problem. Neil Postman, author of *Amusing Ourselves to Death: Public Discourse in the Age of Show Business*, writes, "As late as 1890, advertising, still understood to consist of words, was regarded as an essentially serious and rational enterprise whose purpose was to convey information." Ads appealed to a consumer's understanding, not his passions. However, in the ensuing decades, Postman argues, illustrations, photographs, slogans, and jingles began turning advertising into emotional appeals.

Postman estimates that the average forty-year-old American has already seen well over one million television commercials, and has another million or so to go before the first Social Security check arrives. By using sophisticated psychological techniques that bypass rational decision making, marketers can and do create consumer desires for products that no one knew they needed.

The attitudes of parents toward buying things that aren't really necessary have enormous influence on children. A team led by Penn State University marketing professor Marvin Goldberg developed a test known as the "youth materialism scale" and used it in a survey of 540 parents and 996 children between the ages of nine and fourteen. As part of the test, parents and children alike were asked whether they agreed with statements like "I have fun just thinking about all the things I own. I'd rather spend time buying things than almost anything else. The only kind of job I want when I grow up is one that gets me a lot of money." The test revealed that parents who scored the highest on the materialism scale tended to have the most materialistic children.

But even parents who resist materialistic impulses find it hard to teach their children restraint. Valerie Reddemann, of Chico, California, told us that when her four-and-a-half-year-old son, Sy, saw television commercials advertising "toys or candy or a new cereal, he would start yelling at us from the other room, 'Mom, I want this!'" She said they got "so tired trying to explain to him" why he couldn't have everything he wanted that finally they started telling him, "Put it on your list." At his last birthday, though, Valerie decided to do with Sy what her parents had done with her when she was a child. "My parents didn't have a whole lot. Growing up, we always had food on the table and clothing to wear, but there wasn't a lot of extras for toys and such. I remember for my birthday, my parents would give me a choice. I could either have a birthday party or choose what they called a 'big present.'" She and her husband, Rob, started taking the same approach with Sy this year and they say it has worked out really well so far. Giving children reasonable choices is an excellent strategy, says Jose Szapocznik. "On the one hand, the child learns to make choices, to think for herself. On the other, the parent maintains some control over the outcomes."

We recall that when our daughter Kristin was ten, she had her heart set on getting a parrot. For us, the issue was not so much cost as upkeep. When she promised that she would be entirely responsible for all the work of taking care of the parrot, we required that she do some lengthy research on exactly what that might involve. Once she found that the bird she wanted might live until she was eighty years old, we could sense the tide turning in our favor. She didn't get the parrot, and now, at the age of twenty-five, she's glad she doesn't have a rebellious teenage parrot living with her in Los Angeles.

But even as many families struggle to resist the indiscriminate buying of goods, families who can afford it also find it ever more tempting to buy an increasing number of services. Many of these services replace functions traditionally performed by the family, such as caring for children, caring for the elderly, cooking meals, and cleaning the home. As Arlie Hochschild, one of the country's most thoughtful family scholars, points out, some of these functions well-to-do families may purchase are now surprisingly intimate, such as birthday-party planning, personal gift selection, family album organizing, and taxi services for children. These transactions take place on what Hochschild calls the "commodity frontier," which, she says, "looks out on one side to the marketplace and on another side to the family. On the market side, it is a frontier for companies as they expand the number of market niches for goods and services covering activities [that] in yesteryear formed part of unpaid 'family life.' On the other side it is a frontier for families [that] feel the need or desire to consume such goods and services."

Hochschild believes the trend toward the commodification of traditional family functions is still accelerating, transferring more and more of these functions to the marketplace. As she sees it, the trend is both self-reinforcing and worrisome: "A cycle is set in motion. As the family becomes more minimal, it turns to the market to add what it needs, and by doing so, becomes yet more minimal." Neal Halfon, professor of pediatrics and the director of the University of California at Los Angeles's Center for Healthier Children, Families and Communities, noted that parents are even turning to the marketplace for advice from "experts on parenting, rather than just turning to other parents in the community, or even extended family."

A MATTER OF CHOICE

The more that traditional family functions are purchased in the marketplace, the more people are prone to see spending money as a way to express love and affection. In a culture where everything's value seems to be expressed in monetary terms, families can easily get confused about when spending money satisfies an emotional need and when it satisfies a physical need.

The decisions families make about wants and needs ultimately boil down to decisions about how to spend money. And for a number of reasons, many families are having more than the usual difficulty with decisions about money these days. For one thing, the cost of living has tended to rise faster than average wages have. For another, the desire to please everyone and do the "best" for one's family can easily lead to overspending.

The high amount of debt that many families carry is one symptom of how difficult it can be to balance wants and needs. At the end of 2001, according to the Federal Reserve, consumer debt was at an all-time high: $1.67 trillion. Interest payments alone have risen to 14 percent of disposable personal income, nearly back to the all-time record of 14.4 percent in 1986, when interest rates were much higher than they are now. While much debate surrounds the precise figure, government calculations show that the personal savings rate has flirted with zero.

There is a growing gap between the lifestyle to which many families aspire and their ability to actually attain it. In the constant struggle to first *do right* and then *do better* by their families, too many parents wake up one morning to find themselves struggling to stay afloat in a sea of debt that's teeming with the flotsam and jetsam of all sorts of possessions. And even in such circumstances, they still feel the desire to acquire more things.

Whatever the root cause of financial stress in families, mismanagement of family finances is a common contributing factor and is sometimes the principal cause of the problem. The challenge of making and following a family budget that matches income and expenditures seems much more difficult today than in the past, partly because of the widespread availability of consumer credit.

But there is also evidence that a growing number of Americans simply have not been exposed to the knowledge and skills that make up basic financial literacy. Before the changes of the late nineteenth century, when children were often physically present during their parents' handling of financial transactions, financial literacy could be passed down from one generation to the next during family conversations and everyday life. Nowadays, with the separation of work and home, and with less time available for communication in families, those kinds of family conversations don't take place as often. Among thirteen- to twenty-one-year-olds, only one-quarter report that they have ever actually received guidance from their parents on family finances or how to manage money.

Surprisingly, our school systems rarely fill the resulting gap in knowledge by teaching basic consumer finance—like how a checking account or savings account works. In fact, according to a survey of high school seniors nationwide, only 10 to 20 percent have had any kind of training in personal finances by the time they graduate. Meanwhile, 82 percent of high school seniors failed a test of their basic financial knowledge concerning such topics as loans, savings, interest rates, and credit cards. Barely half of all high school students understand what "compound interest" means.

It's not just young people either. In a recent inquiry of financial literacy, the U.S. Senate Banking Committee found that fewer than 50 percent of American parents draw up a household budget and try to follow it. That's likely one reason that a recent analysis indicated Americans may underestimate their credit card debt by as much as 50 percent. It's also a big reason why, among Americans eighteen to thirty-four, fully 49 percent now say they are living beyond their means.

Lacking basic financial management skills or the minimum balances required by many financial institutions, millions of Americans have established neither a checking nor a savings account. In fact, up to 12 million Americans have no relationship whatsoever with a traditional financial-services company. Fully a third of these households are African-American, 29 percent are Hispanic. Unfortunately, living outside the banking system can be financially disastrous. It is now common in low-income neighborhoods to use "check cashers" who charge outrageous fees for cashing personal checks—some 9 percent of the check amount.

For too many American families, though, the usual response to financial trouble is to borrow heavily on credit cards—the crack cocaine of consumer debt. And some companies are quick to play the role of pusher. The founder of one consumer finance company recently wrote a memo to one of his key executives and explained how to take advantage of people who are desperate for credit: "Is any bit of food too small to grab when you're starving and when there is nothing else in sight? The trick is charging a lot, repeatedly, for small doses of instrumental credit."

According to the industry research group Cardweb.com, the major credit card brands have issued almost twice as many credit cards as there are people in the United States. When you include smaller retail credit cards, an average cardholder has 6.5 credit cards. And as the credit card companies well know, the mere possession of a card can increase a shopper's willingness to buy on impulse. Many families discover that the cost of their impulsive purchases exceeds what they can reasonably afford. Then, once they get behind, too many of these families find that it becomes harder and harder to regain their footing. During the 1990s the average credit card debt per household tripled. One estimate indicates that the average cardholder household carriers in excess of $8,000 on credit cards.

Borrowing on a credit card makes about as much sense as using a check-cashing service, because the typical credit card interest rates are so much higher than what can be obtained by borrowing from a bank. But, like check-cashing services, it is often the only option open to people with meager financial resources. The median interest rate on a credit card is 15 percent. A simple example can illustrate what this means for the average family: if a family carries a credit card balance of $8,000 at 15 percent interest and makes only the minimum monthly payment of 2 percent of the outstanding balance, it would take more than thirty years to pay the debt off. In the process, the family will have paid $12,461 in interest charges alone, for a total of $20,461.

This kind of debt has enormous consequences for families. For one thing, they find that it's impossible to save money and accumulate wealth. So-called family wealth is also an important measure of the options open to a family. For example, even though the income gap between African-American families and white families has been narrowing, median household net worth for African-Americans is still only 14 percent that of whites. Think of the difference that makes to a young entrepreneur with a great idea who turns to his family for investment capital. If he or she comes from a poor family, that great idea is far less likely to be turned into a thriving new business, and the new jobs it would otherwise create in the community never materialize.

As well, the ill effects of excessive debt go far beyond financial troubles or lost entrepreneurial opportunities. Conflicts over finances, including debt, is one of the leading causes of family discord and marital conflict. Debt is now associated with damaged personal relationships, erosion of work performance, sleepless nights, and drug and alcohol abuse.

Given how hard many families have to struggle, and how large the crushing burdens of debt have become, it's not surprising that personal bankruptcy filings are at an all-time high. There were a record 1.5 million personal bankruptcies reported during the twelve-month period ending March 31, 2002, according to the Administrative Office of the U.S. Courts. Americans are carrying a record $711 billion on revolving credit balances. Credit-counseling agencies reported surges in requests for help in 2001, with 2.25 million Americans seeking help. The number of people who sought help for the first time from member agencies of the National Federation of Credit Counseling doubled between 1990 and 2000.

If debt has become an increasing burden to many families, it's also the case that many of today's adults do not have a realistic understanding of what they will or won't have waiting for them when they retire. The introduction of Social Security in the 1930s established the common expectation that income for retirement years was essential and that adult children should no longer be the primary providers of retirement security for their parents. For the first time, retirement plans of various shapes, sizes, and descriptions became an essential expenditure in the eyes of many Americans.

But according to a study recently completed by the AARP, a large number of Americans in the baby-boom generation now preparing for retirement have a false sense of security about their current ability to finance their living costs during retirement. Around 40 percent of people over fifty, for example, believed they had insurance that covers long-term care, whereas in actuality less than 10 percent have such insurance. Not surprisingly, respondents also told the researchers they felt more confident about their retirement prospects than those who had an accurate understanding of what they could finance. Further, with an increasing population of elderly Americans who have special needs—from nutrition requirements to mental-health problems—a majority in the AARP study had an inaccurate understanding of the cost of long-term care, with two out of five confused about whether Medicare would finance long-term care and/or assisted living.

Facing ever greater challenges to their financial well-being, Americans understandably look to the public sphere for relief. But here too, families are whipsawed: although there's a surplus of virtually every kind of product and service that can be purchased in the marketplace, we face a severe shortage of virtually all goods and services in the *public* sphere. Opinion surveys show that Americans want more public after-school and preschool programs, more child-care options, more public efforts to ensure clean water and clean air, more paid leave when their families face crises, more accessible job training and adult-education programs, and more affordable and comfortable public transportation. These needs are difficult if not impossible to satisfy through the purchase of private goods and services, no matter how much money a family makes. They can be gained only through investment in public goods. However, the same opinion surveys show Americans want low taxes and are skeptical of the government's ability to provide quality services at reasonable cost. Therefore, it seems prudent to explore public-private collaboration to create new solutions, and it is essential that the government be run wisely, efficiently, and ethically, in order to regain the people's trust.

It's been clear for years that we have too many cars on our streets and highways, which in turn cause too many time-consuming traffic jams and too much air pollution. Yet we have a severe and growing shortage of public-transportation options, such as light-rail commuter trains, which could save most Americans time, money, and stress. Clean, efficient, affordable public transportation would greatly increase the quality of life for all families while sharply reducing the proportion of family expenditures for transportation, a share that has quadrupled in the last few generations.

Further, we are spending far more per person on health care than any other industrialized society, yet some 40 million Americans still lack health insurance, and we have a pitifully inadequate public-health system. We spend less on community mental-health clinics that provide early diagnosis, treatment, and prevention of mental disorders than we spend dealing with the consequences of preventable mental disorders after they occur.

John Kenneth Galbraith wrote about the sharp contrast between the abundance of private goods and the scarcity of public goods in 1958, in his controversial book *The Affluent Society*. In that book, he declared, "We must find a way to remedy the poverty which afflicts us in public services . . . and which is in such increasingly bizarre contrast with our affluence in private goods." In the years since those words were written, much has been made in our national discourse about the shortcomings, mistakes, waste, and excesses of various public policies and programs. Some people have seemed eager to abandon our historically balanced blend of

private and public goods and work for sharp cuts in public investments (with the exception of national defense). Advocates of this
point of view confidently assert that virtually all needs can be met
by private production purchased in the market system. But realis-
tically, this doesn't seem to work for all Americans. Goods produced privately cannot be expected to reach all American families
who need them to become and remain strong. The strength of families cannot be purchased for any price and is not for sale in any
market. However, family cohesion and time off from work can be
enhanced as public values.

The pursuit of happiness—right up there with life and liberty—
has always been a basic American value. But if many families feel
they are losing ground in their quest for a higher quality of life, it is
partly because they have discovered that many of their deepest
needs are impossible to satisfy through the purchase of private
goods. Increasingly, families say they want more satisfying experiences, not more consumer products that are bought and sold in the
ever-growing private marketplace. What families really want the
most can't be commodified: relaxing and enjoyable time with
loved ones; the appreciation of nature; clean air to breathe and
clean water to drink; peace and quiet; rest, recreation, exercise, and
self-renewal; time to read and learn and be creative; a rich network
of good friends and neighbors who help one another when help is
needed; membership in a real community where people feel a connection to one another and are dedicated to values they respect
and share.

At the root of this growing need is the age-old desire of families
to improve their lot in life. But if some families feel they're making
steady progress toward this goal, many others feel that it is steadily
receding, leaving families running in place longer and faster, ever
more tired, yet still far short of their goal. And to most people,
there is only one possible solution to this unsatisfying equation:
work harder.

THE CORTESES

Eduardo Cortes, Isabela (Bela) Cortes, Laura Castro de Cortes, Isaac (Sacky) Cortes, and Tito the cat

THE LYS

Minh Ly, Sherry Ly, Betty Ly, and Thanh Ly

Chapter 5

WORK

In work, do what you enjoy.
In family life, be completely present.
—LAO-TZU

BALANCING WORK AND FAMILY

Not enough time. Not enough energy. Not enough sleep. Faced with too many competing demands, many families find they simply don't have enough hours in the day to give both work and family their absolute best. With parents putting in stunningly long—and steadily increasing—hours at the workplace, many American families have a problem balancing work and family.

Longer workdays, longer commutes, and economic necessity make it harder for many families to carve out family time. Meanwhile, with children living in an increasingly sophisticated and sometimes dangerous environment, it has become unnervingly clear how critical each hour of family time can be. Trying to do their utter best on all fronts, too many parents are finding there's just not enough of themselves to go around.

Part of the conflict may come from the fact that both work and family are so important to us. For many of us, work is a part of our identity. As children, we see grown-ups working and as we look up to them, we want to be like them. From an early age, we begin to learn that work is what you do to be productive, and that how you approach it says something about your worth as a human being. Al remembers vividly how his father taught him about the work ethic. Every summer Al worked on his family's farm in Tennessee, sometimes by his father's side and sometimes with the other farmhands—but always long hours, from before dawn until suppertime. For a young boy, this experience was character building, but was certainly not something he would have chosen if left to his own devices. Al's father taught him from a young age that there was an intimate relationship between work and the purpose of life, telling him, "Son, you have to *learn* how to work." He repeated that teaching often, always with an emphasis on the word *learn*, because he realized that work did not necessarily come naturally to a young boy, and that learning to work was an important ingredient to living a meaningful life. What needed to be learned was not simply the skills associated with the work task at hand (though they were also important) but, more crucial still, the necessity to *learn* the inner motivation essential to work, the fortitude to work hard and long hours, no matter the sweat, the fatigue, or the desire to be elsewhere. There was a nobility in work, and work itself gave purpose to life.

But later, as young parents, we were forced to go through a transition in our family routines when we realized that this devotion to work was simply not providing enough time for the other, equally vital part of our lives: our family. Al loved his job as a congressman and then senator, and lived by the strong work ethic he had learned. He began to work not only all week long, often late into the evening, but also three weekends out of every four, traveling back to Tennessee on Friday afternoons for town hall meetings through Saturday evening, and then returning to Washington on Sunday to meet Tipper and the children at our church by 11:30 A.M.—halfway through the service. We usually had a nice Sunday family lunch and enjoyed the rest of the day. But on Monday morning, Al was right back into his work routine, so enthusiastic about what he was doing that he didn't notice the impact it was having on our family.

One Saturday when Tipper was really stressed with all the kids, Al called from Tennessee to check in. He asked cheerily, "How is everybody?" Tipper, who was not feeling cheery at all, blurted out, "I'm planning on attending a seminar on single parenting."

Tipper was so frustrated and mad. She understood that Al was the primary breadwinner for the family and that her responsibility was to care for the kids, but work was taking too much of Al's time, and Tipper did not think that there was adequate partnering in the raising of our children. True, Tipper knew she could always count on Al in an emergency, or whenever she strongly insisted, but she really missed his not being a part of the daily rhythms of their life. And the children missed him, too.

Finding the right balance wasn't easy. After Tipper's dramatic announcement over the telephone, Al promised to cut back on the time he devoted to work—and for a short time he did. But before long, the enthusiasm he felt for what he was doing in Congress once again took over and, after a while, it was almost as bad as before. Over the next few years, however, after further discussions between the two of us and especially after Albert's accident, Al finally did make the needed changes—more or less permanently.

Just as we had to figure out a very specific solution based on our individual needs, the complexity and varied circumstances of each family means that the solutions to the work-family conflict have to be worked out one family at a time. Americans' work hours have steadily increased, and unfortunately, most of our institutions and support systems have fallen way behind the new realities. As a result, families have been pushing the limits of creativity and ingenuity to devise new solutions.

How did we get to a point where family is so far below work on America's priority list? The work ethic that Al's father taught him as a child has been passed down in varied forms from generation to generation since the *Mayflower* landed.

Professor Roger Hill of the University of Georgia has studied the work ethic throughout history. He notes that originally, the Judeo-Christian belief system viewed work as a punishment from God for Adam and Eve's transgressions. The Greeks and Romans regarded manual labor with contempt. Throughout the Middle Ages, Christians still considered work a rebuke from God for original sin, but as people came to see work as a means to provide for oneself and to help one's neighbors, it developed a positive aspect too. It was the Reformation, however, that completely changed the dominant view of work, and set the stage for today's work and family conflicts, Hill notes. Martin Luther believed that people could serve God *through* their work and that all "callings were of equal spiritual dignity"—including manual labor. Then, only one generation later, John Calvin taught that success in work was a possible indication that the industrious and monetarily successful individual was one of an "elect" group of persons chosen by God and predestined to inherit eternal life. The catch was that neither the elect nor others could ever know for certain in which category they were predestined to be placed. But, according to Calvinists' beliefs, whether or not they worked hard was an important tip-off. And it helped if they amassed a lot of money.

In any case, attitudes toward hard work changed dramatically. This new view informed the philosophical underpinnings of our nation, including the ideas of diligence, punctuality, discipline, individualism, and deferred gratification.

Although our forebears worked hard, their labors were seasonal; planting and harvesting months were busy, but winter brought some degree of respite. The age of machines, the assembly line, and mass production eventually brought ceaseless monotony to many jobs. And new technologies would usher in an era of increased productivity, higher incomes, and higher standards of living, which led families to place a higher relative value on time spent in the work-place. During the transforming years of the Industrial Revolution, most working-class families—the majority of Americans at that time—could not make a living on one salary alone, unlike middle-class families. As a result, virtually all members of working-class families pitched in to help support the family. Although many women in such families made direct economic contributions to the family by doing paid "outwork," overseeing boarders, or managing the family's finances, their chief responsibilities to the household centered on domestic tasks such as cleaning and cooking.

Children in working-class families often worked too, as their earnings were critical to the family's economic survival. Family members often labored together in factories or mills. Because they could earn a living in the same community, children were not sent to other towns for apprenticeships, as had been customary in the past, and families were able to live together longer than they had previously.

Through all these changes in the labor force and the nation's economy, there was at least one constant: the work ethic was deeply ingrained in secular American culture, and was promoted by factory owners and managers. The work ethic—originally based in religious conviction—became a governing principle of the American workplace, and was embodied in a new popular culture as America became the world's leading industrialized economy.

Frederick W. Taylor, an engineer, standardized production pro-cesses and workers' routines with his concept of "scientific manage-ment" in the late nineteenth and early twentieth centuries. Efficiency measures associated with this management practice—such as centralized personnel decisions and the time clock—lessened the significance of the family within the factory. Women still made up a small proportion of the formal labor force, but when World War II struck, it created a shortage of men, which paved the way for women to enter the workforce in much greater numbers.

Those who would have opposed it had no choice but to accept it. In the postwar years, the migration out of the home accelerated.

Today, many working parents find that they suffer divided loyalties not just from economic necessity but because they find work a fulfilling experience that provides meaning and purpose in their lives. For women in particular, the equal rights revolution and the changes in social attitudes that accompanied it have opened up brand-new opportunities in careers that were once reserved for men—careers that many women have found rewarding. What many women now want is not less work but more options that will enable them to integrate their responsibilities in the home with their responsibilities at work.

THE CORTES FAMILY

Laura Castro de Cortes is a vibrant and warm woman who clearly derives a great deal of joy and fulfillment from the contributions she is able to make through her work. The president and cofounder of her own consulting firm, which advises businesses on how to market to Hispanic customers, Laura is married to her high school sweetheart and calls herself a "Hispanic soccer mom." She and her husband, Eduardo, live in a beautiful home of their own in a charming suburb of Des Moines, Iowa, with their two children, Isabela and Isaac. In addition to running her own business, Laura also cofounded the Iowa Hispanic Chamber of Commerce, is on numerous advisory boards, and is the administrator of an after-school program. Her expertise on and insights into the Hispanic market are so much in demand that at one point she served on fourteen different boards.

Recently she has been making it a goal to get off of as many boards as she can, because she has found it to be too much of a drain on the time she needs to spend with her family. The children say they have noticed the effects of all the hard work on her as well as on their father. "I don't like it when Mom overworks," said twelve-year-old Bela, "because then she gets high-tempered."

Nevertheless, Laura believes that she is a happier person and a more positive role model for her children because of the work she does. She is fulfilled by her job and the contributions she makes to the larger community. And she clearly is energized; her eyes light up when she describes her work.

"Entrepreneurship runs deep in our family," Laura told us. Her maternal grandmother, the matriarch of that family, decided at one point that she wanted to own a flower shop in Juárez, Mexico. "My grandmother saved up one peso at a time to open that shop," Laura said. She worked there herself every day until she was ninety-two, when she passed away. Laura's aunt runs a pork distribution company. Laura's mother, meanwhile, didn't need to work because her husband made enough to support the family, "but she wanted to, so she did!" Laura told us.

Laura's paternal grandfather was the mayor of a small town in Jalisco, Mexico. He was challenged to a duel, in the course of which both he and the other man were killed. Laura's grandmother, fearing that there might be retaliation against the family, moved with her son (Laura's father) and her daughter to Juárez to protect the family. Later, when Laura's father moved from Juárez to El Paso as a young man to learn English, he met and eventually married Laura's mother.

Eduardo and Laura actually met the same way Laura's parents did. Eduardo moved to El Paso so he could attend the high school there and learn English; he needed to know the language to apply for a technical program in college. That is where he met Laura—or rather where Laura spotted and courted him. When she noticed the cute new boy in school, Laura decided she wanted to get to know him and mapped out a plan. She found out everything he liked and all the extracurricular activities he participated in. She then "spontaneously" engaged him in conversations about one of his favorite topics, aviation history, and gradually joined all the clubs he was in. Taking notice of all her new activities, one of her teachers said, "Laura, you are in a lot of clubs." She responded, "Oh yes, Mr. Campbell, I really enjoy all of these clubs." And in fact, she did enjoy the clubs—but more for the company than for the activity. By the end of the year, they were officially a couple.

The second day they were together, Laura sat Eduardo down on the stoop and told him, "Look, this is how it is. I want to have my career and not just a degree for decorating the wall. I want someone who will treat me as a partner, equally. I don't like people who smoke. I don't like beer. This is who I am. Take it or leave it." Eduardo responded, "I want someone who is a partner. I don't want to be the sole income earner. I want someone who will support me in my dreams." Since they shared the same vision of partnership, Eduardo changed his plans to go back to Mexico for college and instead went to the University of Texas at El Paso with Laura. They married while in college, and have been together ever since.

Laura said the first five years of marriage, when they had to make the adjustment to thinking about everything as a couple, were the hardest. And the arrival of a new baby in the midst of it all made it even more challenging. In addition to working and trying to put themselves through college, they now had Bela to take care of. Laura explained that everyone assumed that it was just a matter of time until she dropped out of college. But having seen how many Latinas left school and were never able to come back to finish, Laura was determined to graduate. Although at the time they were living in El Paso, very near their extended family in Juárez, El Paso's sister city just across the Rio Grande, they couldn't rely on their families to help with Bela because the amount of time needed to cross the border was too unpredictable from day to day. They first tried juggling a staggered schedule. Laura took only morning classes and Eduardo took only evening classes, so that there were only a few hours on Tuesday and Thursday mornings when their obligations overlapped. During those hours a friend of theirs who was a nurse watched Bela. But after a while, they realized they couldn't juggle the demands of their jobs, their full courseloads, and the needs of their baby.

They eventually decided that one of them would have to drop out of school. Eduardo said Laura should finish college first, so he dropped out for a while and took care of Bela. Laura took a reduced course schedule for a while and worked at an army supply store, while Eduardo tried a variety of odd jobs, including working his way up at a Mexican restaurant from dishwasher to delivery boy, waiter, cashier, and eventually manager. He also worked weekends as a security guard at a senior citizens' home. They were finally both able to take classes when Laura got Bela accepted into a child-care program at the YWCA. Unlike other child-care programs, Laura and Eduardo could afford this one because it charged on a sliding scale depending on a family's income and because it gave priority to university students. Laura later ended up working as an after-school program coordinator at the YWCA, and she was always grateful to the program. "Eduardo and I could not have both finished school without that child care."

After Laura graduated, it was Eduardo's turn to finish college. As soon as he graduated, he got a great job offer from a major financial-services company—in Des Moines, Iowa. But at that point, Laura didn't want to move the young family in order to accommodate his work, because she was not willing to give up the extended network of family and friends who were such a big part of their lives in El Paso and Juárez.

In order to avoid disrupting those deep family connections, Eduardo agreed to turn down the job and began teaching at a local high school instead. After eight months, however, Laura realized that Eduardo was not happy in that career, and she encouraged him to reapply for the job with the company in Iowa so that he would be happier professionally.

When he indeed got a job offer, they decided to take it. The decision, however, was not driven solely by career advancement for

Eduardo. That was a major factor; but, they told us, they had come to realize that in many ways they wanted to move away from their families of origin for a period of time to a brand-new place because they thought it would be good for their marriage and for their own nuclear family. In El Paso, near both their birth families, there were high expectations that they would spend nearly all their spare time with their extended families. As a result, they felt they never really had time just for themselves.

By moving away, they finally obtained that time and that space. "When something happened, it was just Eduardo and Laura, Bela and Sacky," said Laura. Although sometimes that was difficult, being forced to rely on each other in such a strong way really helped them forge a closer relationship and strengthened their marriage.

The move also created new challenges for the family. Eduardo did so well in his new job that he soon got a promotion. He now makes a good salary; in many respects, Eduardo is the embodiment of the American Dream. A first-generation immigrant, he has worked his way up the ladder of success. He loves his family and enjoys his work. There's only one problem: his work takes so much of his time and energy that there's not enough of either left over for his family.

His daughter, Bela, told us that he often has such large rings under his eyes from working too hard that he "looks like a rac-coon." When he is not working, he is usually at home with his children, but he is often so exhausted that the children don't even ask him to become involved in their play or with their homework.

"I feel bad for Dad because work is mean to him," said Bela, adding that she and her brother, Sacky, are careful to change their pattern of play in order to be very quiet, lest they awaken their dad from his recuperative naps on the sofa. Sacky, who is eight, said he sometimes gets frustrated that his dad can't play with him on Saturdays and adds, "If I had a magic wand and I could change one thing, I would make it so my dad works less."

Eduardo is responsible for the maintenance of a major database that is central to the operations of the company for which he works. Since he got the promotion to that job three years ago, he is frequently paged with work emergencies at any hour of the day or night. "Now everything has to be twenty-four seven," he said, explaining that whenever the system goes down, it costs his company $250,000 per hour. He said that he works such long hours because he has a responsibility to provide for his children. Even though Eduardo is exhausted by his work, he nonetheless describes his career and recent promotion with evident pride and satisfaction. "I was lucky," he notes. "I was at the beginning of the I.T. wave when it started."

Eduardo speaks with some sadness about the fact that his own father always worked so hard that he and his siblings never really had much of a chance to know him as a person, rather than just as a provider. Eduardo grew up on his grandfather's farm. But one year, a bad crop caused his grandfather to lose the farm to the bank. Eduardo's father, who at the time was in school studying agronomy, had to drop out, and the whole family moved to the city, where they opened up a small stationery and school-supplies store. While his father would tend the business, Eduardo and his grandfather would travel together to other cities to buy more supplies for the store. During those trips, Eduardo's grandfather would tell him stories about his days fighting in the Mexican civil war. As a result, Eduardo ended up being much closer to his grandfather than to his father. He mainly remembers his father as always being tired.

Family patterns do have a way of repeating themselves in successive generations. Indeed, although Eduardo's daughter, Bela, bemoans how hard Eduardo works, when we asked her what she would look for in a man when she grows up and is ready to marry, her most important criterion (after someone who is nice and good-looking) was "someone who works hard like my dad." After a moment's reflection, she added, "Maybe not as pressured as my dad, but someone who brings home money and works hard."

THE OVERTAXED RESOURCES
OF TIME AND ENERGY

Many Americans are feeling a time crunch, primarily because work has steadily been taking more and more hours away from the time they have for themselves. This national trend has picked up so much momentum that by 2000, we had become by far the hardest-working people in any developed country.

By contrast, the Japanese, legendary for their diligence and hard work, are now a distant fifth to Americans in terms of the number of hours worked per person per year. Part of the gap may be due to the United States' record economic expansion in the 1990s when Japan suffered a long downturn, but some economists cite different reasons for the increase in work hours and thus the gap: American mothers with children tending to go back to work sooner after their children's births and for more hours per week than young mothers did a decade or two ago; salaried professionals who now often work fifty or more hours per week; manufacturing employees taking advantage of overtime to bring home more money; and low-wage workers who are holding down two or three jobs to make ends meet.

In fact, when you add it all up, the average American works a full three weeks more each year than the average Japanese. And what about the Germans, whose post–World War II production miracle reshaped the economy of Europe? They work an astonishing ten and a half weeks fewer per year than Americans.

We pride ourselves on having the highest productivity per person in the world—almost 40 percent higher than in Japan—but one of the main reasons we do is all the extra hours we put in. In productivity per *hour* worked, as opposed to productivity per *per-*

son, we actually rank behind workers in Belgium and France. They may be more productive when they are *at* work partly because they have more time to rest and recuperate *after* work.

In addition to the increase in the number of hours worked per person, the biggest impact on the effort to balance work and family has come from a dramatic change in the location of our workplaces. For much of human history, the household was the primary unit of economic activity. But over the course of the last century and a half, that changed profoundly. As the Industrial Revolution gathered momentum, family members who used to work from sunrise to sunset on the farm were toiling long hours in factories and mills. Today, just 3 percent of the American workforce is employed in agriculture, compared with 40 percent at the start of the twentieth century.

Late in the 1800s, organized labor made a reduction in the number of hours worked per week one of their principal goals. But in more recent decades this goal has fallen from labor's agenda—partly because, as John Sweeney, head of the AFL-CIO, told us, "Our members are pressed for money and they don't want to give up their overtime." That is beginning to change, however, as the work-family squeeze leads more and more working men and women to ask their employers—and their unions—for help in balancing work and family. In 2001, Al visited with members of Local 1526 of the Machinists Union as they walked a picket line in rural Iowa during their strike against Maytag/Amana. Their demands included fair wages and affordable insurance but also "family time, not overtime." After fifty days, the fourteen hundred members of the local succeeded in getting a new contract.

According to the Economic Policy Institute, from 1989 to 1998 the combined number of hours worked annually by middle-income mothers and fathers in two-parent families with children at home went up by 246 hours. That's six extra full-time weeks a year! Looking at the longer-term trend, from 1979 to 1998, the increase is even more dramatic: 613 hours. That's nearly four months of full-time work per couple each year—and that staggering increase has occurred in just one generation.

So where does all that extra time for work come from? It is taken from time with our families and friends, from civic involvement, from the amount of sleep we get each night, and from the amount of energy we have left when we're not at work. The real time crunch hits when too many things have to happen at the same time. Short of cloning oneself, it's hard to make it all work.

Once, when Al was serving as vice president and was scheduled to attend one of Sarah's soccer games, he needed to meet with the president of an important central Asian country at the White House on the same afternoon. No problem, we thought—just figure out when the game will be over, how long it will take to drive back to the White House, and that's when the meeting will start.

Everything was fine until the game drew to a tie and the overtime period started. What the heck, the plan might still work—and being five minutes late wouldn't matter. But then the first overtime also ended in a tie, and a second overtime began—after a rest break for the players, of course. Now the pressure was on. To make matters worse, it was our family's turn to provide the snacks for the players after the game, and Tipper was out of town making a speech on mental health. Everybody knows how important this ritual is to the child of the snack-bearing parent, and Al had the snacks. So he stayed. The snacks were handed out briskly. The visiting president had to wait a little *too* long, but it wasn't the end of the world. In fact, it turned out that the visiting president was a dad too and had young children about the same age as ours.

Obviously Al's job was not a normal one, and even in that situation, he had more control than most people do. Showing up forty-five minutes late in a lot of jobs can carry a severe penalty, and having to hand out snacks to your daughter's soccer team would probably not be accepted as an excuse.

It should be, though. We've had this huge increase in the number of parents now working outside the home, as well as in the number of hours they spend working. Yet there has been no corresponding change in the structure of work to accommodate the needs of families. Instead, parents have had to devise, on their own, an array of ingenious solutions to preserve time with their children, even as the demands of work increase.

Despite the rapid rise of mothers in the workforce, demographer Suzanne Bianchi found that mothers' time spent with children has actually been quite stable over time. Indeed, mothers today are spending slightly more time each day with children than mothers did in 1965, Bianchi found. Although working more, mothers are also placing higher priority on spending time with children and thus spending less time on housework, volunteer work, and leisure activities. Nevertheless, the hunger for more time with family and less time at work is growing. According to the 1997 National Study of the Changing Workforce conducted by the Families and Work Institute, work negatively affected the personal lives of one quarter to over a third of employees "often or very often." A full 63 percent said they wanted to work fewer hours. And parents are not the only ones who feel this way; many working single people also express the desire to strike a better balance in their lives so they can spend more time with loved ones and pursue personal interests and goals.

The fact is that there is simply no substitute for time shared as a family, special occasions, rituals, play, and activities engaged in by the family as a whole. As a family, we often talk about favorite times we have shared with one another. We remember joint outings, ritual celebrations, special moments, and funny ones—like the time one of our dogs, Shiloh, licked all the icing off Kristin's birthday cake. And you know what? We hardly ever talk about the times when we were apart, working.

Nourishing relationships within a family is critical—not just between parents and children, but between the parents themselves. Yet all too often, parents who make great efforts to focus on their children while also working long hours manage this feat at the expense of time spent with each other as a couple. This is a particularly big challenge for members of all those "split-shift" families, who are seldom all at home and awake at the same time.

The same strategic trade-off takes place in families like ours, where one parent usually worked primarily out of the home and the other primarily in the home. We learned this lesson the hard way. When Al was home, he was intent on spending as much time as possible with the children—assuming that was the best approach for the whole family. He figured his spending time with the children would benefit them and indirectly benefit Tipper also, and that therefore she would appreciate it too.

What was missing was time for the two of us—*just the two of us*—to spend alone, without the children. Yet Al felt guilty going out to dinner or a movie without bringing the children along, so we almost always did activities as a family. Of course, we did have some time alone—late at night and early in the morning. And we were together all those times when we were both with the children. So it wasn't immediately obvious that our relationship was suffering from too little time with each other. After all, we were "together" a lot.

What we finally realized—Tipper first and Al more slowly—was that giving each other time only during the dregs of the day was not enough. We needed time together as a couple when we were not sleepy and exhausted. At first, in our efforts to communicate about this issue, we talked past each other like ships passing in the night. Tipper wanted more time together. Al failed to understand how time together as a family didn't count as time together with Tipper. Tipper was there, wasn't she?

Once we finally agreed we had a problem, we made big changes in our lives, starting with more time at home for Al. We scheduled "dates" with each other to go out and enjoy a dinner almost every week. We took long walks and had talks on weekend afternoons while the kids were occupied elsewhere. And it really worked.

The most important part of the lesson we learned from that experience was that the time we made for ourselves, separate from our children, benefited us—but it also benefited our children. They gained more from the strengthening and deepening of our marriage than they would have from the extra time that would have been spent with them. The overall health and vibrancy of our family life was immeasurably strengthened when each child knew beyond the shadow of any doubt that their parents were deeply in love and couldn't be played off against each other—because we seemed to be in complete accord on what was best for them.

Moreover, the enhanced quality of our communication with each other made it much easier to maintain a healthier balance between work and family on an ongoing basis. We started going over our schedules together, as far in advance as possible. Family events and time just for the two of us started showing up on the calendar many months in advance—before anything else was allowed to be scheduled. We have since learned that many marriage counselors strongly advise adopting a formal process to ensure that adequate time is set aside for family activities, conversations, and rituals—even if it means taking time from work. John Gottman, for instance, recommends weekly dates as a fun, low-key way to stay connected with your partner. Even when a couple solves the problem of how to stay connected, they still probably have to deal with a serious time and energy deficit. Some more affluent families try to buy more time or energy by purchasing technologies to speed up household chores and by heating up ready-to-eat meals. Some may hire other people to help them with tasks that used to be performed by older siblings or members of the extended family. But most families can't afford these options, and they usually don't solve the problem anyway.

Nearly everyone tries to squeeze more hours out of each day by staying up late or getting up earlier at the expense of their sleep. In a recent survey of families with children under five, researchers at UCLA's Center for Healthier Children, Families, and Communities found that 85 percent of parents say they are exhausted by the time they go to sleep each night. But it's not just parents: almost every member of the typical American family is now sleep deprived, said Dr. William Dement, considered to be the father of sleep medicine in the United States. Among those carrying huge sleep debts are parents, adolescent children, shift workers who frequently change their sleep cycles to accommodate their work schedules, and other workers, like Eduardo Cortes, who are trying to respond to the unpredictable demands of today's 24/7 information economy.

Lack of sleep is one of the largest and least understood problems in America, according to Dement. "Sleep deprivation is rampant," he told us. "Most Americans no longer know what it feels like to be fully alert all day long."

According to Dement, who is also the director of the Stanford University Sleep Research Center, average Americans are now sleeping one hour a night less than their parents did after the end of World War II. And millions of shift workers are now averaging less than *five* hours of sleep per day. He likens sleep deprivation to credit card debt: if you get the sleep you need, you have a zero balance, but if you sleep less than your body needs to, over time you go into debt. And if you don't start paying it back, the debt starts increasing and compounding.

But too few of us think about it in those terms; most of us have a poor understanding of the consequences of sleep debt. Individuals with large sleep debt say they feel tired all or most of the time. Feeling unambiguously sleepy is the end stage in this process. In healthy young adults, 99 percent of fatigue is sleep debt. Studies at Stanford University showed that when students obtained sizable amounts of extra sleep, not only did they stop feeling sleepy in afternoon classes, but they stopped feeling tired and fatigued at other times of the day. It has been known for years that adolescents in middle school and high school are extremely sleep deprived. In recent hearings held by the National Academy of Sciences, high school teachers testified that the first two periods were nearly a complete waste because students were too tired and sleepy to do anything but calisthenics, Dement said.

"Children studied twenty years ago were pretty much all wide awake and alert in class. Now they are starting to fall asleep in class," he said. "I date it to cable television and then the Internet." And college students? "Almost every one of them is sleep deprived, the majority at a level we would consider dangerous."

Dement told us that the impact on families can be severe: "We are just starting to study families instead of just focusing on individuals. . . . The negative consequences of sleep deprivation are magnified in family life. Impulse control is greatly undermined, and sudden acts of violence can occur—with the most common being a severely sleep deprived parent striking a baby who won't stop crying." Dement added that sleep deficits due to chronic stress also can contribute to an increased incidence of depression. There may be more truth than we realize in the old saying "The best bridge between hope and despair is a good night's sleep."

With more and more pressure on Americans to work longer hours with less sleep, it's little wonder that Starbucks opened more than fourteen hundred new stores last year, in the midst of a recession. Many who speed themselves up for work with caffeine find it difficult to slow themselves down at bedtime. Those who in turn drink more alcohol at night to slow down compound the problem. And sales of sleeping pills are rising. Where is all this headed? Pharmaceutical companies have developed a new medication that allows people to stay awake for extended periods of time without the "caffeine jitters" and without a serious loss of alertness. In an article for the *New Yorker*, Dr. Jerome Groopman, chief of the Division of Experimental Medicine at Harvard Medical School, notes that some scientists "have even raised the question of whether advances in biopharmacology will ultimately make regular sleep unnecessary." The drug Provigil (its generic name is modafinil) is supposed to be used to treat unusual health problems like narcolepsy, or to help those in unusual work situations, like the pilots of the B-2 stealth bombers who regularly flew nonstop from Whiteman Air Force Base in Missouri round-trip to the Balkans or one-way to Afghanistan in order to drop their bombs—a journey of thirty to forty hours, with no rest. Some experts are studying its capabilities to help people who are required to have unusual sleep patterns, such as shift workers. The number of prescriptions being written for Provigil is already skyrocketing, and although its manufacturer says it's intended only for treating medical problems like narcolepsy, some observers worry that it is being abused by people whose only problem is balancing work and family.

The only safe and reliable way to reduce a sleep debt is by sleeping more. However, we place such a high value on work that it has long since become a point of pride for many to speak about how little they have slept. Never mind that the scientists who study sleep insist that most human beings need, on average, eight hours of sleep per night—or about 15 percent more than most Americans get on average during the week.

In addition to work-related stress, scientists who study sleep disturbances single out pervasive artificial light as a major factor that interferes with sleep. The reason, they say, is that exposure to bright light, whether natural or artificial, can reset our internal body clocks, and play havoc with our sleeping and waking cycles. Thomas Alva Edison, famous for inventing the first practical incandescent light and pioneering the widespread use of electricity, said, "There is really no reason why men should go to bed at all." And what a dramatic change artificial light has caused in the relationship between work and family. In an *Atlantic Monthly* article, Cullen Murphy cites John Staudenmaier, a historian of technology and a Jesuit priest, who wrote several years ago that in the days before lightbulbs, "activities that need good light—where sharp tools are wielded or sharply defined boundaries maintained; purposeful activities designed to achieve specific goals; in short, that which we call work—all this subsided in the dim light of evening. Absent the press of work, people typically took themselves safely to home and were left with time in the evening for less urgent and more sensual matters: storytelling, sex, prayer, sleep, dreaming."

Since the invention of electric light, it has been difficult to recapture the gentler daily rhythms of the pre-electric world. And inside the typical home, the bright light of television is on an average of nearly eight hours a day, many of those hours after sunset. A recent study by sleep specialists found that a staggering 87 percent of all American families spend some portion of the hour just prior to trying to go to sleep watching television, with its bright flickering lights.

In our modern world, light is routing darkness. In our biggest cities, its victory is nearly complete. As Cullen Murphy wrote, "Darkness was once an ocean into which our capacity to venture was greatly limited; now we are wresting vast areas of permanent lightness from the darkness, much the way the Dutch have wrested polders of dry land from the sea. . . . In the United States at midnight, more than 5 million people are at work at full-time jobs. Supermarkets, gas stations, copy shops—many of these never close. I know of a dentist in Ohio who decided to open an all-night clinic and has had the last laugh on friends who believed he would never get patients."

The cumulative effect of this round-the-clock economy can sap the strength of a family and isolate its members from one another. This is a huge loss, because a healthy, happy family has a reality, a vibrancy—a *life*—of its own. Somehow, we must find a way to value families for what they really are and respect them as something greater than a collection of individuals. In busy families today, each member—often including even the youngest child— frequently has his or her own hectic schedule of activities, all of which must mesh together in an elaborate pattern with all the others. But the complicated daily dance of coordinating day-care handoffs, commuting, working, and learning often ignores the need for that intangible extra: some shared time, breath, laughter, and silence, which give families their own special life, their internal strength, and their constant ability to renew themselves.

THE LY FAMILY

Like so many other American families, the Ly family of Massachusetts knows what it means to face the deficits of time, energy, and
sleep every single day. Minh Ly, the father of two teenage daughters, rarely gets more than a few hours of sleep at a time. For the
last eleven years, he has worked nights as a banquet supervisor at
the Four Seasons Hotel while his wife, Thanh, has worked days as a
social worker, so that at least one of them has always been there for
the girls.

Minh can't remember the last time he and his wife did anything
alone together for fun—but that's something he doesn't have too
much time to worry about. His normal routine for many years was
to come home from work early in the morning, just as his wife was
preparing to leave for her job. He would take his daughters to
school, pick his daughters up and take them back to the family's
small apartment, supervise their homework, and begin preparing
dinner, napping intermittently when there were lulls in the schedule. As soon as his wife came home, he would nap while she finished preparing dinner, then wake up to eat with the family before
going back to work.

Of all the families in which both parents work, one third of
them, like the Lys, are headed by parents who have decided to
become "split-shift couples." These families have adopted staggered
work schedules to make sure at least one parent is always available for the children. According to a study conducted in 2000 by
the Working Women's Department of the AFL-CIO, 51 percent
of married women with children under eighteen worked a different schedule from that of their partners. Many of the split-shift
couples we've met say it's the only way they can get enough time
with their children. In fact, there are now so many families working split shifts that they can even buy a calendar created just for
them: the "Working Nights Family Calendar," which provides color-

coded stickers so they can map out the different family members' shift schedules all year long.

For some families, splitting shifts is the only approach to child care they can afford. Minh started working nights when their second child, Sherry, was born, mainly because they couldn't afford day care for two children. Once they got used to their split-shift schedule they decided they preferred it, because it was the only way they could be sure that their children would always have quality care and would never be at home alone. Thanh says, "I never have to worry about my kids' safety, because I know that when I'm not with them, their dad is with them."

When we first met the Ly family, six years ago, Sherry, then nine, told us how hard her parents worked. When we visited with them again a few months ago, inside their modest home in a working-class neighborhood of Brookline, Minh told us that his hours at work have increased. Because the hotel where he works has had to lay off many workers due to the travel-industry slump that followed September 11, he has had to cover unusually long shifts, sometimes working up to nineteen hours a day. Minh's employer is one of the many who are minimizing the number of employees and maximizing the number of hours worked by each one. The extra pay for all the overtime is much less costly than the expense of adding a new employee and a new package of benefits. This trend has worsened the conflict between work and family.

The Lys' older daughter, Betty, eighteen, is a first-year engineering student at Northeastern University, one of a handful of women in the engineering department and the only Asian-American woman in her class in the department. After college, Betty hopes to go to graduate school in engineering. For now, she still lives at home—in part because her father said he would miss her too much if she moved into the dorm. Sherry is now in the tenth grade. She likes techno and trance music as well as modern Korean pop singers. She likes to read everything—especially classics and Asian-American novels—and she's a member of the Asian-American Student Alliance at her high school. But she's at that shy stage, and often Sherry deflects attention to Betty, who she says is "the perfect one," because she is pretty, popular, and gets good grades.

For many years, Betty and Sherry used to go to Chinese school every Saturday and Sunday, and today both daughters speak Cantonese fluently. At home the girls speak Chinese to their parents and English with each other. Both girls are bicultural and, in some respects, torn between cultural identities. Sherry says, "It's crazy growing up as an Asian-American. I can't say I'm Asian. I don't really know. I couldn't deal with being one hundred percent Chinese, but I don't fit in with American society. I have more Chinese values and morals."

The threads of family tradition connecting the Lys are very strong. But there is one tradition that the children of this generation are not certain they will continue. Sherry, when asked whether she thinks she'd want to work a split shift with her husband when she has a family—the way her parents do—shook her head and said, "I don't know if I could make that sacrifice." Now that the girls are both teenagers, Thanh feels it's more important than ever to be around for them, so she and Minh plan to continue their split-shift existence.

Thanh actually has three jobs: she works as a social worker four days a week, as a travel agent two days a week, and for the Massachusetts Department of Mental Health as a Chinese- and Vietnamese-to-English on-call interpreter in hospital emergency rooms and clinics and during court proceedings. When Betty is not in school, she works, too—at a sporting goods store. Betty and Sherry both recently started working Saturdays at the Chinese school they used to attend.

The cumulative effect of the family's seven different jobs is that they are hard-pressed to find occasions when they are all free at the same time. "We have less and less time together now, but we used to go shopping together, and go out to eat once in a while," Thanh told us.

Their annual vacation is one of the few occasions when all four are united in the same place at the same time. These vacations have always been an important time for them to reconnect as a family. This year, however, because of the new expense of Betty's college tuition, they need to save the money that otherwise would have gone to the annual family vacation. Although Betty is eligible for a student loan, Minh feels strongly that he doesn't want his daughter to be burdened with loans when she is finished with her education, so he pays his daughter's tuition every month in cash. "I want her to go to school, not just to work. I don't want her to follow my path," Minh said.

Minh knows what it is like to work and scrape as a child. His family was very poor and he started working at the age of eight to help his parents. At first he worked with his mother, selling goods on the sidewalk. At fourteen, he learned to repair motorcycles. When he was eighteen, he joined the Vietnamese army. Now, as a father, Minh is determined that his children will be well provided for by their parents so that they can learn and achieve their fullest potential. The Lys' many long hours and exhausted days are "all for the children," Minh says, explaining that he wants them to have a better future.

The phrase "balancing work and family" hardly does justice to the heroic parenting efforts of this highly disciplined family—just as it hardly does justice to what millions of other American families are now doing with their lives every day of every week.

For many working families, perhaps the most emotionally difficult aspect of the struggle to integrate work and home is that their loyalties are genuinely divided between the two. After all, most of the money earned at work is earned for the purpose of supporting the family. In families like the Lys', work is just something parents know they must do in order to meet their financial responsibilities to their children. But that still does not make it easy. Thanh said that if she and Minh could have afforded for her to stay at home, she would not have worked when the girls were young. "I still feel that I missed that big piece of being a mother, and that's a very tough feeling," she says.

Ironically, coming home from work can also be difficult, because if parents come home from work exhausted, the relationships in the family may not benefit very much from the time spent together. Thanh is often so worn out at the end of her workday that many evenings she goes straight to the kitchen to cook dinner, with precious little energy left over to sustain an interaction with her daughters. She recalls that Sherry once said to her, "Mommy, do you think you like the kitchen and the washing machine? Because you don't even care about playing games with me." Sherry says that when her mom comes home stressed from too much work, Sherry will "watch TV, go to the computer, or read a book, and pretend she's not even there."

Having the energy to maintain and nourish relationships within a family is critical, both for the parent-child relationship and for the relationship between the parents themselves. This is a particularly big challenge for split-shift couples like the Lys, who are seldom even at home and awake at the same time.

In the early years of their lives together the Lys went through some tough times. Thanh and Minh are both from large, ethnic Chinese families that had lived in Vietnam for many years. Thanh's family used to own a restaurant and butcher shop; Minh's family owned a noodle shop. After the fall of Saigon, Thanh's family had a chance to leave the country, but her father didn't take it, because he said Vietnam had been good to him and his eight children. But in 1978, with the outbreak of the Chinese-Vietnamese war, life became very difficult for ethnic Chinese families. Vietnam tried to expel many ethnic Chinese from the country, and Thanh, the eldest child in her family, was sent to various reeducation camps. Fearing for her safety, her father started working on finding a way to get her out of the country. He scraped together all the money he could to help buy her passage on a boat to flee the country. An uncle who had previously emigrated to Australia helped put together money so three of Thanh's younger siblings could go as well. And Minh, then Thanh's boyfriend, also fled with them in May 1979.

They escaped, but nearly died in the process. During the harrowing journey across the South China Sea, their crowded boat was damaged in a storm and stranded, floating in the middle of the sea for more than ten days. They eventually landed on the Malaysian coast, but were rejected as refugees and were piled onto a second boat and pushed back out to sea. That boat was robbed by pirates during the journey. In the crowd of people loaded onto that boat, Minh and Thanh were separated and were not able to find each other again until after the boat finally arrived on a remote, largely uninhabited island that they were told was part of Indonesia. They spent nearly a year on the island. Because Minh had been a soldier in the South Vietnamese army during the Vietnam War, he was eventually allowed to immigrate to the States, along with Thanh and her three younger siblings. (Initially only Minh was offered the chance to immigrate to the States, but since he and Thanh were to be married, and Thanh and her siblings refused to be separated, they were eventually all allowed to immigrate together.)

Soon after they arrived in the United States in 1980, they got married. Even though Minh had just $100 in his pocket, he was responsible for himself, Thanh, and her three siblings. At first they lived in Dorchester, Massachusetts, then a tough neighborhood of Boston, where they had many problems with both crime and discrimination, partly because they were the first Asian family to move in there. Their windows were smashed, their mailbox was set on fire, and once someone dumped ice all over them. Worse still, Thanh's sister was mugged near the subway stop.

Minh held two jobs. At night he worked in custodial services, cleaning offices and earning $2.90 an hour. During the day, he worked at a Chinese noodle company. "The first few years as immigrants, we had to support our parents, send money back to Vietnam, and had to take care of our kids," Thanh said. Minh said he worked so much because he wanted to take care of the family, and "so the girls could go to school and not follow in my path"—meaning so they wouldn't have to work at manual-labor jobs.

Thanh held three jobs. Days she worked as a caseworker at Catholic Charities, nights she worked with Minh cleaning offices, and weekends she worked at a grocery meat counter. Beyond trying to make enough money for themselves, they were trying to save enough to pay for their parents and siblings to come to the United States. One by one, they succeeded in bringing Minh's brother and parents, as well as Thanh's four older siblings and their whole families. They continued working desperately hard to make the money for the last few trips needed to bring Thanh's parents and reunite the whole family, but just when they were on the brink of having enough to make the arrangements, her mother and then her father passed away.

When Betty was born, three years after they arrived in the States, Thanh took off three months from work. Later, when Sherry was born, she took off only two months, then cut back on her hours for a while, but soon went back to working full-time. Without question, all of the hard work created strife in the family. To begin with, there were problems between husband and wife because they almost never had any time together as a couple. "We fought a lot," Thanh recalls. "We were in crisis." However, now that the children are older and both parents are more settled in their jobs, things are much better between them. Nevertheless, when we asked Thanh what she and her husband do for enjoyment, just the two of them, she was at a loss for words.

And there was conflict between parents and children. Sherry says that she and her mother used to fight a lot. Thanh related that Sherry told her one day, "Mom, you cannot expect me to be perfect. You cannot compare me to the other kids." Thanh concedes that she used to do this and scold her. "I don't think I should have to be perfect," Sherry says, explaining that after she "ranted" at her mother about it, her mother changed. "It was a good thing . . . that made my life a lot easier," Sherry said. As a result, she feels that she can talk with Thanh more on her own terms and as her own person—not just as a child who does or doesn't meet the benchmark set by her older sister.

Even as the Lys coordinate their hectic split-shift schedule to accommodate their child-care needs, they know that at some point they will need to take on additional care responsibilities for Minh's parents. The Lys had purchased a house near their own for Minh's parents, and they and the girls go to visit them often. Although Minh's parents are currently quite independent, Minh and Thanh view it as their responsibility to take care of them as they age, and they intuit that the extra time they may gain as their children get older may be taken up by the need to care for his parents.

THE SANDWICH GENERATION

Like the Lys, an increasing number of families are juggling not just work and family but caring for both children and parents. The challenges these families face can be daunting. In both cases, the middle generation is often harried by not having enough time to do it all themselves, and when they can't, they worry about the quality of care their family members—young or old—are receiving in their absence.

This challenge has become increasingly difficult over the last fifty years, as women, the traditional intergenerational caretakers in a family, have steadily moved into the workforce and have gone back to work even sooner after having children. Meanwhile, the aging of the baby boomers and the general increase in life spans mean there are more families facing the double-barreled challenge of caring for parents and children simultaneously.

Today, more than 70 percent of adults with children at home

are in the workforce. Similarly, nearly two-thirds of adults caring for an elderly relative are in the workforce—most of them in full-time jobs. And more than 40 percent of workers are taking care of *both* children and parents at the same time. Because of the dramatic increase in families where both spouses work, along with the rise in single-parent families, there is now a far greater need for child care than ever before. In 1996, 13 million preschoolers, including 6 million infants and toddlers, were in child care, a third of them in child-care centers. Since 1987, the number of centers per 1,000 children under five has doubled.

In and of itself, however, a growth in the size of the child-care industry hardly provides a panacea. There have to be other options as well. Many child-care centers are so expensive that it is a struggle for families to afford them. For example, Pat and Todd Alexander told us they pay more every month for child care for their two boys than they pay on their home mortgage. And the centers aren't always open or available when a family needs them most. Added to that, stringent pickup times—with some centers charging an extra dollar for every minute a parent is late picking up a child—make any unexpected overtime work a liability. Most problematic of all is that far too many parents drop off their children at day-care centers only to pick up another day's worth of anxiety that their children may not be getting quality care during that time, or that they may be catching yet another cold.

According to several studies, high-quality day care turns out to be just fine for kids—with outcomes virtually as good as those for kids who are cared for by their parents in the home. But the evidence also seems to suggest that less than high-quality day care can be harmful to young children. And here is the hard truth: high-quality day care is rare. In all too many centers, there is insufficient training and compensation and/or high turnover—with a succession of untrained care providers relating to the children for a few weeks at a time, only to be replaced suddenly and without explanation or transition by someone new who has neither knowledge of the child nor adequate skills to quickly form a meaningful connection.

In America we pay day-care workers less than janitors, tree trimmers, or telemarketers. Why so little? One reason is probably that we have not placed a monetary value on the benefits that accrue to growing children from a caregiving environment that meets all their needs. Given how high the stakes are, we should provide subsidies to compensate for this failure in the marketplace. It is ironic that during World War II there was government-subsidized day care—because then it was important to the country to help families deal with the absence of those who were fighting the war. Adding insult to injury, the plight of children in poor day care is often used by reactionary forces to try to push women out of the workplace and back into the home. This is not the answer for those who cannot afford to give up their jobs, nor is it fair to those who find their work fulfilling and don't want to change their lives to suit someone's political agenda. It's a puzzling contradiction that even as working women are encouraged to stay home, welfare mothers are told to go to work.

Universal preschool supported by the federal government would help working parents of young children; it could be a step forward in the improvement of educational outcomes as well. A number of studies have demonstrated that children who attended preschool or other early-education programs scored higher on cognitive tests—and continued to do so later on—compared with children who did not. Yet despite the proven benefits of such programs for children, we still only have 50 percent of our children enrolled in Head Start, Professor Zigler told us, and not one child whose family is one dollar above the poverty line. "We are just ignoring the implications of all the new brain science that shows how critical the first five years of life are to a child's development," he said.

According to the National Institute on Out-of-School Time, approximately 8 million children between the ages of five and fourteen regularly spend time without adult supervision. Many of them are "latchkey children" who come home to an empty house and look after themselves or, in the worst case, get in trouble when no one is around to monitor their activities. According to FBI data, the hours between 3:00 and 7:00 P.M. are the most common time for youth crime and violence. Afternoons are also the time when many teens experiment with sex, tobacco, drugs, and alcohol. Schools and communities could provide universally available after-school programs, again with two objectives in mind: to help parents by keeping their children out of trouble, and to enrich those same children with an array of optional activities such as art, drama, music, athletics, and supervised homework.

Some communities are finding innovative ways to deal with these issues on their own. Hope Meadows, a unique initiative in Rantoul, Illinois, is a terrific example. There, former military base housing has been transformed into a refuge for foster children and their families, who end up adopting a high proportion of the children. A portion of the neighborhood is reserved for senior citizens who benefit from submarket rent and in return devote six hours or more a week to the children and families in the community. The senior citizens offer a supportive network for the families. In the process, the children at Hope Meadows find not only loving parents, but also loving grandparents.

In Florida, we saw a wonderful program that also relies on the unique strength and connection of intergenerational bonds by regularly uniting children from a day-care center with selected residents of a nearby nursing home. When the children come streaming out of their bus and into the common room of the nursing home, they immediately seek out their favorite foster grandparents and play games, read books, or listen to stories.

Sally Newman founded and ran a similar program in Pittsburgh, called Generations Together. She has discovered the great mutual benefits to the elderly and children alike from bringing the generations into contact with each other. The seniors find that, over time, they experience greatly improved mental as well as physical health from being active, engaged, and in contact with young people. And with the guidance, nurturing, and companionship of the seniors, the children develop longer attention spans, cooperate more, and have fewer tantrums—all of which means they are better prepared to learn. Gerontologist Vern Bengtson, at the University of Southern California, wrote that the increase in real and simulated multi-generational families can be a great source of strength and resilience for today's families.

Mitchell Gold, the founder and CEO of a mid-size furniture company in North Carolina, told us that employee morale soared when he decided to introduce free child care for every employee. He was a little surprised to find that a great many of the employees who make use of the service are grandparents—in some cases perhaps because the parents of the children work at locations that do not provide such benefits. Gold welcomes such use of the service by grandparents because the goodwill and the increased morale and productivity more than make up for the cost. One employee used to be universally regarded in the factory as a grouch, Gold told us. Every day at lunch now, his two granddaughters are "draped all over him" as he carries on conversations with a smile. "It just completely changed his entire personality," Gold said.

Coping with the responsibilities of child care and elder care at the same time can be a heavy burden. The number of families having to do so in that situation has never been larger—and it will continue to grow steadily as the baby boomers, and their parents, get older and live longer lives. In a recent AARP study, an overwhelming majority of baby boomers who are currently facing the job of caring for their parents say they do not want their children to feel obligated to take care of them in their own old age.

While families of all ethnicities are shouldering more elder-care burdens, it is most common for minorities to provide care within the extended family. Forty-two percent of Asian-Americans surveyed for a recent AARP study provided care for older family members, compared with 34 percent of Hispanics, 28 percent of African-Americans, and 19 percent of non-Hispanic whites.

But with the cost of a nursing home increasing to more than $55,000 per year, over a quarter of which is paid for out-of-pocket, the pressure to provide elder care in the home is increasing, even as the number of hours worked also continues to increase. Whatever else she does with her life, the average woman in an American family is also a caregiver who spends seventeen years caring for her dependent children and eighteen years caring for her elderly parents or in-laws. As we live to increasingly older ages, the task of long-term care has also become much more complicated than it once was. The Conference Board, a nonprofit organization that studies business-related issues, estimates that within the next several years, there will be more demand for dependent elder–care benefits than for child-care benefits.

Rodney and Missy Crumpton know what it is like to be not just a sandwich-generation family but a club-sandwich-generation family. In 1991, Rodney's mother told them that she had pancreatic cancer and was dying. Rodney, Missy, and the boys immediately moved back to Tennessee from Atlanta, where they had been living. "We moved around the corner from Rodney's parents to help them when they were ill," Missy explained. Unfortunately, Rodney's mother died within a month of their return, leaving Rodney and the family feeling terrible that they had not known to come home and take care of her sooner. Rodney's father died in 1998 and they were glad to have been able to spend more time with him while caring for him in his final years of life. And then, of course, they have their weekends with their grandson Caleb—who, they are pleased to note, met his great-grandfather before he passed away.

The challenges of caring for older and frailer relatives are increasing as the number of "very old" people increases. According to the 2000 census, there are currently more than fifty thousand Americans one hundred or older, and by 2050 the Census Bureau predicts there may be as many as one million. As a result, there is now an increasing number of families that span four generations. It is not just the Crumptons. The "sandwich generation" is becoming the "club sandwich generation."

We got a glimpse of part of the future for the American family when we talked to David Jackson of Seattle, Washington, who at age eighty-seven is the primary caregiver for his mother, Martha Simons, who is 104. He decided to move in with her and take on this responsibility after he became increasingly concerned about her health. As he explained it to us, the time came when he called to check in on her, and she wouldn't always answer. So he "would get in the car and come over here to see what was the matter. After she got so old, and her health deteriorated, I just moved over with her. I know that was the right decision."

David has his own health problems—arthritis and back pain among them—but he has little time to pay attention to his own aches and pains while caring for her. After all, he's only eighty-seven. David does just about everything for his mother. And her dependence on him has made them closer, he says, adding that, in fact, their relationship is "closer than it's ever been."

They eat their meals together, read the paper together, and talk. Martha appreciates him and told us that she thinks the most important thing about family is "to get along together and take care of one another." Martha's grandsons, who are in their forties, also come by and help from time to time, sometimes even staying over for the night.

Although she is dependent on him for so much as her caretaker, some mother-son habits never die. Even after his eighty-seven years of life, she says that one of her biggest complaints about her son is that he doesn't go to church regularly. And after eighty-seven years of trying, she's still working on him.

THE DOUBLE-EDGED SWORD OF TECHNOLOGY

A lot of people hope that they will be able to find new and imaginative answers for their conflicts between work and family with new technologies that may, for example, allow them to be in two places at once—virtually if not physically. There are indeed exciting new advances already helping some families juggle their jobs and their caregiving at home, whether for young children or elderly parents.

For example, Mitch Philpott, who takes care of his disabled son Brett every other day and every other weekend, has been able to succeed as both a loving father and a highly productive caseworker for the Atlanta office of the United States Department of Veterans Affairs. With the familiar combination of a computer, the Internet, a fax machine, and a telephone, he is able to work far more efficiently at home than he could in a centralized office—partly because he can spread his work into the evening hours, when it is more convenient for many veterans to call in for the help they need.

He goes into the office for eight hours a week, split between Tuesdays and Thursdays, to pick up and drop off casework and to consult with his colleagues. The rest of the time he telecommutes and works from his home—which is very near Brett's school. He is always there when Brett comes home from school, and is always nearby and available if the school needs him to come and get Brett in an emergency.

Mitch makes the point that his work arrangement is desirable for his employer and for his "customers"—the veterans—not because it helps him in his role as a parent but because it makes him more productive in his job. Numerous studies conducted of similar work arrangements have shown clearly that rather than allowing family obligations to distract them from their work, employees in these circumstances are often significantly more productive at home than they were when they worked in the office. This may be because employees who have more control over how they divide their time often end up actually spending more time on the job, because it is easier both to meet their obligations at home and to work productively during times when it has little or no impact on the family.

Some workers telecommute in the opposite direction as well—by using videoconferencing to communicate with their children during the day or when they are out of town on a business trip. Similarly, there are now ways to connect soldiers in Afghanistan with their children and families by e-mail and by two-way video connections. These programs, similar to those used during deployments in Bosnia and Kosovo, have also included videotapes of bedtime stories read by deployed parents to their children back at home.

There are also millions of people who simply appreciate the chance to keep in better touch with their families, and have found the new technologies to be a real blessing. Many parents of school-age children now find it much easier to stay in contact on a daily basis. The Lys, for example, have long used Minh's pager as a way of coordinating the family's movements. As early as the age of eight, Sherry would use her father's pager to inform him of changes in her pickup time from school. They developed a simple code: if Sherry sent her father the page 230 230 222, for example, it meant come at 2:30 to pick up your second daughter.

Senior citizens in particular have found the Internet to be a very positive force in their lives. Nearly three in five seniors who use the Internet believe that it helps them communicate better with their families. Indeed, nearly half of all seniors who got Internet access (for reasons other than work or school) say they were encouraged to do so by their family members, according to a 2001 survey by the Pew Internet and American Life Project.

In addition, the Internet has allowed many people to start home businesses, which has proved to be a boon, especially for mothers who run small on-line businesses out of their homes while caring for young children. A famous *New Yorker* cartoon suggested, "On the Internet, no one knows you're a dog." For this segment of the work population, the more relevant saying might be, "On the Internet, no one knows you're changing a diaper while filling an order." For example, Valerie Reddemann, the young mother of four-year-old Sy, started her own Internet company, called Greenfeet.com, to sell environmentally responsible products. The main reason she did it, she told us, was "so I could stay home with my son. I was pregnant at the time I started it. I got tired of doing what is happening with our society—working, working, working, and having no time left for family."

Her husband, Rob, works as the comptroller of a building-supply company in Chico, California, but Valerie said, "When he gets done with his job he comes home and does all my accounting and Web design. It's a family project. Our son is involved. He likes it and he always asks me, 'Do you have their e-mails, Mom?'" She says she is having fun, the business is now making money and starting to grow, and she loves the flexibility it gives her to be with Sy all day.

There are millions of similar success stories in America. Unfortunately though, the anywhere-anytime connectivity also has its downsides. For each person who has set up a home office in order not to leave home to work, there appear to be many more who use the same technologies to log back on and continue working long after they have come home at the end of the day. The challenge is to leave work at work.

And even when workers don't want to continue working, the electronic leashes of pagers and cell phones often find them and digitally insist on being given still more time. For example, the Lys find Sherry's ability to use her dad's pager a great convenience. But Thanh's pager and mobile phone often tether her to her work, even when she is what used to be called "off." Almost every night, her clients and sometimes her supervisors track her down and demand still more of her time. Sherry often complains to her mother, "You're home, but you're still always talking on the phone with other people."

One other downside of the new technology is that it adds significantly to the overall feeling of overwork. The Families and Work Institute reported last year after an extensive study that people who use cell phones, pagers, and other electronic devices and whose employers use them to contact them in off-hours feel far more overworked and stressed than those who are not so connected.

In addition, the sheer volume of information people are now asked to absorb from all of the new communications technologies has itself become a source of stress. A study by the Institute for the Future found that the typical employee in a Fortune 1,000 firm now sends and receives 178 messages per day. An International Labor Organization study concluded that countries in which technology has been widely adopted—including the United States—reported greater incidence of depression and other mental-health problems. A British psychologist, David Lewis, uses the term "information fatigue syndrome" to describe the physical and mental effects of being inundated with information. And in the same vein, Larry Rosen, a professor of psychology at California State University at Dominguez Hills who wrote the book *TechnoStress*, concluded recently, "Even those who are the highest of the high-tech feel like they're behind [in keeping up with the increased information flow] and there's no way of seeing a point where they might get ahead. . . . It makes us feel irritable and frustrated, like we are in an endless loop."

Everybody needs a little relief from the constant grind. Having time off from work is not only good for mental health, it's also good for the workplace. An employee who has no chance to recharge his batteries will likely experience a decline in the quality of his work over time. Many weight lifters pump iron only every other day in order to give their muscles a chance to recuperate. The muscle growth they are seeking doesn't come on the day when they are lifting; it comes on the day when they are resting, when the muscles strained the day before recover, repair damage, and in the process grow stronger. In a similar fashion, everybody needs time off from their jobs to grow in their ability to perform more productively as they gain more experience.

When the time off is not really "off," but can be interrupted at any moment by a pager or a cell phone, there's less chance for the stress levels built up during the day to subside in the evening. A recent survey found that 40 percent of working Americans make contact with their workplace during their vacations, and that nearly a quarter of them are expected to do so. Two-thirds stay in touch by voice mail, 54 percent use e-mail, and 47 percent use a mobile device.

FINDING THE BALANCE

In navigating the competing crosscurrents of work and family, one must, as in sailing, locate a true north by which to navigate. In this case, the true north is one's sense of purpose in life.

When our children were small, we decided to get puppies for our daughters Kristin and Sarah. We then went to a friend who had experience as a dog trainer and requested her help. At the beginning of the very first session she asked, "What is the puppies' purpose?" We looked at each other a bit blankly and mumbled the response, "To be puppies." She gravely, and in all seriousness, shook her head at us and intoned clearly, "A puppy has to have a purpose."

We have never forgotten those words. And we have often been impressed with the realization that if a puppy has to have a purpose, how clearly critical it is for every person to have a purpose. (The puppies, by the way, became excellent playmates for our children and watchdogs for the house at night.)

So what is our purpose? Is it mainly to work? Sigmund Freud once said that people have two basic needs: love and work. Feeling useful and productive can lend dignity and pleasure to life. We have heard many mothers on welfare describe the deep joy they felt when they found their way back into a job. Usually they talk about the pride they feel when they see their children looking at them differently. Eli Segal, the former CEO of the national Welfare-to-Work partnership, a community-business venture that has worked for years with men and women making the transition from welfare to work, noted that for many of the people who were able to get jobs and leave welfare, the increased sense of self-worth and the knowledge that they were providing a positive example for their children were the best motivators in making them dedicated and excited about their jobs.

But work is such a big part of most peoples' lives in America today that it has begun to encroach on the emotional space, time, and energy necessary for love, family, and other activities. If your work is so meaningful that it has become your purpose in life, that's not a problem. But if all of your most important emotional and spiritual relationships are separate from the activity consuming most of your time and energy, then it can seem even harder to figure out what your purpose is. For many, like Eduardo Cortes and the Lys, when asked what the purpose of all their work is, the answer is clear: it's for the children, so they can have a better life. But on a day-to-day basis, the demands of work often tend to monopolize their time and attention. The irony of it all is that in wanting to give our children a better life, many parents are finding themselves working so much and so hard that they are not able to be engaged in their children's lives in a way that helps ensure they indeed have a "better life." And if working hard is often motivated by the desire to increase our family's opportunities, sometimes the tendency to overwork can be indicative of existing family problems.

People who feel that their lives are somehow empty of meaning become vulnerable to all kinds of addictions: alcohol, drugs, and, one of the biggest, work. Workaholics generally have an extremely unhealthy balance between work and family. They have fallen into the habit of using work to avoid a feeling of emptiness and often to avoid intimacy, including with members of their own family. That's a pattern that can quickly become a vicious circle: more work means less time with family means less intimacy means more work. Especially when the "purpose" of many managers in the increasingly competitive marketplace seems to be to pursue the mantra "more, better, faster," it is harder for employees to be able to ascertain "What is enough?" and "When do you stop?"

There can be a natural desire to reunify those parts of their lives that have deep emotional resonance for them with the parts of their lives that involve productive activity. The idea that life can be neatly divided every day into separate parts is inherently uncomfortable. How do we heal this divide and resolve the constant tension between work and family? How can we readdress and redefine the issue so that it is not a constant matter of stealing a few minutes from one side of the ledger to satisfy the other?

One answer lies in fostering a realization within the workplace itself that the tension between work and family isn't good for the bottom line. While demanding more time and energy of workers may seem a natural way to boost productivity, ironically, the current imbalance between work and family ultimately has a clear negative impact on the balance sheet. Productivity suffers when employees are unable to concentrate fully due to nagging concerns about what's happening to family members they feel might need them at the moment. Workplace stress and employee burnout lead to decreased productivity, higher turnover and absenteeism, and increased employee health and disability claims. Larry Howard of Middle Tennessee State University reports the impact of such phenomena on business is estimated to be $344 billion per year. We believe that an unhealthy balance between work and family hastens employee burnout, diminishes employee productivity, and thus is bad for business.

Some leading-edge businesses may be inadvertently adding to the home-job conflict by trying to build a campus or homelike environment in the workplace that provides for many of their employees' social and entertainment needs. Ilene Philipson of the University of California at Berkeley's Center for Working Families finds that many businesses enhance their corporate "campuses" with parties, intramural sports, and other perks to promote corporate morale. They try to become a place where workers find companionship, support, and meaning. They blur the traditional lines between work and family. According to the respected Berkeley sociologist and codirector of the Center for Working Families, Arlie Hochschild, with so much emotional warmth, solicitude, and caring in the workplace, some employees begin to see work as home and home as a place of work. For these employees, the challenge of a time bind is joined by the challenge of a "loyalty bind."

When Hochschild asked working parents at a Fortune 500 company where they felt the most competent, relaxed, and secure, many—especially the parents of young children—said "at work." She studied workplaces that incorporate the best parts of home and compared them to a devalued home realm taking on the alienating attributes of work. "In a cultural contest between work and home," Hochschild told us, "working parents are voting with their feet, and the workplace is winning." Hochschild calls this battle the "major business story of the age," as corporate America wages its fiercest battle with its local rival—the family. "When you're doing the right thing at work, the chances are the boss is patting you on the back. When you're doing the right thing at home, the chances are your teenager is giving you hell for it," said one man she interviewed. Hochschild told us, "What was missing was social support for the invisible work of making a home feel like a home." In a national survey to which Hochschild contributed questions, 47 percent of the respondents said that most of their friends are at work, compared to only 16 percent who said that most of their friends were in the neighborhoods where they lived. And only 6 percent said that most of their friends were at their places of worship.

The separation between work and home that began with the Industrial Revolution has always had an artificial quality. People instinctively try to unify the disparate elements of their lives. Perhaps that is part of the explanation for the trends studied by Hochschild. After taking more time and energy away from families, some workplaces are now taking emotional loyalties away from families as well. But that is not what integrating work and family is all about. Those employers may become more productive in the short term, but if it is at the expense of the connectedness in their employees' families, the gains will not last.

By contrast, many employers who have taken the lead in trying to solve the work-family conundrum are being rewarded with higher productivity, increased longevity, decreased absenteeism, and a new level of loyalty and creativity from their employees— who appreciate being recognized holistically and give more of their best selves to the job in return. One of the first businesses to prove this principle was Boston-based Stride Rite, which in 1971, under then-chairman Arnold Hiatt, was the first corporation in the United States to provide on-site child care for its employees' children. In 1990, Stride Rite opened its Intergenerational Day Care Center to combine employee needs for child care and adult care for aging parents. *Working Mother* magazine has chosen the Stride Rite Corporation eight times as one of the "100 Best Companies for Working Mothers" in America. In 2001, Ford Motor Company, in conjunction with the United Auto Workers, opened the first of what will ultimately be a number of centers offering a range of different services to help families, from round-the-clock child care to tutoring for schoolchildren and financial planning for retirees. In 1996, the nonprofit Business Enterprise Trust identified twelve hundred other examples of companies implementing programs that combine sound management with concern for families to help employees and their communities.

Unfortunately, these workplaces remain the exceptions instead of the rule. The more common practice is still to emphasize the amount of time spent in the workplace and use some version of the punch-card philosophy to measure it precisely, instead of rewarding employees based on the actual results they produce. Juan Sepulveda, who runs a nationally recognized community-empowerment initiative in San Antonio, Texas, told us about a friend of his who bought an extra pair of glasses so that he could leave them on his desk with his computer running in order to create the illusion that he was still hard at work in the office while he had actually left early to meet family needs.

According to an influential Ford Foundation report, "Relinking Life and Work," the organization of most institutions continues to treat work and family as separate spheres, and assumes that responsibilities for each sphere are divided by traditional gender roles. "This situation has created inequities at work that keep men and women from enjoying the same opportunities and responsibilities and from sharing the same constraints," the study reported. It also found that "this separation of work and family undermines both business and employee goals," simultaneously constraining both the desired efficiency of the workplace and the family life's daily ins and outs.

The conflict between duties at work and responsibilities at home is particularly pronounced for women, since working women continue to bear the bulk of household and child-care responsibilities. Most men, unlike Minh Ly, have not filled the gap in hours spent with the children and maintaining the home. Even when couples have what researcher Pepper Schwartz calls "peer marriages," in which spouses view each other as equals on all fronts, the women may do a disproportionate amount of housework and child care, she found. No wonder so many working women half-jokingly say that really both they and their partner need "a wife"—in the traditional sense of the word.

In her book *The Price of Motherhood: Why the Most Important Job in the World Is Still the Least Valued*, Ann Crittenden argues that America fails to recognize the value of mother's work, both economically and socially. The unpaid, hard-to-monetize work of mothers in the home is not accounted for in measures of gross domestic product; if it could be calculated, Crittenden believes, it would rival in size the largest industries. She observes that full-time stay-at-home mothers are the only people who are counted on to work without pay, and points out that the contributions mothers make toward developing the skills of our workforce receive scant attention in traditional economics texts.

Men and women encounter different expectations in most workplaces, and are often judged by different social standards. For example, many fathers who occasionally miss time at work because they have chosen to be with family at a crunch time are often praised by their colleagues for demonstrating progressive values.

Meanwhile, mothers who make the exact same choice often feel they have to keep quiet about what they've done for fear of being seen as insufficiently committed to the job. Or other women may criticize them for failing to maintain the balance American working mothers are expected to achieve. The fact that a mother's conflicts may be more likely to be ongoing and regular also means that multiple late arrivals to work can result in her being shifted onto a "mommy track," a career path with fewer and slower promotions, and with little promise of ever reaching the highest rungs on the corporate ladder. Too many late arrivals could lead to the loss of the job altogether. Indeed, Joan Williams, author of *Unbending Gender: Why Family and Work Conflict and What to Do About It*, notes that the difficult balancing act often means that women have to leave demanding jobs because they aren't compatible with caring for children. She observes that to succeed in elite jobs or executive positions, "workers typically not only must be able to do good work, but also must be able to do it for fifty to seventy hours a week. Few mothers can do this because few women have spouses willing to raise their children while the women are at work."

The world of work can significantly benefit by being more accommodating to families' needs. The Ford Foundation study mentioned earlier also found that "restructuring the way work gets done to address work-family integration can lead to positive, 'win-win' results—a more responsive work environment that takes employees' needs into account and yields significant bottom-line results." These kinds of work environments also benefit the company and the consumer by producing higher-quality products and giving higher-quality service.

Perhaps most important of all, from the business point of view, is that over the longer term, the strength of our economy depends on the strength of our families. And yet we are still not in the habit of calculating price tags for the benefits of a workforce made up of emotionally stable, spiritually healthy men and women who derive those qualities primarily from the families that raise them.

Of course, it is important to remember that the issue of work and family is a very different one for the millions of families who have no work or too little work. For these families, the top priority is finding jobs. Indeed, there are still millions unemployed in the United States who want work and cannot find it. Many lack skills that are in demand, and clearly, part of the answer is to provide more education and job training for the unemployed. But their families' needs are multiplied by unemployment. They experience problems with housing, because often they can no longer pay the rent or make the mortgage payment; the stress of unemployment can lead to behavioral problems, enhanced stress within the family, and even divorce. Those who have no work often have no balance in their lives.

Nevertheless, the issue so many American families struggle with is how to find the time and energy to satisfy the demands of all their obligations at work and at home. There is, however, encouraging evidence that some other families are handling the stress fairly well. The Adult Lives Project, a study of three hundred two-career couples funded by the National Institutes of Mental Health, found that the families created today by dual-earner couples are ones "in which all members are thriving: often happier, healthier, and more well-rounded than the families of the 1950s." The only thing "golden" about the 1950s, this study concludes, is that fewer women needed to work for purely economic reasons. Meanwhile, a different study notes that in 1995 the number of female high school seniors who have been reared with working moms as role models, and who plan to attend college or a professional school, is double what it was in 1980. Interestingly, girls have higher college aspirations for themselves than teenage boys do today.

When all is said and done, the hard truth is that work and family are just wildly out of balance in America. Work is good. But so is family. We all want good jobs, good incomes, and a strong economy. But we also want strong families, good marriages, and the chance to be good parents to our children. We want a good night's sleep and time with loved ones and friends. In short, we want full, well-rounded lives that are fulfilling both at work and at home.

Employers and employees alike in pioneering businesses have demonstrated that meaningful and innovative solutions are indeed available. The real solutions aren't simple and they aren't easy, but they do work: flexible hours, expanded family- and medical-leave rights, on-site child care and elder care, telecommuting, job sharing, paid maternity and paternity leave, a focus on *results* rather than on how many hours are spent in the office, and the right of each employee—unpressured by the boss—to choose for him- or herself between overtime and time off.

Where they have been implemented, these approaches have been successful. But they have not been widely adopted. Either they have collided with deeply ingrained habits of thought or the organization has never considered adopting these new practices. Nevertheless, Americans have a deep and strong yearning to reunify the parts of our lives that feel as if they have been split off from one another. What we're all looking for is not so much a balance between work and family as a healthy integration of the two.

Ultimately, we need to decide how we value our families in relationship to our work—not only how much we value our families, which for most people is not a difficult question at all. The real challenge is how we measure the *relative* value of work and family and how we then manifest our real values in our daily lives. Most people make their choices in life according to their ethics. *Ethics* is a plural word. *Work ethic* is singular; it needs to be seen along with our other ethics and not as the single dominant purpose of our lives.

In our culture, the most common method of assessing value is by quantifying it in dollars and cents. While the workplace can easily assign a dollar value to a worker's time, the value of a parent's time to a child is priceless. And ironically, in the market "priceless" can be interpreted as "valueless." At the very least, at any given moment when a decision between work and family must be made, the workplace has a much stronger ability to quantify and express the immediate cost of neglecting work.

Time may be money, but time is also love. Time is family. Time is relationships. Time is community. And all of these treasures have to be balanced with money on their own terms, not according to their inferred price tag—because they don't have price tags.

Psychologist Abraham Maslow observed that if a hammer is the only tool you have, every problem looks like a nail. If money is the only tool you have for measuring value, then those things that cannot be easily monetized begin to look as if they have no value. Some classic examples are clean air and water and the beauty of a sunset or a mountain clearly visible in the distance. The strength and health of American families should be added to that list. A quarterly report of a corporation can never capture or reflect the immense value these things add—nor can it account for the immeasurable loss we would suffer without them.

THE HOYTS

Bill Hoyt and Jeanne Hoyt

Chapter 6

——•—•——

PLAY

Imagination is more important than knowledge.

——ALBERT EINSTEIN

A LOVE OF PLAY

We have both found a lot of personal fulfillment in work. And our appreciation for the value of hard work has come naturally to us—in part because we brought to our marriage a tradition that each of us had learned in our respective birth families, a tradition that honors achievement and productive work.

But to be honest, what we like best is to play.

As important as work is to sustaining a family, the ability to switch gears and dive wholeheartedly into play is vital to renewing a family on a daily basis. Over the years, some of our family's favorite ways to play together have been silly games that emerged spontaneously. When the children were small, for instance, Al was working such long hours in Congress that the kids would pounce on him the minute he got home. Gradually, this ritual evolved into a playful coming-home game that we called Dinosaur. As Al came through the door, all four children would jump on him as he forged his way up the stairs to the bedroom. Three of the children would scramble onto the bed with him, leaving the fourth to take the first turn as "the dinosaur"—a fearsome beast that would crouch low on the floor by the side of the bed, lurking just out of sight, waiting for the right moment to leap to the attack and try to drag a child off the bed for a growling, high-protein dinosaur meal. There would be a ferocious scramble as the other children would come to the aid of the victim by grabbing arms and legs for a tug-of-war with the dinosaur. If a child was about to go over the edge of the abyss, the others could terminate the attack and save the screaming victim by pressing an invisible emergency button in the middle of Al's chest. But often, just as a child was trying to hit the button, Al would flop onto his stomach and pretend to have fallen asleep, and they'd have to struggle to get to the button. Whoever was dragged completely off the bed had to be the dinosaur for the next round. And then it would start all over again.

Another variation on the game involved the children tiptoeing into the bedroom where Al was "the sleeping monster." They'd never know whether he was truly asleep, or just pretending. As they drew closer and closer in order to check, whispering to one another as they came, he would wait until the last possible second and then *leap* up, snarling and growling, and chase them as they giggled and screamed down the hall to one of their rooms. They'd slam the door shut, just in time, and the monster would claw at it. After a while, he'd go back to bed, and they'd come back out to check on him again. But along the hallway, there were several nooks where he could hide, unnoticed, as they'd open their door and tiptoe back to our bedroom. We've heard them say that there was nothing scarier than when they would open the door to our room, see that the bed was empty, and realize that somewhere just behind them—between them and their place of refuge—the monster was ready to growl and pounce on them.

Whichever game Al and the kids played, all Tipper could hear were screams, running, more screams, laughter, and high-pitched yelps. Eventually, when they were all exhausted by the giddy combination of anxiety, mirth, and mock fear, the game would finally end. The kids absolutely loved playing these games. Al did too. And as any exhausted working parent can probably guess, Al also appreciated the fact that these games involved his spending large portions of the game lying in bed, often "pretending" to be asleep.

The spirit of free-form play in the house was something that we always encouraged. The children knew that our entire home was an open canvas for their creative spirits, and that they could play in all parts of the house and use it fully. Our house may not have been suitable for the pages of *Architectural Digest*, but it was child-proofed and completely safe for them. Tipper knew from her graduate school studies in child development that play fosters learning and exploration, and she wanted our children to feel free to play a lot and use their imaginations fully.

We enjoyed watching how the children's personalities expressed themselves through their play. As the eldest, Karenna was the ringleader, suggesting games, theater productions, and even puppet shows that the kids would perform for us. When staging a play, Karenna would, of course, take care of the casting. Once, when she decided the girls would put on a production of *Annie*, she cast herself as Annie and cast her little sister Kristin, who was just five, as old, bald Daddy Warbucks. However, Kristin vividly remembers that when it came time for the big scene where Daddy Warbucks has his solo, Karenna insisted that they switch, and Kristin suddenly found herself playing the part of Annie—sitting on the side watching Karenna sing Daddy Warbucks's dramatic solo.

The children's love of song, theater, and storytelling was fostered by their grandparents as well. During the summers in Carthage, Tennessee, a big part of the daily ritual was the after-dinner story-telling. Al's father would make up elaborate stories for them about the McGillicuddy family—who happened to have children named Karenna, Kristin, Sarah, and Albert. These McGillicuddy children had all sorts of adventures—and someone always ended up sleeping in the barn with the polecat. Other times, the stories were about Mr. Davis, who worked on the farm, and his nemesis, the coyote, who was always chewing Wrigley's spearmint gum and would drive Mr. Davis's truck off when he wasn't looking. Sometimes, when Al's father really got going, he and Al's mother would burst into song, leading everyone in hymns or other tunes, like "Will the Circle Be Unbroken?"

While family play has often revolved around our children, we have also discovered the value of taking time out for play without our kids—as parents and as partners. As a young married couple, we made a point of going on a number of long camping trips because we wanted to have some adventures—just the two of us, before we had children. The relaxation and fun we were able to enjoy together during those trips helped bring us closer during our early years of marriage; later, when we sometimes found ourselves too busy and tired from all the competing demands of work and family, the trips provided a lasting reservoir of good feelings and good memories.

Even when our lives get absurdly busy, we still find ways to make a little time for play. One kind of fun we indulge in from time to time is playing practical jokes, just to add a little humor to our lives. Once when Al was taking a shower and shampooing his hair, he got out of the shower while the water was still running and walked into the bedroom soaking wet, his hair thick with lather, one eye closed and the other squinting. Holding up a bottle of Neet hair remover, he asked Tipper, "Honey, what *is* this stuff?" Tipper screamed and with great urgency pushed him toward the shower, with instructions to wash it out as quickly as possible. Al started laughing, and Tipper realized that it was a practical joke.

Over the years, Tipper has pulled off some pretty good practical jokes of her own. In the middle of the 1992 presidential campaign, we were each campaigning in separate cities. Al was on *Larry King Live* one night and Tipper was watching from her hotel room. As she watched, she suddenly had an idea. After a few members of the audience had phoned in serious policy questions, Tipper picked up the phone and called in, disguised her voice, and told Al she thought he was really cute and would he go out on a date with her? Both Larry and Al were momentarily stunned. Larry seemed a bit indignant and stammered for a second, while Al searched for words. Watching them on national television, Tipper fell on the floor laughing. And they still did not recognize her voice. Finally, Tipper had to *tell* them who she was.

Getting her prank on national television gave Tipper the higher score in the practical-joke tally. But the point, of course, isn't about competing and winning. What's most important is that these moments remind us of how much fun it is to be together, and thus bring us that much closer.

WHY WE PLAY

At every stage of our lives, play is essential to who we are as human beings and vital to how we find strength and happiness in our families. Play can do much more than many of us realize to restore, reenergize, and rejuvenate families, but only if you forget about goals and objectives and engage in play for its own sake.

Just as family is the place where we learn about love, it is also the place where we learn how to play. In the warmth of our families we learn to delight in simple pleasures, to laugh and giggle, to feel joy, to tell jokes, play games, imagine make-believe worlds, and let our spirits dance. Whether it is playing tag until everyone is out of breath, playing a board game or a card game, making funny faces and silly sounds, or climbing a mountain or skydiving together—whatever it is, the shared experience of play strengthens the family bonds. Just as a history of "turning toward" one another in bids for communication can build up a reservoir of good feelings, trust, and resilience in a relationship, so too can a history of play. Families that play together create pools of good memories, with stored reserves of joy and laughter that can help them weather bad times.

In fact, play is especially important for families. It fosters intimacy and deepens bonds between people; it helps children master the intricacies of complex cultures and learn the essential nature of society's norms; and it facilitates communication. Play strengthens a family in small, incremental ways, but the cumulative benefits are surprisingly large. Just as good communication is essential, so too is play. Ideally it should be a constant, daily ritual that becomes a seamless part of the fabric of family life.

If we are healthy, we are always engaged in all different kinds of play, and usually, without realizing it at the time, we learn different things from play at each stage of life. But regardless of the form it takes, play is as necessary to us as oxygen. When we are children, it is how we explore and learn about the world. When we are adults, it is how we restore and refresh ourselves. As friends, mates, spouses, partners, and parents, play is one way we learn about relating to the people for whom we care most. As older adults, it is how we keep ourselves young and active.

But what exactly is play? Dr. Stuart Brown, president of the Institute for Play, says that play is a "way of being" that frees us from the stress and anxiety that inevitably creep up to join any awareness of what others might be thinking about us, or what we are doing. Play enables us to learn efficiently, and establish mutual trust with our playmates, making it possible to build relationships that have intimacy and cooperation.

Because play involves a freeness of spirit, the same activity may be play for some but not for others, depending on the nature of the experience. A child playing backyard softball, with his older brother pitching and his younger sister acting as catcher and umpire, has an entirely different experience than a child on a highly organized competitive team who feels driven to excel in order to avoid criticism from a parent. As with happiness, the presence or absence of a state of play depends upon the nature of the inner experience—and too much seriousness of purpose can chase it away faster than we can pursue it.

That is not to say that play can't involve a serious and deliberate focus. Who has not delighted in watching the intense single-mindedness of children building a sand castle just a bit too close to the water? Concentrating with furrowed brows, they struggle to shore up the protective walls and prevent the moat from overflowing, making an all-out effort to lug pails of sand into just the right place before the next wave crashes; they demonstrate focused artistic determination as they dribble watery sand through their fingertips to form intricate turrets and steeples. All their imagination and concentration are focused on the task at hand, and all the while they are playing. They are also learning about building a real world while they're exploring a magical one made of sand, where the possibilities are infinite. "Play gives young children experience connecting their ideas with their actions and providing an opportunity for social growth as they share in games with others," said Rich Lerner of Tufts University, an expert in human development.

In short, play pays; to many people, however, the very word *play* inevitably connotes triviality, insignificance, and wasted time. What's worse, anyone who consistently chooses to engage in a lot of nonpurposeful activity is considered irresponsible and somehow immature. Understandably, many families who must struggle mightily to meet the demands of work and family can't make play a priority—or feel as if they can't. For a lot of families, play is something to be squeezed in when possible, but is certainly expected to give way to other, more "serious" endeavors when necessary. And these days, serious work seems necessary more and more often. "People today devalue their play," writes Dr. Lenore Terr, a clinical professor in psychiatry at the University of California at San Francisco Medical School and the author of *Beyond Love and Work: Why Adults Need to Play.* As we have learned from others and from our own family, all too many of us are so focused on work or school, so driven by our daily schedules and to-do lists, and have so thoroughly prioritized our lives that there's hardly any time left for individual and family play. But precisely because work is where Americans spend so much of our time today, it is that much more important for us to rediscover play to renew ourselves and our families—physically, emotionally, mentally, and spiritually.

Of course, most of us say that we'll get around to having fun when we've got time. But then, all too often, we don't—or we decide to wait for a vacation and really enjoy it, because we believe that trying to shoehorn play into an overcommitted schedule would make it impossible to enjoy ourselves anyway. Pat Letke-Alexander, for instance, told us that with the demands of a full-time job and two small children, she doesn't have much time to spare for some of her personal interests. "I like photography but I just don't have time. Time is a real issue right now."

But brain research has now proven conclusively that play is essential. It actually restores our intellectual capacities and renews our spirits. It's essential to good mental health and physical health, and to the reduction of tension. It enhances creativity and allows us to live in the moment—instead of always worrying about the future and fretting about the past. In fact, play is so basic to who we are that evolutionary biologists say that play is one of three major behaviors that distinguish mammals from reptiles. (The other two are audiovocal communication and nursing one's young.)

But while animals' play tends to resemble a few specialized behaviors practiced by the young that will later be important to them when fully mature, human play is far more varied and elaborate, and it persists not only through our extended childhood but also throughout our lives. Psychologists speculate that this may be because we are nature's premier generalists, and we need to prepare ourselves to learn a much broader range of skills. Our play, therefore, serves to help us not only practice a few specialized activities, but adapt constantly to new challenges.

We have, after all, managed to live in or at least visit virtually every ecological niche on earth, from the South Pole to the middle of the Sahara Desert. We can even direct our growth in specific directions by, for example, practicing a golf swing over and over again until the memory is etched in both mind and body memory. It seems to become etched more indelibly not only when we are young, but also when we're having fun. According to George Scarlett of the Eliot-Pearson Department of Child Development at Tufts University, children are able to consolidate and take in a remarkable amount of knowledge through enjoyable play, without actively trying to make sense of the information they are absorbing. The fact that Tiger Woods began swinging a golf club at the age of three is no doubt directly linked to the grace and power, and consistency, of his golf swing today.

One of the first theorists of play, Karl Groos, wrote in the 1890s that in its most basic sense, play is a kind of practice for pure learning. Having a highly developed ability to learn in brand-new situations is what makes us flexible. We're not prisoners of instinct; we're always eager to try something new. In one of his more famous aphorisms, Groos said, "Animals do not play because they are young, but they have their youth because they must play." And the reason play is conducive to learning, according to one of the leading experts on play, psychologist and educator Jerome Bruner, is because play provides a "means of minimizing the consequences of one's action and of learning, therefore, in a less risky situation."

Ironically, Bruner asserted as long ago as the 1970s that if what you're after is a constant ability to change rapidly, a kind of sustained "immaturity" can actually be an advantage. In fact, all of primate evolution, Bruner wrote, can be interpreted as being "based on the progressive selection of a distinctive pattern of immaturity . . . that has made possible the more flexible adaptation of our species."

But in our society, since play is associated with childishness, and childishness has a distinctly trivial, even negative connotation in our goal-oriented society, play is not seen as important. After all, our growth is *toward* maturity, is it not? And the closer we get to maturity, the more progress we are making, right? If we are not yet fully matured, we are lacking in wisdom and judgment, and thus our decisions are more likely to be incorrect or inappropriate.

All that may be true, but it's not the whole truth. If maturity is what we are growing *toward*, then once we reach it, we are no longer growing. So it's a trade-off. The "mature" brain has accumulated a great deal of learning but may be more set in its ways and thus less able to deal with brand-new situations. A brain that is still growing, on the other hand, is more capable of adapting to new circumstances. That is critical for us, because we are constantly changing the technological and cultural context of our lives, and therefore we are always encountering new challenges. We have therefore developed a distinctive evolutionary strategy that keeps us flexible—and thus partly childlike, in a good way.

And that's why play continues to be important no matter how old we are. People often say that play keeps us young, and indeed it does. A proper appreciation for the crucial role held by play depends upon an acceptance that it preserves our ability to change. Play is, among other things, a kind of aerobic workout for the human capacity to change—a freewheeling form of mental, emotional, physical, and spiritual exercise.

PLAY AND LEARNING

Many people believe that for young children, play and learning are the same thing. In fact, twenty-four hundred years ago Plato wrote, "Let your children's lessons take the form of play." And most parents seem to know this intuitively. Just think about the way an adult naturally goes about teaching a baby how to take his or her first bite of solid food. By playing! It automatically becomes a game.

Our own personal experiences certainly taught us that with our babies, toddlers, and young children; there was almost no differentiation between playing and learning. We played with our children from the very first days of their lives. Granted, it was mostly with awe and adoration at first, but our whole way of interacting with babies was a kind of play.

And, of course, most people are the same way. We try to make babies smile and laugh. We make ridiculous faces and sounds to get their attention and to get them to respond. Soon, most of the relationship is made up of play. We bounce them, toss them in the air, nuzzle their necks, and blow on their tummies.

Scientists now know that for infants, play has many benefits. Even seemingly silly, repetitive games like peekaboo help children learn; in that case, the lesson is that something can continue to exist even when they no longer see it. According to UCLA's Neal Halfon, in just the first three years of life, a child is absorbing so much information that her brain forms about one quadrillion synaptic connections. That is twice the number of connections that will ultimately remain in the adult brain. Children's young minds are primed for absorbing new experiences and knowledge of their environments. Children are naturally prepared to engage in countless interactions with people and things they can investigate with each of their senses. As we grow and age, however, our brain starts relying on the more frequently used synapses, and if consistently unused, many of the early synapses that were created as a result of our freewheeling, exploratory experiences and play may go away. That is why it is so critical that babies do play and explore their world, so they have the richest possible set of synapses from which their more lasting neurological patterns can be formed.

Every family comes to its own discovery that the kind of play that proves to be most exhilarating is usually the simplest and requires little more than a lot of imagination. For example, Pat and Todd Alexander told us the favorite game in their family is the nightly ritual of Lamp Shade Chase, an exciting game that just spontaneously emerged one day, when Pat tossed on the floor an old broken lampshade that she was getting ready to throw out.

Nathan, their four-year-old, put it on his head and started running. "Then we started the chase game," Pat told us. "The lamp shade has fallen apart, and all that's left is the ring at the top and the ring at the bottom and some fabric holding the two rings together, but they love this lamp shade and the game we play with it."

No complicated rules, no "educational content," just fun. It builds the bonds of trust between Pat, Todd, and the children. It forges giddy memories. And it helps the growing toddlers improve their reflexes and coordination as everybody runs around the room, trying to catch one another.

Similarly, despite the piles of toys Nathan has, his favorite one is surprisingly simple. Recently he discovered a box of toothpicks, and spilled them all over the floor to make what adults call "a mess." But to Nathan, they became, in his mom's words, "the cool thing, because they were new to him." When we visited in the family's home earlier this year, Nathan eagerly took us upstairs to his bedroom so he could show us the neat "fence" he had made by lining up toothpicks in the carpet. Todd laughed and said that if only they had known, "We could have saved a lot of money and told everybody to just get him toothpicks for his birthday."

For children, play is the living manifestation of freedom, when time itself is theirs to use as they choose. In choosing, they learn about risk and discover boundaries, experiment with independence and gain a positive sense of self. They begin to fill out their physical and mental capacities; they learn about relationships and why good ones are based on mutual respect; and perhaps most important, they learn how to learn.

According to Brown, whose institute is devoted to fostering a deeper understanding of the purpose and importance of play, "Play is the central theme of childhood, and deserves to be honored." It is universally understood that children play. They just do. In fact, they *must*, because it is a critical part of their development.

Play is how they explore the world; it is how they stretch and grow mentally, physically, emotionally, and spiritually. Friedrich

Froebel, who founded the kindergarten system in Germany in the nineteenth century, said, "Play is the highest phase of child development."

Children's play can take many forms, depending on their age and temperament. Physical play can involve running and jumping, throwing and catching, games like tag or hide-and-go-seek, tickling, wrestling, climbing, tests of relative strength—any kind of physical activity or movement that involves fun and in which the participants are not hurting one another. Physical play helps children develop balance, motor skills, dexterity, and eye-hand coordination, while also helping them work through natural tension and crankiness.

Another category of play is social play, the classic example being playing house or any sort of pretend social interaction in which children or others engage in the enactment of actual or imaginative personal or social experiences and relate to one another according to social rules. A third category is creative play, which involves expression through paintings or drawings, or any creation involving materials.

Sometimes, children may simply want time alone for imagining, exploring, or just thinking. In imaginative play, children can take on make-believe identities, brush aside the physical and social rules of the world, and enjoy the company of imaginary playmates or pets. Leading experts in the field of child development, Drs. T. Berry Brazelton and Joshua D. Sparrow, write in *Touchpoints Three to Six: Your Child's Emotional and Behavioral Development* that a child "needs to dream and to wish for a world in which she, not her parents, is in control. Magical thinking is a thrust toward independence at an increasingly thoughtful level."

One of the main lessons our children can so powerfully teach us is that while they may ask for the latest toy they see advertised, what they really treasure most—by far—is time spent playing together as a family. Some parents who are really pressed for time and feel badly about not being able to play more with their kids look for toys that can, in effect, be surrogate playmates in their absence. According to Brian Sutton-Smith, professor emeritus of education at the University of Pennsylvania and a leading proponent of play theory, these kinds of "toys are not only expected to be played with by the child personally, they are also given as part of family bonding. . . . In effect, the parent says, 'I give you this gift to bond you to me; now go and play with it by yourself.' Solitariness often means loneliness, so some of these gifts . . . the child will treat as an imaginary companion."

Despite the Game Boys and other high-tech toys that Dawn Hancock's eight-year-old son, Chase, owns, when we visited his family there was only one toy that Chase took pains to show us: the bright red hand-carved wooden race car that his stepfather Steve (whom Chase calls Daddy) helped him make for his Cub Scouts project. As Chase ran his fingers up and down the curves of the vehicle, he carefully explained how it took his daddy hours to sand it just perfectly so it would be smooth. He then added with a grin that now he wants his dad's help in putting racing spikes on the wheels, so it'll push competing cars off the track.

As children grow, they may forsake the traditional childlike forms of play, but it is critical that they not lose the spirit of play. Mihaly Csikszentmihalyi, a renowned professor of psychology and the author of *Flow: The Psychology of Optimal Experience*, found that preteens who labeled virtually all their activities as "play" turned out to be better adjusted as teenagers than preteens who labeled most of their activities as "work." Experts also say that preteens who enjoy play and feel competent at it are better at social interaction later on and are much less likely to engage in violence or risky behavior as teenagers.

According to census figures, teens who involve themselves in extracurricular play are far more likely to succeed academically and have fewer behavioral problems. Jette Halladay, associate professor of theater education at Middle Tennessee State University, recently surveyed research that documents how teens who participated in youth arts and music programs earned better grades, demonstrated better communication and conflict-resolution skills, scored higher on their SAT scores, and were less likely to drop out of school. But of course, none of that is the point.

Beyond the ways in which play can improve a teen's achievements, the pure bliss that can be found in play itself must not be overlooked. Indeed, it is often through play that we discover some of our deepest and truest passions in life. And some of those passions can turn into careers that qualify as "work" but also have a lasting element of joy in them.

Whatever the kind of play, the ability to participate in it fully is a critical part of building a child's sense of self-worth and happiness. We learned that lesson most eloquently and powerfully from an amazing young man named Matthew Cavedon from Berlin, Connecticut, who uses a wheelchair and has become a spokesperson and leader in helping to make sure that playgrounds are accessible for all children. We first met Matthew when he was ten years old. Matthew works with an organization called Boundless Playgrounds that helps communities design universally accessible playgrounds where children of all different abilities can play side by side.

Matthew relied upon his own experiences in playgrounds to design a "boat swing," which was made to accommodate two children in wheelchairs as well as six children without them and lets them swing together. Explaining to us what motivated his efforts, he said that, with proper design, "a playground is one place differences disappear. If I can play next to you, then I am your equal. If I have to just watch you from the sidelines, I am separate. I want every kid to be laughing on a playground independently." Interestingly, his invention has had benefits beyond those he originally envisioned. For example, among the favorite users of his boat swing are not only children in wheelchairs but also elderly grandparents who are delighted to share in some active play with their grandchildren or other young family members.

One of Susan Fadley's fondest childhood memories is of her

paternal grandfather's special birthday celebrations. "He had the greatest sense of humor of any person I've ever met and probably will ever meet. He had a real way of letting you know that you were a special person to him." Susan explains that while he didn't have a lot of money, he found creative ways of making certain your day was a special one. She recalls how he made the most of the fact that her brother Tim loved ravioli. One year, he got Tim two large cans of ravioli. However, instead of simply presenting Tim with them, he wrapped them up, tied string around them, and then wound the string all around the entire house. He handed the excited birthday boy the end of the string, and instructed Tim to follow it until he found his surprise. "Let me tell you what, Tim had myself and a bunch of cousins all behind him, trying to find whatever was at the end, and it took well over an hour probably, to locate this gift." Susan said her grandfather's games were something they looked forward to every year, and that his gift was always the best gift, largely because of the creativity and love that went into each and every one.

Perhaps the most common misconception about play is that it is—or should be—mostly limited to childhood. In fact, play serves an essential role in promoting a healthy and balanced experience at every stage of life. According to Lenore Terr, play "gives us pleasure, a sense of accomplishment, of belonging," and "without huge risk our cares, worries, sadness, secrets are released."

For young couples starting out together, an element of play in their lives is an important part of keeping the joy and romance in their relationship. Before the hard challenge of raising a family and juggling child care and work and all the rest, it is important that the couple make a point to have lots of fun, private times that help cement their relationship. That's part of what courtships and honeymoons are all about—but it can't stop there.

The time couples spend having fun—either alone together, or with their larger family—is critically important for the well-being of their marriage and the well-being of the family as a whole. Parents model playfulness for kids. It shows the children and everyone in the extended family that there is joy and love and laughter in the family's heart.

Being able to have fun and play together is an important part of feeling connected to the other person. It is a part of what may contribute to people feeling that their spouse is not just a partner in parenting but a best friend, a soul mate, a partner in play. This, in turn, is critical for parents' ability to be playful, responsive, and patient with their children.

Gabrielle and Chris Wagener enjoy going out to dinner, traveling, playing tennis, and skiing. But much more than the activities themselves, what they most enjoy is being able do these things together. "If I can't do it with Gabrielle, I'd just as soon not do it. It's just more fun with her," Chris says.

Having a history of play as a couple and as a family is also important when spouses become empty nesters. Judith Wallerstein, author of *The Good Marriage: How and Why Love Lasts*, told us that a capacity for play can help these couples rebuild their relationship in a new way once the children have left home. That can be extremely difficult for couples who concentrated all of their energies on taking care of their children and neglected to find time for each other while the children were still home.

Numerous studies have shown that older individuals who are involved in community activities, sports, and other sources of play are healthier, happier, and live longer. And older people who have remained active all their lives have greater strength, endurance, and stamina. Rather than becoming less important as one ages, play is equally important at all ages.

WHEN PLAY BECOMES WORK

As Americans work more and more, we are—unsurprisingly perhaps—playing less and less. Increasingly, time that used to be for play is being reallocated for work. And even when busy families set aside time for play, it is often much more harried and scheduled—sometimes leading people to feel like they're working at play. According to a recent Harris Poll, last year adults reported having only twenty hours of leisure per week, combined with fifty hours of work per week. That's a full nine more hours of work per week and six fewer hours to play per week than we had just one generation ago. In the struggle to balance work and family, unstructured time for play is increasingly getting short shrift.

Not only is play harder to come by, it has also undergone a fundamental transformation. Rather than being a relatively unstructured, unsupervised free-form activity done mostly outdoors, play today has taken on a highly organized nature, and many parents find themselves encouraged to take their children's play seriously—in some cases perhaps *too* seriously. They try to use play as an opportunity for their children to acquire extra skills and absorb specific, useful knowledge. A recent cover story in *Time* magazine chronicled the new trend among parents who are striving to raise so-called superkids, concluding, "Many parents are consumed by the idea that if they can't perfect their children, they must at least get them as close to that ideal as possible."

For some well-intentioned parents, the process begins even before birth. Inspired by some research findings that certain cognitive skills may be improved by exposure to classical music, there are now whole cottage industries based on making and selling CDs with titles like *Mozart Makes You Smarter, Mozart for Mothers-to-Be, Build Your Baby's Brain Through the Power of Music*, and of course, the ever popular *Baby Needs Mozart*. Other studies have called into question whether any such benefits are sustainable or even measurable. But the CDs remain popular. At least it can relax the expectant mother, which is not a bad thing!

And that's just the beginning. As their children grow, instead of playing catch or engaging in some other simple and spontaneous form of play, many parents eagerly fill their children's time with classes and their closets with educational toys. Studies have shown that, regardless of income level, a large proportion of parents are using flash cards and other "educational toys" with their children from very early ages.

But the results can often be self-defeating, because of a simple irony: play is beneficial for learning largely because of the absence of stress; when stress is put back into the activity, no matter how good the intention or the plan, the educational potential is often negated. Today some children as young as five years old are actually showing signs of stress similar to stressed adults.

According to George Scarlett, "In reality there really is no such thing as an educational toy. Toys and play material are educational only with respect to what children do with them. . . . Pass by the expensive, complicated toys and go for the stuff that children really use." In fact, many children who are encouraged to play with overly designed educational toys sometimes lose touch with creative play altogether. Instead of high-tech "interactive" toys, babies and young children really need interactive *people*. And contrary to the implications of much toy marketing, toddlers are simply not prepared for learning letters and numbers or engaging in symbolic learning; they just want to play. "Don't bother with toys meant to teach preschoolers to read, write, and calculate; that's not a good use of their time," Scarlett said.

Nonetheless, busy parents can't always create the space or time in their lives for long periods of unstructured play. They often need to devise schedules as intricate as ballet routines to orchestrate when each member of the family will work, commute, eat, study, and play. Whether it is racing to dance practice, art class, a soccer game, or Little League, many of today's children—and parents too—are starting to feel exhausted by what can become a never-ending game of logistics management. When multiple children in a family participate in different age-appropriate activities, it can be even more exhausting, as parents split up to drive in separate circuits for the better part of the weekend. Play sometimes feels like it's no longer a fun family activity, but instead one more chore added to the list.

Not only has individual child's play become much more organized, but children are also increasingly often playing together in highly organized leagues. According to Bob Bigelow, Tom Moroney, and Linda Hall, authors of the book *Just Let the Kids Play: How to Stop Other Adults from Ruining Your Child's Fun and Success in Youth Sports*, "organized youth sports involve an estimated 30–35 million children each year, and along with them, their parents. Youth sports are second only to school in the amount of interest, investment, and involvement of parents on behalf of their children. For some people, strictly measured by those three gauges, youth sports actually come in first."

Inevitably, however, some parents get caught up in the competitive nature of these activities and lose control of their better judgment. Anyone who has spent time on the sidelines at these games knows the phenomenon well: some mothers and fathers yell at their children and curse the referees, or even the children on the other team. The authors of *Just Let the Kids Play* refer to some of these highly scheduled team activities as "organized anxiety programs." A survey of participants in a Minnesota sports league several years ago found that 45 percent of those surveyed reported being called names, being yelled at, or being insulted while engaging in sports; 18 percent reported being kicked, hit, or slapped; and 8 percent said they had been encouraged to intentionally harm others. This trend reached its extreme in the summer of 2000 in the death of a young hockey player's father at the hands of another player's father.

When competition is within healthy limits, there are, of course, many benefits to organized youth sports activities. Despite all the travel time, we found that the organization and scheduling required to have all four of our children participate in sports leagues and other activities made it easier for us to spend more time with them. Part of the appeal is that parents can participate—at least as observers and supporters.

What is behind this intense organization of play activities is a much deeper transformation in the nature of play. Scarlett believes we are witnessing a revolution in the way children play in modern America that has its roots in shifts in family structure and community cohesion. Several generations ago, when it was the norm for families to have one parent at home during the day, and when the outdoors was considered a generally safe environment for children, the common practice was to encourage children to go outside and play. The parent who was at home could often look out the window and down the block to see their children playing with others—and they had the assurance that the other parents were probably looking out from time to time as well, forming an informal but nonetheless real safety net.

Today that is no longer the case. Working parents seek out more structured forms of play for their children while they're not home. Children's play is increasingly organized and controlled, through playground supervision, physical education, and athletic leagues. Their behavior is far more controlled and perhaps less creative than it was when children were more independent in their play. Sutton-Smith says, "The major play event of the past 300 years has been the ever-increasing domestication of children's play. By that I mean the increasing control and supervision of play to get rid of its physical dangers and its emotional licenses." In addition, the rise of suburban developments—which often don't have sidewalks or enough safe spaces to play—means that children now spend much more time indoors with electronic toys, specifically television. Parents find that watching television, whatever its negatives, does keep children more or less confined to one location inside the house. Ironically, according to UCLA Associate Vice Chancellor of Community Partnerships Frank Gilliam, television itself—specifically local television news—appears to distort the frequency and pervasiveness of violent crime and artificially magnify the tendency of parents to protect their children by keeping them indoors.

Despite these findings, both television and computer video games have become major replacements for physical play—for children and adults alike. Some now use the term "screen addict" to describe the children who are mesmerized not only by TV, but by computer games, Game Boys, and other electronic devices. According to an article by Robert Kubey and Mihaly Csikszentmihalyi in *Scientific American*, "on average, individuals in the industrialized world devote three hours a day to the pursuit [watching television]—fully half of their leisure time, more than on any single activity save work and sleep. At this rate, someone who lives to seventy-five would spend nine years in front of the tube." Among other things, that represents a lot of play deprivation.

According to the article's analysis of the scientific literature, the addictive power of television most likely derives from its exploitation of our brains' automatic response, something called the "orienting response." Put simply, this means that our brains are programmed to compel us to pay attention to a sudden movement in our immediate surroundings, so that we can quickly orient ourselves to whatever new circumstances might have just been created. One can visualize early humans reacting to a rustle of leaves caused by a leopard stalking the group. Those who reoriented quickly and reacted to the movement survived. Those who did not react did not become our ancestors. In any case, this response has remained part of human behavior across our evolution. It leads us to look in the direction of the flickering movements displayed on the television screen.

Most of us have had the experience of engaging in conversation while a television set is on in the room. No matter the import of the conversation, and even if the television's sound is muted, it is virtually impossible to refrain from occasional glances at the screen. It is no accident that commercials typically trigger this orienting response an average of once every second. Even ordinary programming constantly engages us by using it, producing a glazed, almost hypnotic effect. Importantly, studies show that the emotional impact of television watching is both seductive and pernicious: specifically, the immediate impact on mood at the beginning of a TV-watching session is a feeling of relaxation, but as soon as the watching ceases, the illusion of relaxation quickly disappears and is replaced by a feeling of having been "drained."

THE COSTS OF TOO LITTLE PLAY

While play is often the first thing to go when families are pressed for time, play deprivation can have harsh consequences, both for individuals and for families. The lack of play can signal underlying problems, such as depression or social maladjustment, explains Scarlett. "The presence of play is . . . associated with general vitality."

Many specialists also believe that the reduction of opportunities for self-renewal through play has become a significant factor contributing to stress-induced depression among American adults and children. After conducting an extensive study of eight thousand students in their teens and early twenties, University of Michigan psychologist Harold Stevenson found that two-thirds reported that they suffered from too much stress at least one day a week, and one-third reported that they had too much tension and stress every day. Furthermore, according to the Institute for Play, children who are deprived of play are more susceptible to behaving impulsively when provoked. Other researchers have found that children who do not engage in physical play are more likely to become tense and grumpy and less likely to learn the social skills that are often essential to dealing with pressure.

In a sense, play benefits work in the same way that sleep benefits wakefulness. In fact, John Gottman told us, "Play is really the waking equivalent of dreaming, and like dreaming and REM sleep, it is restorative." Play restores our capacity for purpose and in the process strengthens it. But the purpose of play transcends its instrumental value in enhancing our capacity for work. One could also say that work makes it possible for us to play—though it does have some inherent value of its own.

Many people describe play as the activity that makes them feel most alive. Moreover, the inherent need for play does not go away. It continues to assert itself just as someone intentionally holding his breath reaches the point where it is impossible not to gasp for air. If we deprive ourselves of play for long enough, and lose the ability to indulge the play instinct in a healthy way, our need for the psychic release that play can provide will often reassert itself in an unhealthy way. For example, one of the many reasons for the epidemic of alcoholism and drug abuse in America may be our failure to carve out an appropriate place for regular play that can allow our spirits to breathe freely, without stifling them in such a way that they're forced to, in effect, "gasp for play."

For thousands of years, people have used alcohol and other intoxicants as such a release. A 3,800-year-old recipe for beer written in cuneiform on Babylonian tablets was recently found by archaeologists in Syria. Since at least then, some individuals have been vulnerable to an overreliance on intoxicants or addictive behaviors as a means of "losing themselves"—in an effort to escape the constant and, for many, oppressive internal discipline that they find difficult to switch off at will.

Could it be that a society with a diminished appreciation of play becomes more vulnerable to the widespread abuse of substances that promise to simulate the psychological release that play is intended to provide? In many social settings, drinking rituals are relied upon to provide a rationale—or excuse—for entering a state of play, so much so that some find it difficult to imagine "having fun" without becoming at least partially intoxicated.

Moderate alcohol consumption of a drink or two a day is not harmful for most adults, according to the National Institute on Alcohol Abuse and Alcoholism at the National Institutes of Health.

But the NIH estimates that "currently, nearly 14 million Americans—1 in every 13 adults—abuse alcohol or are alcoholics." That estimate doesn't include several million more who regularly drink heavily or even engage in binge drinking. A study conducted at all-women colleges that was published earlier this year by the *Journal of American College Health* found that from 1993 to 2001, there was a 125 percent increase in frequent binge drinking by young women.

It needs to be said that there is little in America today that has anything approaching the negative impact on families as does substance abuse, particularly alcohol abuse. "About 43 percent of U.S. adults—76 million people—have been exposed to alcoholism in the family," reports the Centers for Disease Control. More than 10 percent of all children, "live with at least one parent who is in need of treatment for alcohol- or drug dependency," according to the Substance Abuse Mental Health Services Administration, "and one in four children under the age of eighteen is living in a home where alcoholism or alcohol abuse is a fact of daily life." At least as much as the adults who need help with substance abuse problems, these children need help as well.

Children who live in such homes face a number of challenges. They are far more likely to experience emotional problems, health problems, and learning difficulties. Children of alcoholics are also four times more likely to become alcoholics themselves. When there is drug addiction in the home as well, children face still more difficulties. They are three times more likely to experience verbal, physical, or sexual abuse and are four times more likely to be neglected. And because the children often feel obliged to take on parental responsibilities, many of them also lose the carefree experience of childhood.

Of course, substance abuse is far from the only artificial substitute for play that is used in an effort to "turn off" inhibitions or internal discipline that has become oppressive in some way. Some people turn to overeating. Others turn to overwork. But all addictive behaviors have one thing in common: they serve the purpose

of *distracting* conscious attention from an internal experience that
is a source of distress.

Certainly there are a vast number of personal factors and situations that contribute to an addiction. Families need help dealing
with and managing addictions as they try to find a solution. Play is
not a cure-all. But as play can provide a sense of freedom and
release, developing a healthy tradition of play can be one step
toward helping a family deal with the complicated problem of
addiction.

THE HOYT FAMILY

On her honeymoon in Alaska, Jeanne Hoyt was driving a team of
five dogs for the first time. Standing on the runners of the sled, she
turned into the icy wind and headed straight across the frozen lake
to try to catch up with her husband, Bill, who was also trying
something new: skijoring, that is, zipping across the ice and snow
on skis while being pulled at top speed by another dog.

"It was wonderful," Jeanne said, beaming. "Most people—especially old women—don't do that, but it was a wonderful experience to be out and it was really wilderness living for a week."

You could also say that most people in their seventies don't do
that either. But Jeanne and Bill did—and that was in 1992. Now
both in their eighties, Jeanne and Bill are as vibrant and active as
ever. Together, they run, climb mountains, kayak, and do whatever
else strikes their fancy.

Since their marriage, they have continued to revel in how much
their ability to share in play has strengthened their relationship as
a couple. "We've got a perfect life, because we're into these sports
and we do all of these things together. It's just ideal," says Jeanne.

They downhill ski twenty to thirty days a year. Every other day,
they ride ten to twelve miles on their mountain bikes, "and if we
can't bike, we walk for an hour," Jeanne says. Jeanne and Bill have
enjoyed sports and outdoor activities all their lives. But as they

have gotten older, they have made a conscious effort to keep up and even increase their level of activity. They are prime examples of the benefits of an active and playful lifestyle.

They make a point of doing some form of activity at least five days a week for at least an hour. "I figure the older you get, the more physical and mental you have to be, or you lose it," says Jeanne. Play keeps them happy and healthy, Bill says. Jeanne concurs: "A person who goes to bed with a smile on their lips lives longer."

Jeanne also loves to dance. Reminiscing in their home in Redlands, California, Jeanne recalled how as a girl she took a ballroom-dancing class where she and one boy in particular, Gower Champion, became a natural dancing team. They loved dancing together, and their joy showed.

One day, a dance contest was put on at the Coconut Grove nightclub in downtown Los Angeles. Five hundred couples entered the contest. "And we said, 'Let's go in—it'd be fun,'" Jeanne recalls. Just sixteen years old, they were the youngest ones in the contest. They made the cut that first night to reach the finals, and, as Jeanne tells it, "The next night the audience was just with us one hundred percent, so we won."

They then went on a thirteen-week tour, became a professional dance team, and ended up dancing together on Broadway and for an extended run at Radio City Music Hall in New York City. They continued dancing together for six years, until Gower went off to fight in World War II. Although Jeanne doesn't dance professionally anymore, she still loves it.

Bill, meanwhile, was a talented athlete as a young man who once played in the Rose Bowl for UCLA and later taught physical education and coached track, cross-country, and football at San Bernardino Valley and Crafton Hills Colleges. But it was only when they married each other—a second marriage for both—that they were able to share these activities with their spouses.

"My wife was a movie actress with no athletic ability or desire to do anything like that. Jeanne's husband: same way," Bill said. Then, breaking into a smile, he added, "So now, all of a sudden, we're doing these things together, instead of alone." Both of them, in fact, fairly glow with happiness when they describe the joys of being able to indulge in these forms of play together.

Earlier in their lives, each of them had to choose between time together with their spouses and the activities that for them were so much fun—like Bill's thirty-seven years on ski patrol at Snow Valley. But when they married each other, all of that changed. "We were so compatible when we got married that we just started doing everything together," Bill told us.

Even though they have been married for only ten years, Bill and Jeanne have known each other for forty-seven years all together. They and their spouses were neighbors and friends. It was Bill who taught Jeanne to ski when she was fifty-five. Jeanne and her first husband had divorced twenty years before she married Bill, a year and a half after Bill's wife passed away.

When we asked how they handle disagreements, Bill jokingly said, "You can't win with a woman," to which Jeanne sweetly suggested, "Well, you could just listen to me." Addressing the question seriously, Bill added, "We don't have any problems at all. If we have a disagreement, we yell at each other a couple minutes, and then it's all over. Life's too short for that sort of thing, and we both feel that way." Jeanne added, "We have too much to do, too much yet to enjoy, so why waste time arguing?"

For Jeanne and Bill, the other part of their secret to keeping young is staying not just physically active but also mentally active, through their commitment to the Civilian Volunteer Patrol (CVP), a unit of the Redlands Police Department in Redlands, California. They each volunteer an average of sixty hours each month (much more than the required sixteen hours) and between the two of them have put in over nine thousand hours of service since they joined the program in 1996. As CVP members, they do everything police officers do except carry a gun, confront violence, or give citations for moving violations. But they can tape off a crime scene, direct traffic, and give parking tickets. They wear badges and even drive their own patrol car. They also conduct activities for the young people of the community, such as giving school groups tours of the police department or educating them on gun safety.

And certainly Bill and Jeanne also benefit, not just from their interactions with young people in the community, but also from time with their own children and five grandchildren. During the summers, they have the grandchildren over for a week at a time. Jeanne says, "When we first had them—they were from age five to eleven at that time—their parents said, 'Do you think you can handle them?' I said, 'Don't worry about it.' So, they came. I had all the meals cooked ahead of time, all the things I knew kids would like. And we had everything planned: swimming one day, kayaking one day, mountain climbing one day. When they got home, one of the fathers called and said, 'What did you do to our kids? They've been sleeping for two days.'"

Jeanne has also taught her grandchildren the power of quiet play and enjoyment. When she takes them hiking, she advises them to listen for the sounds around them. "I want you to be quiet. I want you to enjoy nature. I want to hear what you can hear— whether it's a woodpecker, an anthill, anything." She told us how important that kind of mental quiet space and release has been for her throughout her life. When she was raising her children, that quiet was instrumental to her ability to think about and solve problems. "If I had a problem coming up, I'd go out and sit in my orange grove, where nature was around."

On a typical day, Jeanne and Bill are up at 5:45 A.M. Before breakfast, they usually go for their daily run, walk, or bike. During the day, they spend much of their time on volunteer activities. And of late, they've been asked to be speakers at senior citizen groups to talk to their peers about adopting more active, playful lifestyles.

"There are so many who just vegetate, and that's sad," Jeanne said, adding that they tell her, "We've had it hard all of our lives, we want to take it easy."

"I say, 'That's your biggest mistake,'" Jeanne told us. "The brain does not deteriorate just because of age; it's only when you stop using it. You need a positive attitude. If you're negative, you're gone. So, we tell them what we're doing, and how we're doing it."

PLAY AND FAMILY RITUALS

Surprisingly, some of our family's most vivid memories of playing during the years we lived in the official residence of the vice president, at the Naval Observatory in Washington, come from the tense thirty-six-day period after the 2000 presidential election, when we were striving to get the Florida votes counted.

More than once, in the late evening, everyone gathered spontaneously around the grand piano in the entrance hall—first one person, then another and another. Usually Kristin played the piano, then Sarah took out her saxophone, and Karenna played her flute. Pretty soon, as music filled the house, everybody was there—Albert and Tipper played the two sets of drums, while Al played the harmonica. And on it went.

The "jam session" might not have impressed anyone outside the family as good, but that was not the point. It wasn't a performance; it was just really fun, a release, an opportunity for renewal. In other words, it was play. We thought of those sessions when Stuart Brown and others told us about the importance of play in handling stress. Sharing a few laughs can do a lot more than simply temporarily taking one's mind off problems. Then we can return to confront our challenges refreshed and renewed. With our hope, motivation, creativity, and energy restored, we are often able to provide more creative solutions. Family rituals are also an important kind of play. They create cohesion and produce a feeling of comfort. In fact, when families talk about their shared experiences, it is often the times of play that everyone remembers best and enjoys talking about the most.

Meg Cox, the author of *The Heart of a Family: Searching America for New Traditions That Fulfill Us*, writes that family traditions, holidays, and other special days can be infused with a much deeper meaning that will give them special, lasting significance for children. While the traditional holidays and such milestones as birthdays are common rituals that most families observe in one way or another, Cox suggests creating new family rituals that will make an event special for the family. These can range from special meals on certain occasions to family toasts, or special meetings—or even "ritualizing" everyday activities like having breakfast, getting on the school bus, or putting children to bed. Worshiping together in one's faith tradition is another way families can share in rituals, connections, and renewal.

Like many parents, we discovered that the repetitive nature of rituals can strengthen a child's sense of security. They can also help children deal with transitions that can otherwise be disorienting. Rituals also serve as a way for parents to impart values and pass on a family's heritage. When parents enact the rituals they may have performed with their own parents or grandparents, it can help children feel a connection to those relatives—even those they may never have known personally. Perhaps most important, rituals can be a source of joy both when they are lived and when they are remembered. There are many benefits to family rituals of all kinds, according to Cox. They help give children a sense of their own identity and their place in the family and community.

Of course, there is the classic ritual of family reunions—which seem to be growing increasingly popular. According to Edith Wagner, editor of *Reunions* magazine, there are now more than 200,000 family reunions a year in the United States, with an average of fifty extended family members attending each gathering. Margo Strong, a public school teacher in Holt, Michigan, told us her family has had an active tradition of family reunions. For the past fifty-two years, her mother's side of the family has gotten the extended family together. Since Margo's mother is the oldest of eight, there are usually at least fifty people present, and often sixty or seventy or more. They even have an official family meeting at the reunion—and someone always takes minutes so that family members who couldn't make it will know what was discussed.

Margo says her husband, Jay, who is also a school teacher, enjoys it, too—especially because these gatherings are quite different from those in his own family, which is much smaller. She explains, "He knows two cousins and one aunt. That's it. And then I come from a family where I have like fifty cousins—first cousins—and I'm the youngest on my dad's side, cousin-wise, so some of my older cousins who are sixteen years older than I am have kids my age, and so we're like two and three generations, so when we get all together, there's quite a few of us." Jay added, "I just feel bad because it took me twenty-five years to learn most of their names."

While not every family may want to have the kind of large, formalized reunions that Margo's family has, it is important to realize, Cox notes, that even if a family does not adopt positive family rituals, they will still have rituals nonetheless. But in the absence of attention, those rituals may well turn out to be negative ones—such as repetitive fights, or sitting every night silently in front of the television, or ignoring children's storytelling. Negative rituals such as these can create lasting patterns of tension, resentment, or unease in a family.

Play also serves as a principal focal point for families to interact with other families in their community. Community events organized around play—whether school raffles, festivals, athletic events, or old-fashioned county fairs—are the most likely to draw families from all parts of the community together and to provide environments within which everyone can interact on equal footing and in which children can feel safe.

In our family, Halloween has always been a ritual that felt special, in part because of the way it integrated our family into the neighborhood where we lived for most of the time when Congress was in session during the years Al was a representative and senator. It was the same neighborhood where Tipper grew up, in Arlington, Virginia—a neighborhood with sidewalks and friendly neighbors who all knew one another. Lots of children played in the narrow, quiet streets and cul-de-sacs and in one another's yards. In a neighborhood like this, when all the houses are dressed up with lights and scary decorations, Halloween can take on a wonderful and magical feeling.

Of course, a big part of the fun—and not just for the children— was in adopting the identity and persona of some character or archetype completely at odds with our everyday life. So more than the usual energy went into choosing and then making costumes. We hardly ever bought costumes; we encouraged the kids to make them from stuff in the house. And somehow we developed a family tradition that each year the children could pick Al's costume.

One year, they presented a real challenge by deciding that he would be a carrot for Halloween. So with great fanfare and effort, a sheet was colored orange and wrapped around him with the idea that it would narrow toward his feet—like a carrot. It all worked fine, until he started to walk and the bindings came loose. Even though the children had imagined that he might hop all evening from house to house, his solution was to tell them to "use your imagination." He looked more like a confused orange ghost than a vegetable. The kids loved it. And the neighbors had a good laugh. But the best part of our Halloween night was that the whole family—and indeed, the whole neighborhood—played together.

THE WALLACES

Linda Wallace and Anthony (Tony) Wallace

Chapter 7

RESILIENCE

Although the world is full of suffering,
it is also full of the overcoming of it.
—HELEN KELLER

THE CAPACITY TO REBOUND

Constant change is an inevitable reality for all families. Much of the change is welcome, but some is not. Every family faces numerous crises, setbacks, disappointments, heartaches, and devastating blows. Some can be avoided, but not all can be—no matter the family's wisdom or wealth, no matter their character or virtue.

The difficulties families experience are of three kinds. First, there are the predictable but still challenging transitions that usually occur in the life cycle: painful transitions such as losing a parent, and happy but nevertheless turbulent transitions such as getting married or having a child. Second, there are the wholly unpredictable crises, such as losing a job or struggling with a serious illness. Third, there are the difficult problems that arise when one or more family members inflict emotional or physical pain upon another. This is, of course, often the most destructive kind of difficulty. In whichever case, these events can put enormous strains on a family, and the traditional relationships in a family may need to be fundamentally redefined and reforged in a way that enables the family to better handle the stress of whatever difficulty they are experiencing. Then, having found a new equilibrium, the family members can regroup, gather strength from one another, and push back out into the world. This ability to bounce back is the essence of resilience, a quality demonstrated by all healthy families.

Froma Walsh, a professor of psychiatry at the University of Chicago and the author of *Strengthening Family Resilience*, defines resilience as "the capacity to rebound from adversity strengthened and more resourceful." She goes on to describe resilience as not simply the endurance of life's travails but as an active process by which we as individuals grow stronger in response to the crises and challenges we face throughout our lives. As Walsh explains, resilient children can "heal from painful wounds, take charge of their lives, and go on to live fully and love well."

But this kind of resilience does not exist only within the hearts and minds of individuals. Resilience also resides in the coping and support mechanisms that exist inside the family, and it's sometimes found in resources and help within the community as well. Families can cultivate and build their resilience in order to help one another as individuals—and the unit as a whole—weather tough times. According to Walsh, "how a family confronts and manages a disruptive experience, buffers stress, effectively reorganizes itself, and moves forward with life will influence immediate and long-term adaptation for every family member *and* for the very survival and well-being of the family unit." Resilience requires a shared belief in why it is important for the family *to* prevail, a shared confidence that it *can*, and most important, a shared determination to make sure that it *will*.

Taken together, these qualities make up resilience, an attribute that successful families almost always nurture, even if few of them use the word *resilience* to describe it. We learned from Hamilton.

McCubbin, a former dean of the University of Wisconsin School of Human Ecology and now the CEO of Kamehameha Schools in Hawaii, and his colleagues that family members collectively make sense of the challenges they face. They do so either with the positive attitude that together they can manage stress and change, or with the negative assumption that they are victims. The development of family resilience, as Froma Walsh describes it, is an interactive process over time; in healthy families, members share a deep belief in and commitment to one another—strengths that are reinforced each time they are confronted with and successfully navigate a challenging new situation.

Families have always relied on resilience and perseverance to succeed, but recently, resilience has taken on a new dimension. It is no longer enough just to keep hearth and home together, to nourish and protect the family's physical needs. By itself, stalwart perseverance is insufficient. Now it is equally important to maintain a rich and constant emotional connection between and among the members of a family. Mutual support, open communication, candid expression of feelings, unconditional love—all these give a family the confidence that it can withstand any crisis. And in turbulent times such as these, with almost every family struggling to cope with the enormous social, structural, and demographic changes in our society, the ability to discover and nurture emotional resilience in the face of hardship is now more important than ever.

THE WALLACE FAMILY

As a child growing up in Mississippi, Tony Wallace experienced more than his share of hardship. His resilience and strength of character were tested often, but never more so than on the day he saw his father murdered in his family's home. "The shot came in through the window. And I saw him laying there in a pool of blood, with basically his shoulder torn off," Tony said, by "a shotgun blast at close range."

His mother frantically called 911, but help was slow to get there. "I can remember the ambulance coming down the road—it was two hours late," Tony recalled. After a pause, he added, "He had already bled to death right there on the bedroom floor when the ambulance came."

Tony was three years old.

The paramedics, who were white, "were pretty much jovial when they arrived. They were laughing and joking, things like that," he said. His mother, who had tried in vain to save her husband's life, was "pretty hysterical when they got there. She jumped into one of them, and was kind of pounding his chest because of what had happened, and he just threw her off and kind of knocked her around a little bit. 'Remember who you are' was basically the attitude that they had. You know, you're black and this is Mississippi in 1958."

Some family members believed that the murderer was a jealous husband or a jilted lover. "Apparently Daddy was a ladies' man," Tony explained. His mother moved the family to Indiana after the murder, in hopes that she and her children could find a new start.

But new starts were hard to come by. "Pretty much, she just struggled from there," Tony said. "A lot of poverty, different boyfriends, and things that come with being a single mom trying to find her way. And having all of these children didn't help. Mom was fifteen when she started having babies. She was a baby herself. She was growing up." His mother made a lot of bad choices in the men she took in. Many of them, Tony remembers, "were not good people." Indeed, some were abusive.

And the boyfriends cared little for the well-being of her five children. Some would exploit the family's already meager resources. Tony remembers one of the men in particular, who would regularly eat all the food in the house. "We were on welfare," Tony recalled, with traces of bitterness still lingering after so many years. "He would bring in food for her, and they would go to the room and eat the food. And we could smell the food, but we didn't get any. Sometimes, for us, dinner would become peanut butter on spoons, and we would sit there and eat it like lollipops. Going to school under those conditions wasn't very easy, when you're sitting there trying to learn, and you're starving."

Another boyfriend, Johnny, put Tony's mother in the most turmoil. "She tended to chase him around quite a bit. She got into this mode where she'd try to find out where he was going, and would drag me along with her. I don't know if I was like a security blanket or what. I was in shock mostly." By then Tony was about ten. "We got into some places where we would run into some of his old flames, and there were physical fights. Once she got whupped up pretty good with a pipe by one of the women. I think she broke her arm."

With that kind of childhood, Tony Wallace might have turned out to be pretty disturbed as an adult. Indeed, Tony said his older brother Henry, who also witnessed his father's murder, had many problems as a result. Tony said that he himself, as a teenager, was "a little bit wild" and got into some fights.

Yet today, Tony Wallace is a highly respected community leader and successful businessman in Indianapolis. He has a beautiful and strong family. He is a loving husband and father, and now a proud grandfather of five grandchildren—two of whom are named after him. Tony Wallace exemplifies the ability to rebound from potential disaster; his inner strength and resilience enabled him to triumph over adverse conditions.

So how did this product of a fatherless, unstable home—plagued by poverty, hunger, and violence—somehow find the ability to survive, and then prevail? Part of the answer is that someone came into Tony's life who developed a positive relationship with his mother, helped her stabilize her family, and served as a role model for Tony. "His name is Herman Washington," Tony says. "He's my hero. He's the best man in the world, as far as I'm concerned." He and Tony's mother married just before Tony started high school and have been together ever since.

The real turning point, however, came when he met Linda—to whom he has been married for twenty-eight years. When they met in a high school art class, they were almost exact opposites in temperament. Linda remembers that Tony was always getting into trouble in class, "because he would turn around and talk to me. So I said to the teacher, 'Just put him behind me.' I had more control; he had none." Soon thereafter, Tony began to change. "She kind of took me under her wing and settled me down. Things just got better as we went along," Tony said, nodding toward Linda. "Mainly because of her."

He fell in love not only with Linda but also with the strength of her family. "I didn't have any idea about some of the things that children are supposed to have, until I met Linda," he said. "I could not believe how fantastic her family was, from the grandparents on down to the cousins. Everybody seemed so close."

Tony says he learned most of what he now knows about fatherhood and character from Linda's family, particularly her maternal grandfather, Lafayette Whitney, "one fantastic guy who made a big difference in my life. I didn't know at that time what the role of a man was," he said. "Didn't have a clue. I learned so much."

Lafayette Whitney was the patriarch of Linda's extended family. Everyone looked to him as an example of the righteousness and moral fiber that they felt he had instilled in the whole family. "He was my role model," Linda said. "I thought if there was anyone in the world I could pattern my life after, it was him." Tony also recognized Lafayette's great character the first time he met him. "He was like the glue in the family."

Tony began spending a lot of time with Lafayette, and began to understand the ways in which Linda was carrying on his example. The positive influence of Linda and her family actively nurtured the resilience and the optimism that was deep inside Tony's spirit. It was the combination of that basic resilience and the encouragement from her family that enabled Tony to discover the courage and determination to create a strong and successful family.

There was no doubt in Tony's mind that the kind of family he wanted would require a lot of work. According to Tony, "I was going to be there for my children no matter what. They would have a strong man in the house, a provider in the house, and I would share with them all of the things that I missed in my life growing up."

Tony and Linda arranged to work split shifts at their jobs so that their children would always have a loving parent available to them. "We've never in our lives had to pay a baby-sitter, because one of us was always there," he said. Indeed, Tony was committed to fulfilling every aspect of parenting to the fullest, rejecting the notion that there were roles or responsibilities that fathers should leave only to mothers. "I've changed the diapers, I've used the bottle. I figure I'm as strong as they come, and I don't think it takes anything away from my manhood. I'm a parent. I'm a father. It's my responsiblity to nurture as well as to be the strong protector."

It is not uncommon for someone who spent his childhood in a weak or dysfunctional family to try to build in his new family the kind of strength and stability that he never had. Linda, who is highly disciplined and goal-oriented, somehow transmitted to Tony what she carried within her—the resilience and strength of character that can come from a stable and loving family. And she, in turn, says that her decision to model her approach to life and family after her grandfather is the basis for that resilience, determination, and loyalty for which she is now generally known by her family and friends.

Linda Wallace has always had an inner strength. As a child, she took on major responsibilities at home because her mother didn't want to run the household or do any work. "My mother was a spoiled child. She really was," Linda said. "I love her, but I used to always want to jump in her body for a minute and take over. I cooked and cleaned, and I can remember standing on a doggone box doing dishes because I wasn't big enough to reach the sink. And between my older sister and I, we took care of the house, we did the laundry, and we did everything, because those were things that my mother just didn't do."

Both of her parents were young when she was born, particularly her mother, and when Linda and her sister got a little older, "We were more like her friends, instead of her being our mother. We just kind of helped raise her. Our father would go to work, and he didn't understand why she wasn't doing things, and then you'd hear the bickering start."

Her grandparents on her mother's side, Lafayette and Rivers Whitney, had a major influence on her life, but her other grandparents were more distant. Her paternal grandmother treated Linda differently than her two sisters—apparently because Linda's skin was darker than theirs. "My two sisters are real fair-skinned," Linda explained. "And my father's father was born in Paris, France. So he always has this thing where he says he's not a black man but a black Frenchman. So his wife, my grandmother, always thought I was not my father's child."

They all attended the same church and her grandmother would always greet her sisters warmly as they entered the pew. But when it was Linda's turn to be greeted, "Every Sunday she would go, 'Now, who are you? Which one are you?' Until she died, it was, 'Who are you?' It got so bad that some of the other people in church would say, 'Now, you know that's your granddaughter. That's Linda!'"

The experience was searing, but she turned the pain into a source of strength and resilience with the help of one of her maternal great-grandmothers, Catherine Austin, who patiently counseled her. "She used to always tell me, 'Don't ever get upset like that, because if you let things like that hurt you inside, it messes you up!'" She also learned from her great-grandmother Austin that she should not respond in kind because life is full of "every kind of hurt, racial hurts, and just people in general who try to hurt you." Her great-grandmother told her she shouldn't worry about hurtful comments because in the afterlife God will exact the appropriate vengeance on the wrongdoers. She gave young Linda a feeling of peace and justice by assuring her that Grandmother Tyler's hatefulness toward her would surely be punished. "She used to tell me, 'That's okay, because she's got to pay for that.'"

Tony has lighter skin than Linda, and after hearing this story, we asked if Linda's darker complexion was an issue with his family before the wedding. Tony said, "No" at the same moment that Linda much more firmly said, "Yes." They both laughed and Linda continued: "That's why his mother did not want him to marry me." By the time the children were born, Linda no longer noticed any remnant of that attitude.

Linda found the strength she needed, thanks to some loving family members, as well as, in great part, her religious faith. Tony, too, found support in his religious faith, in the support of the family as a whole, in his community, and, belatedly, in his own birth family, when his mother married Herman Washington. He also found it in his relationship to Linda and in the strength of the commitment they made to each other.

Perhaps more remarkably, Tony used his pain as a source of inspiration. "It wasn't the best childhood in the world," he says, with considerable understatement. "I think that's one of the reasons I was determined to always be there for my children. I was determined that they wouldn't have to go through all the things I went through."

RESPONDING TO CRISIS AND TRANSITION

Despite the vital role resilience plays in supporting families, it is surprisingly under-recognized as a quality that one can and should nurture. As children, we all learned the virtues of honesty, cooperation, sharing, open-mindedness, and perseverance. As we grow up, we learn that adhering to these values serves us well in our relationships with people. But we are rarely taught to nurture the quality of resilience for its own sake.

Thankfully, we can learn resilience even when it is not specifically taught. Tipper remembers as a child having to cope with
some of the emotional and social challenges of having divorced
parents in the 1950s, when it was hardly as common or accepted as
it is today. At a time when the family ideal was a *Father Knows Best*
stereotype, with two parents—Dad working and Mom staying
home—Tipper often felt very different living primarily in a family
made up of three generations of women (after her grandfather
passed away)—herself, her mother, and her grandmother. It
required more adjusting to stepbrothers and stepsisters across
town after her father remarried.

While such a situation is hardly unusual today, at the time it
made Tipper feel that her family was going against the grain and
that she was an outsider. On the one hand, she felt the typical
childhood guilt that she must have somehow caused the trouble
between the adults that led to her family being so unusual for the
times. Yet she also felt a lot of love coming from each of her family
members to support her. Even as a little girl struggling with how to
deal with the situation, she had the benefit of role models in her
mother and grandmother, women who found their own sources of
inner strength and the courage to forge their own paths in life,
despite societal disapproval. Tipper feels that in many ways she
developed resilience because she was forced to, just as her grandmother and mother were forced to—and because she intuited that
she had to trust herself to embrace the challenges life presented
and use them to make her stronger. She was taught "Your problems
can be your best friends if you learn and grow from them" and "Get
back on the horse if you're thrown off" and "Get up and smile in
the face of adversity."

While persistence and resolve are a large part of resilience,
sometimes the solution to a problem isn't always "Try, try again."
Sometimes the way forward is to step back, look at the situation
from a new perspective, think deeply about what matters most,
and then find a new way to honor and be true to those values and

priorities. Oftentimes resilience simply comes from deep within. It can be something you develop unconsciously or something you quietly accumulate in the process of overcoming the challenges with which you have been presented. An early researcher studying resilience, psychiatrist Michael Rutter, suggested that it arises out of a "belief in one's own self-efficacy and ability to deal with change . . . [and] a repertoire of social problem-solving skills." University of California at Davis child-development psychologist and professor emeritus Emmy Werner and her colleagues also found that close bonds with a caring, supportive adult helped children develop self-esteem and problem-solving abilities.

Susan Fadley told us that she thinks she learned resilience in college, when she somehow found within herself "just how to bounce back, how to deal with things, little things that happen. How to keep your family intact, when there are little bumps, and not totally lose it." She acknowledged that sometimes "you totally lose it every once in a while," but then you find a way to get perspective on the situation. After her divorce, Susan had long conversations with her minister, who encouraged her to think deeply about what had helped her get through the tough times in her childhood and as a young adult. She finally realized that at the toughest times in her life, "I kept hearing a voice saying that it's going to be okay. It's going to be okay. Not from a living person, but I just kept hearing it. I just think that I had a connection somehow, some way, and I really, truly believe it was the Lord helping me."

Wherever it comes from, resilience is required not only when there is a dramatic crisis. It's often required during the normal family transitions that just about everyone experiences: marriage, childbirth, the coming-of-age of children, and children's separation as they move to form families of their own. After all, every family, no matter how constant it may appear, is in a continuous state of change. In a way, looking at a family over time is like standing on the seashore and watching the ocean swell, then break, then swell again. Each wave is different and brings a different swirl of change, but the ocean itself remains a lasting force—always there and always in motion. In much the same way, successful families experience wave after wave of change but retain their strength and consistency.

It's also true that any major change in the life of one family member almost always brings about a significant change in the family as a whole, as when Tony Wallace's mother met Herman Washington. Moreover, most transitions bring simultaneous changes to several family members at once, causing the emergence of new patterns of interaction that can seem radically different. The deterioration in the quality of an emotional bond between two people in a family, such as in the case of a divorce, can radically alter every other relationship in the family, shifting the balance and requiring each member to find a new level of comfort and a new way of interacting with the others. Sometimes roles within the family may be completely reversed, with a new principal breadwinner or with a new leader of the family emerging. This may, in turn, lead to significant changes in the roles and duties of everyone else.

The most significant transitions are often those that result in a change in the daily composition of a family, when a new member of the family is added to the household or when one leaves. These transitions may occur for happy reasons—such as a marriage, or a birth or adoption, or a remarriage that adds members to a family, or from the graduation of a child from high school, if that leads her to leave the parental home. Or they may result from separation or divorce—which can be the equivalent of a personal earthquake of devastating proportions that has an enormous impact on the child or children. Even an amicable divorce has a profound effect on the children because of changes in family relationships, residences, and financial conditions that it sets in motion. Alternatively, the changes may come about because of the evolving needs of family members, such as when an elderly family member begins to require more day-to-day assistance, and moves in with one of the adult children. Or they may come as the result of tragedy, such as when the death of a family member leaves a void in the daily rhythms of the family. At such times, many families turn to religious traditions, which have developed rituals for dealing with loss that help the family come together, talk about and share the loss, commemorate it, and move forward.

Whatever the cause, and whatever the emotions that accompany the transition, all such changes in the daily fabric of family life have the potential to induce stress. Stress is cumulative; as a result, sometimes even the small amounts of stress generated by a transition can become the straw that breaks the camel's back—by increasing the cumulative stress load beyond an individual's or a family's ability to deal with it.

Fortunately, though, some of these transitions can be anticipated and even planned for. Probably the most respected authority on the natural stages of an individual's life is the late psychoanalyst Erik Erikson, who persuasively argued that every person passes through up to eight psychosocial stages, each of which is associated with a different challenge that needs resolution. Erikson emphasized that the way each challenge was resolved had a profound impact on whether or not an individual could move successfully through the next stage. Our research into families leads us to believe that families must also navigate predictable transitions or passages from one stage to the next. And as with individuals, the way a given challenge is resolved—or not resolved—has a direct effect on the family's ability to grow.

For simplicity's sake, we think of a family as an ever evolving entity that experiences a four-season life cycle. The first season is marked by a family's *formation*, when spouses or partners decide to join together. The second season occurs when a family enters a period of *productivity* by having and raising children, or by focusing their energies on productive endeavors. In the third season, as the children mature and begin to separate from the family of origin, both generations find *independence* from the primary nurturing relationship that has bound them to each other. In the final season, the family of origin, having reached the last stage of its life, watches the cycle begin again and focuses on *generativity*—a concern for future generations.

Each of these seasons or stages tests a family's resilience. Of course, success is not guaranteed at any stage and, unfortunately, failure to handle one transition may make failure at the next more likely. But the good news is that every transition a family navigates successfully makes the family stronger and enriches it with a larger storehouse of shared experiences, gives its members a deeper understanding of one another, and ensures a greater likelihood of successfully managing future waves of disruptive change with stability, security, comfort, and grace. Even a weak family bond can grow much stronger if a stern test of its strength forges closer cooperation. And even the most difficult and disorienting transition can bring with it great opportunities for positive transformation and growth.

FAMILY FORMATION

One of the biggest transitions in the life of any family is the first one—the *formation* of a new family unit, when two individuals come together and join in a committed relationship. The conscious act of commitment to each other, the decision to join hearts and become a family, is a momentous one that changes the internal dynamics of the relationship that existed prior to that mutual commitment.

Pat Letke-Alexander, for example, told us that after she and Todd married, it was a big emotional change for her when she realized that she could no longer sometimes say to Todd, "No, I don't feel like getting together today," because every single day he was "very much a part of my life." When Todd reminded her that she never told him to stay away even before they were married, Pat rejoined, "Yes, but I had the option." After their marriage, Pat said she realized that "I had just committed to this person for the long haul, and I know that I approached the relationship very differently looking at it through those glasses."

Even the growing number of couples who live together before making a conscious decision to commit to each other as long-term partners may note a transition in the dynamic of their relationship once they have taken their vows. This happened with Gabrielle and Chris Wagener. Committed couples usually feel a newfound security, but they experience other changes as well—some of them expected and some that come as a shock.

A complete change in living arrangements, for example, can be disorienting. When Chris and Gabrielle moved from a town house in Washington, D.C., to a suburban neighborhood in Birmingham, Alabama, the change affected Chris more than he thought it would. In some ways it was startling.

Chris recalled one day when the reality of his new life hit him. "It's just kind of a weird revelation for me. I'm going to be twenty-nine in January, and here I am standing out on my front lawn in this suburban hell. . . . We used to be this young, vibrant couple in Washington, D.C., and the next thing you know I've got a garden hose in my hand and I'm watering the lawn, waving hello to my neighbor Bob, and thinking, 'What has happened?' "

Upon marriage, partners expect to feel changes in terms of their legal status, their financial situation, and their sense of identity. But, unexpectedly, they may also experience tension between the allegiance they feel they still owe to their birth families and the commitment they have made to their newly formed family. This can come into play as couples start to worry about their aging parents. One spouse may need to devote significant amounts of time to care for an aging parent—or even want him or her to come live with them—while the other spouse wants to spend time forging the new nuclear family together. Young couples may simply feel a need or obligation to spend time with their birth families, but also to carve out time together—much the way Laura and Eduardo Cortes did when they finally decided, after a few years of marriage, that they needed to move away so they could bond as a couple and a nuclear family. And as with any significant life transition, new couples may feel the stress of the outward change in their inner emotional state and in the nature of their outlook on life.

The couple may also discover that they had seemingly slight—but in reality, significant—differences concerning their expectations for the marriage. There are a lot of issues for a new couple to resolve, from the mundane details of housekeeping to larger issues such as where they will live, how they'll set up their finances, and (especially for women) whether they'll change their last name.

As couples navigate these transitions, it is important that they remember and remain true to the love that brought them together in the first place, according to University of California at Berkeley psychologists Carolyn and Philip Cowan. It is crucial that they find ways to communicate openly and honestly with each other about their feelings and thoughts concerning these issues as they arise. Even if the pleasant afterglow of their newlywed status enables them to sail through all these potential tensions, the underlying stress the issues cause may not completely go away. Indeed, many marriages end during the first year, at least in part due to the emotional turbulence created by so many changes taking place at the same time.

PRODUCTIVITY

One of the most intense transitions for any couple is the birth of their first child, which begins the stage we call productivity. Productivity is not only about having children; it is about raising them while they are entirely dependent. And productivity, in this sense, is not only for couples that give birth to or adopt children. For couples that don't have children this season is about channeling their energy into creative endeavors or community services, or starting a business. The hectic nature of this period—families are usually busiest during this stage—produces more challenges than ever, because of the centrifugal forces that now pull them apart, including the longer hours at work and the attendant negotiation needed to redefine traditional parenting roles and duties between partners.

Once a couple does decide to conceive or adopt a child, it can be a time of great adventure and closeness for them. Like millions of couples, we found experiencing the birth of our child together was a very important bonding experience. And like many others, we prepared for this experience by taking lessons together in the Lamaze childbirth technique. For us, it was a chance to participate together in the entire process, and to learn a new way of approaching the birth of a child that had been unknown to any previous generation in either of our families. The birth experience itself was profound, exhilarating, exhausting, spiritual, and euphoric. Tipper described it as "the best church service I ever attended." What we learned (and the time we spent together learning it) vastly enhanced our shared joy during our transition from a family of two to a family of three. In the process, we also discovered new things about each other that we appreciated and found some strengths in each other that we hadn't known we had.

Each of the four births we experienced together was miraculous in its intensity, and each brought us closer together. As a result, we emerged from each experience with a stronger and more intimate relationship. Moreover, there is no question that the strength we added to our family bonds during these transitions turned out to be needed and was put to good use during other, less happy times that tested our family's resilience.

It's important to pay extra attention to a couple's relationship after their baby is born because of the profound change it brings to the emotional dynamic. When each partner suddenly gets less attention from the other, that can create a feeling of emotional neglect—even if the reasons for it are perfectly rational and understandable. Some couples don't handle that shift as well as others.

For example, some men who have depended emotionally on an intense relationship with their wives can be thrown for a loop by the sudden loss of attention—attention that is now devoted to the baby. By the same token, some new mothers who are not emotionally prepared for the intensity of the mother-infant relationship have great difficulty adjusting to it while simultaneously attending to the relationship with their husbands. More than a few new mothers find the transition immeasurably more difficult if they also experience postpartum depression, a phenomenon that is normally relatively mild but can in some cases be quite severe. No matter the emotional need, after the baby's birth, neither spouse can single-mindedly devote his or her attention, love, and time to the other.

One other unanticipated effect of the birth of a child is that it may cause the partners to drift toward more traditional roles—even in "peer marriages," where tasks and responsibilities had been shared more or less evenly. Understandably, the parents may find themselves frustrated by the traditional roles they end up adopting. According to Heather Helms-Erickson, assistant professor in the Department of Human Development and Family Studies at the University of North Carolina at Greensboro, the timing of when a couple has its first child can influence how the couple divides household chores. Numerous studies have found that the younger a couple is when it has its first child, the more likely that couple will be to follow traditional divisions of household labor. On the other hand, the older a couple is when they become parents, the more likely they are to adopt a more collaborative division of labor, because the women are more likely to have a career.

Another interesting finding comes from Carolyn and Philip Cowan, who maintain that when young parents begin to have serious problems soon after their first baby is born and their young family starts to fall apart, it is almost never the arrival of the baby itself that causes the marital problems. Their research shows that the seeds of those problems were almost always sown long before.

Indeed, they discovered that couples who reported the most marital difficulty after having a baby tend to be the same ones who were experiencing the most strain in their relationships before they became parents; and the couples who felt that they had productive ways of working out their differences reported the least dissatisfaction and distress in the first few years of parenthood. Many couples who are having problems trick themselves into believing that if they have a child things will get better. Invariably, just the opposite happens. Dawn Hancock, for example, told us that shortly after she became pregnant, her then husband suddenly started accusing her of having "tricked him into marrying" her. Ten minutes after they came out of the delivery room, she says, he told her he wanted another baby. But just eight months later, he effectively ended their marriage.

Jay and Margo Strong of Holt, Michigan, who have two children, both of whom are adopted, told us about an even bigger challenge they faced during their first transition to having a baby in the house. Like most adoptive parents, they noticed that for them the transition was sharper and more sudden because they did not go through the nine-month process of pregnancy and all the gradual changes—personal and social—that accompany it.

"When you have a baby naturally, you have time to prepare. You know, you can actually see the mom getting bigger," said Jay. "With an adoption, it's like you have no baby, nothing, you're just doing your regular life. And then all of a sudden, one day you have a baby! It's different. It's almost like you didn't have the time to mentally prepare, even though you think you are prepared, and then when you actually get the child in your arms, all of a sudden, it's there. It's just kind of a shock. It's like this sudden realization when you're holding this child, 'Okay, now I have this child for the rest of my life.' "

With both adoption and biological birth, so much attention is paid to the arrival of the first child and to the transition from "none to one" that sometimes families are not prepared for the bracing challenge that accompanies the arrival of subsequent children. To begin with, the relationship between the first child and the second is very important for the whole family—and can depend heavily on how well the parents manage the emotional transition for their first child and prepare him or her for the sudden presence of a sibling, with whom he or she will have to compete for the parents' attention and affection.

Margo Strong told us that when they adopted their second child, Anna, their son, Nick, was at first quite nonchalant. They introduced her and told him, "This is Anna, your sister." His initial reaction was "Oh, okay," Margo said. But Anna was a colicky baby and spent most of her first few days at home crying. "One day, he looks at us and goes, 'How long is she going to stay here?' "

In adopting Nick and Anna, Margo and Jay had two different experiences that demonstrate some of the changes occurring in adoption practices these days. Each of the biological mothers selected Jay and Margo through the adoption agency as the parents to adopt her baby. The first time, when they adopted Nick, the Strongs were only given very basic general information about the birth mother, but never met her or learned her name, and have not had any contact with her over the years. When they adopted Anna, however, they actually met the woman before the birth, had lunch with her, and then saw her in the hospital the day after Anna was born. Although they are not in touch directly with one another, they have maintained contact over the years. Anna's birth mother periodically sends things to Anna. The Strongs, in turn, send Anna's birth mother pictures of Anna and information about her.

As children grow and develop, each new stage creates yet another transition. The terrible twos, for example, are legendary for their potential to cause stress in the family system. Couples who have found it difficult to cope with the transition of childbirth and the transformation from a family of two to a family of three sometimes enter the terrible twos in a weakened and exhausted state, and may be especially vulnerable to conflict with each other when the typically difficult temperament manifested in many two-year-olds takes the family to the breaking point.

One of America's leading experts on child development, Dr. T. Berry Brazelton, describes "touchpoints" that infants and toddlers experience. He sees these as particularly challenging but also fruitful times when children are learning and mastering new tasks. Much as these touchpoints are pivotal points for children, we as families also go through any number of touchpoints, such as dealing with intense sibling rivalry or a child's first day of school. These are times of change, but if we realize that these are also times of incredible potential that offer the chance for growth, we can embrace them with courage and with determination to use them to strengthen our families and our ability to tackle new challenges together.

INDEPENDENCE

In most families, the typhoon of transitions is the onset of puberty, which often brings dramatic changes in family relationships as your children morph into teenagers before your eyes. Other than the first year of life, this is the period of a child's development that produces the most rapid growth and the most far-reaching series of changes. And all too often, as the adolescent child's internal equilibrium is thrown into a chaotic state, so too is the equilibrium of the family system. As any parent of a teenager knows, every relationship in the family changes as a result, and resilience is put to a stern test.

The turbulence comes in part because both the child's transformation in puberty and the young adult's departure from home are part of a healthy individuation process. It is a process in which both the birth family and the child-who-is-no-longer-a-child become independent of the primary nurturing bond, and it marks the beginning of a new season of independence for the family as a whole. (It's worth noting, however, that the young adult's separation and departure from his family is not universal; rather, it is particularly marked in mainstream American culture. In traditional Latin American cultures, departure may not occur until marriage. In traditional Chinese culture, there is also no such marked separation between a mother and her son, Jose Szapocznik said.)

Each of our children had his or her own way of separating from the family, as they spent more time with his or her friends. We recognized that they each behaved according to his or her own personality, and dealt with each difficult transition differently. When Karenna became a teenager, for example, her relationship with us definitely changed. She became much more rebellious and tried to buck our parental authority to see how far she could push the boundaries. The emotional skirmishes quickly settled into trench warfare along either side of the most assaulted boundary line: the curfew. She also began to spend less time with her younger siblings, causing them to recalibrate their patterns of play.

Even though all parents know in advance that the challenges of puberty and the teen years will come, most don't feel ready when they arrive. Laura Cortes, whose daughter, Bela, was about to turn twelve when we visited the family, told us, "Nobody prepared me for how early they start getting what I call the 'teenager attitude.' Oh, my God. You know, I just assumed that somehow a switch got flipped at thirteen, and I just wasn't ready when it happened sooner. You see little glimpses of it at ten, and then it just gets progressively more and more apparent."

When Bela started testing her limits, Laura told us that she spoke very directly to her daughter about what was happening. "I didn't want Bela to be at all confused about our relationship, so I told her, 'Your job as a teenager is to push toward your freedom and independence, and that's totally correct. That's what should be happening. But our job as parents is to push it the other way and make sure you understand that there are consequences to any actions that you take.'"

She said she and Eduardo are often surprised by Bela's precocious assertion of independence, and they compare her "teenager attitude" to their own teenage experiences. "I would never have talked to my parents the way Bela sometimes talks to us," Eduardo said. "But then we always realize she's living a very different reality from our reality, and those allowances have to be put into place," Laura added.

Eduardo and Laura's fond remembrance of their own adolescence in a time that seemed more innocent is no doubt partially nostalgic, but it is also true that the task of raising teenagers has grown increasingly complex. For one thing, the age of puberty has actually been dropping significantly. Over the last hundred or so years, the average age that girls begin menstruating has dropped from approximately fifteen to twelve, with some girls exhibiting other signs of puberty as early as nine or ten years old. The overall declining trend is similar for boys, although boys reach puberty on average about two years later than girls. As a result, children are having to deal with these often confusing physical changes long before they are emotionally or intellectually ready.

For many reasons, an uncomfortable gawkiness can overtake the relationship between boys and girls at this age. Our daughter Kristin remembers, "Thirteen was no fun, because I still had braces. I felt very gangly, and I was in a new school. I remember fourteen getting better." And when both boys and girls get older, some of the gawkiness can show up in the father of the girls. Each of our girls' first boyfriend represented a significant transition for them—and sometimes a traumatic one for Al.

Laura and Eduardo Cortes, who are watching their children grow up rapidly, are amazed by the differences they see. "They're both trying so desperately to make their own mark," Laura observed, adding that it is both wonderful and strange to see your children maturing before your eyes. Both parents love talking with the children about school and the world as a whole because "their observations are so different."

Conflicts between teens and parents can spill over into the relationship between the parents. Not only can the tensions of dealing with a teenager exacerbate differences between parents, it can also simply rob them of the time and energy they need to invest in their own relationship as a married couple. After all, relating to a rebellious teenager can be emotionally exhausting.

Another test of resilience for the entire family is when a child leaves home, whether to go to college or for some other reason. The parents' excitement at having their child begin a new phase of life is mixed with sadness that their "baby" is moving on. And younger siblings who have come to rely on the departing sibling for mediation with the parents or for daily advice can feel particularly wounded by the departure. In our family, Kristin's departure for college was especially tough on Sarah—who was suddenly left home without her big sister and best friend. The night before Kristin left for college, Sarah wrote her a note that Kristin still keeps to this day.

Kristin,
You're going away to college tomorrow and I can't stop crying. I'm so proud of you, and I always knew you'd do whatever you set your mind to. I don't think you realize how much I'll miss you. How much I value your opinion, your advice, and your respect. How much I love your humor. How much I love being around you. How much I love you. You are my best friend and now that you're leaving, I worry that things are never going to be the same anymore. I just imagine running into your room at night—itching to tell you something and finding only your empty bed. Sure I can call you, but it's not the same. I'll just have to visit ALL the time.

. . . Sarah

GENERATIVITY

When the last child leaves home, the transition for the parent or parents is especially challenging. It marks the beginning of a season of *generativity*, when thoughts turn to what can be done for future generations. This "empty nest" stage of life is relatively new in our history because it was not until the last century that it became common for parents to be left alone. In earlier times, larger families with children of a wide age range, coupled with shorter life expectancy, provided little opportunity for middle-aged parents to live alone in the home, Tamara Hareven said.

A couple facing an empty nest has to learn or relearn ways to relate to each other without the constant presence of children. In many ways it is a mirror image of the transition they went through when the first child was born. Martha Farrell Erickson, director of the University of Minnesota's Children, Youth, and Family Consortium, advises couples to revisit the relationship they had before their lives were organized around the children and celebrate their new time together. The renewal of the primary relationship in a family does more than benefit the couple. Erickson says, "One of the best gifts you can give your young adult children is the example of a strong, loving, playful relationship."

But for some couples or individuals, there is a great feeling of loss, which can result in sadness, grief, or even depression. According to Shelley Bovey, author of *The Empty Nest: When Children Leave Home*, the moment a child leaves home can represent either a longed-for liberation or an irredeemable loss, for women in particular. Just as a child faces a shift in his primary identity, from being a member of a family to being a member of society at large, some empty-nest parents who have identified themselves primarily in terms of raising their children can suddenly face identity confusion when the children are no longer there. It is no mystery why some couples drift apart during this stage of their marriage, particularly those who have been "holding it together for the children," consciously or unconsciously. But as Bovey also observed, during the empty nest stage, "many couples find renewed vigor in their relationship and enjoy the opportunity to have the house to themselves, to do things again as a couple, and to share in the pleasure and sense of achievement of having done the job of parenting well."

We became empty nesters just last year, when our youngest child went off to college, and it has indeed been a significant change for us. But along with the sadness, we have been pleasantly surprised at how much we have enjoyed this transition. In particular, the freedom to leave home for days at a time without making detailed arrangements for the children has enabled us to do more traveling together.

In addition to facing the now abnormally tranquil house, empty nesters must also confront their own aging, since having grown children is certainly one reminder that the years are flying by. As the baby boomers reach midlife, middle-aged Americans are the fastest-growing age group. But it's also true that the better health care and longer life spans have led to the happy trend of "down-aging"—the phenomenon illustrated by the fact that today's eighty-year-olds feel comparable in well-being to sixty-year-olds two generations ago. Significantly, in a recent survey by the National Council on Aging, 40 percent of people ages sixty-five to seventy-four said they considered themselves middle-aged, and 26 percent of those seventy-five or older called themselves middle-aged.

Rodney Crumpton, for one, has discovered the rewards of generativity in his vibrant relationship with his grandson Caleb. Rodney is thriving in his middle age more than ever before in his life. "We are at the peak of our wisdom right now. They call me 'the oracle.' I want to do something with it now before it starts going down hill at sixty-five. I am at peak decision-making ability now." He wants very much to find a good job after completing his college degree so that he can continue to provide a positive example of success to his sons and grandsons. He told us proudly that little Caleb said to him recently, "You are the first to graduate, Oompa, but I will be the smartest."

For women, of course, midlife brings menopause. Fortunately, understanding of menopause has increased dramatically in recent decades, and this knowledge is empowering. But there is still insufficient awareness of how it can affect the family as a whole. When Tipper went through menopause, for instance, she had trouble with her memory. It got so bad that she finally called the whole family together, listed the symptoms of menopause, and said that she was experiencing all of them. She still remembers one night when Albert cracked up laughing because her memory was so bad. The kids also got a kick out of what Tipper fondly liked to call "word-search." It was as if her brain couldn't think critically anymore about the meaning of individual words, but could only think of categories of words. Tipper compared it to playing charades with people during casual conversation—except that they don't know the game is on. Again, education and communication enabled Tipper to get the support she needed from within the family and demysti-fied menopause.

One of the unique joys of middle age is the special sweetness and mellowness of a growing friendship with children who become adults. We have certainly experienced this phenomenon with the three of our children who have graduated from college and begun to make their way in the world. And we are beginning the same transition with our youngest, who is starting his second year in col-lege. The candor and depth of communication in such relation-ships is often exceeded only by that between couples.

Of course, the arrival of grandchildren is perhaps the happiest and least stressful transition of all, mainly because it has such a high "joy-to-hassle" ratio. We now appreciate the bumper sticker that says, "If we'd known grandchildren were so much fun, we'd have had them first." It is gratifying to have the opportunity to share that feeling with the other grandparent or grandparents and watch the creation of your family taken to the next level. We have loved sharing this joy with our son-in-law Drew's parents, David and Lisa Schiff, and Lisa and Tipper frequently e-mail each other with news about Wyatt or Anna.

Even as middle age brings changes in one's relationship with children and grandchildren, it also represents a transition in the relationship with one's parents. From the standpoint of adult children, the establishment of a new, equal relationship with older parents as they enter another stage of their lives can, in some cases, be surprisingly difficult. The awareness that death is closer than birth inspires many to reflect, and then act in new ways, according to Marc Freedman, the author of *Prime Time: How Baby Boomers Will Revolutionize Retirement and Transform America*. At middle age, we not only confront the reality of our own mortality, but those of us with aging parents have found that there are a host of other issues that must be resolved. These include how to communicate with loved ones about needs: medicine, loneliness, love, forgetfulness, selling the house, etc. Working through all these issues can be extremely difficult for everyone involved, as psychologist Mary Pipher, the author of *Another Country: Navigating the Emotional Terrain of Our Elders*, points out.

Declining health further complicates the relationship with one's parents. Americans are living longer than ever before, and ever higher numbers of families are involved in providing long-term care for aging parents. In many cases, prolonged periods of illness or infirmity mean that the elderly need the help and support of family members or an institution. Some 40 percent of caregivers are currently helping an aging parent, and that percentage is expected to increase as the baby boomers retire. In the future, elder care could well overtake child care as a primary family responsibility. The transition to parenting your own parents can be very delicate. After spending so much time looking up to your parents as strong and indomitable figures, it can be disconcerting to begin seeing them as dependents. Accepting this new position is also difficult for the elderly parents. It may be stressful for them to pass on to their children the responsibilities for their financial affairs as well as their health and long-term care arrangements—but it also can lead to a very tender, rewarding phase of the relationship, as the parents allow themselves to *be* parented.

As we move from one season in life to the next, it's important to remember that it is transitions that test the resilience of families. Yet most members of strong families know they must be there for one another, even when a person—regardless of his or her age—may seem exceedingly difficult or irrational or hard to be around. Life's inevitable transitions test our constancy, even as they help us accept changes in the people we love and in our relationships to them.

EMOTIONAL RESILIENCE IN FAMILIES

In addition to having to deal with the predictable transitions in the life cycle, at some point most families will have to face a crisis or event for which they're completely unprepared. During such moments, members of a family mobilize instinctively by reaching out for one another, because in a time of crisis there is a deep need to be connected and honored by the people who make up our own family. For most families, a time of crisis puts their emotional resilience to a harrowing test. On the most basic level, the way we as individuals and families deal with predictable transitions and unexpected crises is the same, but there are some crucial distinctions to make. For example, when we're aware of an upcoming change, such as becoming parents for the first time, a certain amount of psychological and emotional preparation takes place. But no amount of preparation could have helped young Tony Wallace, for example, be better able to cope with the murder of his father. Experiencing such a trauma is where emotional resilience really comes into play.

At times like these, we need to be flexible enough to adjust quickly to the unexpected, which, of course, is easier said than done. One unpredictable event, all too common these days, is sudden job loss. In addition to financial stress, the family may be buffeted by powerful emotional and psychological forces. Since many breadwinners have a sense of self that is based on their work, that identity may be shaken by the loss of a job. Ellen Galinsky, cofounder of the Families and Work Institute, says that such an event "affects not only your daily routine, but it affects how you're living, and the money that you have. It also affects your sense of identity, because all of us have at least part of our identity in who we are at work."

Children are especially affected and should receive special attention during this time. In fact, parents should use the adversity as an opportunity to teach children how to cope with difficult changes. Galinsky adds, "I know that's a real burden when families are going through such a tough time, but it's better if you can try to show your kids how to cope. . . . Show them the plans that you're making or that you may feel upset, but you're working on it. . . . [T]here are studies that show that this can affect the children but it depends on how we present it to them. We can present it as a story on coping and a story on dealing with tough things— and all lives contain those tough things—or we can present it as a story of defeat, or anger, or despair, and I hope that those aren't the lessons that we give our children."

Whatever the issue, a tradition of open communication between family members is invaluable. Dominic Cappello told us, "The families that can talk about their feelings are the ones that tend to have better tools to cope when bad things happen. These are tools that help a child through life. That leads to a resilient child, which leads to a resilient adult, which leads to a resilient parent."

In the same way that emotional resilience can help families cope with a sudden change in the family's finances, it can also help them deal with the death of a loved one. Of course, when you are aware that a person in your family is likely to die from his or her illness, it's best if you can prepare your children and yourself and then help the person leave this world and have the time to say what needs to be said. Although death and loss are never to be underestimated, when the death is unexpected or due to accident, it is obviously much harder to cope with. Let's face it: explaining to our children that we die is one of the most difficult teaching challenges for families. Facing the fact that we must die is one of the hardest truths about living. Fortunately, a lot of useful information about the grieving process is available from organizations like Hospice, which takes a holistic approach to the family. Hospice realizes that preparing for the death of a family member can be a much more complicated and difficult transition than anyone realizes, until they go through it themselves.

Regardless of the age at which it happens, the death of a parent, for example, can cause enormous ripple effects throughout the family and redefine roles and relationships throughout the extended family. Even as they grieve, adults with children must think about the effect of their parents' death on their children. When Tipper's mother died, the children got together and decided that Sarah, our third daughter, would give her eulogy because she had developed an especially close relationship with Anyha. In her remarks, Sarah shared the life lessons that Anyha had shared with her over the years; Anyha would often even encourage Sarah to take notes. During one such conversation, Anyha told Sarah about five guiding principles for cultivating balance in life. The last principle was "Let go and let God."

Al lost his father four years ago, just three weeks before his ninety-first birthday. We knew beforehand that his death was approaching, so we talked about it as a family and began preparing the children. As the time drew nearer, all the children came to Tennessee over Thanksgiving to be with their grandfather and to comfort their grandmother Pauline. Each child spent time alone with him, telling him stories, rubbing his shoulders, and holding his hand. Karenna told him she was pregnant with his first great-grandchild, and he understood and was so happy. He loved each of his grandchildren fiercely, and his passing was a mighty roar in their lives, which they heard clearly because they were all at peace.

The hospice professionals helped all of us by providing timely and healing information about the dying process and making it possible for Al's father to die at home. Al held his father's hand for the final hours of his life, talking him gently home. In our family, Al's father was a man like Lafayette Whitney was in Linda Wallace's family, a tower of strength and integrity. At the memorial service, Al said, "My father was the greatest man I ever knew in my life."

In the midst of their grief, death often forces families to deal with complex financial transitions. It is partly for this reason that everyone should prepare for the eventuality of loss by having legally acceptable wills; this vastly simplifies the transition a family must navigate in the midst of an emotionally vulnerable time. The advances in medical science and technology have now created miraculous cures but have also made it possible to keep many patients technically alive for an indefinite period of time, even if there is no consciousness or brain activity and no quality of life. As a result, more and more families are faced with excruciatingly difficult caregiving decisions for terminal patients. Living wills have been of tremendous value to families wrestling with these decisions; knowing the exact wishes of the patient can minimize the conflicts of the surviving members of the family and lessen the burden of emotional distress caused by the loss of the loved one.

If the parent has experienced a lengthy illness, during which the adult child has been the primary caregiver, death can come as a sort of relief. By the same token, if an adult child has been taking care of an elderly parent for a long time, the loss of those duties requires a dramatic refocusing of energy. For example, Edna Henderson, of Seattle, Washington, was the primary caregiver for her mother, the Reverend Hattie Paul, for almost ten years, until her death in December 2001. Edna, who is seventy-three and previously had back surgery, cared for her mother, who suffered from Alzheimer's disease. It was difficult because her mother needed to be lifted in and out of bed, the bathtub, and chairs. But for Edna, there was no question that she would do it.

Since her mother passed away, Edna told us, "the biggest change is I just can't get used to her not being here. I wake up during the night sometimes and go downstairs thinking, 'I got to go down and make sure I got the cover on her.'"

The adjustment to no longer having her mother as a daily presence in her life was almost incapacitating. "I do have some time right now. I haven't been able to get myself together. I can't hardly even get out of the house anymore." Like many long-term-care providers who have lost the person they cared for, Edna said that she felt depressed. She had trouble concentrating and sometimes found herself crying during the day, and at night. She recognized that she could use some help, and intended to seek medical treatment.

When we talked to her again, several months later, she told us that she had indeed sought treatment and is now doing very well. Her resilience in bouncing back and regaining her joy for life is a testament to how important it can be to reach out for help when it is needed.

A HELPING HAND

Unlike Edna Henderson, many people are afraid to get professional mental health care because of the stigma attached to such care. In fact, a lot of people experiencing mental anguish are afraid to seek treatment because they don't want anyone to know. They are afraid of being discriminated against at work, possibly even losing their job and health benefits. Parents often refuse to acknowledge emotional problems or mental illness in a child because they don't want their child "seen" as different in that way, or "labeled," and they are sometimes concerned that administrators will put their child on a different track in school. What a sad state of affairs this is, when one in four families has an experience with mental illness.

Because of this shameful, ignorant, and sometimes just downright mean attitude toward depression and mental illness, many Americans don't get the help they need to continue leading productive lives. According to a 1999 comprehensive Mental Health report of the Surgeon General, "the *majority* of those who need mental health treatment do not seek it."

Attitudes must mature and keep up with the science of the brain. Mental illnesses are diagnosable, treatable, and if not curable, then manageable, just like diabetes, high blood pressure, and heart disease. Only when a majority of people understand these illnesses and their treatments will we finally eradicate the totally unjustifiable stigma, and discrimination aimed at people who suffer from mental illnesses.

There is precedent for ending the stigma associated with disease. Many Americans our age remember when cancer was so fearsome and shrouded in mystery that victims were stigmatized, many to the point that they were reluctant to talk about their illness. Fortunately, we have long since banished the prejudice that used to be associated with that disease, and now there is some encouraging evidence that we're making progress against the stigma attached to mental illness. For instance, families can now go to support groups like the National Alliance for the Mentally Ill, a support and advocacy group that has state chapters as well.

When someone suffers from depression or another kind of mental illness, their family suffers with them. Sometimes an important part of family resiliency is knowing when the family needs to reach out and ask for professional help. Resources available in the extended family, faith communities, and other outside support systems can help families weather crises. And when families need to get help, they should see it not as a sign of weakness, but as one of strength. When there is a crisis, everyone is affected. But just as each family member is affected, each family member can also be part of a healthy response that can increase the family's reservoir of resilience.

We learned this lesson the hard way after Albert's accident. When he was first in the hospital, we did exactly the wrong thing by sheltering his sisters from his injury as much as possible. We believed that, as the parents, we should shoulder all the burden and the stress, and we thought it best if the girls kept to their normal routine while we took turns staying by Albert's bedside twenty-four hours a day. Fortunately, the staff at the hospital saw that as a family we were having a difficult time managing the crisis, and that we weren't tapping into all the support that was available to us. They recommended family counseling—and through that counseling we realized that Albert's sisters not only wanted to participate (we already knew that) but *needed* to participate in the healing and be a part of their brother's recovery. They were worried about him and didn't want to just go about their own schedules as usual. Further, they needed to feel connected to us and therefore needed to be able to help share the burden of our worries and work. By being allowed to help fully, they were able to learn how to channel their concern into healing action that helped their brother, helped us, and helped them—and made our whole family much stronger as a result. So our effort at being stoic adults had not been the right response. We needed to trust our children enough to share the pain. We did, and they were awesome, and we were so proud of their maturity and willingness to shoulder serious responsibilities, their deep abilities to nurture, and their growing capacity for love.

What we learned about family resilience was not only that it was a mistake to think that the two adult members of a family had to be the pillars of strength for the whole family and relieve everyone else from participating. We also learned why no one person could go off and be happy on his or her own when someone else in the family is suffering. To the contrary, helping the family in a time of crisis is healthy and healing for everyone in the family. Any illness affects every member of the family, and all can be a part of the healing process. If the whole family knows and understands what needs to be done, it contributes to the proper handling of the crisis. In the process, that understanding can help mitigate its effects on other family members. The choice is simple: they can be mystified or they can be a part of the solution.

Over the course of a year, Albert did recover. We brought him home from the hospital in a body cast. For the next six weeks, we turned our dining room into his bedroom. And each of his sisters worked hard to help him—for example, by taking turns sleeping near him all night, where all the medical gear was set up. Our friends and neighbors were great, our church was terrific, and the public school even sent a teacher to our home. Albert eventually recovered completely and went on his merry way. Thank God. But then it was Tipper's turn.

At the end this grueling experience, Tipper realized that she had spent so much time taking care of everyone else—as wives and mothers often do—that she had neglected her own needs. Something was wrong and she knew it, but she just didn't know what it was. She tried to pray her way out of it, to will her way out of it, to exercise her way out of it. She still couldn't get at it. After a number of long talks with friends, she realized she needed help. She consulted mental-health professionals and was diagnosed with clinical depression. The doctor prescribed both therapy and medication—and it worked.

Fortunately, Tipper's experience as a child with her mother's depression helped her understand that she needed to seek help. Her mother, Margaret Ann, was a single working mother who, when struck with a bout of depression, lost her job. But she sought treatment and then rebuilt her life all over again. Unfortunately, she went through that cycle several times.

Tipper and her mother were fortunate, because they lived with Tipper's grandparents. When Margaret Ann was ill, they had the support of a loving extended family. Tipper could always count on her father, who was attentive and understanding during these difficult times. What made these periods especially difficult was that mental illnesses and treatments just weren't discussed outside the family. Even as a young child, Tipper was aware of the fear and the stigma that surrounded her mother's disease, but she was even more aware of how brave her mother had to be each time she reclaimed her life.

For several years after her own experience with clinical depression, Tipper didn't discuss the matter with anyone but our family and close friends, believing that personal medical information should be kept private—even if you are living a public life. But slowly she came to realize that her story might help people who were afraid to seek help. When Al became vice president, Tipper became convinced that she should use whatever platform she had to help change attitudes about mental health. She became the special adviser to the president for mental-health policy and traveled around the country speaking about the issue.

Another experience that brought home the importance of her message occurred a couple of days after the 1999 school shooting at Columbine, when Tipper met with students in New Hampshire. When she asked them if they knew someone considering suicide, almost all of the hands went up. The teachers gasped. Tipper asked them why they or their friends didn't seek help, and they said it was because they were afraid of being labeled. That distressing experience helped Tipper realize that despite the many medical advances, the shame and fear surrounding mental illness are nearly as prevalent today as they were in her mother's generation. Unfortunately, the stigma is being passed to our children's generation.

Since Tipper began speaking out about mental-health issues, hundreds of people of all ages and from all walks of life have stopped her—on airplanes, in coffee shops, when she's out jogging or walking down the street—to tell her about their own mental-health experiences. In June 1999, Tipper chaired the first White House Conference on Mental Health. It was an important opportunity to dispel myths about mental illness, highlight the many scientific advances that have been made in understanding the brain, deal with discrimination in insurance practices, and eradicate the stigma associated with mental-health care. Before chairing the conference, Tipper spoke publicly for the first time about her experience with clinical depression.

We have often been surprised to learn that someone we knew had been silently suffering from depression. For instance, when we last visited with Brett's parents, Mitch Philpott and Cindy and Lee Nalley, Mitch told us that he now realizes that he was slipping into depression immediately after Brett's surgery, when we'd first met. "I'd leave work and just sit in the car and I'd cry," he told us. So during the same period that we received help to better cope with the stresses of Albert's recovery, Mitch went undiagnosed and had to work through the depression by himself. He now believes that his depression contributed substantially to his and Cindy's divorce. During the last years of their marriage, Mitch admits, "I was irresponsible. I'm tickled to death Cindy found someone like she did." We couldn't help but think how things might have been different for Mitch and Cindy if he had been diagnosed and received treatment at the time. But seeing the happiness of Cindy and Lee, and their amazing two-home family for Brett, we remembered Susan Fadley's statement that things didn't work out the way she'd imagined they would when she was younger. She concluded with these words: "It didn't happen that way, unfortunately—or fortunately, because then we wouldn't have who we have now."

It has been over a year now since the terrible terrorist attack on the United States struck directly in New York, Pennsylvania, and Washington, D.C. Those places felt the full force of the tragedy immediately, but the shock waves were felt by all Americans, and we have had to draw on our reserves of resilience and strength as a nation, much as an individual family does. In the wake of not only the attacks but also the anthrax deaths, the associated anxiety, and the warnings from the government of other imminent attacks, people across the nation have been examining the issue of mental illness and distress and are seeing it in a different light. For example, we all realize that our nations' children are particularly vulnerable at times like this. Researchers from Columbia University studied young students in New York City six months after the attacks and found that one out of four children registered at least one symptom of mental anguish. Children across the nation continue to show signs of anxiety, depression, and stress as well as of recovery and resilience. Tipper, as honorary chair of the National Mental Health Awareness Campaign, worked with a number of organizations to produce mental-health town hall meetings in Washington and New York, to examine how people could best be directed toward mental-health assistance and to help people recognize the signs of posttraumatic stress disorder, anxiety and depression, and substance abuse—just a few of the aftereffects of the attacks. Experiencing any of these signs in response to the attacks and the heightened sense of anxiety that we are all living with in a post-9/11 world is a normal response to an abnormal situation. Without question, Americans are a resourceful and strong people. Most will not develop mental-health problems as a result of the new reality we are all adapting to, but some will experience serious problems, and they should be comforted by the thought that they can get assistance if they need it. Participating in support groups, talking with friends and coworkers, going to religious services, volunteering in your community, talking to family members, and having a plan of action in case there is more terrorism are all positive steps we can take to get through difficult times. We should see ourselves as one big, resilient American family—unified in response to challenge and strong enough to help one another.

CULTIVATING RESILIENCE

Just as resilience can come from the individual, from family relationships, or from the community, fragility can reside in any of those same places. An individual who may be having a difficult time coping with adversity or managing stressful situations does not necessarily have a character flaw or weakness. Indeed, a person may be incredibly strong and resilient in certain situations but at other times may be extraordinarily fragile. The strength and grace to cope with crises is not eternal or invincible. If we are overtired or hungry or stressed or simply overtaxed by the cumulative challenges of life, there may be times when our inner reserves of strength can be exhausted. And sometimes we may despair that we simply can no longer carry the load we have been given.

ering a crisis in an already weakened state can make some-
less able to bounce back from adversity. If a family is already
stressed by constant arguments or overwork, the additional burden
of one family member developing a problem with substance abuse,
depression, a health crisis, or job loss may prove too much for the
family to bear together.

Whatever the cause, when a family becomes overburdened and
is not able to bounce back, the consequences can be devastating
and even tragic. It can manifest itself in the form of substance
abuse, physical or verbal abuse, or even suicide. All too often, just
as children learn resilience from their parents, they can also learn
fragility. Family experts believe that this type of learning may be
one reason, unfortunately, that such destructive behaviors often
repeat themselves from one generation to the next, creating a
tragic family legacy.

For all the joy and fulfillment they can provide, families can also
be the source of profound emotional suffering—which is the third
kind of difficulty families face. The very closeness that is part of the
essence of family serves to magnify the pain that family members
sometimes cause each other. Domestic abuse—of spouses, children, and other family members—occurs all too frequently in
America. Likewise, sexual abuse of children by members of their
families—while not often discussed—is, according to experts, far
more common than Americans would like to admit. When a family member persists in inflicting physical abuse on another family
member, experts say the best and safest course of action is usually
to leave the home—quickly. And in many communities, there are
now shelters to protect victims of family abuse.

Unfortunately, the victim may find that the family's emotional
bonds become almost like invisible chains, preventing escape from
harm. A more subtle version of this effect is a phenomenon
known as "enmeshment," in which differences of opinion are dangerous to express because, emotionally, they are not tolerated.
Emotional abuse is far more common than physical abuse—and

can sometimes be just as harmful. In healthy families, all of the individuals are respected for who they are, and their uniqueness is acknowledged.

Within families, people inflict many varieties of pain on each other, including betrayal of trust and abandonment. John Gottman singles out several behaviors—criticism, contempt, defensiveness, and stonewalling—and notes that these can be especially corrosive to a relationship. In fact, he believes these four behaviors are so damaging and such accurate predictors of failed relationships that he calls them the "Four Horsemen of the Apocalypse" for relationships. Further, Gottman says that these harmful behaviors can build upon one another when partners fail to recognize and change them, thus causing a dangerous escalation of the conflict.

Problems in a relationship can also be magnified if one or both partners are bringing unresolved emotional wounds from childhood into the marriage. For example, some people have such low self-esteem due to difficulties during childhood that they look to their spouses for constant validation, and chronically overreact to anything remotely like criticism. As parents, these fragile individuals can be so lacking in a healthy concept of themselves that they use their children as a kind of emotional looking glass, searching for emotional support *from* their children instead of giving it *to* them. In the process, their children are deprived of the nurturing they need for healthy growth, and when they become parents themselves, they sometimes repeat the cycle of emotional abuse.

But painful legacies do not have to repeat themselves. Trauma is not destiny. Many admirable individuals take the painful experiences they have endured and transform them into a powerful determination to heal themselves and to ensure that the pattern will not repeat itself. In some families, one member sometimes emerges as a "tower of strength" and leads a family out of trauma and dysfunction by living life with true integrity and thus demonstrating what it means to have character, courage, and devotion to family. This sort of leadership—leadership by example—can make all the difference in a family, and its influence can affect many generations. One especially inspiring example is Linda Wallace's maternal grandfather, the late Lafayette Whitney, whose example of family leadership lives on today in Linda—and in Tony Wallace as well.

Although some people—especially men—react to crises with stoic silence, the ability to draw resilience from relationships requires being able to open up and communicate freely with those closest to you when times are hard. For many, that is easier said than done, but doing it once makes it easier the next time. It is a building block, if you will—a foundation that the family members can rely on as something they learned and put into practice.

In our family, the tradition of family meetings has become just this kind of foundation over the years. Even now, in times of crisis or unusual stress, one of our children will say, "Hey, we need a family meeting," and we will all find a date and a place to gather. Or sometimes when we're all together, they just happen. Early last year, for example, before Tipper's mother died, her illness unexpectedly became the topic of a spontaneous family meeting. Each of us was contributing in our own way to her mother's care and we all thought that we were giving Tipper the support she needed. But it turned out we weren't. Tipper was the only one who was investing enough time to really understand just how ill her mother was, and the speed with which she was getting worse. Yet even though Tipper knew what was happening, she was not able to talk about it and—in a pattern that is common in many families—she privately hoped and, indeed, assumed, that the rest of the family would intuit the situation and spontaneously begin supporting her more fully. But that didn't happen, in part because no one had the same vantage point on the situation as she did, and therefore didn't realize exactly what she needed.

Finally, one day Tipper blurted out, "Why aren't you all helping me more with Mother? She is dying." The children were shocked. When some of them started crying, Tipper realized they didn't know how ill her mother really was. Only then did Tipper come to understand that she had not wanted to admit the truth to herself either.

That impromptu family meeting was a turning point that helped all of us come face-to-face with the fact that we were about to lose a beloved family member and that Tipper—in particular—needed extra support. Once we understood that, we were able to help one another through the last stages of Margaret Ann's illness, and ultimately adapt to the profound emotional changes resulting from her death.

Resilience in families also comes from a plain, old-fashioned sense of commitment and responsibility. When we asked Cindy Nalley how they all find it in themselves to face their son Brett's health challenges day after day, she said simply, "You find the strength. You just have to. Who's going to take care of Brett if you don't? It's a commitment." She makes it sound like the most natural thing in the world when she says, "People don't realize that if they were in the same situation, they'd do the same thing." Now, as a teenager, Brett is facing some new growth challenges and may need another major operation, but all three parents are taking it in stride.

Mitch Philpott watched his grandmother take care of his grandfather for seventeen years after his stroke, doing everything for him, even though she herself was frail. Mitch's aunt and uncle, similarly, have been caring lovingly for their son, who is forty years old and mentally handicapped and still lives with them. From his family, Mitch learned a powerful lesson. "You don't leave people," Mitch said.

Mitch and Cindy, upon reflection, acknowledge that a number of coworkers over the years have urged them to consider easing their burden by putting Brett into an institution and just visiting him on weekends, but that is something that neither of them would ever dream of doing. Mitch, Cindy, and Lee have all had opportunities to focus more attention on their careers and themselves personally, but the compass of their life has always pointed to true north, and their unwavering commitment to Brett has in many ways given their lives uncommon strength and certainty. "I don't know how much longer we're going to have him, and I just want to be with him as much as I can be," said Cindy.

But sometimes, as Mitch, Cindy, and Lee also know, families need to accept assistance from others. Late one night, when Brett was a toddler, just before it was time to take him to Johns Hopkins for his first surgery, Cindy and Mitch were awakened by the sound of a neighbor throwing rocks at their window. They woke up to discover that flames were coming out of the roof of their house. They had to lower Brett out of their second-floor bedroom window to the neighbors waiting below and then crawl out themselves. All three escaped safely, but they then had to stand outside and watch their home, and all their belongings, burn down. Mitch still remembers that in his total exhaustion, feeling the pressure of all of the burdens in his life, he said, "God, what else can you do to me?" They had no insurance, no belongings, and no savings.

Yet in retrospect they now say, "It was a blessing." They discovered the powerful way in which community can help shore up a family. Neighbors took them in for several weeks, until they could find another house to rent. A local TV network affiliate and the local paper did a story about the fire and Brett's medical problem. A radio personality even organized a fund-raiser to help the family. "People were great. One guy gave twenty thousand dollars. It saved us," says Mitch. The family ended up living off of that money for the next year while Mitch and Cindy were both unemployed, spending nearly all of their time in hospitals with Brett. When Mitch and Cindy were truly at the end of their rope and had done all they could to help themselves, they learned that sometimes the resilience that a family needs can be found only in the community.

Resilience means, among other things, having enough flexibility to bend without breaking. And flexibility, in turn, means having options. In general, the more options that are available within the community, the more resilient families can become.

Just as the source of resilience is sometimes found in the community, there are other times when it must be found in the nation as a whole. For example, Cindy was forced to quit her job because her employer refused to let her take leave for her son's illness. As a result of meeting them and getting to know them, when we were finally able to leave the hospital with our son, one of the things Al did upon returning to the Senate was cosponsor Senator Chris Dodd's bill on family medical leave—to give parents like Mitch and Cindy the legal right to take time off from work in a medical emergency without losing their jobs. Then Al worked with Senator Dodd and others to help get the bill passed. After it was vetoed twice during the Bush-Quayle administration, we felt a special sense of joy when it became the first law signed by President Clinton when the Clinton-Gore administration took office. And the Philpotts helped Al and the president explain to the American people how the new law would help families like theirs.

LILY YEH AND THE VILLAGE FAMILY

Elizabeth Bargar, H. German Wilson (crouching), *Kelly Brooks Tannen,*
James "Big Man" Maxton, and Lily Yeh

Chapter 8

COMMUNITY

Only by restoring the broken connections can we be healed. Connection *is* health.

—WENDELL BERRY

THE YEH FAMILY

Lily Yeh, a Chinese-born artist, freely admits that she never set out to be a community leader when she first began a small project to build a garden in a run-down neighborhood in North Philadelphia. The only reason she started it was because Arthur Hall, the head of the historic African-American cultural center in Philadelphia, approached Lily and asked her to create a small outdoor garden in the abandoned lot next to his building. She was not at all sure she wanted to work in this urban wasteland surrounded by dilapidated buildings and abandoned lots, but she agreed to apply for a grant. Even after she got the grant, she almost backed out of the project because she had no experience in designing public spaces and was an outsider to the low-income neighborhood.

"I was really scared," she told us, and she remembered thinking, "Maybe I shouldn't do this. It's a little over my head." But somehow she couldn't quite let it go: "As I was preparing the letter to withdraw from the proposal, there was a little voice in me, just very frail, but very clear, and it said, 'If you don't rise to the occasion, the best of you will die, and the rest will not amount to anything.'" So she forged ahead, improvising as she went along. She went back to the abandoned lot, and standing there, not knowing how to even begin to reclaim it and build a garden, she let instinct guide her. "The lot looked chaotic, because it didn't have a sense of orientation. So I picked a stick up, and right in the center, I drew a circle. I said, 'This is the center. From here we are going to build.'"

The early days of the project were difficult, because most of the adults in the run-down neighborhood were extremely skeptical and critical of this "crazy Chinese woman" coming in from the outside with the goal of improving their neighborhood, Lily said. They laughed at her and said that her project was nothing more than a woman and some children playing in the dirt. The person who helped her slowly build a connection to the adults in the neighborhood was an African-American man named JoJo Williams, who, although unemployed and suffering from a drug addiction, was a generous man with a strong spirit. He agreed to help her clear out the debris from abandoned lots for a small amount of money, eventually becoming Lily's anchor and protector, as well as a real force in the neighborhood. It was with his help that she first overcame the community members' skepticism and gradually enlisted their aid.

When that first little garden was finished, Lily initially thought her work was done and that she would leave. But she remained drawn to the place and couldn't stop coming back. Sixteen years later, Lily is still there. And the garden has grown and been joined by many other gardens, parks, and activity centers all around the small neighborhood, which is now known as the Village of Arts and Humanities. What was once just one small garden is now an entire village, complete with sculptures, murals, vegetable gardens, a theater, a dance program, a community newspaper, and a working tree farm that employs area adults and youth.

"I have to confess," Lily said, "I didn't start this because I was a philanthropist at heart. I did it because I needed to do it to make my life meaningful. I didn't go as the person who had all the answers. I went as a person who was in need—in need of help and in need of understanding."

Lily told us that after coming to the States as an adult, she managed to do well professionally. Her art was accepted by galleries and museums and she received a prestigious teaching position at the University of the Arts in Philadelphia. Yet she always felt a bit out of place. "I came from China, and I just felt the values didn't fit what I was taught. I couldn't find a space that was sacred, that was spiritual. Everything here is very secular." But if the galleries and the university were never able to provide that sacred space, somehow the ragged canvas of the broken neighborhood provided the place where she could create it for herself. "My weakness became a strength, and created the opportunity for other people to come in with their strength. That's how it really started."

Lily says her project is in many ways rooted in her love for her late father, who gave her "unconditional love" and instilled within her a passion for Chinese landscape painting. "He got me started in painting landscapes and that has everything to do with me working in North Philadelphia."

Her father was a general in the Nationalist Army of Chiang Kai-shek. Orphaned at age six on Hainan Island, he had only a second-grade education because his family was so poor. Lily's mother, on the other hand, was born into an aristocratic family. Her parents married, Lily said, because "opposites attracted, but then they grew apart because of the differences."

Three months into the marriage, her mother wanted out. But her mother's father forbade a divorce, and so she stayed in the marriage, which produced five children. Lily's father had had three children with his first wife (in an arranged marriage) before marrying Lily's mother.

Born during World War II, Lily graduated from college before coming to the United States in 1963 to do graduate work at the University of Pennsylvania. She married an architect, David, who shared her artistic and musical interests. Together they had a son, Daniel, now thirty, who is presently working as a filmmaker in China. But neither Lily nor David ever quite felt entirely settled in the marriage, Lily said, and after six years of marriage, when Daniel was two, they divorced. Currently they live just two blocks away from each other and have a good relationship. They were careful to stay on good terms throughout Daniel's childhood. David is remarried now and Lily says she really likes his new wife.

Most of Lily's family eventually came to the United States, including her mother's mother. Meanwhile, once her son was grown, Lily tried marriage again. In 1989 she married Steven, a lawyer who was very interested in education and community building in the inner city. His interest in these issues encouraged Lily to expand their garden into a cultural center. In fact, they started the Village together.

"It's kind of like our child. It was a difficult labor." But after just two years, their marriage failed. Their intense work on the Village was hard on their relationship—especially because they disagreed about how to manage it. For example, she said Steven thought that people who used drugs should not be allowed to work at the Village, but Lily felt that the Village was for the people who lived there and that she would not exclude someone because of an addiction problem. "I really felt my heart was torn apart. I really felt I spilled blood." The Village was "split at the core" by their differences, and the dissolution of their marriage left Lily depressed. Lily and Steven divorced in the early 1990s, and Lily gained "custody" of the Village, she said.

Lily persevered, and what was once a stretch of abandoned crack houses and empty yards full of garbage and broken glass is now a remarkable and inspiring place. The neighborhoods around the Village haven't changed much; the run-down buildings and vacant lots are a reminder of what the Village used to look like. But the Village itself glows as an oasis of warmth and color and sparkle. The brownstone buildings are well maintained, and elderly women sitting out on their stoops greet Lily and visitors as they pass by. Formerly empty lots are now bursts of color; instead of broken windows, bright bits of broken tile have been artistically arranged in stucco walls to create beautiful mosaics of sunsets, flowers, and trees. The bits of tile are also used in whimsical designs along the sidewalk, vividly creating a sense of wholeness and beauty in the neighborhood.

Lily sees the mosaics of broken tile as a metaphor: "Mosaic is something broken, but from brokenness we create something whole, and that's really what our family is. We have to think of our deficits as our resource, and so you start to build a community in any way that you can. It's like when a family breaks down; when a community breaks down, it needs to be rebuilt." She also speaks of each of us as individuals being broken and needing to find a way to bring our broken pieces together—just as she has done with her community. In the Village, Lily gathers together "the people that nobody wants, the disenfranchised community, abandoned lots, and somehow, somehow in all this dysfunctional scenario, we come together; we hold each other dear; we remake it. We transform places, and people become transformed."

The beautiful works of art now show the unmistakable signs of an intact community that is healing itself. The many acts that created that beauty—and that sense of community—actually transformed the lives of those who became involved. Lily is proud of the examples set by two former drug addicts, JoJo Williams and James "Big Man" Maxton. Both discovered that they were artists and community builders. Sadly, JoJo passed away a few years ago, but Lily holds her hand over her heart and says, "He's always here."

Big Man told us about how Lily and the Village helped change his life. In 1987, after years of substance abuse, he said he "got to a point where I was just sick and tired of being sick and tired." While most people wouldn't give a drug addict much of a chance, Lily put Big Man to work. At that time, Lily thought it was important to get everyone involved in order to get the project as deeply rooted in the community as possible. She notes that today, however, because the Village is now a nonprofit organization with many different funders, they are required to certify that no one who works on the project uses drugs.

Big Man said he first started to work with Lily because his friend JoJo told him that Lily would pay him "lots of money." Big Man told us, "What I didn't realize was that I'd be drawn to this particular place night after night, and listen to JoJo talk about Lily's hopes and dreams for this community. I was a person who had no dreams or hopes or anything, so I was fascinated by it." He remembered Lily once pointed to a pile of old garden chairs piled up against the side of a building and told him that he would transform them into beautiful serpentine benches that would turn an abandoned lot into a park where neighborhood residents would sit. He said he couldn't imagine how it was going to be, but was amazed when, sure enough, Lily's prediction fulfilled itself through his hands and he did indeed create those benches.

The experience of having been shunned by the community but then validated by it was transformational for Big Man. People would walk by and admire the statues and mosaics he was creating, telling him he was doing a wonderful job. He said he had never before received that kind of praise; he called it the best kind of "instant gratification" he'd ever known. One park is surrounded by a row of guardian angels he made, and they shimmer with tiny pieces of mirror amid the colorful broken tile pieces.

Lily changed the way Big Man thought about the neighborhood. "I had seen the community as an overlooked, neglected kind of place," he said. "It had no kind of resources. It didn't get no kind of municipal services, things like that. I felt the same way. I felt neglected. I felt unwanted, unable to perform in a mainstream kind of setting, and Lily came and gave me an alternative."

As Big Man discovered the artist within him, he knew that his work was not about money at all. "It was about me saving my life, about me doing something positive and doing good, about myself and the talent that was hidden, that I never knew was there—to be able to connect with people, to be able to be a positive influence in the community." Big Man considers Lily his "guardian angel."

The process of transforming the Village and its community also transformed Lily herself. As a young woman, she was an introverted artist, but over the years she became an outspoken community leader, overcoming all her fears and hesitations. Lily fully realizes that with her beautiful mosaics and parks she has not only pieced together artwork and woven together the threads of the lives of the community members but she has also, in fact, created a family—which includes, among others, Big Man and H. German Wilson, the theater director at the Village. "It's a long-term commitment," Lily told us, "especially when people start to entrust you with their innermost stories. People have a responsibility to each other." Lily's son, her parents, and her siblings remain her family, of course, but Lily has formed such close relationships with people at the Village that she considers them family as well. "What is family?" she asked. "You feel a bond. You feel that deep love nurtured by going through different experiences together and by being together through thick and thin. This big family in the Village has given me the opportunity to realize who I am."

Her loving relationship with her birth family made it possible for Lily to open her heart to others. "The reason I can do this now is because of the love from my parents—their devotion, their unconditional support," she said. She now defines the bond of family as "that moment when you are really there for another person, and you are really connecting. You're fully present at that time."

As a result of her experience in Philadelphia, Lily Yeh believes that art and culture, music and dance can play crucial roles in reweaving the web of community and reestablishing the connection between family and community. She found that families who had been quite cynical about the community became actively involved because they wanted to be a part of her blossoming labor of love.

THE CHANGING COMMUNITY

Just as we turn to our family for comfort, support, and resilience, communities should also be there when families need some place to turn—and be there as well for individuals who want to expand their connections to an extended family. Unfortunately, some of the same trends that have brought about the transformation of the American family have had a negative impact on American community life. Too many hours at work, long commutes, too little free time, too much television—these and other factors have produced a sharp decline in civic participation. Most Americans are devoting far less time to community functions than they did two generations ago. In a number of respects, the bond between families and communities has weakened.

What exactly is a community? Like a family, it is a complex system, and its essence is found in connections. Communitarian theorist Amitai Etzioni defines community as a web of relationships among individuals that "often crisscross and reinforce one another." In addition, he says community involves a "measure of commitment to a set of shared values, norms, and meanings, and a shared history and identity—in short, to a particular culture."

Of course, the definition of community, like the definition of family, can change over time. Just as individuals and families change, the community also responds to influences from economic and social conditions. One expert with especially deep knowledge about changing American communities is Robert Putnam, a professor of public policy at Harvard's Kennedy School of Government. Putnam has spent the last twenty-five years conducting extensive research into how involved individuals and families are in the life of their communities. What he has discovered is the story of a dramatic decline in the degree to which Americans join civic organizations and participate in community functions.

In the early 1900s, Americans were dedicated and very creative community builders. In fact, they started many of the most widely known community organizations in our country today, such as the 4-H and the Rotary Club. Civic involvement increased steadily in the first half of the century, except during the Great Depression. Then, the "Greatest Generation"—the one that fought in World War II—also became a generation of great joiners, organizers, and supporters of clubs and civic organizations.

But by the late 1950s, the swell of community involvement began to taper off, and it has fallen steadily over the last thirty to forty years. Membership in some civic organizations is now down to the low levels last seen during the Depression. The generations preceding the baby boomers were more apt to seek out community connections, while their children's and grandchildren's generations are not—at least not when measured by the traditional benchmark of civic involvement. Putnam and other social scientists see this trend as a cause for concern. Putnam, like several scholars before him, describes the connections between individuals, families, and the greater community as "social capital," a resource just as real as money, only created by establishing and maintaining good relationships.

Because families have undergone such profound changes over the last fifty years, it should not be surprising that our requirements from and interests in the community may be quite different than those of our grandparents. For example, some older groups aimed primarily at men may not be responsive to the needs of a single mom raising two kids and holding down two jobs. If we are looking for something different from our communities today, we are therefore challenged to discover new forms of community organizing and civic involvement that will resonate with our needs, just as clubs and associations did for our parents' generation. In fact, at a time when families face so many disruptive changes and challenges in their busy lives, the connections they forge to community can potentially become more important than ever.

We have been inspired by many people we've met who are taking the initiative to get involved in their communities and create completely new, innovative ways of rejoining the transformed institution of family with today's rapidly changing communities. Americans today are less likely to belong to organizations that seem to have social gatherings as their main purpose. But many are gravitating toward organizations that are formed to address a particular social need or particular interest, such as helping the homeless, mentoring at-risk children, protecting the environment, or raising money and awareness to fight AIDS or other public-health problems. And there are some indications that the current generation of young people is more apt to volunteer for such causes than the previous generation. Community organizations for families are also forming based around shared needs: for example, community action groups, single-parent groups, and support groups for families of children with special needs.

Long before children are consciously aware of the wider community in which they live, they and their families are profoundly influenced by it. To begin with, the general health and well-being of the community significantly affects a child. Is it a place free of pollution and violent crime, and endowed with amenities like parks, playgrounds, and grocery stores with affordable and nutritious food? Are there affordable sources of high-quality child care? Is there accessible health care in the neighborhood? Do neighbors come together to discuss ways to improve their surroundings?

With more dual-income families, more single parents, and fewer relatives living nearby, many families with young children would like to rely more than ever on supportive communities. When parents return to work, they need to be able to depend on other caring, trusted adults to help with child care and make that experience enjoyable for child and parent alike.

In some communities, families cooperate with their neighbors for baby-sitting and carpooling. But if you don't have a group of stay-at-home parents in your immediate circle, finding someone to take a car full of kids to a soccer game at four in the afternoon can be pretty hard. And since Americans are putting in ever longer work hours, there is an increased need for innovative solutions, such as on-site child care for employees and easier availability of flex-time or part-time work for those who want it.

Interestingly, community cohesion also turns out to be a highly accurate predictive factor where quality of health is concerned—both for individuals and for families. Persuasive evidence shows that being engaged in civic activity is not only beneficial to the community but has significant and measurable health benefits for individuals and families.

Health, after all, can be measured not only individual by individual but also family by family and even community by community. Dr. Edward Schor of the Commonwealth Fund in New York has studied these broader measures of health, and he makes a strong case that community cohesion is one of the keys to the quality of health throughout the United States. He cites a detailed study by Ichiro Kawachi of Harvard and his colleagues that correlates rates of death with attitudes of people toward their neighbors. Among other results, they tabulated the answers to a question asked by pollsters across America: "Do you think most people would take advantage of you if they got the chance?" Then they showed that to a significant degree, age-adjusted mortality rates correlated with the percentage of people who agreed with the pollster's statement.

Summarizing many other studies, Putnam reports that, statistically, belonging to *no* clubs or community groups is actually as bad for your health as smoking cigarettes. Moreover, joining even *one club* or group cuts in half the risk that an individual will die the following year.

Similarly, communities that have adopted a family-centered approach to health care have seen significant improvements in the health of their citizens. After all, family members are the most important deliverers of health care, from taking a child's temperature and administering antiasthma medication to operating a home kidney dialysis machine or monitoring a serious illness. Supportive communities can also strengthen families by providing practical information, such as advice on prenatal nutrition. Some communities have improved the health of children by providing parenting education programs and teaching new parents about children's early development. Other communities have even organized home visits to help new mothers adjust.

One inspiring example of the beneficial effect a community can have on its citizens is the Elizabeth Learning Center, a school located in Cudahy, a Los Angeles neighborhood. The Learning Center provides free health care for all its students and their families as well as other members of the community through a partnership with St. Francis Hospital. Although the neighborhood is crime-ridden and spotted with graffiti, the school is rarely a target because the community protects it as a special resource, and the school itself takes care of those in the community. The campus is open for activities from 7:00 A.M. until 9:00 P.M., and a portion of the campus is set aside for adult activities throughout the day. The school strives to include parents and other community members in its decision-making process and even offers a course on school governance to parents and community members so they know how the school administration operates and how they can best get involved. When Al visited the school two years ago, Emilio "Ed" Vasquez, the now retired principal, told him, "Giving members of the community a voice in the life of our school brings a fresh perspective and new ideas about how our school is run, but it also reinforces an important point—the success of the community is linked to the success of the school, and its students."

COMMUNITIES AND PUBLIC SAFETY

Communities, like families, have an integrity all their own. And the degree and nature of social interaction among the families that live in a community determine the community's overall vitality and well-being. Nowhere is this more evident than in a community's ability to protect itself against crime.

Community cohesion protects against crime just as unbroken skin protects against infection. Healthy and happy families almost always have vibrant connections to their neighbors and to the other families in the communities where they live. Families do not live in isolation; just as we are family-oriented animals, we are also most comfortable living in communities—for mutual support, for child rearing, for productive activities, and for self-defense. It is our nature.

Fighting crime in the absence of community cohesion is almost always a long, losing battle. But the good news is that when families are linked to the community and social cohesion is high, the tide turns quickly against crime and violence. One community that is an excellent illustration of how to do this well is Redlands, California, a community of seventy thousand people sixty miles east of Los Angeles, where Bill and Jeanne Hoyt live. Jim Bueermann is the head of the police department, and his official title lets you know that they're doing things a little differently here: it's "chief of police and director of housing, recreation and senior services."

By merging these different departments, Redlands has become a leader among communities in reducing crime rates and strengthening the fabric of society. It is focusing not just on reducing crime but on building those positive forces that protect and shore up communities by supporting strong and resilient families, mentoring young people, and creating safe and sustainable neighborhoods.

Jim Bueermann grew up in Redlands. When he was eighteen years old he drove a school bus through a low-income section of the city and got to know a lot of youngsters from a part of the community that was very different from the neighborhood where his family lived. During his college summer vacations, he and a friend became mentors to some of those same youngsters—but the relationships were broken off when it was time to go back to school, and he lost track of the young people with whom he had worked so closely. A few years later, when he was back in town as a rookie cop, he chased down a young man who had just committed a murder. He pinned him to the ground, turned him over, and recognized one of the boys he had mentored when he was younger. The man was sent to jail, but he became a career criminal and was eventually killed in a gang execution, Bueermann said.

Bueermann thinks of that young man as he explains why he has adopted what he calls "family-centered community policing" in his community. He focuses not only on crime prevention but on the active promotion of strong families and community cohesion. In doing so, he is building on a relatively new but growing trend in law enforcement.

In 1982, James Wilson and George Kelling came up with what has proven to be one of the most powerful new strategies in many decades for fighting crime: the "broken windows" theory. They wrote, "[I]f a window in a building is broken and is left unrepaired, all the rest of the windows will soon be broken. This is as true in nice neighborhoods as in rundown ones. . . . [O]ne unrepaired broken window is a signal that no one cares, and so breaking more windows costs nothing." That in turn is a signal to potential criminals that there is no community force to prevent things from going downhill. In such a place a crime is more likely to go unpunished, unpursued, or even unnoticed.

If, on the other hand, a potential criminal walks into a neighborhood where all the windows are repaired and there's no graffiti, where there are flowers and trees, carefully tended lawns, and well-kept homes, the unspoken but powerful message is: "If you're looking for a place to commit a crime, don't even think about committing it here, because we take pride in our community. The families who live here stick together. We watch out for one another. You see the seamlessness of the beauty and the order in this community? You see the pride we take in what happens? We pay attention. If you even start to do anything wrong, there are going to be lots of eyes on you, and in the same way we established the order that you see all around you, we will clamp down on your criminal activity immediately."

Community cohesion is the key. And it begins with social connections between families and the community. Robert Putnam summarizes in shorthand the single best predictor of how much crime will take place in any given neighborhood: how well the families who live there know the first names of their neighbors. That is because interconnections among the families and relationships of trust and reciprocity among them mean that they look out for one another.

Establishing and manifesting strong community cohesion is crucial, because the outward signals a community sends can speak volumes about the inner life of that community. One of the most effective ways to signal strong community cohesion is to actively involve the families in the community in the overall effort. That's how Jim Bueermann met Bill and Jeanne Hoyt and began working with them in their role as members of the Civilian Volunteer Patrol (CVP).

Neighborhood children know the Hoyts as the nice couple that gave them the tour of the police station and taught them about gun safety. Home owners appreciate them as the concerned citizens who make sure their houses aren't broken into or vandalized while they are away. Residents at senior centers know them as the couple who tell them to "get up and walk around!" Redlands police officers see them as committed members of their CVP, which was begun in 1997 to make Redlands a nicer place to live. Bill and Jeanne love their work because, as she says, "We love Redlands. It's our way of returning something. It's a unique town."

Bill and Jeanne and their fellow CVP members are a key element of Jim Bueermann's strategy to control crime before it occurs and to provide guidance to young people. Despite a recent resurgence of crime that's part of a national trend, the Redlands program has clearly had success. For example, major crimes citywide fell by 15 percent in 1999, but dropped almost 50 percent more in areas where Redlands concentrated on increasing community members' attachment to their neighborhood. Meanwhile, some fifty-six hundred young people are served by their after-school program. "It's clear to me that when we can develop this kind of program, we can have a real, positive impact," Chief Bueermann said.

Other communities around the country are adopting similar programs. In Manchester, New Hampshire, three community police officers were assigned permanently to help prevent problems in the community. When they discovered that drug deals almost always occurred on streets with poor lighting, they had the city's public-works department install better lighting. Similarly, in Flint, Michigan, the Neighborhood Violence Prevention Collaborative acts in cooperation with local organizations and community agencies to address the underlying causes of violence by strengthening the community at the grassroots level. More than fifteen thousand hours of volunteer service have been donated toward that goal, through a variety of community workshops, projects, and festivals.

One of the biggest obstacles to enlisting the aid of citizens has been the media portrayal of crime in most communities. Television coverage in particular often exaggerates the amount of violent crime in a town or city and creates an artificial sense that it is more dangerous to go outside than it really is. This leads to an increased fear of violence, which can keep people from reaching out and making connections within the community and tends to increase support for punitive approaches to crime. Media experts Frank Gilliam of UCLA and Shanto Iyengar of Stanford University have explored how news coverage can be episodic in nature (focusing on coverage of events by themselves, one by one, in isolation from any context) or thematic (reporting on specific news events but also placing them in a larger context). Their research on local television coverage of crime shows that episodic coverage, by focusing on violent crimes and their perpetrators, can stoke fear and raise suspicions. On the other hand, thematic coverage, which includes consideration of broader societal factors that contribute to a problem and points to appropriate solutions to the problem, can function as an invaluable, ever present community resource for promoting understanding of both problems and solutions, Gilliam told us.

The media can serve as a catalyst to encourage pride and ownership in the community, to help families and communities know themselves and one another better, and thus mobilize for positive social change. As Gilliam told us, "How media frames an issue has fundamental relevance to attributions of responsibility for the problem as well as pointing to solutions." Especially when trying to turn around communities in need, "the trick is to convince the broader public that the problems are tractable and that the solutions have direct relevance to other communities."

We all know that our nation's young people represent a remarkable resource, full of hope and creativity and inspiration for the future—if only we will give them the chance. But according to *Off Balance: Youth, Race, and Crime in the News,* a report published in 2001 by Lori Dorfman of the Berkeley Media Studies Group and Vincent Schiraldi of the Justice Policy Institute, Americans see a steady stream of negative portrayals of the young people in the age groups called Generation X and Generation Y. Despite the fact that violent crime by youth was at its lowest point on national record, 62 percent of poll respondents in 1998 thought juvenile crime was increasing. And 71 percent of respondents in another poll said they considered a school shooting "likely" in their community, when there was only a 1 in 2 million chance of being killed in an American school during the 1998–99 school year.

Although media overemphasis on violence can make community building more difficult, there are inspiring exceptions to the rule. In response to the Los Angeles riots in 1992 following the Rodney King verdict, Diane Bock, a mother of two in San Diego, California, set out to fight racism. Two years later, she and her husband, Larry, founded Community Cousins, a program that works against prejudice at the grassroots level by helping families of different ethnicities and backgrounds to become acquainted with one another and develop a personal stake in each other's lives. The paired families, or "cousins," who live in the same city, are encouraged to meet often during the year, at ball games, picnics, and the like, and to attend a few all-cousins events. Bock began by passing out pamphlets and held a party with forty families. Within five years, three hundred families had participated, and today, Community Cousins chapters are being established in other cities.

COMMUNITIES AND EDUCATION

After a community's public safety is ensured, public education rises to the top of the agenda for most families—particularly those with school-age children. The fate of schools and communities are inextricably linked. Good schools increase property values, while higher property values and a higher tax base mean more funds available for schools. In turn, more funds for schools can translate into more resources for better teachers, less teacher turnover, and better education, although they don't always do so. Conversely, poor neighborhoods often have poor schools that are strapped for resources and good teachers. And because they cannot provide the same quality of education, they usually cannot open as many doors for the children they educate as can better-financed schools in more affluent communities.

Community-centered schools, and school-centered communities, could provide the connections families are seeking. They certainly used to. One news story quoted Joe Agron, the editor of *American School and University*, who said, "In the early twentieth century, the schoolhouse was widely regarded as an indoor town square—the place to go for a speech, play, or meeting." After World War II, both our schools and neighborhoods changed. "Kids were piling through the doors, and schools were being built very rapidly and often cheaply," according to Agron. Separate civic centers, stadiums, and other public forums rose to replace the neighborhood-centered school.

In many communities, families now find it difficult to connect to their children's schools in a satisfying way. This is unfortunate, because parental involvement is the single most powerful way to improve our children's education. Studies show that children whose parents are involved in their schooling are more likely to earn high grades than children whose parents are not involved. Further, children of involved parents—those who attend parent-teacher conferences, PTA meetings, and school events, and are generally attuned to what's going at their children's schools—are more likely to have higher educational aspirations and a higher motivation to achieve, and are less likely to have behavior problems in school.

But when principals and teachers do not take the initiative to build a closer relationship with the families of their students, many families have little connection to their schools. Sometimes it seems as if the schools almost prefer that parents keep their distance. Too often, parents are not made to feel welcome in the schools, except for parent-teacher conferences, or to discuss problems their children may be having, or to cheer them on at a sporting event. And many teachers and administrators do not necessarily know about their students' lives outside of school. Many people believe that the notion that there should be a clear and sharp demarcation between school life and home life has gone too far. Jim Connell, president of the Institute for Research and Reform in Education, put it this way when he joined a session of a course Al was teaching, called Family-Centered Community Building: "The foundation of everything that is done in these schools that has been successful is that there are strong, long-standing, and mutually accountable relationships among students, between students and teachers, and among students, teachers, and families. These relationships become, then, the foundations and the beginning of the conversations we can then have about a young person's progress in the form of grades and other indicators of progress—but we have to have the foundation of relationships to do that."

The less than friendly posture of schools toward families can be seen in the failure to adapt school schedules to the work schedules of the vast majority of modern families. Routinely, millions of children are released from school two to three hours before parents are able to leave work, and the resulting lack of supervision is certainly a major reason for the high incidence of teen violence, experimentation with drugs, alcohol, and tobacco, and unwanted teen pregnancy in the after-school hours. Aware of this burden on families, some communities are now reaching out to establish after-school programs, often right in the school buildings themselves. When schools do fill this gap, many parents feel much less concerned about their children's safety, which in turn allows them to be more productive at work.

When educators solicit greater involvement from parents, it's important for them to be sensitive to both the personal and the cultural needs of each family and to provide opportunities for involvement that meet those needs. For example, because it is now more common for students not to be living with both biological parents, educators and policy makers need to develop different methods to enlist the participation of both mothers and fathers—perhaps separately—in their children's school lives.

And there's no question that getting parents to participate pays off in higher achievement by their children. The National Center for Education Statistics (the U.S. Department of Education's clearinghouse for education data) has used the National Household Education survey to help communities better understand parental involvement. Their study showed that students living in families headed by single fathers are the most likely of all students to have highly involved fathers. Further, there is a greater chance of students earning mostly A's if fathers are involved, including stepfather and single-parent father situations. The involvement of mothers is also associated with a higher likelihood of students getting mostly A's, regardless of family structure.

Anne McGintis, coordinator of parent, school, and community involvement at the Hamilton County Schools in Chattanooga, Tennessee, talked to us about how involving parents in the local schools made huge differences not only in the quality of the schools and the children's performance but also in the parents' self-esteem. The Chattanooga School District recognized that it needed to make it easier for parents to become involved, which meant it had to be flexible in terms of parents' schedules. For example, PTA meetings and parent-teacher conferences are now scheduled in the morning, during the lunch hour, or on the weekends—when parents who are tied up at other times can actually attend—and child care is provided at the schools during those meeting times. Then, to ensure that parents had an opportunity to become *trained* in the subjects and issues facing their children, the district created parental-involvement sessions to help parents become more involved in their children's education and lives. In these sessions, the district teaches parents about the standards it uses, so that parents understand how their children's homework and tests are evaluated; offers English classes to those parents for whom it's a second language; and finds creative solutions to include parents who don't think they have anything to offer in school activities.

As students move from elementary to secondary school, parental involvement tends to decrease. Because the children are older and seem more self-sufficient, school personnel may not exert as much effort to involve families as they did when the children were younger. Also, the larger student bodies in high schools can make it more difficult to create and sustain a caring, supportive, and cohesive community. Even so, parental involvement as children get older remains vitally important.

Linda and Tony Wallace provided a good example of this point. When their children entered Indianapolis's Arlington High School—the same school where Linda and Tony had first met, years earlier—they were startled and disturbed by the sharp contrast between their experience and what they saw their children going through. The school had become chaotic and at times violent.

Most of the problems were being caused by older boys who

didn't seem to be responding to the school's effort to impose discipline. So Tony and Linda came up with a plan. They designed a black T-shirt for Tony that said, in big yellow letters, SECURITY DAD. Then, in cooperation with Jacquie Greenwood, the new school principal, Tony began to hang out in the hallways to encourage civility and order. And what started to happen next was a little like magic. Other fathers wanted to play a part—and wanted to wear a shirt just like Tony's. Before long there were lots of security dads. They organized themselves into shifts, and started going to extracurricular events as well.

The school's students—especially those who didn't have fathers at home—were tremendously impressed by fathers like Tony who cared so much that they would rearrange their work schedules and come to school to help impose discipline. The young people understood that they had to respect the men's moral authority—because they were there in their capacity as fathers. Soon, discipline was restored and the problems with violence and disorder were reduced considerably. It worked so well, in fact, that Tony and Linda have been asked to come to other schools to teach the parents how to start the same kind of program.

Parents who get deeply involved with their children's schools tend to have a stronger sense of community when their schools regularly inform them of their children's progress and school events—through school newsletters, letters from the principal and teachers, and the Internet, for example—and when there are frequent, meaningful opportunities for them to be involved, from tutoring to shelving library books to taking a shift as a security dad. Schools can also foster this sense of community by conducting activities with partners in the community such as universities, local cultural institutions like museums or orchestras, and nonprofit organizations. Teachers tend to have a stronger sense of community when the activities geared for families directly support their classroom programs. For example, the Vaughn Next Century Learning Center, a charter school in Los Angeles, has put this idea into practice by making the school a "full-service community hub," principal Yvonne Chan told us. At Vaughn they have established a universal preschool, infant care, GED courses, and counseling services on how to apply for Social Security or for a new job. They even run a bilingual adult education program where the teachers teach parents what their children will be taught a week later. That way parents can help the teachers by reinforcing the lessons at home. The program also improves family relationships. "Middle school kids often look down on parents if their English isn't proficient. We stopped that nonsense," Chan said.

Oakridge Elementary School in Arlington, Virginia, the public school that our children attended, was a wonderful center of the community in which we had a home during Al's congressional years. This healthy integration of school and community was largely the result of a concerted effort by Betty Belt, who had been principal for twenty-five years, to get the parents and the families involved in the school. Every year she organized the Oakridge School Festival, a major community event for parents and kids. Parents would come to the school for planning meetings weeks in advance. The whole school would turn out for this fair, where students, teachers, and parents could play games, eat good food, and even dunk a teacher.

In addition to making parents feel that they're a part of the school community, the fair also benefited the school because the money raised was used for bonuses to attract the best teachers to Oakridge. We parents had lots of reasons to enjoy supporting this school-centered family event, which has been bringing people together in the neighborhood for many years. Tipper has fond memories of attending it when she herself was a student there, and she would buy special treats for her grandmother.

Other schools, too, are making active efforts to reach out to parents. Chan told us that her reasoning behind establishing her school's community library, job training center, and other community resources was simple: "We need to initiate and maintain an ongoing conversation with our families to fully engage them in their children's education." To help parents better balance work and family and to support the school, Vaughn established a "parent exchange service bank" where parents can barter services—such as, "I will take your child to child care if you take a few kids to the library on Saturday." If parents don't have a specific thing to offer, Chan will take an I.O.U. for contributing time to the school, and then she'll call the parents in whenever there's a project to be done. As a result, parents are at Vaughn all day long, every day, contributing in any way they can—as teacher's helpers, community builders, classroom renovators, or even performers.

When you think about it, why should schools close at 3:00 P.M. every day and remain closed all weekend? After all, as Joy Dryfoos noted in her book, *Inside Full-Service Community Schools*, schools are centrally located and offer amenities such as gymnasiums that community center personnel can work with to provide activities and services. Welcoming adult education and cultural activities into the school ensures that the school is not deserted after the last bell rings. And as schools and classrooms across the country have connected to the Internet—helped in large part by the E-Rate, which ensures that all schools can afford to take advantage of the educational opportunities of the Internet—teachers and schools now have another valuable tool. Connections in the classroom can be used not only to improve learning outcomes, but also to build community by enhancing the dialogue with parents and community members.

Today, many schools and communities are also either encouraging voluntary community service or requiring a specified number of community-service hours for young people as a condition of graduation. One of the best things about community service is that it helps foster a productive connection between students and the community that often lasts for life. We have had the pleasure of working with many community leaders and public servants over the years, and a very high percentage of them say that they got their start in community activities when they were still in school.

Providing teens with ways to contribute to their communities can help broaden their experience and enhance their self-esteem. One example is Communities In Schools, an impressive community development organization that focuses on building supportive communities around children, giving them the resources to prepare for life. Organizing around schools, especially ones with a high proportion of so-called at-risk youth, CIS serves 1.9 million young people around the country each year and has been described as the largest drop-out prevention program in America. CIS espouses five critical things that all children should have: a one-on-one relationship with a caring adult, a safe place to learn and grow, a healthy start and a healthy future, a marketable skill to use upon graduation, and a chance to give back to peers and the community.

CIS recognizes that the chance to give back is a powerful motivation for teens and a critical part of their developing sense of themselves as valuable members of the community who are not "at risk" but, rather, can be resources for their families and their communities. CIS founder and president Bill Milliken told us, "Help is not always helpful. The greatest gift we can give a kid is to allow him to give something to us. We have to create communities and learning environments where we expect young people to give back. Once they find out they have something to give, that improves their self-esteem, because they realize they are valued."

Youth development programs such as this one need to be based on a sound understanding of exactly what teens are going through. While parents and families will always be the most important force in the lives of teens, communities can provide additional support and value to their lives during this time of great change. After all, this is the time of life when young people are beginning the process of establishing their own independence. When communities get involved with adolescents, the tendency has been to focus youth programs on the prevention of such high-risk behaviors as teen pregnancy, drug abuse, and violence. As Karen Pittman of the Forum for Youth Investment notes, however, "problem free is not fully prepared." To illustrate the point, Rich Lerner of Tufts University offers this example: "Say I own a delicatessen and a young person who is applying for work says in a job interview, 'I don't drink, I don't do drugs, and I don't engage in violent crime.' I would say, 'That's fine—but what can you do to help make my business successful?'"

The point is that being problem free is not enough. True youth development focuses not only on prevention but also on developing assets, making young people more resilient, and giving them skills and job training. It is important to prepare them for the next level of education and help them develop social skills, communication skills, and leadership skills.

Toward that end, Communities In Schools works to ensure that students graduate with the skills and abilities they need to succeed in the world—not only life skills, but also a marketable professional skill. Through its independent state and local programs, the initiative builds partnerships between schools, community leaders, and businesses. But, as Milliken told us, the most critical elements of the program are the simplest: a mentor relationship with a caring, involved adult and the support of the community. "Everything boils down to the relationships and creating community. It is relationships that change people, not programs. A 'good program' has simply created an environment where healthy relationships are happening between adults and children, where everyone gives and everyone receives," said Milliken.

COMMUNITIES AND SPACE

According to some newer definitions of the word, community can be found in cyberspace or in a group of far-flung members who communicate with one another about a shared interest. But the kind of community where families actually live is a place. And places are physical spaces that determine our comings and goings, define the structure of "here" and "there," draw the boundaries of "us" and "them," and shape the patterns of our days and nights.

To paraphrase Winston Churchill, we make our spaces, but then our spaces make us. And because man-made spaces are created from asphalt and concrete, wood and plastic, steel and stone—not flesh and blood—they usually outlast us by several generations. It is common, therefore, that each new generation of families is shaped by spaces they had no hand in making. As the Judeo-Christian religious tradition tells us: we live in cities that we did not build. By the same token, it's past time to accept responsibility for the fact that our great-grandchildren will live in cities that we built.

Unfortunately, however, a great many of the spaces in which we live have been made and unmade according to a design that does not particularly take families into account. As Samina Quraeshi of the University of Miami told us, "The guiding principle shaping the design of our American communities is simply this: Make certain that all the cars are happy."

One of the most serious problems families encounter today in trying to establish meaningful connections with the places where they live is that the physical structure of many communities works against them. If a poorly designed subdivision makes it difficult for a family to routinely interact with their neighbors and to share inviting public spaces, a sense of community will be seriously hindered. A family that lives in a neighborhood with sidewalks, playgrounds, and pleasant stores within walking distance has a very different relationship to the community than a family that must drive to purchase even the most basic amenity.

The physical landscape of our neighborhoods and towns has changed markedly since World War II. U.S. metropolitan areas have been decentralizing, leading to longer commute times, fewer neighbors and community activities within walking distance from one's home, the isolation of homes from retail stores and professional offices, and the segregation of houses according to size and type through zoning.

Community cohesion is also severely damaged when families

frequently relocate from one community to the next. One of the reasons for the constant movement is that many zoning laws require houses of roughly the same size and value to be clumped together, so that a couple looking to buy a larger home to accommodate a growing family finds that they must change neighborhoods. After the children are grown, when the couple wants a smaller, more affordable place to live on their retirement income, they have to move yet again—once more pulling their family out of the community by the roots.

Over the last fifty years, the traditional neighborhood model has been replaced by an "idealized, artificial system," according to Andres Duany, Elizabeth Plater-Zyberk, and Jeff Speck, authors of *Suburban Nation: The Rise of Sprawl and the Decline of the American Dream.* New real estate developments consisting of housing subdivisions, shopping centers, and office parks, all connected by highways, are increasingly becoming the norm. Ironically, communities become fragmented by the powerful and persistent impact of their own growth. If a community experiences a period of growth through expansion, and sprawls across the surrounding countryside, home builders, developers, and lending institutions all get used to financing that growth pattern, which causes yet more sprawl and fragmentation.

Meanwhile, families often look for their dream house in the suburbs—just a little farther out than the last one—and the pattern builds upon itself. Soon public subsidies are built into community policies, and then national policies begin to encourage and help finance urban and suburban sprawl. Duany, Plater-Zyberk, and Speck cite the example of loan programs sponsored by the Federal Housing Administration and Veterans Administration after World War II. The loans helped families finance more than 11 million new homes, but they "discouraged the renovation of existing housing stock, while turning their back on the construction of row houses, mixed-use buildings, and other urban housing types," thus helping to set the stage for suburban sprawl.

Todd and Pat Letke-Alexander have firsthand experience of this displacement. Pat notes that the suburban area north of Baltimore where she and Todd live now has "no sense of community." Although they're pleased with the local schools and feel that they live in a safe area, they don't find as many opportunities to interact with their neighbors and others as they'd like. Todd says, "Our community is basically Patty's family."

Suburban sprawl is also accelerated by the migration of jobs from cities to suburbs. According to the *2000 State of the Cities Report* by the U.S. Department of Housing and Urban Development, suburbs gained far more jobs in the mid-1990s than city centers did. In Atlanta, for example, less than half of the jobs in the metropolitan area now remain within ten miles of the city center, according to Harvard economist Edward Glaeser and his colleagues.

Fortunately, a number of towns and cities are now recognizing that families must be able to connect to the community on a human scale—and that the only way this can happen is if the community connects organically with the larger region in which it is located. Some communities are now forming partnerships with surrounding rural areas and suburbs in an effort to reverse the pattern of sprawl. This new approach, called "smart growth," is an emerging strategy that can slow sprawl, enhance investment in urban centers, protect the environment, and improve access to community.

Maryland's Smart Growth and Neighborhood Conservation Program, initiated by Governor Parris Glendening in 1997, is an example of how a thoughtful, coordinated approach to growth issues can achieve these goals. The approach balances a concern for economic growth with other, less tangible—but no less important—objectives. Under the plan, growth is welcomed but is directed away from pristine, undeveloped places; brownfields (contaminated, abandoned industrial sites) are rehabilitated; older downtown areas are revitalized; investment in historic preservation is promoted; and workers are encouraged to move closer to their places of work.

In her book *Designing the City: A Guide for Advocates and Public*

Officials, Adele Fleet Bacow asserts that good design can accomplish public goals by making communities more livable, economically stable, more efficient to travel within and through, and more affordable. Recently, townspeople in <u>Elizabethton</u>, a small town in eastern Tennessee, were concerned about both development issues and protecting their environment, Bacow notes. Through a coordinated planning process—including substantial input from residents—a plan was devised that bolstered the local economy by creating an industrial park and revitalizing the downtown; protected the environment by controlling erosion with a riverfront park that also increased access to the river; and preserved the community's sense of history by enlarging the historic district. That's exactly the sort of effort needed in more communities across America.

Good community design is an ongoing process involving not only businesses and real estate developers, but also local government, citizens, and community groups. Buildings, neighborhoods, the environment, freeways, cities, and people have their own life cycles, within which needs, circumstances, priorities, and patterns of living change and evolve. In practice, however, when only a few stakeholders are actually involved in the process of community design, they can end up effectively controlling it for their own benefit. Unfortunately, in too many cases the system fully recognizes only those values that can be expressed in money, while giving a much lower priority to those values that can't be priced in dollars and cents—values such as family cohesion or a community's quality of life. In recent decades the field of environmental justice has emerged as a means to give voice to those communities where landfills, freeways, and the like were built without appropriate consideration of the impact on residents. We need a "family justice" movement as well.

To take one example, the <u>presence of parks</u> can do a great deal to enhance the quality of life for families that want to spend unstructured time together outdoors in a beautiful place. Low-cost and free opportunities and venues for family play are certainly in the best interest of the community. Public spaces bring vitality to communities. Places where people can congregate for organized activities or simply take a walk or a break from work help keep communities healthy. The Village of Arts and Humanities in North Philadelphia exemplifies how the revitalization of a public space can reinvigorate a community. Yet the perceived need for real estate development opportunities (and thus the chance for a community to make a profit in the short term) is frequently allowed to override the longer-term interests of the community.

As the physical spaces of our communities change, so too do our patterns of transportation. The nature of a community's transportation system exerts a powerful influence on the quality of life, determining, for example, whether or not there are traffic jams that generate extra pollution and prevent parents from getting home in time to read a bedtime story. The transportation system is also critical to the ability of low-income families to travel easily—on public transportation, if necessary—from inner cities to jobs in the suburbs.

The amount of time needed to commute is another powerful barrier to social connection in the community. The increase in commuting time has contributed to the sharp decline in civic participation rates. Robert Putnam's research reveals that every ten minutes of additional commuting time reduces all forms of family and community connectedness by 10 percent.

Beyond the impact of the built environment, communities are now finding that clean air, clean water, and a beautiful natural environment are not only good for the soul but have enormous economic benefits as well. When companies have some choice in where to build a new facility, they now frequently look for an area with a clean environment and a wide range of cultural amenities, so that the families of the future employees and executives will be happy—which translates into lower turnover and higher productivity. Richard Florida and Derek Davison of Carnegie Mellon University note that a "growing number of companies have pioneered new strategies for integrating the environment into their overall business strategy and for simultaneously improving their environmental and business performance." It's no longer true that communities need to choose between employment and a pleasant environment.

Without question, then, the physical shape and structure of the communities in which we live can have an enormous impact on the shape and quality of our family lives. "The idea of community is related to the sense of families at home, sharing common bonds and interests, building the infrastructure that is necessary to protect themselves from want and fulfill the needs of faith and ambition," Quraeshi said, adding, "When a place feels disjointed and beyond the ability of its residents to react, its integrity can be threatened by demoralization and flight. When the currents of change and the reactions to them act in concert, the place feels whole, engaging, and rewarding to those who inhabit it."

RESTORING THE BROKEN CONNECTIONS

Healthy communities are similar in some ways to healthy families. They may not be joined at the heart, but their members do feel an emotional identification with others who live in their community. In a family, if individuals don't communicate with one another, everyone suffers. Similarly, when one part of a community feels little or no connection to the community as a whole, the impact can be devastating. We can use the concept of attachment theory from the field of human development to illustrate this point. If an infant establishes a healthy attachment to a caregiver, she learns to feel secure and empowered, but if she is ignored or mistreated, she learns a sense of powerlessness. In the same way, if a community fails to understand or respond appropriately to persistent signals of distress from a small group within the community, that group may learn a sense of powerlessness and, eventually, rage. However the separation begins, divisions between different parts of a community will increase, and they are like the proverbial "broken windows": they serve as a magnet for crime, prejudice, and poverty.

Many experts who study American communities believe that discrimination based on race, ethnicity, religion, or sexual orientation represents the most serious obstacle to the establishment of cohesion. As America grows ever more diverse, finding ways to bring families of different racial and ethnic backgrounds together is more crucial than ever to the future of our community connectedness. America is still a nation of immigrants, and future growth in the United States' population will be driven primarily by immigrants and their children. One in five children today is an immigrant or the child of an immigrant; more than 60 percent of those children are Hispanic and more than 20 percent are Asian. "The emergence of racial and ethnic minorities as the majority population is occurring most rapidly, and will become a reality first, among children," Donald Hernandez said. "Immigrant children live in very strong families. Most of them live with two parents. Their parents come with very high educational aspirations and hopes for their children. They are working very hard. In all of those ways, they exhibit American values—things we have valued in the United States historically." In building a rich and diverse nation, our children will be leading the way. Creating community among people of different backgrounds is imperative for the health and resilience of the nation in which our children are growing up.

Just as our brains automatically combine the slightly different view from each of our eyes and give us depth perception, so can we see community problems much more clearly if we take advantage of the different points of view in a diverse community. African-Americans, Asian-Americans, Native Americans, Hispanics, and Anglos, women and men, gays and straights, Gentiles and Jews, Muslims and Hindus, young and old, able and disabled—these and other distinctions among people can be sources of wisdom for communities. By learning how to combine the different perspectives and share our respective truths, we can see each challenge and each opportunity more clearly.

Every community in America faces some version of this challenge.

If, like Lily Yeh, people are determined to work together and embrace all community members, our country will be all the richer for it. Communication across racial lines has historically been a source of tension in American communities, but when the problem is approached in a thoughtful way it can be transcended.

At times, families may feel powerless to tackle major problems facing a community. But many families and communities prove that it is possible to make a difference. Diane Bock, who started Community Cousins, told us that racism "is considered a macro problem but it's practiced by individuals." And Diane continues to put her beliefs into practice. In the wake of the terrorist attacks on September 11, 2001, her organization is reaching out to more families of Middle Eastern heritage to further increase the cross-cultural understanding in their community. A Muslim woman who is one of Diane's "cousins" is now starting a new chapter in Garden Grove, California, where California's largest mosque is located and where one third of the families in the chapter will be Muslim.

Diane believes that "racism is as serious as any of the major diseases we are fighting. We should put similar effort into battling racism as we do to finding treatments for cancer or heart disease. Involving individuals and encouraging them to buy into a solution will ultimately be the most effective way to change people's hearts and minds—from the bottom up." And while bringing people together one family at a time may seem insignificant to some people, Diane constantly reminds us of the power of small, positive steps repeated again and again. She told us that her favorite proverb is "The most foolish man is he who did nothing because he could only do a little."

Lily Yeh is another inspiring example of someone who is committed to bringing positive change to her community, and her faith in the power of this commitment was apparent from the start. When she first began creating her artwork, some of the neighbors who supported her told her that she would have to build walls to protect the art from the "dangerous neighborhood." As Lily told them, "I can't put up walls, because I came to build this beautiful garden for the community. I can't say, 'This is ours.' Everybody is welcome in here."

Although she faced a number of setbacks at first—and experienced some vandalism from neighborhood youths—Lily did not give up. Rather than building walls or fences, she decided to befriend the children, including those who vandalized her work. She had her construction crew help them build a clubhouse, and thereby won their respect. She eventually got them involved in her project and named them "The Eleventh Street Youth Construction Team."

In Lily Yeh's community, communication across ethnic and racial lines isn't necessarily a particular goal—it's just something that happens in the course of building and nurturing the Village. Among the people Lily works with, such barriers have mostly slipped away. German Wilson, the Village's theater director, told us with a laugh that he never expected to have a Chinese little sister, but that's exactly what Lily is to him. Lily's mosaic community knits together many people of different races and backgrounds, and is a vivid symbol of the potential that we have as a country.

For the people whose lives have been transformed by the enormous contribution that Lily Yeh has made to the community with her art and her gardens, the Village is much more than a symbol. Lily remembers with particular fondness that when she looked around the impoverished neighborhood early in the project, she decided that it desperately needed water. But the only way she could afford to bring the children water was to paint a wall mural of an ocean with a sunset—so she did. Later, when she couldn't take the children to the countryside, she brought a small bit of the countryside to them in the form of rich, black earth to plant a real, live garden. "I never thought black dirt had such power," Lily said. "But the first full load they dumped, with the steam rising, and the butterflies, and dragonflies, and the children chasing them, that brought tears to people's eyes. In this very stark place, it was the beginning of hope."

CONCLUSION

If you believe, as we do, that strengthening American families is important, then there is much to do. We have worked on issues related to families for the past quarter century, and over the past decade, as we have held our annual Family Re-Union gatherings, we have felt a growing sense of urgency about the need to change the way families are seen, supported, nurtured, and respected in America.

The stakes are very high. We all know that for each of us, having a strong and healthy family and good relationships can make the difference between living a happy, successful life or living a life of constant struggle and hardship. But the strength and health of American families are also crucial to the soundness and character of our nation and to the way we relate to one another as citizens. Think about it: over time, when families function well internally and forge strong bonds to the community, social problems diminish.

But when families—for whatever reason—function poorly, social problems begin to mount up.

In addressing the challenges that confront the American family, it's important to keep our current problems in context. The history of the family reveals cyclical patterns and by most measures, the American family slowly grew stronger during the 1990s, after declining during the 1980s. The divorce rate, the out-of-wedlock birthrate, and the amount of time fathers spent with their children, for example, all improved slightly in the latest figures available. Moreover, comparisons to the so-called golden age for families in the 1950s can be misleading, because the 1950s were so different from any other decade before or since.

Even so, a comparison of the family of today to the family of 1960 suggests that many of the problems we now face in America are unprecedented and demand attention. Over the past two generations, the number of children born to unmarried mothers has increased at a shocking rate; too many fathers are absent from the home; and the divorce rate, though improved, appears to have stabilized at a very high level—twice that of 1960. The economic stress on low- and middle-income families is dangerously high, and the time crunch is depleting the reserves of family cohesion.

Stresses The *quality* of family life is suffering because so many working parents are now chronically exhausted, stretched thin, and stressed out. In the last twenty years, the sharp increase in the number of hours worked outside the home by mothers as well as fathers— along with the dramatic increase in the number of single parents— has placed intense new strains on families. Large expenses that are relatively new for many families, like child care, and huge increases in traditional expenses, like housing and health care, have combined to put the squeeze on family budgets. In the struggle to make ends meet, personal debt—especially credit card debt—has reached alarming levels.

And in trying to balance the growing demands in their workplaces with the needs of their families, many are cutting back on sleep, time off, and recreation. As a consequence, the extra demands of the workplace have now begun to crowd out not only the time available for family, but also some of the emotional resources that used to be available. That's especially worrisome, because at a time when emotional connection and intimacy are the most important "tie that binds," the average family may be less resilient and more vulnerable to new pressures that threaten that connection.

One of our purposes in this book has been to describe the transformation of the American family over the last few decades. For the first time in history, the definition of family relies less on structure and more on subjective experience. We have also discussed the many new pressures challenging today's families. We have met some wonderful people doing difficult, extraordinary things to honor their families and nurture their children, even as they cope with enormous pressures. We have looked closely at the everyday experience of American families—one family at a time.

In the end, we have come to believe more deeply than ever that if we are serious about strengthening families, then every sector of American society has a role to play. In a democracy, we are all responsible for supporting healthy family life. No one can or should tell families how to raise their children, but we can all use help, and we can cheer others on in a multitude of ways. Many of the needed changes don't necessarily involve the federal government, but most do require national leadership.

Our communities have a big role to play. Indeed, a great many initiatives at the community level can make families more self-sufficient. And some communities, like Redlands, California, are taking the lead in showing the way—with a chief of police whose philosophy is explicitly "family-centered." We think it could serve as an excellent model for other communities.

Universities can also play a major role. We've been working with a group of forward-thinking universities to create and teach a course in "Family-Centered Community Building" at Fisk University, Middle Tennessee State University, and the University of California at Los Angeles. Those three, along with more than a dozen others, including Columbia, Tufts, and Vanderbilt, have been willing to look past the traditional departmental boundaries to combine the best aspects of many disciplines—including psychology, urban design, sociology, criminology, architecture, law, business, education, environmental studies, health sciences, and child development—to offer integrated courses of study and advance broad-based research that will support families and their communities.

The philanthropic community, long active in and a critical contributor to family support services and community development, should play an even larger role. Individual donors as well as charitable and corporate foundations need to reexamine the boundaries created by their sources of funding and look across the disciplines, across the generations, and across the issue categories to fund pioneering responses to families and their communities. Our foundation partners in Family Re-Union have done just that.

The faith community, traditionally a leader in supporting families, can do still more to help families adjust to the pressures of the modern world while remaining true to their oldest values. Many congregations and faith leaders are leading the charge—like Reverend T. D. Jakes, whom we visited at the dedication of his new church in Dallas, the Potter's House. Jakes combines traditional religious instruction with a sophisticated blend of family therapy and couples counseling to deliver a powerful, healing message for families. Other faith leaders are working hard to promote interfaith activities to build tolerance and an understanding of what all of the major faith traditions have in common.

Corporate America can also be more creative in offering flexible arrangements for hours worked and the location where the work takes place. One of the experts on family we consulted, Lynne Casper, who is launching a new initiative to study work and family for the National Institutes of Health, told us: "Corporations and employees are basing everything on a 1950s framework, and the family has long since moved past that. What needs to be done is a restructuring of work." And one of the keys is to reward productivity and results, not just "face time." Once again, some corporations, like Stride Rite in Boston, are leading the way. Stride Rite provides child care, parental leave, and an array of family-friendly policies. Other companies are pioneering flexible work hours and telecommuting for employees. As more companies discover that their own enlightened self-interest is promoted by policies oriented to the new American family, there will be a greater recognition of the productivity gains, increases in worker satisfaction, and decreases in absenteeism that come with supporting their employees' desire to be at least as committed to their families as they are to their jobs.

Of course, families themselves must begin to demand the flexibility they need at work, and to reach out to one another to help with the challenging roles involved in families, such as the job of parenting. Each of us must decide for ourselves what we are willing to do for our own family and our neighbors and then, as active citizens, decide what we are going to demand and work for. Perhaps most important, we must commit ourselves to teaching our children that the central role of family—in all its wonderfully various forms—should be respected and honored in everything we do.

We have long believed that the first and most important step our country can take to help families is to change our way of *thinking* about families. For many people, the change will be both more difficult and more profound than they expect. Specifically, what's required is a shift from focusing exclusively on the individual to focusing on the family as a complex system, a system whose essential meaning is found in the relationships among the individuals who are connected emotionally and committed to one another as family—those who are, as we put it here, joined at the heart.

radical? new thought

*

For several hundred years, the principal thrust of social thought in the West has been focused on the dignity and rights of the individual. Indeed, the ascendancy of the nuclear family over the past millennium has accompanied and enhanced the development of individual rights. But any strength can become a weakness if taken to an illogical extreme. It is becoming increasingly apparent that an exclusive focus on individuals, to the exclusion of the family and the community, and on individual rights, to the exclusion of responsibilities, is in fact illogical and counterproductive.

Earlier, we compared the family to the community; we also believe that in some ways, the family is like the environment. In all three cases, connections and relationships are what matter most, and when something goes wrong in one part, it usually affects all the rest. One big difference between family issues and environmental issues lies in our individual degree of control and influence. If we decide to bring about healthy changes in our families—and convince other family members to join in the effort—we are likely to succeed, whereas changing the environment requires convincing a lot more people, some of whom have a financial stake in continuing behaviors that cause environmental harm.

Like the environment, each family is a sum greater than its parts, an entity that must be respected on its own terms, not just as a collection of individuals. If we can change our way of thinking and take families as well as individuals into account, we will open up a new way of seeing what is truly valuable to us and what is not. The choices we make about how to conduct our lives can be made with a fuller appreciation of all that is at stake.

For example, time off from work may seem to have little value if our way of thinking about the use of time is dominated by the marketplace value of each individual's hours. After all, employers pay time-and-a-half for overtime work. But if the needs and rewards of family life are taken fully into account, then the choice between more overtime at work and more time off with family looks very different.

We should encourage employers to create incentives so that employees have a real choice between overtime and family time. One approach is to permit employers to structure their employee benefits so that compensation for overtime could be either in the form of time-and-a-half *wages* for each hour, or time-and-a-half *time off* for each hour. But the key to the fairness and acceptability of such an approach is to ensure that the option is always in the control of the employee, with no penalty or retribution allowed if the employee chooses family time.

Corporate America has also got to become more responsive to the need for quality child care. Hardworking parents are now forced to rely on a community-based child-care system for their young children that is largely, in the judgment of the leading experts, a national disgrace. High-quality child care has been shown to be healthy for children, but most of the child care presently available in America is of either mediocre or low quality, which research has confirmed is harmful to children. So what should we do—ignore the crisis and continue to subject the majority of a generation to a massive experiment? Of course not; instead, we urgently need to develop a variety of new approaches to ensure that the quality of affordable child care is quickly elevated. Among other things, that means taking steps to recruit and train a large number of new, highly qualified child-care workers and finding a way to make sure they are adequately compensated. Our goal should be to ensure that all children develop their full potential and are well prepared for school.

At the other end of the age spectrum, the cost to families of elder care has gone up dramatically as life spans have increased and medical bills have soared, thus worsening the squeeze on what some are now calling "the club-sandwich generation." Meanwhile, many family caregivers—for both infirm elders and disabled children or other family members—are laboring and suffering in silence, mostly hidden from public awareness, because they are in their homes seven days a week taking care of a loved one. They need help, and at a minimum, providing respite care and adult day care for part of the week can be a life saver. But they also need financial help with medical bills that many simply cannot afford to pay. And they need a commitment from our nation to a program of long-term care that helps families adapt to the new reality of longer life spans and more chronic, but treatable, conditions—and the new family expenses that result.

On the other hand, many more elderly people are now healthy and active. Here, too, we should change our thinking—in this case, about the role of the elderly in families. We should see them as assets, not burdens. We should make a concerted effort to mobilize their talents and considerable energies, and encourage them to contribute by serving their communities, providing wisdom to younger generations, and helping all of us address new challenges. Older Americans may, for example, be able to help families pass on the values they most cherish in a cultural environment that seems to work against them, with too many adolescents exploring without guidance the violent and explicit content in the dark corners of our culture. Bringing teens and older members of a community together might go a long way toward helping adolescents sort out these pressures and develop a solid sense of self.

Our increasingly pervasive and omnipresent media culture is a source of serious competition for families. It's not only the exposure to questionable content but also the very nature of our interaction with some media—like television—that have a seductive and compelling attraction for us. Far too much prime family time is being replaced by hours upon hours of television-watching, and the combination of all the new technologies for communicating— e-mail, cell phones, pagers, and instant messaging—seems sometimes to have caught families in a kind of hypnosis, leaving them surrounded by a seamless cocoon of electronic stimuli and messages that steadily take up more and more of the time, space, and attention that families used to set aside for family activities and interaction.

As vice president, Al worked with President Clinton to give parents more control over TV programming that they thought was inappropriate for their children by requiring a "V-chip" and a rating system. We successfully argued for regulation to require broadcasters to air three hours of educational programming for children each week, and for the "E-Rate" program, which has been providing the funds to help close the so-called digital divide—by connecting school classrooms and libraries to the Internet. Today, more than 98 percent of schools are connected, as are more than 90 percent of classrooms. But there is still much more that needs to be done, and no one should underestimate the depth of problems created for low-income families by the digital divide.

American families face many other decisions about values that must also be resolved successfully if we are to ensure a bright future. For example, the transformation of the American family has brought astonishing new diversity and pluralism in the kinds of families that make up our country, creating a need for more acceptance and understanding of differences. Laws protecting civil rights should be vigorously enforced and, where necessary, strengthened. During this century, racial and ethnic minorities will become the majority of the population, and this will happen first among young people. In fact, according to the Census Bureau, children under eighteen who are currently part of a racial or ethnic minority will make up more than half of all American children in just a little more than thirty-five years.

Meanwhile, we must work together to promote greater understanding of the rich diversity of cultural traditions in our country and thus draw on the many different strengths we all can contribute. We also need to be more accepting of the different kinds of families that Americans are choosing for themselves. We should reserve our intolerance for genuine threats to the family, such as domestic violence, child abuse, prejudice, and discrimination; the failure to offer treatment for substance abuse; employers who are insensitive to the needs of families; and outdated attitudes and shortsighted policies and programs that do not take family into account.

The powerful link between the health of families and the health of communities requires that we provide much more support for community-based policing, which focuses on preventing crime by strengthening both families and neighborhoods. Communities became safer during the latter two-thirds of the 1990s as a result of a variety of policy changes. But after declining for most of the decade, violent crime rates are unfortunately going up again. In addition to tough enforcement, communities can work toward safety and security by involving families at every step in the process, by promoting crime prevention with more playgrounds and parks and sports facilities, and by developing more community-based and school-based arts, theater, and music programs. Our communities will also become stronger when we address the serious shortage of affordable housing for low- and middle-income families with a new public commitment to create incentives for expanding the supply and improving the quality of affordable housing.

In a similar vein, the two of us have a special commitment to fighting on behalf of families for community-based mental-health care—and for insurance coverage that is at parity with the coverage of all other health care. We believe that part of this coverage should also involve providing quality coverage of substance-abuse treatment and prevention.

At the community level, our most important task may be providing meaningful reform of public education for families with children, including changes in local governance and state financing—backed up by a commitment of adequate federal resources to make the improvements real. New emphasis is needed on early education, especially since we now know that the period of early child development is one of the most crucial for success in later life. We must also build on efforts to involve families actively in their children's education, since their participation benefits the schools, the children, and the families themselves.

We urgently need universal preschool, formed in partnership with communities and public-private alliances, in order to simultaneously relieve family expenses for child care and provide the stimulating environments that facilitate healthy child development during the most critical years of life. Ideally, the hours should match the hours that parents are at work. A similar joint effort to provide high-quality after-school youth development programs for elementary and high school students is also needed. Such a program would simultaneously ease the minds of parents who are still at work during weekday afternoons when adolescents are especially at risk for getting into trouble and also make available enriching activities for young people at a time in their lives when they most need attention from leaders and role models. And we should offer new courses in financial literacy to all students and expand the already existing commitments to service learning.

Shortsighted views about our global community also have a negative impact on families, most especially when it comes to the environment. Cleaning up the air and water and preventing more cases of asthma among children should be considered more important than bailing out a polluter who doesn't want to clean up his own mess. Finding the political will to stop global warming and save the global climate for our grandchildren depends upon placing an accurate value on the well-being of those grandchildren. Laws creating strong incentives for cleaner cars—and yes, phasing out the internal combustion engine, in much less than twenty-five years—and investments in attractive, efficient, and affordable public transportation would do a great deal to help family budgets and promote smart growth as an alternative to sprawl—and, in the process, reduce disease-causing pollution.

Families could also benefit if they could convince communities to make a special effort to preserve beautiful places where families can gather and enjoy themselves. Communities attuned to families' needs could plan more family-oriented patterns of development so that shopping, meaningful jobs, and good, safe housing are available in close enough proximity to one another. One simple way to enhance the dialogue between families and communities is to insist upon "community health report cards" to make it easier for families to hold their communities accountable. Such a report card could assess a local community's assets against a "best practices" guide or, even better, against the goals chosen by the citizens themselves.

Finally, we feel compelled to say that if families want to get results through the political system—in their community, state, or nation—they must become involved in the process. Many of the same pressures harming family cohesion are also hurting communities and weakening the connections between families and communities—and that loss of connection has, in turn, damaged our democracy and diminished our capacity for self-government. Put simply, chronically exhausted, isolated, and stressed-out family members naturally find it harder to be active as citizens, go to town hall meetings, debate community issues, and maintain a healthy involvement with democracy. Moreover, the cheapening of our political dialogue by the replacement of thoughtful discourse with impressionistic thirty-second television advertisements has served to obscure the real issues and further discourage participation by feeding cynicism.

This declining involvement by average citizens and their families in the political process has enhanced the influence of special interest groups who have enough wealth to disproportionately influence the process, and has magnified the power of small groups who have enough passion to vote in disproportionate numbers. It seems at times as if, in the words of W. B. Yeats, "The best lack all conviction, while the worst are full of passionate intensity."

Whatever the reason, voting participation, and thus the political influence of average families, has declined. In this environment, some groups who believe public programs usually do more harm than good have mounted a sustained effort to reduce supports and services for families (and individuals) and reduce the investment of tax dollars in social programs in order to eliminate claimed distortions of and interference in the marketplace.

We take exception to several prevailing policies that we believe are proving harmful to many low- and moderate-income families, including tax policies that favor the wealthiest in the nation, as well as the uncompromising opposition to collective bargaining rights, employee benefits, minimum wage increases, and child-care assistance. We urge a reconsideration of these policies and a close look at what we believe are inconsistencies between their stated goals and their overall approach. For example, the criticism of welfare mothers of young children who do not work combined with the criticism of middle-class mothers who do not stay at home with their children is a paradox that we have never understood and that leads to strange policies at best. We also oppose attempts to undermine the current design of the Social Security program and replace it with a hybrid public-private system that most actuaries and analysts say would require average families to pay a much larger share of the costs of retirement.

Of course, many of the economic problems facing families have been building for a long time, and some of the causes of the growing economic pressure on families are complex. One example is the strong downward pressure on wages, which is driven by new competition in the global marketplace from nations with large populations and much lower wage rates—nations that now have greater access to technology and capital investment. Further, the disproportionate strength of the wealthy in our political system is due in part to the growing importance of money in politics, mainly to buy television advertisements, and to a long decline in the percentage of America's workforce that is unionized—although this trend may have been stopped and even reversed in the last few years.

But whatever the causes of the economic pressures on families, what is clearly needed is a set of family-friendly policies that address the most critical ways in which families need help from the community. There are many legitimate differences of opinion about what works and what doesn't, and vigorous political debate about the best ways to design policies to help and strengthen families is needed and highly desirable. What we believe is unacceptable— from the standpoint of families—is for nobody to take responsibility for meeting these critical needs. When government and business and political figures keep passing the buck, families pay the costs and children are harmed.

During eight years in the White House, Al and President Clinton looked long and hard at how a wide range of policies would affect families. By considering governance from this perspective, we were able to implement many policies specifically designed to help average families. For one thing, we developed an economic plan that greatly expanded a tax credit for low- and middle-income working families, known as the "earned income tax credit," to put cash in the hands of 15 million of the hardest working families who most needed help. We created Community Development Financial Institutions and raised the minimum wage, helping 10 million workers. We increased housing assistance and championed the reinstatement and increase of new housing vouchers. We eliminated the budget deficits while expanding and improving services in almost every area where families needed help. The nation prospered: the economy grew at an average of 4 percent annually from 1993 to 2000—the longest economic expansion on record—leading to the creation of more than 22 million new jobs, the lowest poverty rate in twenty years, and the strongest economy on record.

Because we believed that our nation's future depends in large part on the commitment we make to our children and their families, we worked to nearly double funding for the Head Start program, and to create the Early Start program targeted to development of younger children. For the same reason, we won the largest expansion of health insurance for children since the creation of the Medicaid program, helping 2.5 million children receive health insurance.

With our Reinventing Government initiative, we helped communities that had created comprehensive and carefully conceived plans for helping families and children to focus on their own goals. We provided greater flexibility so they could use federal dollars more efficiently and helped them to measure their results and to share with other communities what they had learned. We also created a program called "Boost4Kids" that helped communities achieve goals such as increased health care coverage for children and better school readiness. We enabled these communities to streamline their interactions with federal agencies and to cut red tape so that this initiative didn't cost a single additional federal dollar. We did the same thing at the state level with "performance partnerships" like the one we established with the state of Oregon, in which the state agreed to set clear goals and to measure its performance in return for the removal of strict guidelines and detailed requirements that traditionally have been attached to the spending of federal dollars. Flexible and creative partnerships like these allow people at the local level to determine what families really need, instead of focusing on what the government thinks they ought to have.

In order to address the real needs of families, we have to be prepared to make some difficult decisions again. And ultimately, the decisions we make as a nation concerning the importance of families will come down to judgments about values. In deciding what values should guide us as a country, we ought to reflect on the values demonstrated by the millions of healthy and successful American families. The values that guide the families we interviewed in depth for this book are, we believe, compelling examples of the love, courage, and commitment that so many families display every day in the way they care for one another. By their own admission, the families we interviewed are far from perfect. But at their best, they are truly inspiring, and if we could follow their lead in the way we care for one another, that's really all it would take to restore families to their rightful place at the center of American life.

As the two of us reflect on the great strengths of the families we interviewed for this book, here is what stands out in our minds:

Mitch Philpott, Cindy Nalley, and Lee Nalley demonstrate what commitment and dedication are all about in the extraordinary way they provide two loving homes that give joy, comfort, and caretaking to their disabled son, Brett. We have never seen a more inspiring example of the commitment to love one another that is truly at the core of family. What our country most needs is a commitment to one another that aspires to be as strong as the commitment Brett's parents have made to him.

Rodney and Missy Crumpton taught us a lot about family with the brave decision they made to radically change the course of their lives by going to college in their forties. No one in their family had ever gone to college, and they wanted to give their beloved young grandson Caleb a legacy of family achievement that would inspire him to reach for higher goals in his life. The empowering love they feel for their grandson has made them not only role models for Caleb, but models of determination for all of us. Can we as a nation match the Crumptons' example and care enough for the next generation to make major changes in our lives for their sake?

Susan and Dick Fadley emerged from false starts, divorces, and broken dreams to weave a seamless, loving, blended family with six children born in different circumstances. The stamina and creativity they have brought to their marriage are exactly the qualities our nation needs to make sense of the new complexities in American families. The Fadleys show us that the key to success is hanging in there and working it out—no matter what.

Jeanne and Bill Hoyt helped us realize how important it is to renew ourselves by making time for play and joy. When we're in our eighties, we hope to feel as young and vibrant as they do in theirs! Though human beings are meant to play and need to play regularly, we often make it our last priority. The Hoyts also show us the extraordinary contribution that seniors, and indeed all citizens, can make to improving the quality of community life for families. The Hoyts can teach us how to be active and enjoy life in all of its stages, and how the generous contribution of time can make any community a more family-friendly place for all.

Tony and Linda Wallace are living examples of how resilient the human spirit can be. Overcoming difficult circumstances in their youth, they found and strengthened each other. And with Security Dads, the program they created to involve fathers in the schools as mentors, role models, and security monitors, Tony and Linda also found a way to bring love, commitment, and the power of a positive example to young people who desperately need it. Like the Wallaces, we need to reach out beyond our own families to provide an example of family to those who do not have one.

Minh and Thanh Ly are good examples of the sacrifice parents so often make to ensure a better life for their children than they had for themselves. Like so many immigrant families that have enriched America in every generation, the Lys bring extraordinary energy and drive to the challenge of forging a good family life in the new country. Faced with discrimination and prejudice, they paid it no heed but instead kept on working because, as Minh told us, "It's all for the children." They work extraordinarily hard so their daughters won't have college debt and will never have to work menial jobs.

Dawn Hancock filled us with respect for the courage and grit necessary to break free of poverty and escape a cycle of abuse that she told us involved her father and then her first husband. Dawn not only transcended her abuse, she escaped from a difficult and dangerous predicament as an impoverished, single teen mother with no home and no job, to become an outstanding college graduate and postgraduate student. And along with her new husband, Steve, she is now providing a wonderful, loving home for her son— and Steve's stepson—Chase.

The Logan family taught us how perfectly ordinary many families are even if they do not fit the traditional definition of family. As the parents of two young children, John and Josh have the same concerns, the same hopes, and the same challenges that most parents of young children have. Their simple goal is to create a loving family and do right by their sons. Does it really matter that they are gay? That their sons are multiracial? That their boys are adopted? That one was born to a mother who was HIV-positive? They don't think so, and neither do we. The point is that they are providing a loving home and doing a great job as parents to two children who are fortunate to have them as fathers—and who might have no parents at all, if not for the decision by Josh and John to adopt them. We believe that it's long past time to demand an end to the narrow-minded condemnation of good families that happen to be different.

Eduardo and Laura Cortes demonstrate to us the dynamism of a peer marriage in which both partners are active professionally and share the duties of parenting, even as they pass on the traditions of two cultures to their children, that of Mexico and that of West Des Moines, Iowa. Eduardo also embodies for us the dilemma faced by so many millions of Americans who find themselves working more than their families would like.

Lily Yeh inspired us with her creative dream that formed an extended family in a desolate neighborhood of North Philadelphia that others had abandoned. With her artistic vision and vibrant spirit, she brought together previously isolated community members and created with art the vital connections and bonds of intimacy that in turn create family.

Pat and Todd Alexander embody the ease and grace with which an interracial couple can transcend the obsolete social boundaries of bygone decades. The differences that outsiders may perceive are irrelevant to them; with a simple yet strong commitment to try to make each other happy, and to care for and prepare their sons for the challenges ahead in life, they have created a loving family. They also taught us some important lessons about the importance of clarity in communication within families.

Jay and Margo Strong touched our hearts with the bright intensity of the love they feel for their adopted son and daughter. Perhaps because they were a little older than most when they were able to adopt, they seem to have as strong a sense of what blessings children are as anyone we've ever met. Maybe it's because they were both teachers of young children for a long time before they had children, but whatever the reason, they showed us how to make spending time with their children their top priority without completely changing their lives.

Gabrielle and Chris Wagener are newlyweds and don't have children yet. But to us they represent something about the future of families in America. Like many couples these days, they lived together for a while before deciding to get married. Like most married couples, they both work. And like an increasing number of families, they have effortlessly blended different traditions, in their case a Jewish-Catholic marriage. They have given sustained thought to what they need before they have children and what they want for those children when they do have them. Young people today, like Gabrielle and Chris, in spite of the problems and challenges confronting families, are optimistic about the families they plan to create for themselves. And that's one of the biggest reasons we are optimistic too.

In spite of the serious challenges we believe America must address on behalf of families, we are optimistic because we believe that our nation is strong and creative and bighearted enough to rise to meet these challenges. For us, as for most Americans, family is our bedrock, and we believe the strength of the American family is the nation's bedrock. Now, because of the profound transformation of American families over the last forty years, it is time to examine all of the changes that have taken place. It is time to boldly address the urgent need to provide every appropriate support to every kind of family—and so make it possible for all of us to discover the lasting joy and deep sense of connection experienced by those who are joined at the heart.

Resources

Following is a brief list of some of the resources that we turned to for information, advice, or expertise during the process of writing this book. This is in no way intended to be an exhaustive or comprehensive list of the many wonderful groups, organizations, and resources for families. Still, we hope this list will be helpful to readers interested in finding out more about some of the topics discussed in this book.

GENERAL FAMILY RESOURCES

Alianza Dominicana
2410 Amsterdam Avenue, 4th floor
New York, NY 10033
(212) 740-1960
http://www.alianzadom.org

The Child Welfare League of
    America
440 First Street, NW, 3rd floor
Washington, DC 20001
(202) 638-2952
http://www.cwla.org

The Children's Defense Fund
25 E Street, NW
Washington, DC 20001
(202) 628-8787
http://www.childrensdefense.org

Council on Contemporary Families
http://www.contemporaryfamilies.
    org/about.htm

Family Re-Union
Child and Family Policy Center
Vanderbilt University
1207 Eighteenth Avenue South
Nashville, TN 37212
(615) 322-8505
http://www.familyreunion.org

Family Support America
20 North Wacker Drive, suite 1100
Chicago, IL 60606
(312) 338-0900
http://www.familysupportamerica.
   org

Family Voices
3411 Candelaria NE, suite M
Albuquerque, NM 87107
(505) 872–4774 or (888) 835-5669
http://www.familyvoices.org

Kids Count
The Annie E. Casey Foundation
701 St. Paul Street
Baltimore, MD 21202
(410) 547-6600
http://www.aecf.org/kidscount

National Alliance of Children's Trust
   and Prevention Funds
http://www.ctfalliance.org

National Council on Family
   Relations
3989 Central Avenue, NE #550
Minneapolis, MN 55421
(888) 781-9331
http://www.ncfr.org

EARLY CHILDHOOD

Connect for Kids
http://www.connectforkids.org

Family Communications, Inc.
4802 Fifth Avenue
Pittsburgh, PA 15213
(412) 687-2990
http://www.fci.org

I Am Your Child Foundation
P.O. Box 15605
Beverly Hills, CA 90209
(310) 285-2385
http://www.iamyourchild.org/

National Association for the
   Education of Young Children
1509 Sixteenth Street, NW
Washington, DC 20036
(202) 232–8777 or (800) 424-2460
http://www.naeyc.org

Zero to Three
2000 M Street, NW, suite 200
Washington, DC 20036
(202) 638-1144
http://www.zerotothree.org

ADOLESCENCE

National Campaign to Prevent Teen
   Pregnancy
1776 Massachusetts Avenue, NW,
   suite 200
Washington, DC 20036
(202) 478-8500
http://www.teenpregnancy.org

National Youth Development
  Information Center
http://www.nydic.org/nydic

Search Institute
The Banks Building
615 First Avenue NE, suite 125
Minneapolis, MN 55413
(612) 376-8955 or (800) 888–7828
http://www.search-institute.org/

Talking with Kids About Tough
  Issues
http://www.talkingwithkids.org/

FAMILY AND THE MEDIA

National Institute on Media and the
  Family
606 Twenty-fourth Avenue South,
  suite 606
Minneapolis, MN 55454
(612) 672-5437
http://www.mediafamily.org

UCLA Center for Communication
  Policy
P.O. Box 951586
Los Angeles, CA 90095
(310) 825-3711
http://ccp.ucla.edu/index.asp

BALANCING WORK AND FAMILY

Bright Horizons Family Solutions
200 Talcott Avenue South
Watertown, MA 02472
(617) 673-8000
http://www.brighthorizons.com

Center for Working Families
University of California, Berkeley
2420 Bowditch Street, MC 5670
Berkeley, CA 94720
(510) 642-7737
http://workingfamilies.berkeley.edu

Families and Work Institute
267 Fifth Avenue, 2nd floor
New York, NY 10016
(212) 465-2044
http://www.familiesandwork.org

Information about the Family &
  Medical Leave Act
United States Department of Labor
200 Constitution Avenue, NW
Washington, DC 20210
(866) 4-USA-DOL
http://www.dol.gov/esa/fmla.htm

National Partnership for Women &
  Families
1875 Connecticut Avenue, NW,
  suite 650
Washington, DC 20009
(202) 986-2600
http://www.nationalpartnership.org

The Stride Rite Corporation and
  Philanthropic Foundation
191 Spring Street
Lexington, MA 02420
(617) 824-6000
http://www.strideritecorp.com

Work/Family Directions Consulting
200 Talcott Avenue West
Watertown, MA 02472
http://www.wfd.com

PLAY

Boundless Playgrounds
One Regency Drive
Bloomfield, CT 06002
(860) 243-8315
http://www.boundlessplaygrounds.
  org

Institute for Play
46 West Garzas Road
Carmel Valley, CA 93924
(831) 659-1740
http://www.instituteforplay.com

FATHERHOOD

Center for Fathers, Families, and
  Workforce Development
3002 Druid Park Drive
Baltimore, MD 21215
(410) 367-5691
http://www.cfwd.org

The Fatherhood Project
Families and Work Institute
267 Fifth Avenue, 2nd floor
New York, NY 10016
(212) 465-2044
http://www.fatherhoodproject.org

The Fathers Network
http://www.fathersnetwork.org/
  page.php?page=554&

The National Center for Fathering
P.O. Box 413888
Kansas City, MO 64141
(800) 593-DADS
http://www.fathers.com

The National Center on Fathers and
  Families
Dr. Vivian Gadsden
Director of NCOFF
University of Pennsylvania
3440 Market Street, suite 450
Philadelphia, PA 19104
(215) 573-5500
http://www.ncoff.gse.upenn.edu

The National Center for Strategic
  Non-Profit Planning and
  Community Leadership
2000 L Street, NW, suite 815
Washington, DC 20036
(202) 822-6725
http://www.npcl.org

National Fatherhood Initiative
101 Lake Forest Boulevard, suite 360
Gaithersburg, MD 20877
(301) 948-0599
http://www.fatherhood.org

National Practitioners Network for
Fathers and Families, Inc.
1003 K Street, NW, suite 565
Washington, DC 20001
(202) 737-6680 or (800) 34N-PNFF
http://www.npnff.org

ADOPTION AND FOSTER FAMILIES

Center for Adoption Research at the
University of Massachusetts
365 Plantation Street, suite 100
Worcester, MA 01605
http://www.umassmed.edu/adoption/

Generations of Hope
1530 Fairway Drive
Rantoul, IL 61866
(217) 8934673
http://www.hope4children.org/
index.htm

National Adoption Information
Clearinghouse
The Administration for Children
and Families
U.S. Department of Health and
Human Services
330 C Street, SW
Washington, DC 20447
(888) 251-0075
http://www.calib.com/naic

MULTIGENERATIONAL FAMILIES

Generations Together
University of Pittsburgh
121 University Place, suite 300
Pittsburgh, PA 15260
(412) 648-7150
http://www.gt.pitt.edu

Generations United
122 C Street, NW, suite 820
Washington, DC 20001
(202) 638-1263
http://www.gu.org

National Family Caregivers
Association
10400 Connecticut Avenue #500
Kensington, MD 20895
(800) 896-3650
http://www.nfcacares.org/home.html

RESILIENCE AND MENTAL HEALTH

Mothers Against Violence in
America (MAVIA)
Students Against Violence
Everywhere (SAVE)
105 Fourteenth Avenue, suite 2A
Seattle, WA 98122
(800) 897-7697
http://www.mavia.org/default.asp

National Clearinghouse on Child
Abuse and Neglect Information
The Administration for Children
and Families
U.S. Department of Health and
Human Services
330 C Street, SW
Washington, DC 20447
(800) 394-3366
http://www.calib.com/nccanch

National Domestic Violence Hotline
(800) 799-SAFE
http://www.ndvh.org/

The National Institute of Mental
Health
6001 Executive Boulevard, room
8184, MSC 9663
Bethesda, MD 20892
(301) 443-4513
http://www.nimh.nih.gov

National Mental Health Awareness
Campaign
(877) 495-0009
http://www.nostigma.org

Substance Abuse and Mental Health
Services Administration
United States Department of Health
and Human Services
5600 Fishers Lane
Rockville, MD 20857
http://www.samhsa.gov

FAMILY AND ECONOMICS

The Child Care Action Campaign
330 Seventh Avenue, 14th floor
New York, NY 10001
(212) 239-0138
http://www.childcareaction.org

National Alliance to End
Homelessness
1518 K Street NW, suite 206
Washington, DC 20005
(202) 638-1526
http://www.naeh.org

National Center for Children in
Poverty
Mailman School of Public Health
Columbia University
154 Haven Avenue
New York, NY 10032
(212) 304-7100
http://cpmcnet.columbia.edu/dept/
nccp

National Low-Income Housing
Coalition
1012 Fourteenth Street, NW,
suite 610
Washington, DC 20005
(202) 662-1530
http://www.nlihc.org/index.html

COMMUNITY BUILDING

The Asset Based Community
  Development Institute (ABCD)
2040 Sheridan Road
Evanston, IL 60208
(817) 491-8712
http://www.northwestern.edu/ipr/
  abcd.html

BetterTogether
http://www.bettertogether.org

Civic Practice Network
http://www.cpn.org

Civilian Volunteer Patrol
Redlands Police Department
P.O. Box 1025
Redlands, CA 92373
(909) 798-7681
http://www.ci.redlands.ca.us/
  207.html

Coalition of Community
  Foundations for Youth
15639 Leavenworth Road
Basehor, KS 66007
(800) 292-6149
http://www.ccfy.org

The Common Enterprise
2321 Grove
Boulder, CO 80302
(303) 939-8605
http://www.cpn.org/cpn/sections/
  affiliates/common_enterprise.
  html

Mar Vista Family Center and
  Institute
5075 Slauson Avenue
Culver City, CA 90230
(310) 390-9607

Maryland's Smart Growth
Maryland State House
100 State Circle, room 208
Annapolis, MD 21401
(401) 974-5292
http://www.smartgrowth.state.md.us

National Civic League Alliance for
  National Renewal
1445 Market Street, suite 300
Denver, CO 80202
(303) 571-4343
http://www.ncl.org/anr

National Violence Prevention
  Collaborative
1198 Robert T. Longway Boulevard
Flint, MI 48503
(810) 235-7210
http://www.nal.usda.gov/pavnet/
  whitehouse/catalog/models-3.html

Peace Games
285 Dorchester Avenue
Boston, MA 02127
(617) 464-2600
http://www.peacegames.org

Village of the Arts & Humanities
2544 Germantown Avenue
Philadelphia, PA 19133
(215) 255-3949
http://www.villagearts.org

COMMUNITY INVOLVEMENT IN EDUCATION

Communities In Schools, Inc.
277 S. Washington Street, suite 210
Alexandria, VA 22314
(800) CIS-4KIDS
http://www.cisnet.org

Elizabeth Learning Center
4811 Elizabeth Center
Cudahy, CA 90201
(323) 562-0175
http://www.eslc.k12.ca.us

Hamilton County Department of
   Education
Parent, School and Community
   Involvement Dept.
6703 Bonny Oaks Drive
Chattanooga, TN 37421
(423) 209-8595
http://www.hcde.org/parents/
   liteson/mission.htm

The Partnership for Family
   Involvement in Education
400 Maryland Avenue, SW
Washington, DC 20202
http://pfie.ed.gov

Safe and Drug Free Schools
400 Maryland Avenue, SW
Washington, DC 20202
(202) 260-3954
http://www.ed.gov/offices/OESE/
   SDFS

The School Mental Health Project
   at UCLA
P.O. Box 951563
Los Angeles, CA 90095
(310) 825-3634
http://smhp.psych.ucla.edu

Security Dads, Inc.
Arlington High School
4825 North Arlington Avenue
Indianapolis, IN 46226
http://www.ips.k12.in.us/s722/
   secdad/background.html

Vaughn Next Century Learning
   Center
13330 Vaughn Street
San Fernando, CA 91340
(818) 896-7461
http://www.vaughn.k12.ca.us

DIVERSITY

Community Cousins
140 Encinitas Boulevard, suite 220
Encinitas, CA 92024
(760) 944-CUZZ
http://www.cuzz.org

Human Rights Campaign
919 Eighteenth Street, NW,
   suite 800
Washington, DC 20006
(202) 628-4160
http://www.hrc.org

Parents and Friends of Lesbians and
  Gays PFLAG
1726 M Street, NW, suite 400
Washington, DC 20036
(202) 467-8180
http://www.pflag.org

Teaching Tolerance Project
Southern Poverty Law Center
http://www.splcenter.org/teaching
  tolerance/tt-index.html

RESEARCH-BASED FAMILY RESOURCES

The Annenberg Public Policy Center
  of the University of Pennsylvania
320 National Press Building
Washington, DC 20045
(202) 879-6700
http://www.appcpenn.org

Children and Family Research at
the National Institute of Children
  and Health Development
Rockledge I, suite 8030
6705 Rockledge Drive
Bethesda, MD 20892
(301) 496-6832
http://www.cfr.nichd.nih.gov

Children, Youth and Family
  Education and Research Network
http://www.cyfernet.org

Tufts University Child and Family
  WebGuide
Eliot-Pearson Department of Child
  Development
105 College Avenue
Medford, MA 02155
(617) 627-3355
http://www.cfw.tufts.edu

UCLA Center for Healthier
  Children, Families, and
  Communities
10945 Le Conte Avenue
Ueberroth Building, suite 1401
Box 956939
Los Angeles, CA 90095
(310) 825-8042
http://healthychild.ucla.edu

University of Minnesota Children,
  Youth and Family Consortium
McNamara Alumni Center, suite
  270A
200 Oak Street, SE
Minneapolis, MN 55455
(612) 625-7849
http://www.cyfc.umn.edu

Yale University Child Study Center
230 South Frontage Road
New Haven, CT 06520
(20) 785-2513
http://info.med.yale.edu/chldstdy

Notes

CHAPTER 1. FAMILY REDEFINED

14   *rate of teenage pregnancies:* Lynne M. Casper and Suzanne M. Bianchi,
      Continuity and Change in the American Family (Thousand Oaks, Cal-
      ifornia: Sage Publications, 2002): 75, fig. 3-3.

15   *fewer married-with-children families:* U.S. Department of Commerce,
      U.S. Census Bureau, Historical Table, "Families, by Presence of Own
      Children Under 18: 1950 to Present," 29 June 2001, <http://www.
      census.gov/population/socdemo/hh-fam/tabFM-1.txt>; U.S. Depart-
      ment of Commerce, U.S. Census Bureau, Historical Table, "House-
      holds, by Type: 1940 to Present," 29 June 2001, <http://www.census.
      gov/population/socdemo/hh-fam/tabHH-1.txt>.
      Single parents head more families: U.S. Department of Commerce, U.S.
      Census Bureau, "Living Arrangements of Children Under Eighteen
      Years Old: 1960 to Present," 29 June 2001, <http://www.census.gov/
      population/socdemo/hh-fam/tabCH-1.txt>; U.S. Department of
      Commerce, U.S. Census Bureau, "Families, by Presence of Own Chil-
      dren Under Eighteen: 1950 to Present," 29 June 2001, <http://www.
      census.gov/population/socdemo/hh-fam/tabFM-1.txt>

born to unmarried mothers: National Center for Health Statistics, "Nonmarital Childbearing in the United States, 1940–99," *National Vital Statistics Reports* 48, no. 16 (18 October 2000): 17.

15   *are working outside the home:* U.S. Department of Commerce, U.S. Census Bureau, *Statistical Abstract of the United States 1995* (Washington, D.C.: U.S. Government Printing Office, 1996): 406; U.S. Department of Commerce, U.S. Census Bureau, *Statistical Abstract of the United States 2000* (Washington, D.C.: U.S. Government Printing Office, 2001): 409.

entire marriageable population: U.S. Department of Commerce, U.S. Census Bureau, Historical Table, "Marital Status of the Population 15 Years Old and Over, by Sex and Race: 1950 to Present," 29 June 2001, <http://www.census.gov/population/socdemo/hh-fam/tabMS-1.txt>.

cohabiting unmarried couples: U.S. Department of Commerce, U.S. Census Bureau, *Profile of General Demographic Characteristics for the United States: 2000,* <http://www.census.gov/Press-Release/www/2001/tables/dp_us_2000.PDF>; U.S. Department of Commerce, U.S. Census Bureau, Historical Table, "Unmarried-Couple Households, by Presence of Children: 1960 to Present," 7 January 1999, <http://www.census.gov/population/socdemo/ms-la/tabad-2.txt>.

families are forming later: U.S. Department of Commerce, U.S. Census Bureau, Historical Table, "Estimated Median Age at First Marriage, by Sex: 1890 to the Present," 29 June 2001, <http://www.census.gov/population/socdemo/hh-fam/tabMS-2.txt>.

16   *children are coming much later:* U.S Department of Health and Human Services, National Center for Health Statistics, *Health, United States, 2001* (Hyattsville, Maryland: National Center for Health Statistics, 2002): 133, <http://www.cdc.gov/nchs/hus.htm>.

average family had 2.3 children: U.S. Department of Commerce, U.S. Census Bureau, Historical Table, "Average Number of Own Children Under 18 per Family, by Type of Family: 1955 to Present," 29 June 2001, <http://www.census.gov/population/socdemo/hh-fam/tabFM-3.txt>.

average life span: U.S. Department of Health and Human Services. National Center for Health Statistics, *Health, United States, 2001,* 2002, <http://www.cdc.gov/nchs/hus.htm>: 163.

cared for by grandparents: U.S. Department of Commerce, U.S. Census Bureau, "Grandchildren Living in the Home of Their Grandparents:

1970 to Present," 29 June 2001, <http://www.census.gov/population/socdemo/hh-fam/tabCH-7.txt>; U.S. Department of Commerce, U.S. Census Bureau, 1960 Census of Population and Housing, "Family Status of Persons Under 14 Years Old by Age and Color, By Presence and Marital Status of Parents, for the United States, By Type of Residence, and for the South: 1960" (Washington, D.C.: U.S. Government Printing Office, 1960).

about 90 percent white: Tabulations from U.S. Census Bureau Census 1960; U.S. Department of Commerce, U.S. Census Bureau, *Profile of General Demographic Characteristics for the United States: 2000,* <http://www.census.gov/Press-Release/www/2001/tables/dp_us_2000.PDF>.

16   *interracial couples:* U.S. Department of Commerce, U.S. Census Bureau, Historical Table, "Race of Wife by Race of Husband: 1960, 1970, 1980, 1991, and 1992," 20 June 1998, <http://www.census.gov/population/socdemo/race/interractab1.txt>; U.S. Department of Commerce, U.S. Census Bureau, Historical Table, "Interracial Married Couples: 1980 to Present," 4 February 2002, <http://www.census.gov/population/socdemo/hh-fam/tabMS-3.txt>; U.S. Department of Commerce, U.S. Census Bureau, Married Couple Family Groups, by Presence of Own Children/1 In Specific Age Groups, and Age, Earnings, Education, and Race and Hispanic Origin/2 of Both Spouses: March 2000, <http://www.census.gov/population/socdemo/hh-fam/p20-537/2000/tab FG4.txt>.

17   *two-thirds of the housework:* Joan Williams, *Unbending Gender: Why Family and Work Conflict and What to do About It* (New York: Oxford University Press, 2000), 2; Scott Coltrane, "Research on Household Labor: Modeling and Measuring the Social Embeddedness of Routine Family Work," *Journal of Marriage and Family* 62, no. 4, 1211, 1223.

majority of college degrees: U.S. Department of Education, *Digest of Education Statistics 2000,* 2001, <http://nces.ed.gov/pubs2001/digest/tables/PDF/table248.pdf>.

as much money as men: U.S. Department of Labor, Bureau of Labor Statistics, "Highlights of Women's Earnings in 2000," August 2001, <http://www.bls.gov/cps/cpswom2000.pdf>.

power of working-class men: Lawrence Mishel, Jared Bernstein, and John Schmitt, *State of Working America, 2000–2001, An Economic Policy Institute Book* (Washington, D.C.: Economic Policy Institute, 2001): 124–26.

18   *"everyone was working":* Conversation with Donald Hernandez, professor of sociology, University at Albany, State University of New York.

"women not to work": Conversation with Tamara Hareven, professor of history at the University of Delaware.

19   *long period of helplessness:* Meredith F. Small, *Our Babies, Ourselves: How Biology and Culture Shaped the Way We Parent* (New York: Doubleday, 1998): 6–8, 14.

has a soft spot: Ibid., 8–12.

"never been a time": Conversation with Steven Ozment, professor of ancient and modern history at Harvard University.

"distinction between family": Conversation with Maris Vinovskis, professor of history at the University of Michigan.

21   *key factor in the modernization of Western civilization:* Conversation with Brigitte Berger, professor emeritus of sociology at Boston University (retired); Brigitte Berger, *The Family in the Modern Age: More Than a Lifestyle Choice* (New Brunswick, New Jersey: Transaction Publishers, 2002).

twelfth and thirteenth centuries: Conversation with Ozment.

22   *"from the very beginning":* Conversation with Vinovskis.

23   *"little commonwealth"*: Steven Mintz and Susan Kellogg, *Domestic Revolutions: A Social History of the American Family* (New York: The Free Press, 1988): xiv–xv.

"an emotional bond": Steven Mintz, "The American History Files: Family," <http://www.myhistory.org/historytopics/articles/family.html>.

"economic significance declined": Ibid.

24   *Longer life spans:* U.S. Department of Health and Human Services, National Center for Health Statistics, *Health, United States, 2001* (Washington, D.C.: U.S. Government Printing Office, 2002): 163, <http://www.cdc.gov/nchs/hus.htm>.

25   *incidence of divorces:* U.S. Department of Health and Human Services, National Center for Health Statistics, "Advance Report of Final Divorce Statistics, 1989 and 1990," *Monthly Vital Statistics Report* 43, no. 9(S) (22 March 1995): 9, <http://www.cdc.gov/nchs/data/mvsr/supp/mv43_09s.pdf>.

divorce rate is now about twice: U.S. Department of Health and Human Services, National Center for Health Statistics, *Vital Statistics of the United States 1960*, vol. 3, 1964, <http://www.cdc.gov/nchs/data/vsus/mgdv60_3acc.pdf>; National Center for Health Statistics, "Births, Marriages, Divorces, and Deaths: Provisional Data for January–December 2000," *National Vital Statistics Reports* 49, no. 6 (22 August 2001): 1, <http://www.cdc.gov/nchs/data/nvsr/nvsr49/nvsr49_06.pdf>.

one in three first marriages: Matthew D. Bramlett and William D. Mosher, "First Marriage Dissolution, Divorce, and Remarriage: United States," *Advance Data,* no. 323 (31 May 2001): 5, <http://www.cdc.gov/nchs/data/ad/ad323.pdf>.

26   *one million children are involved in:* Estimate based on U.S. Census data and U.S. Department of Health and Human Services, National Center for Health Statistics, "Advance Report of Final Divorce Statistics," *Monthly Vital Statistics Report* 39, no. 12(S2) (21 May 1991): 1, <http://www.cdc.gov/nchs/data/mvsr/supp/mv39_12s2.pdf>.

"were really enhanced after divorce": Conversation with Mavis Hetherington, professor emeritus of psychology at the University of Virginia.

27   *length of family relationships:* Casper and Bianchi, *Continuity and Change in the American Family,* 7.

"very positive about the institution of marriage": Conversation with Lynne Casper, health scientist administrator and demographer in the Demographic and Behavioral Sciences Branch at the National Institute of Child Health and Human Development.

eventually remarry: Casper and Bianchi, 27.

unmarried couples living together: U.S. Department of Commerce, U.S. Census Bureau, *Social and Economic Characteristics: United States,* 1993; U.S. Department of Commerce, U.S. Census Bureau, *Profile of General Demographic Characteristics for the United States: 2000,* <http://www.census.gov/Press-Release/www/2001/tables/dp_us_2000.PDF>.

lower than those in many European countries: The Clearinghouse on International Developments in Child, Youth, and Family Policies at Columbia University, "Fewer and Later Marriages, Increase Divorce Rates, and More Cohabitation," December 2001, <http://www.childpolicyintl.org/contexttabledemography/table216.pdf>.

more than half of all women: Larry Bumpass and Hsien-Hen Lu, "Trends in Cohabitation and Implications for Children's Family Contexts in the U.S.," *Center for Demography and Ecology Working Papers,* no. 98–15 (March 1999), <http://www.ssc.wisc.edu/cde/cdewp/98-15.pdf>.

28   *marry the same person:* Linda Regensburger, *The American Family: Reflecting a Changing Nation* (Detroit: Gale Group, 2001): 116.

still headed by married couples: U.S. Department of Commerce, U.S. Census Bureau, *Profile of General Demographic Characteristics for the United States: 2000,* <http://www.census.gov/Press-Release/www/2001/tables/dp_us_2000.PDF>.

spend some time in a stepfamily: Stepfamily Association of America,

"Stepfamily Fact Sheet," 10 June 2000, <http://www.saafamilies.org/faqs/index.htm>.

29   *no different than those who:* E. Mavis Hetherington and John Kelly, *For Better or for Worse: Divorce Reconsidered* (New York: W. W. Norton and Company, 2002): 3–16, 28–29.

30   *psychological scars that divorce:* Judith S. Wallerstein, Julia M. Lewis, and Sandra Blakeslee, *The Unexpected Legacy of Divorce: A Twenty-five Year Landmark Study* (New York: Hyperion, 2000): 298–301.

    depended largely on the quality: Conversation with Hetherington, founder of the Judith Wallerstein Center for the Family in Transition.

31   *"It's self-doubt about":* Conversation with Judith Wallerstein, senior lecturer emerita at the University of California at Berkeley.

    "choice of spouse becomes really important": Conversation Hetherington.

32   *"ability to elicit social support":* Ibid.

    "regain a sense of hope": Conversation with Wallerstein.

33   *"group of people who love":* Alternatives to Marriage Project, "Frequently Asked Questions," <http://www.unmarried.org/faq.html>.

    nearly 2 million couples: U.S. Department of Commerce, U.S. Census Bureau Census 2000, <http://www.census.gov/population/socdemo/hh-fam/p20-537/2000/tabFG4.txt>.

34   *already had dated interracially:* Karen S. Peterson, "Interracial Dating: For Today's Teens, Race 'Not an Issue Anymore,'" *USA Today*, 3 November 1997.

35   *children being raised primarily:* U.S. Department of Commerce, U.S. Census Bureau, "Grandchildren Living in the Home of Their Grandparents: 1970 to Present," 29 June 2001, <http://www.census.gov/population/socdemo/hh-fam/tabCH-7.txt>; U.S. Department of Commerce, U.S. Census Bureau, "Family Status of Persons Under 14 Years Old by Age and Color, by Presence and Marital Status of Parents, for the United States, by Type of Residence, and for the South: 1960," Table 1.

    household headed by a grandparent: Ibid.

37   *"a lot of intergenerational influences":* Conversation Lynne Casper.

38   *children in father-only families:* U.S. Department of Commerce, U.S. Census Bureau, Historical Table, "Living Arrangements of Children Under 18 Years Old: 1960 to Present," 29 June 2001, <http://www.census.gov/population/socdemo/hh-fam/tabCH-1.txt>.

    "more expected for fathers": Conversation with Casper.

    of gay or lesbian couples: U.S. Department of Commerce, U.S. Census Bureau Census 2000, <http://factfinder.census.gov>.

38   *all but 255 of all 3,141 American counties:* Conversation with Gary Gates, research associate, Urban Institute.

in an estimated 800,000 families: Dan Black et al., "Demographics of the Gay and Lesbian Population in the United States: Evidence from Available Systematic Data Sources," *Demography* 37, no. 2 (May 2000): 139–54.

at least one gay parent: American Civil Liberties Union, "ACLU Fact Sheet: Overview of Lesbian and Gay Parenting, Adoption, and Foster Care," 6 April 1999, <http://www.aclu.org/issues/gay/parent/html>.

39   *a spouse who shares their own religion:* Barbara Dafoe Whitehead and David Popenoe, "Who Wants to Marry a Soul Mate? New Survey Findings on Young Adults' Attitudes About Love and Marriage," *The State of Our Unions: The Social Health of Marriage in America*, 2001, <http://marriage.rutgers.edu/TEXTSOOU2001.htm>.

life expectancy increases: U.S. Department of Health and Human Services, National Center for Health Statistics, *Health, United States, 2001* (Hyattsville, Md.: National Center for Health Statistics, 2002): 163, <http://www.cdc.gov/nchs/hus.htm>.

39   *faster than the rate of inflation:* Phyllis Shelton, *Long Term Care: Your Financial Planning Guide* (New York: Kensington Books, 2001): 3.

42   *one who could talk about feelings:* Whitehead and Popenoe, 2001.

43   *for about eight years before marriage:* Alan Guttmacher Institute, "Teen Sex and Pregnancy," September 1999, <http://www.agi-usa.org/pubs/fb_teen_sex.html.>

marriage is hard work: Whitehead and Popenoe, 2001.

CHAPTER 2. LOVE

54   *withered away from lack:* Rene A. Spitz, with W. Godfrey Cobliner, *The First Year of Life: A Psychoanalytic Study of Normal and Deviant Development of Object Relations* (New York: International Universities Press, Inc., 1965): 277–81

55   *slowly started to change:* Conversation with Steven Mintz, associate professor of history at the University of Houston.

"to be happy in marriage": Conversation with Steven Ozment, professor of ancient and modern history at Harvard University.

"transfer of a variety of functions": Talcott Parsons and Robert F. Bales, *Family, Socialization and Interaction Process* (Glencoe, Illinois: The Free Press, 1960): 9.

56   *"locus of intimacy"*: Conversation with Graham Spanier, president, Pennsylvania State University.
     "nuclear family members": Jan E. Dizard and Howard Gadlin, *The Minimal Family* (Amherst, Massachusetts: The University of Massachusetts Press, 1990): 11.
     Martha Minow: Conversation with Martha Minow, professor of law, Harvard Law School; Martha Minow, "Redefining Families: Who's In and Who's Out?" *University of Colorado Law Review* 62, no. 2 (1991): 270, 272.

57   *partners of victims of the September 11*: Jane Gross, "U.S. Fund for Tower Victims Will Aid Some Gay Partners," *New York Times*, 30 May 2002.
     family life survives for two: Conversation with Spanier; Graham Spanier, "Bequeathing Family Continuity," *Journal of Marriage and the Family* 51 (February 1989): 9.

63   *Judith Wallerstein*: Conversation with Judith Wallerstein, senior lecturer emerita, University of California at Berkeley, and founder of the Center for the Family in Transition.

69   *"would get goose flesh"*: Benjamin Spock, *The Pocket Book of Baby and Child Care*, illus. by Dorothea Fox, 5th ed. (New York: Pocket Books, 1947): 15.
     "don't look at it for the first two years": A. E. Hotchner, *Papa Hemingway* (New York: Random House, 1966): 87.

70   *children in homes without fathers*: Annie E. Casey Foundation, *Kids Count Data Book 2002* (Baltimore: The Annie E. Casey Foundation, 2002): 38, Sara McLanahan and Gary Sandefur, *Growing Up With a Single Parent* (Cambridge, Massachusetts: Harvard University Press, 1994: 1–2.

71   *"vast majority of children"*: David T. Ellwood, *Poor Support: Poverty in the American Family* (New York: Basic Books, 1988): 46.
     essays about the meaning of fathers: National Center for Fathering, *Father of the Year Essay Contest*, "What My Father Means to Me," 1994.

72   *fathers are more satisfied*: Richard Louv, *FatherLove: What We Need, What We Seek, What We Must Create* (New York: Pocket Books, 1993): 98–100.

CHAPTER 3. COMMUNICATION

81   *According to Deborah Tannen*: Conversation with Deborah Tannen, professor of linguistics at Georgetown University; Deborah Tannen, *I*

Only Say This Because I Love You: How the Way We Talk Can Make or Break Family Relationships Throughout Our Lives (New York: Random House, 2001): xvii.

82　*two completely different parts of:* Jaak Panksepp, *Affective Neuroscience: The Foundations of Human and Animal Emotions* (New York: Oxford University Press, 1998): 42–43, 57–58, 70–72.

84　*all watching television while they eat:* William J. Doherty, *The Intentional Family: How to Build Family Ties in Our Modern World* (Reading, Massachusetts: Addison-Wesley Publishing Company, Inc., 1997): 22.
making teenagers feel highly connected: Michael D. Resnick, et al., "Protecting Adolescents from Harm: Findings From the National Longitudinal Study on Adolescent Health," *Journal of the American Medical Association* 278, no. 10 (September 10, 1997): 823–32.
the more parents have family: The National Center on Addiction and Substance Abuse at Columbia University, "Family Day—a Day to Eat Dinner with Your Children," <http://www.casacolumbia.org/newsletter1457/newsletter_show.htm?doc_id=82275>.

90　*calls this process "bidding":* Conversation with John Gottman, professor of psychology at the University of Washington and cofounder of the Gottman Institute; John Gottman and Joan DeClaire, *The Relationship Cure: A 5 Step Guide for Building Better Connections with Family, Friends, and Lovers* (New York: Crown Publishers, 2001): 16–18, 38–50.

92　*"gradual erosion of intimacy":* Conversation with Gottman.

93　*stabilize the relationship by "triangling in":* Michael E. Kerr and Murray Bowen, *Family Evaluation* (New York: W.W. Norton & Company, 1988), 134–62; Maggie Scarf, "Intimate Partners," *Atlantic Monthly* 258, no. 5 (November 1986): 45–58, <http://www.theatlantic.com/issues/86nov/scarf.htm>.

94　*think and speak differently:* Carol Gilligan, *In a Different Voice* (Cambridge, Massachusetts: Harvard University Press, 1982), 17, 73, 100, 163.
"long-distance calls": Robert Putnam, *Bowling Alone: The Collapse and Revival of American Community* (New York: Simon and Schuster, 2000): 94–95.

95　*twenty years before women do:* Teri James Bellis and Laura Ann Wilber, "Effects of Aging and Gender on Interhemispheric Function," *Journal of Speech, Language, and Hearing Research* 44 (April 2001): 246–63.
"male versus female communication differences": American Speech-

Language-Hearing Association, press release, "Age, Gender Affect Auditory Measures of Interhemispheric Function During Middle-Age Years," April 4, 2001, <http://www.asha.org/press/age_gender.cfm>.

95   *remembering emotional events:* Turhan Canli, John E. Desmond, Zuo Zhao, and John D. E. Gabrieli, "Sex Differences in the Neural Basis of Emotional Memories," *Proceedings of the National Academy of Sciences* 99, no. 16 (August 6, 2002): 10789–94.

harder time processing emotions: Michael Gurian and Patricia Henley with Terry Trueman, *Boys and Girls Learn Differently: A Guide for Teachers and Parents* (San Francisco: Jossey-Bass, 2001): 21, 29, 31–33.

96   *"the importance of communion":* William Line, "The Nature of Human Nature," *Empathic Parenting* 3, no. 1 (winter 1980): 16–21.

97   *Romanian orphans:* Richard Yallop, "The Children Who Learnt to Cry the Tears of Love," *The Independent* (London), 12 June 1990; *Nightline*, "Abandoned," 19 January 2000.

98   *attachment theory:* Martha Farrell Erickson and Karen Kurz-Riemer, *Infants, Toddlers, and Families: A Framework for Support and Intervention* (New York: The Guilford Press, 1999): 54–67; Conversation with Dr. Martha Farrell Erickson, director of the University of Minnesota's Children, Youth, and Family Consortium.

"opportunities for teaching": John Gottman with Joan DeClaire, *Raising an Emotionally Intelligent Child: The Heart of Parenting* (New York: Simon & Schuster, 1998): 21.

99   *"parents as lepers":* Conversation with Dominic Cappello, family communication expert and author.

101   *history of talking to their children:* Conversation with Jose Szapocznik, professor in Department of Psychiatry and Behavioral Sciences and director of the Center for Family Studies, University of Miami School of Medicine.

102   *think they're talking to their children:* Nickelodeon, Kaiser Family Foundation, and Children Now, "Talking with Kids About Tough Issues: A National Survey of Parents and Kids," 8 March 2001, <http://www.talkingwithkids.org/nickelodeon/summary.pdf>.

effective parent-adolescent communication: Conversation with Szapocznik.

reducing high-risk behavior: Kim S. Miller and Daniel J. Whittaker, "Predictors of Mother-Adolescent Discussions About Condoms: Implications for Providers Who Serve Youth," *Pediatrics* 108, no. 2 (August 2001): e28.

103   *"kids will find them elsewhere"*: Conversation with Dr. Pepper Schwartz, professor of sociology, University of Washington.

advice teens would give: National Campaign to Prevent Teen Pregnancy, "Talking Back: Ten Things Teens Want Parents to Know About Teen Pregnancy," April 1999, <http://www.teenpregnancy.org/resources/reading/tips/talk_back.asp>.

"more positive the relationship": Anthony R. D'Augelli, "Mental Health Problems Among Lesbian, Gay, and Bisexual Youths Ages 14 to 21," *Clinical Child Psychology and Psychiatry* 7, no. 3 (July 2002): 457.

for those teens who did: Anthony R. D'Augelli, Scott L. Hershberger, and Neil W. Pilkington, "Lesbian, Gay, and Bisexual Youths and Their Families: Disclosure of Sexual Orientation and its Consequences," *American Journal of Orthopsychiatry* 68, no. 3 (July 1998): 361–71.

104   *being able to communicate:* Ritch C. Savin-Williams, *Mom, Dad. I'm Gay. How Families Negotiate Coming Out* (Washington, D.C.: American Psychological Association, 2001): 219–38.

107   *than in school each year:* TV Turnoff Network, "Facts and Figures About Our TV Habit," <http://tv-turnoff.org/images/facts&figs/factsheets/Facts%20and%20Figures.pdf>.

107   *with any type of screen media:* Emory H. Woodard IV and Natalia Gridina, "Media in the Home 2000: The Fifth Annual Survey of Parents and Children," Annenberg Public Policy Center of the University of Pennsylvania, 26 June 2000, <http://www.appcpenn.org/mediainhome/survey/survey7.pdf>.

107   *four and a half hours of television:* Henry J. Kaiser Family Foundation, "Kids and Media at the New Millennium," November 1999, <http://www.kff.org/content/1999/1535/KidsReport%20FINAL.pdf>.

108   *no rules whatsoever:* TV Turnoff Network.

"the art of chatting": Conversation with Szapocznik.

information through a passive visual medium: Conversation with Dr. Penney Brooks, speech-language pathologist, Columbus Public Schools, Columbus, Ohio.

"watch 'Friends' instead of having friends": Presentation by Robert Putnam to Family-Centered Community Building, course taught by Al Gore at Middle Tennessee State University, 31 October 2001.

109   *16,000 simulated murders and 200,000 acts of violence:* American Psychiatric Association, "Psychiatric Effects of Media Violence," <http://www.psych.org/public_info/media_violence.cfm>.

violence that young people see: American Psychiatric Association, "Psychiatric Effect of Media Violence," <http://www.psych.org/public_info/media_violence.cfm>.

can lead to aggressive behavior: Aletha C. Huston et al., *Big World, Small Screen: The Role of Television in American Society* (Lincoln, Nebraska: University of Nebraska Press, 1992): 2, 43–46, 54–57.

110   *fear that it will happen again:* American Counseling Association, "Responding to Tragedy," "Helping Children Cope with Trauma," <http://www.counseling.org/tragedy/trauma.htm>.

113   *biracial couples report "widespread tolerance":* Darryl Fears and Claudia Deane, "Biracial Couples Report Tolerance," *Washington Post*, 5 July 2001, A1.

115   *family as an "emotional system":* Kerr and Bowen, 23–24, 50.

CHAPTER 4. FOR RICHER, FOR POORER

124   *An estimated 800,000:* Martha R. Burt, "What Will It Take to End Homelessness?" *Urban Institute Brief*, September 2001, <http://www.urban.org/UploadedPDF/end_homelessness.pdf>.

125   *fair-market rent:* National Low Income Housing Coalition, *Out of Reach 2001: America's Growing Wage-Rent Disparity*, 2001, <http://www.nlihc.org/oor2001, 2001>.

approximately 170,000 Americans: U.S. Department of Commerce, U.S. Census Bureau, *Emergency and Transitional Shelter Population: 2000*, 2001, <http://www.census.gov/prod/2001pubs/censr01-2.pdf, 2001>.

children have numerous problems: Eugene M. Lewit and Linda Schuurmann Baker, "Child Indicators: Homeless Families and Children," *The Future of Children: Financing Child Care* 6, no. 2 (summer–fall 1996): 146, <http://www.futureofchildren.org/usr_doc/vol6no2ART7.pdf>.

127   *11 percent of Americans:* U.S. Department of Commerce, U.S. Census Bureau, *Poverty in the United States: 2000*, September 2001, <http://www.census.gov/prod/2001pubs/p60-214.pdf>.

128   *largest single expenditure:* U.S. Department of Labor, Bureau of Labor Statistics, "Housing Expenditures," *Issues in Labor Statistics*, March 2002, <http://www.bls.gov/opub/ils/pdf/opbils47.pdf>.

average sale price for a new home: U.S. Department of Commerce, U.S. Census Bureau, *Median and Average Sales Prices of House Sold in United States*, <http://www.census.gov/const/uspricemon.pdf>.

rent has been increasing: Tabulations from U.S. Department of Labor, Bureau of Labor Statistics Consumer Price Index, <http://www.bls.gov/cpi/>.

128   *6.2 million families:* U.S. Department of Commerce, U.S. Census Bureau, *Poverty in the United States: 2000,* September 2001, <http://www.census.gov/prod/2001pubs/p60-214.pdf>.

the formula has been based: Gordon M. Fisher, "The Development and History of the Poverty Thresholds," *Social Security Bulletin* 55, no. 4, (winter 1992): 3–14.

food costs represented the single largest expense: Ibid.

food costs are less than 15 percent: Tabulations from U.S. Department of Labor, Bureau of Labor Statistics Consumer Expenditure Survey, <http://www.bls.gov/cex/>.

below the official poverty line: U.S. Department of Health and Human Services "2002 Poverty Guidelines," *Federal Register,* vol. 67, no. 31 (14 February 2002): 6931–33.

129   *one in six American children:* U.S. Department of Commerce, U.S. Census Bureau, *Poverty in the United States: 2000,* September 2001, <http://www.census.gov/prod/2001pubs/p60-214.pdf>.

40 percent of all children: National Center for Children in Poverty, *Low-Income Children in the United States: A Brief Demographic Profile,* March 2002, <http://cpmcnet.columbia.edu/dept/nccp/YCPfact302.pdf>.

"Nothing undermines a family more": Conversation with Graham Spanier, president of Pennsylvania State University.

less likely to have health insurance: Karen Seccombe, "Families in Poverty in the 1990s: Trends, Causes, Consequences, and Lessons Learned," *Journal of Marriage and Family* 62, no. 4 (November 2000): 1103.

tend to have worse nutrition: Ibid.

higher rates of infant mortality: Ibid.,1102.

less likely to succeed academically: Ibid., 1104.

130   *more likely to be victimized by crime:* Ibid.

translate into higher mortality rates: Hyun Joo Oh, "An Exploration of the Influence of Household Poverty Spells on Mortality Risk," *Journal of Marriage and Family* 63, no. 1 (February 2001): 224–34.

132   *60 percent of the 2.3 million jobs lost:* Kim Clark, "A Youthful Recession," *U.S. News and World Report,* 25 February 2002.

134   *"established by nature":* Aristotle, *Politics,* trans. Benjamin Jowett (Mineola, New York: Dover Publications, Inc., 2000): 27.

incentive for younger siblings: David Popenoe, *Disturbing the Nest* (New York: Aldine de Gruyter, 1988): 62.

"cooperative economic enterprise": Steven Mintz and Susan Kellogg,

Domestic Revolutions: A Social History of the American Family (New York: The Free Press, 1988): 49–50.

135   *"haven in a heartless world"*: Mintz and Kellogg, xv, 23.

136   *a trend of "intensive mothering"*: Sharon Hays, *The Cultural Contradictions of Motherhood* (New Haven: Yale University Press, 1996): 9, 128.

137   *42 percent of single women:* John Pawasarat and Frank Stetzer, "Removing Transportation Barriers to Employment: Assessing Driver's License and Vehicle Ownership Patterns of Low-Income Populations," July 1998, <http://www.uwm.edu/Dept/ETI/dot.htm>.

Stafford college loan commitments: U.S. Department of Education Office of Postsecondary Education, *Federal Student Loans Program FY1997–FY2000 Data Book*, <http://www.ed.gov/offices/OPE/Data/FSLPData97-01>.

138   *a bachelor's degree or more:* Tabulations from U.S. Department of Labor, Bureau of Labor Statistics Current Population Survey, <http://www.bls.gov/cps/>.

gains from higher education: Ibid.

139   *child care costs $4,000 to $10,000:* Karen Schulman, "The High Cost of Child Care Puts Quality Care out of Reach for Many Families," *Children's Defense Fund Issue Brief*, 2000, <http://www.childrens defense.org/pdf/highcost.pdf>.

one out of four families: Tabulations from U.S. Census Bureau Current Population Survey, <http://www.census.gov/hhes/income/dinctabs. html>.

over half of all parents: Humphrey Taylor, "Harris Poll on Child Care," Harris Poll #5, 28 January 1998, <http://www.harrisinteractive.com/harris_poll/index.asp?PID=200.>

could be rated as "good": National Center for Early Development and Learning, "Quality in Child Care Centers," *Early Childhood Research and Policy Briefs* 1, no. 1 (summer 1997): 1, <http://www.fpg.unc. edu/~ncedl/PDFs/brief11.pdf>.

"but no one can afford it": Conversation with Dr. Edward Zigler, professor of psychology at Yale University and director of the Bush Center in Child Development and Social Policy.

140   *women with children over six who work:* U.S. Department of Labor, Bureau of Labor Statistics, *Report on the American Workforce 2001* (Washington, D.C.: U.S. Government Printing Office, 2001): 127, table 6, <http://www.bls.gov/opub/rtaw/pdf/table06.pdf>.

140   *close to 20 percent of total earnings:* Linda Giannarelli and James Barsi-
      mantov, *Child Care Expenses of America's Families* (Washington, D.C.:
      The Urban Institute, 2000): 9, table 1, <http://newfederalism.urban.org/
      pdf/occa40.pdf>. *Assessing the New Federalism Occasional Paper* no. 40.
      keeping mothers on welfare: Wilder Research Center, "Filling the Gaps
      in Welfare Reform: The Minnesota Welfare-to-Work Partnerships Ini-
      tiative," August 2001, <http://www.wilder.org/research/reports/pdf/
      mcknightreport8-01.pdf>.
      "decisive factor in promoting work": Deborah Phillips, ed., National
      Academy of Sciences, Institute of Medicine, *Child Care for Low
      Income Families: Summary of Two Workshops* (Washington, D.C.:
      National Academy Press, 1995): <http://www.nap.edu/readingroom/
      books/childcare/chap4b.html>.

141   *the average family spent 40 percent:* Clair Brown, *American Standards
      of Living* (Cambridge: Blackwell Publishers, 1994): 12.

142   *sugar helped our ancestors:* S. Boyd Eaton and Stanley B. Eaton III,
      "Evolution, Diet, and Health," paper prepared for the 14th Inter-
      national Congress of Anthropological and Ethnological Sciences,
      <http://www.cast.uark.edu/local/icaes/conferences/wburg/posters/
      sboydeaton/eaton.htm>.
      obesity among adults: U.S. Department of Health and Human Ser-
      vices, *The Surgeon General's Call to Action to Prevent and Decrease
      Overweight and Obesity,* 2001, <http://www.surgeongeneral.gov/
      topics/obesity/calltoaction/CalltoAction.pdf>.
      soon overtake tobacco: Ibid., xiii.
      Some 300,000 deaths: Ibid.
      meals prepared away from the home: U.S. Department of Agriculture,
      Economic Research Service, "Food Consumption: Household Food
      Expenditures," 2001 <http://www.ers.usda.gov/briefing/consumption/
      Expenditures.htm>.

143   *money to bolster their budgets:* abcnews.com, "Vending Maching Con-
      troversy: Is the Student Body Buying Too Many Snacks?" 29 October
      2001, <http://abcnews.go.com/sections/GMA/GoodMorningAmerica/
      GMA011029Junk_food_kids.html>.
      typical portion: Lisa R. Young and Marion Nestle, "The Contribution
      of Expanding Portion Sizes to the U.S. Obesity Epidemic," *American
      Journal of Public Health* 92, no. 2 (February 2002): 246–49.
      plates themselves have increased in size: American Institute for Cancer

Research, "AICR Introduces the New American Plate," 5 September 2000, <http://www.aicr.org/r090500.htm>.

"live through things": James B. Twitchell, *Lead Us into Temptation: The Triumph of American Materialism* (New York: Columbia University Press, 1999): 19.

144 *"a lot of impulsive buying"*: Conversation with Juliet Schor, professor of sociology at Boston College.

"stronger religious orientation": Conversation with Schor.

"human beings are hard-wired": Paul Krugman, "Money Can't Buy Happiness. Er, Can It?" *New York Times*, 1 June 1999, A23.

"not only the commodities": Adam Smith, *An Inquiry into the Nature and Causes of the Wealth of Nations*, fifth edition of 1789, Edwin Cannan, ed. (New York: Modern Library, 1937): 821.

145 *a shift in the distribution of income:* Conversation with Schor.

146 *"serious and rational enterprise"*: Neil Postman, *Amusing Ourselves to Death: Public Discourse in the Age of Show Business* (New York: Penguin Books, 1985), 59–60.

146 *"youth materialism scale"*: Pennsylvania State University, Smeal College of Business Media Relations Office, "Materialistic Children Expect More During 'Season of Giving,'" 29 November 2001, <http://www.smeal.psu.edu/news/releases/dec01/children.html>.

148 *well-to-do families may purchase:* Arlie Russell Hochschild, *The Commercialization of Intimate Life and Other Essays* (Berkeley: University of California Press, forthcoming in January 2003).

advice from "experts on parenting": Conversation with Dr. Neal Halfon, professor of pediatrics, University of California at Los Angeles School of Medicine and director of the UCLA Center for Healthier Children, Families and Communities.

149 *consumer debt was at an all-time high:* Federal Reserve Statistical Release, "Consumer Credit," <http://www.federalreserve.gov/releases/g19/hist/cc_hist_sa.html>.

Interest payments alone have risen: Federal Reserve Statistical Release, "Household Debt-Service Burden," 16 July 2002, <http://www.federalreserve.gov/releases/housedebt/>.

150 *ever actually received guidance:* Senate Committee on Banking, Housing, and Urban Affairs, *A Financial Education and Literacy Primer,* report prepared by the majority staff, 107th Cong., 2d sess., 2002.

up to 12 million: Fannie Mae Foundation, *Financial Services in Distressed*

Communities: Issues and Answers, August 2001, <http://www.fanniemae foundation.org/programs/financial.pdf>.

151   *"the trick is charging a lot":* Chuck Squatrigia, "Questions on Corporate Crime Cop," *San Francisco Chronicle*, 13 July 2002, A13.

twice as many credit cards: Cardweb.com, "Cardlearn—Frequently Asked Questions," 30 September 2001, <http://www.cardweb.com/cardlearn/faqs/2001/nov/20.amp>.

average credit card debt per household: U.S. Senate Committee on Banking, Housing, and Urban Affairs, 2002.

median interest rate: Arthur B. Kennickell, Martha Starr-McCluer, and Brian J. Surette, "Recent Changes in U.S. Family Finances: Results from the 1998 Survey of Consumer Finances," *Federal Reserve Bulletin* 86, no. 1 (January 2000): 23, <http://www.federalreserve.gov/pubs/oss/oss2/98/bull0100.pdf>.

152   *income gap:* U.S. Department of Commerce, U.S. Census Bureau, *Money Income in the United States: 2000*, September 2001, <http://www.census.gov/prod/2001pubs/p60-213.pdf>.

leading causes of family discord: William Betcher and Robie Macauley, *The Seven Basic Quarrels of Marriage: Recognize, Defuse, Negotiate, and Resolve Your Conflicts* (New York: Villard Books, 1990): 97.

1.5 million personal bankruptcies: Administrative Office of the U.S. Courts, "Bankruptcy Filing Hit Record—Again," 16 May 2002, <http://www.uscourts.gov/Press_Releases/bk302.pdf>.

record $711 billion: Federal Reserve Statistical Release, "Consumer Credit," 8 July 2002, <http://www.federalreserve.gov/releases/g19/hist/cc_hist_sa.html>.

Credit-counseling agencies reported surges: Michael E. Staten et al., "The Impact of Credit Counseling on Subsequent Borrower Usage and Payment Behavior," *Credit Research Center Monograph*, no. 36 (March 2002): i, <http://www.nfcc.org/mo/commark/news/counseling_study032102.pdf>.

153   *false sense of security:* AARP, *Beyond 50: A Report to the Nation on Economic Security*, May 2002, <http://www.aarp.org/beyond50>.

154   *spending far more per person:* Howard Oxley and Maitland MacFarlan, "Health Care Reform: Controlling Spending and Increasing Efficiency," *OECD Working Paper*, 15 December 1994, <http://www.oecd.org/pdf/M00001000/M00001088.pdf>.

"bizarre contrast with our affluence": John Kenneth Galbraith, *The Affluent Society*, 40th Anniversary ed. (New York: Houghton Mifflin, 1998): 223.

CHAPTER 5. WORKS

160 *work ethic throughout history:* Roger B. Hill, "The Work Ethic as Determined by Occupation, Education, Age, Gender, Work Experience, and Empowerment" (Ph.D. dissertation, University of Tennessee, Knoxville, 1992).

161 *could not make a living:* Steven Mintz and Susan Kellogg, *Domestic Revolutions: A Social History of American Family Life* (New York: The Free Press, 1988): 88.
Children in working-class families: Conversation with Steven Mintz; Ibid., 83–95.
Frederick W. Taylor: Arlie Russell Hoshchild, *The Time Bind: When Work Becomes Home and Home Becomes Work* (New York: Henry Holt and Company, 1997): 48–49.
women to enter the workforce: Mintz and Kellogg, 161–62.

162 *migration out of the home: Economic Report of the President* (Washington, D.C.: U.S. Government Printing Office, 2000): 169, chart 5–1.

168 *the hardest-working people:* International Labor Organization, *Key Indicators of the Labor Market, 2001–2002* (New York: Routledge, 2001): 219–22.
By contrast, the Japanese: Ibid.
go back to work sooner: Lawrence Mishel, Jared Bernstein, and John Schmitt, *State of Working America, 2000–2001* (Washington, D.C.: Economic Policy Institute, 2001): 94, 102–103.
often work fifty or more: Barry Bluestone and Stephen Rose, "Unraveling an Economic Enigma," *American Prospect* (March/April 1997).
taking advantage of overtime: Ibid.
holding down two or three jobs: Ibid.
when you add it all up: International Labor Organization, 219, 222.
highest productivity per person: Ibid., 636–37, 640.

169 *employed in agriculture: Economic Report of the President* (2000): 279.
"don't want to give up their overtime": Conversation with John J. Sweeney, president, AFL-CIO.
number of hours worked annually: Mishel et al., 98.

171 *slightly more time each day:* Suzanne M. Bianchi, "Maternal Employment and Time With Children: Dramatic Change or Surprising Continuity?" *Demography* 37, no. 4 (November 2000): 401–14.
wanted to work fewer hours: James T. Bond, Ellen Galinsky, and Jennifer E. Swanberg, *The 1997 National Study of the Changing Workforce* (New York: Families and Work Institute, 1998): 62–67, 73–74.

173   *a fun, low-key way:* Conversation with John Gottman, professor of psychology at the University of Washington and cofounder of the Gottman Institute.

exhausted by the time they go to sleep: Conversation with Dr. Neal Halfon, professor of pediatrics, University of California at Los Angeles School of Medicine and director of the UCLA Center for Healthier Children, Families and Communities.

174   *family is now sleep deprived:* Conversation with Dr. William C. Dement, professor of psychiatry at Stanford University and founder and director of the Stanford University Sleep Research Center.

nearly a complete waste: Conversation with Dement.

175   *"make regular sleep unnecessary":* Jerome Groopman, "Eyes Wide Open," *New Yorker* 77, no. 38 (3 December 2001): 52.

176   *experts are studying its capabilities:* Timothy Gower, "A New Pill to Stretch Your Day," *Los Angeles Times,* 15 April 2002.

eight hours of sleep: Conversation with Dement; National Sleep Foundation, "2001 Sleep in America Poll," <http://www.sleepfoundation.org/publications/2001poll.html#3>.

"why men should go to bed at all": Wyn Wachhorst, *Thomas Alva Edison: An American Myth* (Cambridge, Massachusetts: MIT Press, 1981): 163.

"dim light of evening": Cullen Murphy, "Hello, Darkness: Dealing With Yet Another Deficit," *Atlantic Monthly,* March 1996, <http://www.theatlantic.com/issues/96mar/darkness/darkness.htm>.

177   *nearly eight hours a day:* TV Turnoff Network, "Facts and Figures About Our TV Habit," <http://tv-turnoff.org/images/facts&figs/factsheets/Facts%20and%20Figures.pdf>.

some portion of the hour: National Sleep Foundation, "2001 Sleep in America Poll," <http://www.sleepfoundation.org/publications/2001poll.html>.

"all-night clinic": Murphy, 1996.

178   *worked a different schedule:* Working Women Department, AFL-CIO, "Working Women Say . . . ," (2000): <http://www.aflcio.org/women/survey1.htm.>

185   *more than 70 percent of adults:* U.S. Department of Labor, Bureau of Labor Statistics, "Employment Characteristics of Families," Table 4: Families with Own Children: Employment Status of Parents by Age of Youngest Child and Family Type, 1999–2000 Annual Averages, <http://www.bls.gov/news.release/famee.t04.htm>.

186   *adults caring for an elderly relative:* National Alliance for Caregiving, "Caregiving in the U.S.: Findings from a National Survey" (1997): <http://www.caregiving.org/content/reports/finalreport.pdf>.
more than 40 percent of workers: Ibid.
13 million preschoolers: U.S. Department of Education, National Center for Education Statistics, "Child Care and Early Education Program Participation of Infants, Toddlers, and Preschoolers" (October 1996): <http://nces.ed.gov/pubs/95824.html>.
per 1,000 children: U.S. Department of Commerce, U.S. Census Bureau, "State Estimates of Child Care Establishments: 1977–1997," by Grace O'Neill and Martin O'Connell, August 2001, <http://www.census.gov/population/www/documentation/twps0055.html>, Working Paper Series No. 55.
high-quality day care turns out to be just fine: National Institute of Child Health and Human Development, National Institutes of Health, "The NICHD Study of Early Child Care," ongoing study, <http://www.nichd.nih.gov/publications/pubs/early_child_care.htm>; Lawrence J. Schweinhart and David P. Weikart, "High/Scope Perry Preschool Program Effects at Age Twenty-Seven," in *Social Programs That Work*, Jonathan Crane, ed. (New York: Russell Sage Foundation, 1998): 148–61.
training and compensation: National Council of Jewish Women, "Opening a New Window on Child Care: A Report on the Status of Child Care in the Nation Today" (1999): 10–12; <http://www.ncjw.org/news/childcare/NCJWfinal.pdf>

187   *we pay day-care workers less:* U.S. Department of Labor, U.S. Bureau of Labor Statistics, "Occupational Employment Statistics," <http://www.bls.gov/oes/home.htm#tables>.
"not one child whose family": Conversation with Zigler.
National Institute on Out-of-School Time: National Institute on Out-of-School Time, "Fact Sheet on School-Age Children's Out-of-School Time" (March 2001): <http://www.wellesley.edu/WCW/CRW/SAC/factsheet.pdf>.

188   *According to FBI data:* U.S. Department of Justice, Office of Juvenile Justice and Delinquency Programs, "Juvenile Justice and Victims: 1999 National Report" (1999): <http://www.ncjrs.org/html/ojjdp/nationalreport99/chapter3.pdf>.
when many teens experiment: Save the Children, "United States Children Are at Risk: The Risk During Out-of-School Time," <http://www.savethechildren.org/afc/americasforgottenatrisk2.html>.

189 *multigenerational families can be a great source:* Vern L. Bengston, "Beyond the Nuclear Family: The Increasing Importance of Multigenerational Bonds," *Journal of Marriage and Family* 63, no. 1 (February 2001): 1–16.

obligated to take care of them: AARP, "In the Middle: A Report on Multicultural Boomers Coping with Family and Aging Issues" (July 2001): <http://research.aarp.org/il/in_the_middle_1.html>.

190 *cost of a nursing home increasing:* MetLife Mature Market Institute, press release, "Nursing Home Costs Average $153 Per Day in U.S.," July 24, 2000, <http://metnews.metlife.com/archive/newsdocs/pressrelease/pr0822000a.html>.

paid for out-of-pocket: U.S. Department of Health and Human Services, Centers for Medicare and Medicaid Services, *National Health Care Expenditures Projections Tables,* <http://www.cms.hhs.gov/statistics/nhe/projections-2000/t13.asp>, "Table 13: Nursing Home Expenditures Aggregate and per Capita Amounts, Percent Distribution and Average Annual Percent Change by Source of Funds: Selected Calendar Years 1980–2010."

average woman in an American family: U.S. Department of Labor, Advisory Council on Employee Welfare and Pension Benefit Plans, "Report, Findings, and Recommendations of the Working Group on Long-Term Care," November 14, 2000; <http://www.dol.gov/pwba/adcoun/report2.htm>.

dependent elder–care benefits: Diane E. Lewis, "Helping to Give Kids a Safe Place Online Among New Benefits," *Boston Globe,* 14 May 2000, H13.

Americans one hundred years or older: U.S. Department of Commerce, U.S. Census Bureau, "The 65 Years and Over Population: 2000" (2001): 7, <http://www.census.gov/prod/2001pubs/c2kbr01-10.pdf>; U.S. Department of Commerce, U.S. Census Bureau, "Projections of the Total Resident Population by 5-Year Age Groups, and Sex with Special Age Categories: Middle Series, 2050 to 2070," January 13, 2000, <http://www.census.gov/population/projections/nation/summary/np-t3-g.pdf>.

193 *telecommute in the opposite direction:* Sue Shellenbarger, "Parents See Benefits for After Work, Too," *Wall Street Journal,* 15 August 2000, B1.

seniors who got Internet access: Pew Internet and American Life Project, "Wired Seniors: A Fervent Few, Inspired by Family Ties," 9 September 2001.

"On the Internet": Peter Steiner, "On the Internet, No One Knows You're a Dog," *New Yorker* 69, no. 20 (5 July 1993): 61, illus.

195   *more overworked and stressed:* Ellen Galinksy, Stacy S. Kim, and James T. Bond, *Feeling Overworked: When Work Becomes Too Much.* Families and Work Institute (New York: Price Waterhouse Coopers, LLP, 2001).

178 messages per day: Institute for the Future, *Annual Ten-Year Forecast, 1998* (Menlo Park, California: Institute for the Future, 1998): 177.

and other mental health problems: Clayton Harrison, "Tech Workers Advised to Ward Off Depression," *Dallas Morning News*, 22 October 2000, 21L.

"information fatigue syndrome": Marsha White and Steve Dorman, "Confronting Information Overload," *Journal of School Health*, 1 April 2000.

"in an endless loop": Harrison, 2000.

during their vacations: careerbuilder.com, "Workers Often Pack Flip-Flops and Laptops During Summer Getaways, careerbuilder Survey Finds," June 26, 2001, <http://corp.careerbuilder.com/cfm/newsview.cfm?type=release&ID=122>.

196   *Sigmund Freud once said:* Sigmund Freud, "Civilization and Its Discontents" (1930), in trans. and ed. James Strachey, *The Standard Edition of the Complete Psychological Works of Sigmund Freud*, vol. 21 (London: Hogarth Press, 1961): 101.

positive example for their children: Conversation with Eli Segal, former CEO of the national Welfare-to-Work partnership.

198   *$344 billion per year:* Larry W. Howard, "An Empirical Examination of the Relationships Among Organizational Justice, Job Demands, and Occupational Stress," Paper presented at the Academy of Management, Denver, Colorado, August 2002.

enhance their corporate "campuses": Ilene Philipson, "Married to the Job," *San Francisco Chronicle*, 30 January 2000, Z1.

199   *work as home and home as work:* Hochschild, 198–99.

200   *chosen the Stride Rite Corporation:* Kim L. Tan, "MIT Makes Moms' List," *Boston Herald*, 6 September 2000; "Fleet Is Recognized by Working Mother," *Boston Globe*, 24 September 1999; Davis Bushnell, "Family-Flexible Jobs Pay Off for Firms," *Boston Globe*, 27 September 1998.

with the United Auto Workers: Ford Motor Co., "Dedication of Family Cetners Salutes UWA, Ford and Visteon Vision for Stronger Families,

Better Communities," 19 October 2001, <http://media.ford.com/ newsroom/release_display_test.cfm?article_id=10610&id=432&art_ids= 12048,11221,10371,10033,10610,9790,9650,8702,7740,6700&sec]>.

200   *combine sound management:* Family Re-Union 5: Family and Work, "Forum 2: The Workplace and Community Perspective" (1996): <http://www.familyreunion.org/five/fr5_proceed_forum2.html>.

Ford Foundation report: The Ford Foundation, "Relinking Life and Work: Toward a Better Future," 1 November 1996, <http://www. fordfound.org/publications/recent_articles/life_and_work/relink_toc. html>.

201   *"peer marriages":* Conversation with Schwartz.

value of mothers' work: Ann Crittenden, *The Price of Motherhood: Why the Most Important Job in the World Is Still the Least Valued* (New York: Henry Holt and Company, 2001): 8, 10, 65–66, 73–74, 77.

202   *difficult balancing act:* Joan Williams, *Unbending Gender: Why Family and Work Conflict and What to do About It* (New York: Oxford University Press, 2000): 5.

"restructuring the way work gets done": Ford Foundation, 1996.

203   *dual-earner couples:* Rosalind C. Barnett and Caryl Rivers, *She Works He Works: How Two-Income Families Are Happier, Healthier, and Better Off* (San Francisco: Harper San Francisco, 1996): ix–x, 1–2, 17–20.

female high school seniors: Yupin Bae, Susan Choy, Claire Geddes, Jennifer Sable, and Thomas Snyder, "Trends in Educational Equity of Girls and Women," *Education Statistics Quarterly* 2, no. 2 (summer 2000): <http://nces.ed.gov/pubs2000/quarterly/summer/6cross/q6–1. html>.

CHAPTER 6. PLAY

212   *"way of being":* Conversation with Dr. Stuart L. Brown, founder of the Institute for Play.

213   *"share in games with others":* Conversation with Dr. Rich Lerner, Bergstrom Chair in Applied Developmental Science, Eliot-Pearson Department of Child Development at Tufts University.

"People today devalue": Lenore Terr, *Beyond Love and Work: Why Adults Need to Play* (New York: Scribner, 1999): 25.

214   *play is one of three:* Paul D. MacLean, *The Triune Brain in Evolution* (New York: Plenum, 1990): 389, 559.

we are nature's premier generalists: Jerome S. Bruner, "The Nature and Uses of Immaturity," in *Play: Its Role in Development and Evolution,*

Jerome S. Bruner, Allison Jolly, and Kathy Sylva, eds. (New York: Basic Books, 1976): 13–14, 28.

215   *children are able to:* George Scarlett, "Not Just Fooling Around: Supporting Your Child's Play," in *Proactive Parenting: Guiding Your Child from Two to Six* (New York: Berkeley Publishing Group, forthcoming).
play is a kind of practice: Karl Groos, "The Play of Animals: Play and Instinct," in *The Play of Animals*, trans. by Elizabeth L. Baldwin (New York: D. Appleton, 1898): 65–67.
play is conducive to learning: Jerome S. Bruner, "The Nature and Uses of Immaturity," in *Play: Its Role in Development and Evolution*, 28, 38.

216   *"Let your children's lessons":* Francis M. Cornford, ed. and trans., *The Republic of Plato* (Oxford: Oxford University Press, 1951): 536 d–e.

217   *one quadrillion synaptic connections:* Miles Hochstein and Neal Halfon, The California Center for Health Improvement, "Brain Development: Nearly Half of California Parents Unaware of Important First Three Years," <http://www.cchi.org/pdf/GUW7.pdf>.

218   *"Play is the central theme":* Conversation with Dr. Brown.

219   *"Play is the highest":* Fredrich Froebel, *The Education of Man*, ed. W. T. Harris and trans. W. N. Hailmann (1887; reprint, Clifton, New Jersey: Augustus M. Kelley Publishers, 1974): 54.
work through natural tension: Kim Wallace, ParentCenter, "How Your Child Benefits From Play," <http://www.parentcenter.com/refcap/fun/games/5607.html?CP_bid >.
according to social rules: Ibid.
"Magical thinking is a thrust": T. Berry Brazelton and Joshua D. Sparrow, *Touchpoints Three to Six: Your Child's Emotional and Behavioral Development* (Cambridge, Massachusetts: Perseus Publishing, 2001): 119.

220   *"toys are not only":* Brian Sutton-Smith, "Does Play Prepare the Future?" in *Toys, Play, and Child Development*, Jeffrey H. Goldstein, ed. (Cambridge: Cambridge University Press, 1995): 141.
"preteens who labeled": Institute for Play, "Playing at Work," <http://www.instituteforplay.com/7playing_at_work.htm>.
teens who involve themselves: American Association of School Administrators, "Reliance on Child Care Continued to Grow in the 1990s: Census Report," 23 February 2001.
teens who participated in youth: Presentation by Jette Halladay to Family Centered Community Building, course taught by Al Gore at Middle Tennessee State University and Fisk University, 11 February 2002; James S. Catterall et al., "Involvement in the Arts and Human

Development: General Involvement and Intensive Involvement in Music and Theater Arts"; College Board, *Profile of SAT and Achievement Test Takers*, 1990–2000.

221   *"a playground is one place"*: Conversation with Matthew Cavedon, chair of Boundless Playgrounds's Junior Advisory Board.

222   *"gives us a pleasure"*: Terr, *Beyond Love and Work*, 30, 40.

223   *a capacity for play*: Conversation with Judith Wallerstein, psychologist and author of *The Unexpected Legacy of Divorce: A Twenty-Five-Year Landmark Study*.

  healthier, happier, live longer: John Rowe and Robert Kahn, *Successful Aging* (New York: Pantheon Books, 1998); Ellen Langer, *Mindfulness* (New York: Perseus, 1990).

224   *last year adults*: Humphrey Taylor, "Reading, TV, Spending Time with Family, Gardening and Fishing Top List of Favorite Leisure-Time Activities," The Harris Poll #38, 8 August 2001, <http://www.harrisinteractive.com/harris_poll/index.asp?PID=249>.

  new trend among parents: Jeffrey Kluger and Alice Park, "The Quest For a Superkid," *Time*, 30 April 2001, 50–55.

  certain cognitive skills: Frances H. Rauscher, Gordon L. Shaw, Linda J. Levine, Katherine N. Ky, and Eric L. Wright, "Music and Spatial Task Performance: A Causal Relationship," paper presented at the American Psychological Association 102nd Annual Convention, Los Angeles, California, 12–16 August 1994.

  sustainable, or even measurable: Kenneth M. Steele, Karen E. Bass, and Melissa D. Crook, "The Mystery of the Mozart Effect: Failure to Replicate," *Psychological Science* 10, no. 4 (July 1999): 366–69.

225   *using flash cards*: Kluger and Park, 2001.

  similar to stressed adults: Ibid.

  "stuff that children really use": Scarlett, "Not Just Fooling Around, forthcoming.

226   *"organized youth sports involve"*: Bob Bigelow et al., *Just Let the Kids Play* (Deerfield Beach, Florida: Health Communications Inc., 2001): 5, 103–104.

  Minnesota sports leagues: Ibid., 246.

227   *we are witnessing a revolution*: letter from George Scarlett, deputy chair of the Eliot-Pearson Department of Child Development at Tufts University, 8 March 2002.

  "increasing control and supervision": Brian Sutton-Smith, "Does Play Prepare the Future?" in *Toys, Play, and Child Development*, 137.

228 *television itself—specifically local:* Children Now, "Local TV News Distorts Real Picture of Children," 23 October 2001, <http://www.childrennow.org/newsroom/new-01/pr-10-23-01.cfm>.

replacements for physical play: Dennison et al., "Television Viewing and Television in Bedroom Associated with Overweight Risk Among Low-Income Preschool Children," *Pediatrics* 109, no. 106 (June 2002): 1028–35.

more than any single activity: Robert Kubey and Mihaly Csikszentmihalyi, "Television Addiction Is No Mere Metaphor," *Scientific American* 286, no. 2 (February 2002): 74–80.

commercials typically trigger: Ibid.

229 *emotional impact of television:* Ibid.

two-thirds suffered from too much stress: Lisa Collier Cool, "Raising Kids in a World of Internet Speed," *Child*, <http://www.child.com/your_child/media_and_technology/internet_speed.jsp>.

children who are deprived of play: Institute for Play, "Preventing Violence," <http://www.instituteforplay.com/9preventing_violence.htm>.

children who do not engage: ParentCenter, "How Your Child Benefits from Play," <www.parentcenter.com/refcap/fun/games/5607.html?CP_bid>.

"Play is really the waking equivalent": Conversation with Dr. John Gottman, professor of psychology at the University of Washington and cofounder of the Gottman Institute.

230 *recipe for beer written in cuneiform:* Associated Press, "Ancient Beer Recipes Found," *Modern Brewery Age* 47, no. 52 (19 November 2001): 1.

Moderate alcohol consumption: National Institute on Alcohol Abuse and Alcoholism, "Alcoholism, Getting the Facts,", <http://www.niaaa.nih.gov>.

231 *nearly 14 million Americans:* Ibid.

between 1993 and 2001: Allyson Schafter, "Girls and Alcohol: Closing the Gender Gap," National Clearinghouse for Alcohol and Drug Information, 17 April 2002, <http://www.health.org/newsroom/rep/188.htm>.

"exposed to alcoholism": Charlotte A. Schoenborn, "Exposure to Alcoholism in the Family: United States, 1988," Advance Data from Vital and Health Statistics of the National Center for Health Statistics, no. 205 (Hyattsville, Maryland: National Center for Health Statistics, 1991): 1.

More than 10 percent: U.S. Department of Health and Human Services, Substance Abuse and Mental Health Services Administration,

"You Can Help: A Guide for Caring Adults Working with Young People Experiencing Addiction in the Family," <http://www.samhsa.gov/
centers/csat/content/intermediaries>.

231   *alcohol abuse is a part of their daily lives*: Ibid.

more likely to experience emotional problems: U.S. Department of
Health and Human Services, National Clearinghouse for Alcohol and
Drug Information, "Children of Alcoholics: Important Facts," <http://
www.health.org/nongovpubs/coafacts>.

four times more likely to develop alcoholism: Ibid.

verbal, physical, or sexual abuse: Joseph A. Califano, Jr., "Haven for the
Children," The National Center on Addiction and Substance Abuse at
Columbia University, 26 January 1999, <http://www.casacolumbia.
org/newsletter1457/newsletter_show.htm?doc_id=7526>.

236   *importance of play in handling stress*: Conversation with Dr. Brown.

237   *creating new family rituals*: Meg Cox, *The Heart of a Family: Searching
America for New Traditions that Fulfill Us* (New York: Random House,
1998).

more than 200,000 family: Terri D. Reeves, "Reinventing the Family
Reunion," *St. Petersburg Times*, 31 July 2001.

CHAPTER 7. RESILIENCE

242   *"the capacity to rebound"*: Froma Walsh, *Strengthening Family Resilience*
(New York: Guilford Press, 1998): 4.

"family confronts and manages": Ibid., 14.

243   *make sense of the challenges*: Hamilton I. McCubbin et al., "Ethnicity,
Schema, and Coherence: Appraisal Processes for Families in Crisis," in
Stress, Coping, and Health in Families (Thousand Oaks, California:
Sage Publications, 1998), 59–64; Anne W. Garwick et al., "Variations
in Families' Explanation of Childhood Chronic Conditions: A Cross-
Cultural Perspective," in *The Dynamics of Resilient Families*, Hamilton
I. McCubbin et al., eds. (Thousand Oaks, California: Sage Publica-
tions, 1999): 166.

an interactive process: Walsh, *Strengthening Family Resilience*, 21–25.

251   *"ability to deal with change"*: Michael Rutter, "Resilience in the Face of
Adversity: Protective Factors and Resistance to Psychiatric Disorder,"
British Journal of Psychiatry 147, no. 6 (December 1985): 598–611.

a caring, supportive adult: Emmy E. Werner, "Risk, Resilience, and
Recovery: Perspectives from the Kauai Longitudinal Study," *Development and Psychopathology* 5, no. 3 (September 1993): 503–15.

253   *eight psychosocial stages:* Erik H. Erikson, *Childhood and Society,* 35th anniv. ed. (New York: W.W. Norton & Co., 1985); Erik H. Erikson, *Identity, Youth, and Crisis* (New York: W.W. Norton & Co., 1968).

256   *find ways to communicate openly:* Carolyn Pape Cowan and Philip A. Cowan, *When Partners Become Parents: The Big Life Change for Couples* (New York: Basic Books, 1992).

258   *how the couple divides household chores:* Heather Helms-Erikson, "Marital Quality Ten Years After the Transition to Parenthood: Implications of the Timing of Parenthood and the Division of Housework," *Journal of Marriage and Family* 63, no. 4 (November 2001): 1107–108.
      traditional divisions of household labor: Ibid., 1100–102.
      have serious problems: Cowan and Cowan, *When Partners Become Parents,* 11.

261   *"touchpoints":* T. Berry Brazelton, *Touchpoints: The Essential Reference* (Reading: Perseus Books, 1992).

263   *average age girls begin menstruating:* James M. Tanner, "Menarche, Secular Trend in Age of," in Richard M. Lerner et al., eds., *Encyclopedia of Adolescence,* vol. 2 (New York: Garland Publishing, 1991): 637–41; Marcia E. Herman-Giddens et al., "Secondary Sexual Characteristics and Menses in Young Girls Seen in Office Practice: A Study from the Pediatric Research in Office Settings Network," *Pediatrics* 99, no. 4 (April 1997): 505–12.
      similar for boys: Marcia E. Herman-Giddens et al., "Secondary Sexual Characteristics in Boys: Estimates from the National Health and Nutrition Examination Survey III, 1988–1994," *Archives of Pediatrics and Adolescent Medicine* 155, no. 9 (September 2001): 1022–28.

265   *shorter life expectancy:* Conversation with Tamara Hareven, professor of history, University of Delaware; Tamara Hareven, "Family Time and Historical Time," *Daedalus* 106, no. 2 (spring 1977: The Family): 61.
      "example of a strong, loving, playful relationship": Martha Farrell Erickson, "Empty Nest," *Growing Concerns,* 12 September 1995.
      moment a child leaves home: Shelley Bovey, *The Empty Nest: When Children Leave Home* (New York: Rivers Oram Press, 1995).

266   *fastest-growing age group:* U.S. Census Bureau, *Age: 2000,* October 2001, <http://www.census.gov/prod/2001pubs/c2kbr01-12.pdf>.
      trend of "down-aging": Marilyn Elias, " 'Middle Age' Stretches Toward 80," *USA Today,* 3 August 2000, 10.
      survey by National Council on Aging: National Council on Aging,

American Perceptions of Aging in the Twenty-first Century (2002): 6, <http://www.ncoa.org/study_aging.pdf>, 6.

268   *awareness that death is closer:* Marc Freedman, *Prime Time: How Baby Boomers Will Revolutionize Retirement and Transform America* (New York: Public Affairs, 1999), 28–29.

with aging parents: Mary Pipher, *Another Country: Navigating the Emotional Terrain of Our Elders* (New York: Riverhead Books, 1999), 1–12.

Americans are living longer: Federal Interagency Forum on Aging-Related Statistics, *Older Americans, 2000: Key Indicators of Well-being* (Washington, D.C.: U.S. Government Printing Office, 2000), <http://www.agingstats.gov/chartbook2000/default.htm>.

Some 40 percent of caregivers: U.S. Department of Health and Human Services, *Informal Caregiving: Compassion in Action,* June 1998, <http://aspe.hhs.gov/daltcp/reports/carebro2.pdf>.

270   *"affects your sense of identity":* Ellen Galinsky, interview by Lian Dolan and Liz Dolan, *Satellite Sisters,* WNYC Radio and Oregon Public Broadcasting, 9 March 2002.

"families that can talk about their feelings": Conversation with Dominic Cappello, family communication expert and author.

273   *"who need mental health treatment":* U.S. Department of Health and Human Services, Substance Abuse and Mental Health Services Administration, Center for Mental Health Services, National Institutes of Health, National Institute of Mental Health, *Mental Health: A Report From the Surgeon General* (Rockville, Maryland: U.S. Department of Health and Human Services, 1999): 453, <http:www.surgeongeneral.gov/library/mentalhealth/home.html>.

278   *one out of four children:* Applied Research and Consulting LLC, the Columbia University Mailman School of Public Health, and the New York Psychiatric Institute, *Effects of the World Trade Center Attack on NYC Public School Students: Initial Report to the New York City Board of Education,* 6 May 2002, 24, <http://www.nycenet.edu/offices/spss/wtc_needs/firstrep.pdf>.

280   *known as "enmeshment":* Conversation with Dr. Salvador Minuchin, family therapist.

281   *"Four Horsemen of the Apocalyspe":* John Gottman with Nan Silver, *Why Marriages Succeed or Fail: What You Can Learn from the Breakthrough Research to Make Your Marriage Last* (New York: Fireside, 1994): 71–98.

CHAPTER 8. COMMUNITY

294 *as a web of relationships:* Amitai Etzioni, "Creating Good Communities and Good Societies," *Contemporary Sociology* 29, no. 1 (January 2000): 188–90.

295 *dramatic decline:* Robert D. Putnam, *Bowling Alone: The Collapse and Revival of American Community* (New York: Simon and Schuster, 2000): 16, 53–64.
fallen steadily: Ibid.
community as "social capital": Ibid., 18–25.

296 *social gatherings as their main purpose:* Ibid., 54–55.
more apt to volunteer: Ibid., 133, 148, 180.

297 *benefits for individuals and families:* Ibid., 329–31.
detailed study by Ichiro Kawachi: Ichiro Kawachi et al., "Social Capital, Income Inequality, and Mortality," *American Journal of Public Health* 87, no. 9 (September 1997): 1491–98.
joining even one club: Putnam, *Bowling Alone*, 331.

298 *"success of the community is linked":* Conversation with Emilio Vasquez, principal (retired) of the Elizabeth Learning Center.

300 *"broken windows" theory:* James Q. Wilson and George L. Kelling, "Broken Windows: The Police and Neighborhood Safety," *Atlantic Monthly* 249, no.3 (March 1982): 29–38.

301 *first names of their neighbors:* Presentation by Robert Putnam to the Family Centered Community Building course taught by Al Gore at Fisk University and Middle Tennessee State University and Fisk University, October 2001.
dropped almost 50 percent: Conversation with Jim Bueermann, chief of police and director of Housing, Recreation, and Senior Services, City of Redlands, California.

302 *young people are served:* Conversation with Bueermann.
streets with poor lighting: U.S. Department of Agriculture and U.S. Department of Housing and Urban Development, *What Works! In the Empowerment Zones and Enterprise Communities*, 1999.
fifteen thousand hours of volunteer service: Ibid.
news coverage can be: Franklin D. Gilliam Jr. and Shanto Iyengar, "Prime Suspects: The Corrosive Influence of Local Television News on the Viewing Public," <http://www.sscnet.ucla.edu/issr/ccc/papers/primesus.html>; Presentation by Frank Gilliam to the Family Centered Community Building course taught by Al Gore at Fisk University and Middle Tennessee State University, 18 March 2002.

303   *"How media frames an issue"*: Conversation with Frank Gilliam, asso-
      ciate vice chancellor for community partnerships at the University of
      California at Los Angeles.
      portrayals of the young people: Lori Dorfman and Vincent Schiraldi,
      Off Balance: Youth, Race, & Crime in the News, April 2001, <http://
      www.buildingblocksforyouth.org/media/media.pdf>.
      violent crime by youth: Ibid., 3.
      killed in an American school: Ibid., 3–4.

304   *"indoor town square"*: Associated Press, "More Schools Double as
      Community Centers," 26 October 2001.

305   *earn high grades:* Putnam, *Bowling Alone*, 303.
      higher educational aspirations: Ibid., 296–306.
      "mutually accountable relationships": Presentation by Jim McConnell
      to the "Family Centered Community Building" course taught by Al
      Gore at Fisk University and Middle Tennessee State University, 24
      September 2001.

306   *high incidence of teen violence:* U.S. Department of Justice, Office of
      Juvenile Justice and Delinquency Programs, "Juvenile Justice and Vic-
      tims: 1999 National Report," 1999, <http://www.ncjrs.org/html/
      ojjdp/nationalreport99/chapter3.pdf>.
      getting parents to participate: U.S. Department of Education, National
      Center for Education Statistics, *Fathers' and Mothers' Involvement in
      Their Children's Schools by Family Type and Resident Status*, <http://nces.
      ed.gov/pubs2001/2001032.pdf>.

309   *"full-service community hub"*: Conversation with Yvonne Chan, princi-
      pal of the Vaughn Next Century Learning Center.

310   *schools are centrally located:* Joy Dryfoos and Sue Maguire, *Inside Full-
      Service Community Schools* (Thousand Oaks, California: Corwin
      Press, Inc., 2002).

311   *"problem free is not fully prepared"*: Karen J. Pittman, "Community,
      Youth, Development: Three Goals in Search of Connection," *New
      Designs for Youth Development* 12, no. 1 (winter 1996): 5.

312   *mentor relationship:* Conversation with Bill Milliken, founder of Com-
      munities In Schools.
      "what can you do to help make my business successful": Conversation
      with Rich Lerner, Bergstrom Chair in Applied Developmental Sci-
      ence at Tufts University.

313   *"all the cars are happy"*: Conversation with Samina Quraeshi, Luce
      Professor in Family and Community at the University of Miami.

metropolitan areas have been decentralizing: Andres Duany, Elizabeth Plater-Zyberk, and Jeff Speck, *Suburban Nation: The Rise of Sprawl and the Decline of the American Dream* (New York: North Point Press, 2000), 3–12.

314 *"idealized, artificial system":* Ibid., 4–7.
11 million new homes: Ibid., 7–8.

315 *suburbs gained far more jobs:* U.S. Department of Housing and Urban Development, *The State of the Cities 2000: Megaforces Shaping the Future of the Nation's Cities,* June 2000: 9, <http://www.hud.gov/library/bookshelf18/pressrel/socrpt.pdf, June 2000>.
less than half of the jobs: Edward L. Glaeser, Matthew Kahn, and Chenghuan Chu, "Job Sprawl: Employment Location in U.S. Metropolitan Areas," May 2001: 5, <http://www.brook.edu/dybdocroot/es/urban/publications/glaeserjobsprawl.pdf.>.
Maryland's Smart Growth: Governor's Office of Smart Growth, State of Maryland, "Smart Growth in Maryland," <http://www.op.state.md.us/smartgrowth>.

316 *good design can accomplish public goals:* Adele Fleet Bacow, *Designing the City: A Guide for Advocates and Public Officials* (Washington, D.C.: Island Press, 1995), 6, 76.

317 *increase in commuting time:* Putnam, *Bowling Alone,* 213.
"new strategies for integrating the environment": Richard Florida and Derek Davison, "Gaining from Green Management: Environmental Management Systems Inside and Outside the Factory," *California Management Review* 43, no. 3 (spring 2001): 64–67.

318 *physical shape and structure:* Conversation with Quraeshi.

319 *one in five children:* Donald J. Hernandez, "The Changing Demographics of Families During the Course of American History," in Jody Heymann and Chris Beem, eds., *Work, Family, and Democracy* (Princeton, New Jersey: Princeton University Press, forthcoming).
"immigrant children live in very strong families": Conversation with Donald Hernandez, professor of sociology, University at Albany, State University of New York.

Bibliography

AARP. In the Middle: A Report on Multicultural Boomers Coping with Family and Aging Issues. <http://research.aarp.org/il/in_the_middle_1.html> July 2001.

abcnews.com. "Vending Maching Controversy: Is the Student Body Buying Too Many Snacks?" 29 October 2001. <http://abcnews.go.com/sections/GMA/GoodMorningAmerica/GMA011029Junk_food_ kids.html>.

Administrative Office of the U.S. Courts. "Bankruptcy Filing Hit Record—Again." 16 May 2002. <http://www.uscourts.gov/ Press_Releases/bk302.pdf>.

American Association of School Administrators. *Reliance on Child Care Continued to Grow in the 1990s: Census Report.* 23 February 2001.

American Psychiatric Association. "Psychiatric Effect of Media Violence." <http://www.psych.org/public_info/media_violence.cfm>.

Applied Research and Consulting, LLC, Columbia University Mailman School of Public Health, and New York State Psychiatric Institute. *Effects of the World Trade Center Attack on NYC Public School Students: Initial Report to the New York City Board of Education.* 6 May 2002. <http://www.nycenet.edu/offices/ spss/wtc_needs/firstrep.pdf>.

Aristotle. *Politics.* Benjamin Jowett, trans. Mineola, New York: Dover Publications, Inc., 2000.

Associated Press. "Ancient Beer Recipes Found." *Modern Brewery Age* 47, no. 52 (19 November 2001): 1.

Bacow, Adele Fleet. *Designing the City: A Guide for Advocates and Public Officials*. Washington, D.C.: Island Press, 1995.

Bae, Yupin, Susan Choy, Claire Geddes, Jennifer Sable, and Thomas Snyder. "Trends in Educational Equity of Girls and Women." *Education Statistics Quarterly*, volume 2, issue 2 (summer 2000). <http://nces.ed.gov/pubs2000/quarterly/summer/6cross/q6-1.html>.

Barnett, Rosalind C. and Caryl Rivers. *She Works He Works: How Two-Income Families are Happier, Healthier, and Better Off*. San Francisco: Harper San Francisco, 1996.

Bell, Nancy J., Elizabeth G. Haley, Ginny Felstehausen, and Charlie Adams. "The Healthy Neighborhood Project," in *Serving Children and Families Through Community-University Partnerships: Success Stories*, Thomas R. Chibucos and Richard M. Lerner, eds. Boston: Kluwer Academic Publishers, 1999.

Bellis, Teri James and Laura Ann Wilber. "Effects of Aging and Gender on Interhemispheric Function." *Journal of Speech, Language, and Hearing Research* 44 (April 2001): 246–63.

Bengston, Vern L. "Beyond the Nuclear Family: The Increasing Importance of Multigenerational Bonds." *Journal of Marriage and Family* 63, no. 1 (February 2001): 1–16.

Berger, Brigitte. *The Family in the Modern Age: More Than a Lifestyle Choice*. New Brunswick, New Jersey: Transaction Publishers, 2002.

Betcher, William and Robie Macauley. *The Seven Basic Quarrels of Marriage: Recognize, Defuse, Negotiate, and Resolve Your Conflicts*. New York: Villard Books, 1990.

Bigelow Bob et al. *Just Let the Kids Play*. Deerfield Beach, Florida: Health Communications Inc., 2001.

Black, Dan, Gary Cates, Seth Sanders, and Lowell Taylor. "Demographics of the Gay and Lesbian Popluation in the United States: Evidence from Available Systematic Data Sources." *Demography* 37, no. 2 (May 2000): 139–54.

Bluestone, Barry and Stephen Rose. "Unraveling an Economic Enigma." *The American Prospect* (March/April 1997).

Bond, James T., Ellen Galinsky, and Jennifer E. Swanberg. *The 1997 National Study of the Changing Workforce*. New York: Families and Work Institute, 1998.

Bramlett, Matthew D. and William D. Mosher. "First Marriage Dissolution, Divorce, and Remarriage: United States." *Advance Data*, no. 323 (31 May 2001): 5. <http://www.cdc.gov/nchs/data/ad/ad323.pdf>.

Brazelton, T. Berry and Joshua D. Sparrow. *Touchpoints Three to Six: Your Child's Emotional and Behavioral Development*. Cambridge, Massachusetts: Perseus Publishing, 2001.

Brazelton, T. Berry. *Touchpoints: Your Child's Emotional and Behavioral Development*. Reading: Perseus Books, 1992.

Brazelton, T. Berry and Stanley I. Greenspan. *The Irreducible Needs of Children*. Cambridge: Perseus Publishing, 2000.

Brazelton, T. Berry and Joshua D. Sparrow. *Touchpoints Three to Six*. Cambridge: Perseus Publishing, 2001.

Brooks, Robert and Sam Goldstein. *Raising Resilient Children: Fostering Strength, Hope, and Optimism in Your Child*. Chicago: Contemporary Books, 2001.

Brown, Clair. *American Standards of Living*. Cambridge: Blackwell Publishers, 1994.

Bruner, Jerome S. "The Nature and Uses of Immaturity," in *Play: Its Role in Development and Evolution*. Jerome S. Bruner, Allison Jolly, and Kathy Sylva, eds. New York: Basic Books, 1976.

Bruner, Jerome S., Allison Jolly, and Kathy Sylva, eds. *Play: Its Role in Development and Evolution*. New York: Basic Books, 1976.

Bumpass, Larry and Hsien-Hen Lu. "Trends in Cohabitation and Implications for Children's Family Contexts in the U.S." Center for Demography and Ecology Working Papers, no. 98-15 (March 1999). <http://www.ssc.wisc.edu/cde/cdewp/98-15.pdf>.

Burt Martha R. "What Will It Take to End Homelessness?" Urban Institute Brief, September 2001. <http://www.urban.org/UploadedPDF/end_homelessness.pdf>.

Burt, Martha, Laudan Y. Aron, and Edgar Lee with Jesse Valente. *Helping America's Homeless: Emergency Shelter or Affordable Housing?* Washington, D.C.: The Urban Institute Press, 2001.

Califano, Jr., Joseph A. "Haven for the Children." National Center on Addiction and Substance Abuse at Columbia University. 26 January 1999. <http://www.casacolumbia.org/newsletter1457/newsletter_show.htm?doc_id=7526>.

Canli, Turhan, John E. Desmond, Zuo Zhao, and John D. E. Gabrieli. "Sex Differences in the Neural Basis of Emotional Memories." *Proceedings of the National Academy of Sciences*, vol. 99 no. 16 (6 August 2002): 10789-94.

Cappello, Dominic and Pepper Schwartz. *Ten Talks Parents Must Have With Their Children About Sex and Character*. New York: Hyperion, 2000.

Carnegie Corporation of New York, Carnegie Council on Adolescent Development. *A Matter of Time: Risk and Opportunity in the Non-School Hours*. New York: Carnegie Corporation of New York, 1992.

———. *Starting Points: Meeting the Needs of Our Youngest Children*. New York: Carnegie Corporation of New York, 1994.

———. *Turning Points: Preparing American Youth for the Twenty-first Century*. New York: Carnegie Council on Adolescent Development, 1989.

Annie E. Casey Foundation. *Kids Count Data Book 2001*. Baltimore: The Annie E. Casey Foundation, 2001.

Annie E. Casey Foundation. *Kids Count Data Book 2002*. Baltimore: The Annie E. Casey Foundation, 2002.

Casper, Lynne M. and Suzanne M. Bianchi. *Continuity and Change in the American Family*. Thousand Oaks, California: Sage Publications, 2002.

Cato, Jo, Deborah Wilkes, Susan Maxwell, J. Lee Kreader, Anne Wharff, and Christine M. Todd. "Improving Child Care Systems in Illinois and Georgia: Partnerships Between the Land-Grant Universities and State Agencies," in *Serving Children and Families Through Community-University Partnerships: Success Stories*, Thomas R. Chibucos and Richard M. Lerner, eds. Boston: Kluwer Academic Publishers, 1999.

Catterall, James S., Richard Chapleau, and John Iwanaga. "Involvement in the Arts and Human Development: General Involvement and Intensive Involvement in Music and Theater Arts." The Imagination Project at UCLA Graduate School of Education & Information Studies, September 1999.

Children Now, "Local TV News Distorts Real Picture of Children." October 2001. <http://www.childrennow.org/newsroom/new-01/pr-10-23-01.cfm>.

Christian Science Monitor. "Families: The Ties That Bind." 19 January 2000, 14.

Clearinghouse on International Developments in Child, Youth, and Family Policies at Columbia University. "Fewer and Later Marriages, Increased Divorce Rates, and More Cohabitation." December 2001. <http://www.childpolicyintl.org/contexttabledemography/table216.pdf>.

Coles, Robert and Randy Testa, eds., with Michael Coles. *Growing Up Poor*. New York: The New Press, 2001.

College Board. *Profile of SAT and Achievement Test Takers, 1990–2000*. Princeton, NJ: The College Board, 2001.

Coltrane, Scott. "Research on Household Labor: Modeling and Measuring the Social Embeddedness of Routine Family Work." *Journal of Marriage and Family* 62, no. 4, 1208–33.

Cool, Lisa Collier. "Raising Kids in a World of Internet Speed." *Child*. <http://www.child.com/your_child/media_and_technology/internet_speed.jsp>.

Coontz, Stephanie. *The Way We Never Were. 2000 Edition*. New York: Basic Books, 2000.

Cornford, Francis M., ed. and trans. *The Republic of Plato*. Oxford: Oxford University Press, 1951.

Cox, Meg. *The Heart of a Family: Searching America for New Traditions That Fulfill Us*. New York: Random House, 1998.

Crittenden, Ann. *The Price of Motherhood: Why the Most Important Job in the World Is Still the Least Valued*. New York: Henry Holt and Company, 2001.

Csikszentmihalyi, Mihaly. *Creativity*. New York: Harper Perennial, 1996.

————. *Flow: The Psychology of Optimal Experience*. New York: Harper Perennial, 1990.

D'Augelli, Anthony R. "Mental Health Problems Among Lesbian, Gay, and Bisexual Youths Ages 14 to 21." *Clinical Child Psychology and Psychiatry*, vol. 7, no. 3 (July 2002): 439–62.

D'Augelli, Anthony R, Scott L. Hershberger, and Neil W. Pilkington. "Lesbian, Gay, and Bisexual Youths and Their Families: Disclosure of Sexual Orientation and its Consequences." *American Journal of Orthopsychiatry*, vol. 68, no. 3 (July 1998): 361–71.

de Graaf, John, David Wann, and Thomas H. Naylor. *Affluenza: The All-Consuming Epidemic*. San Francisco: Berrett-Koehler Publishers, Inc., 2001.

Dement, William C. and Christopher Vaughn. *The Promise of Sleep*. New York: Dell Publishing, 1999.

Dizard, Jan E. and Howard Gadlin. *The Minimal Family*. Amherst, Massachusetts: The University of Massachusetts Press, 1990.

Doherty, William J. *The Intentional Family: How to Build Family Ties in Our Modern World*. Reading, Massachusetts: Addison-Wesley Publishing Company, Inc., 1997.

Dorfman, Lori and Vincent Schiraldi. *Off Balance: Youth, Race, & Crime in the News*. April 2001. <http://www.buildingblocksforyouth.org/media/media.pdf>.

Dryfoos, Joy and Sue Maguire. *Inside Full-Service Community Schools*. Thousand Oaks, California: Corwin Press, Inc., 2002.

Duany, Andres, Elizabeth Plater-Zyberk, and Jeff Speck. *Suburban Nation: The Rise of Sprawl and the Decline of the American Dream*. New York: North Point Press, 2000.

Eaton, S. Boyd and Stanley B. Eaton III. "Evolution, Diet, and Health." Prepared for the 14th International Congress of Anthropological and Ethnological Sciences. <http://www.cast.uark.edu/local/icaes/conferences/wburg/posters/sboydeaton/eaton.htm>.

Economic Report of the President (2000). Washington, D.C.: U.S. Government Printing Office, 2000.

Ehrenreich, Barbara. *Nickel and Dimed*. New York: Metropolitan Books, 2001.

Elias, Marilyn. "'Middle Age' Stretches Toward 80." *USA Today*, 3 August 2000, 1D.

Ellwood, David. *Poor Support: Poverty in the American Family*. New York: Basic Books, 1988.

Erickson, Martha Farrell and Karen Kurz-Riemer. *Infants, Toddlers, and Families: A Framework for Support and Intervention*. New York: The Guilford Press, 1999.

Erikson, Erik H. *Childhood and Society*, 35th anniversary edition. New York: W. W. Norton and Company, 1963.

————. *Identity, Youth, and Crisis*. New York: W. W. Norton and Company., 1968.

Etzioni, Amitai. "Creating Good Communities and Good Societies." *Contemporary Sociology* 29, no. 1 (January 2000): 188–90.

Fannie Mae Foundation. *Financial Services in Distressed Communities: Issues and Answers*. August 2001. <http://www.fanniemaefoundation.org/programs/financial.pdf>.

Federal Interagency Forum on Child and Family Statistics. "America's Children: Key National Indicators of Well-Being 2001." Federal Interagency Forum on Child and Family Statistics, Washington, D.C.: U.S. Government Printing Office, 2001.

Fisher, Gordon M. "The Development and History of the Poverty Thresholds." *Social Security Bulletin*, vol. 55, no. 4 (winter 1992): 3-14.

Florida, Richard and Derek Davison. "Gaining from Green Management: Environmental Management Systems Inside and Outside the Factory." *California Management Review* 43, no. 3 (spring 2001): 64–84.

Ford Foundation. "Relinking Life and Work: Toward a Better Future." November 1996. <http://www.fordfound.org/publications/recent_articles/life_and_work/relink_toc.html>.

Fredriksen-Goldsen, Karen I. and Andrew E. Scharlach. *Families and Work: New Directions in the Twenty-first Century*. New York: Oxford University Press, 2001.

Freud, Sigmund. "Civilization and Its Discontents" (1930) James Strachey, trans. and ed. *The Standard Edition of the Complete Psychological Works of Sigmund Freud*, vol. 21. London: Hogarth Press, 1961.

Froebel, Friedrich. *The Education of Man*. W. T. Harris, ed. and W. N. Hailmann, trans. 1887. Reprint, Clifton, New Jersey: Augustus M. Kelley Publishers, 1974.

Galbraith, John Kenneth. *The Affluent Society*, 40th anniversary edition. New York: Houghton Mifflin, 1998.

Galinksy, Ellen, Interview by Lian Dolan and Liz Dolan. *Satellite Sisters*. WNYC Radio and Oregon Public Broadcasting, 9 March 2002.

Galinksy, Ellen, Stacy S. Kim, and James T. Bond. *Feeling Overworked: When Work Becomes Too Much*. Families and Work Institute, New York: PriceWaterhouseCoopers, LLP, 2001.

Garwick, Anne W. et al. "Variations in Families' Explanation of Childhood Chronic Conditions: A Cross-Cultural Perspective," in *The Dynamics of Resilient Families*, Hamilton I. McCubbin et al., eds. Thousand Oaks, California: Sage Publications, 1999.

Giannarelli, Linda and James Barsimantov. *Child Care Expenses of America's Families*. Washington, D.C.: The Urban Institute, 2000. <http://newfederalism.urban.org/pdf/occa40.pdf>. *Assessing the New Federalism*, Occasional Paper no. 40.

Gilliam, Franklin D. Jr. and Shanto Iyengar. "Prime Suspects: The Corrosive Influence of Local Television News on the Viewing Public." <http://www.sscnet.ucla.edu/issr/ccc/papers/primesus.html>.

Gilligan, Carol. *In a Different Voice.* Cambridge, Massachusetts: Harvard University Press, 1982.

Glaeser, Edward L., Matthew Kahn, and Chenghuan Chu. "Job Sprawl: Employment Location in U.S. Metropolitan Areas." May 2001. <http://www.brook.edu/dybdocroot/es/urban/publications/glaeserjob sprawl.pdf.>.

Goldberg, Marvin E. et al. "Understanding Materialism Among Youth." *Journal of Consumer Psychology.* Forthcoming.

Gordon, Robert J. "Does the 'New Economy' Measure Up to the Great Inventions of the Past." *National Bureau of Economic Research.* August 2000. <http://www.nber.org/papers/w7833>.

Gottman, John, with Joan DeClaire. *Raising an Emotionally Intelligent Child: The Heart of Parenting.* New York: Fireside Books, Simon and Schuster, 1997.

———. *The Relationship Cure: A 5 Step Guide for Building Better Connections with Family, Friends, and Lovers.* New York: Crown Publishers, 2001.

Gottman, John and Nan Silver. *The Seven Principles for Making Marriage Work.* New York: Crown Publishers, 1999.

———. *Why Marriages Succeed or Fail: What You Can Learn from the Breakthrough Research to Make Your Marriage Last.* New York: Fireside, 1994.

Gower, Timothy. "A New Pill to Stretch Your Day." *Los Angeles Times,* 15 April 2002.

Groopman, Jerome. "Eyes Wide Open." *New Yorker,* vol. 77, no. 30 (3 December 2001).

Groos, Karl. *The Play of Animals,* Elizabeth L. Baldwin, trans. New York: D. Appleton, 1898.

Gurian, Michael, Patricia Henley, and Terry Trueman. *Boys and Girls Learn Differently: A Guide for Teachers and Parents.* San Francisco: Jossey-Bass, 2001.

Hackstaff, Karla B. *Marriage in a Culture of Divorce.* Philadelphia: Temple University Press, 1999.

Hareven, Tamara. "Family Time and Historical Time." *Daedalus* 106, no. 2 (spring 1977: The Family). 57–70.

Harris, Judith Rich. *The Nurture Assumption: Why Children Turn Out the Way They Do.* New York: Touchstone Books, 1999.

Harrison, Clayton. "Tech Workers Advised to Ward Off Depression." *Dallas Morning News,* 22 October 2000, 21L.

Hays, Sharon. *The Cultural Contradictions of Motherhood.* New Haven: Yale University Press, 1996.

Helburn, Suzanne W. and Barbara Bergmann. *America's Childcare Problem*. New York: Palgrave for St. Martin's Press, 2002.

Helms-Erikson, Heather. "Marital Quality Ten Years After the Transition to Parenthood: Implications of the Timing of Parenthood and the Division of Housework." *Journal of Marriage and Family* 63, no. 4 (November 2001): 1107–108.

Herman-Giddens, Marcia E. et. al. "Secondary Sexual Characteristics and Menses in Young Girls Seen in Office Practice: A Study from the Pediatric Research in Office Settings Network." *Pediatrics* 99, no. 4 (April 1987): 505–12.

Herman-Giddens, Marcia E., Lily Wang, and Gary Koch. "Secondary Sexual Characteristics in Boys." *Archives of Pediatrics and Adolescent Medicine* 155 (September 2001): 1022–28.

Hernandez, Donald J. *America's Children: Resources from Family, Government, and the Economy*. New York: Russell Sage Foundation, 1995.

———. "The Changing Demographics of Families During the Course of American History." In Jody Heymann and Chris Beem, eds. *Work, Family, and Democracy*. Princeton, New Jersey: Princeton University Press, forthcoming.

Hetherington, E. Mavis and John Kelly. *For Better or for Worse: Divorce Reconsidered*. New York: W. W. Norton and Company, 2002.

Hill, Roger B. "The Work Ethic as Determined by Occupation, Education, Age, Gender, Work Experience, and Empowerment." Ph.D. dissertation, University of Tennessee, Knoxville, 1992.

Hochschild, Arlie Russell. *The Commercialization of Intimate Life and Other Essays*. Berkeley: University of California Press. Forthcoming January 2003.

———. *The Time Bind: When Work Becomes Home and Home Becomes Work*. New York: Henry Holt and Company, 1997.

Hochstein, Miles and Neal Halfon. "Brain Development: Nearly Half of California Parents Unaware of Important First Three Years." The California Center for Health Improvement. <http://www.cchi.org/pdf/ GUW7.pdf>.

Hoffman, Saul D. and Greg J. Duncan. "The Effect of Incomes, Wages, and AFDC Benefits on Marital Disruption." *The Journal of Human Resources* 30, no. 1 (winter 1995): 19–41.

Hotchner, A. E. *Papa Hemingway*. New York: Random House, 1966.

Howard, Larry W. "An Empirical Examination of the Relationships Among Organizational Justice, Job Demands, and Occupational Stress." Paper presented at the Academy of Management, Denver, Colorado, August 2002.

Huston, Aletha C., et al. *Big World, Small Screen: The Role of Television in American Society*. Lincoln, Nebraska: University of Nebraska Press, 1992.

Institute for the Future. *Annual Ten-Year Forecast, 1998*. Menlo Park, California: Institute for the Future, 1998.

International Labor Organization. *Key Indicators of the Labor Market, 2001–2002.* New York: Routledge, 2001.

Kabat-Zinn, Jon and Myla. *Everyday Blessings.* New York: Hyperion, 1997.

The Henry J. Kaiser Family Foundation. Kids and Media at the New Millennium. November 1999. <http://www.kff.org/content/1999/1535/KidsReport%20FINAL.pdf>.

Kawachi, Ichiro, Bruce P. Kennedy, Kimberly Lochner, and Deborah Prothrow-Smith. "Social Capital, Income Inequality, and Mortality." *American Journal of Public Health* 87, no. 9 (September 1997): 1491–98.

Kennedy, Marge and Janet Spencer King. *The Single-Parent Family.* New York: Crown Trade Paperbacks, 1994.

Kennickell, Arthur B., Martha Starr-McCluer, and Brian J. Surette. "Recent Changes in U.S. Family Finances: Results from the 1998 Survey of Consumer Finances." *Federal Reserve Bulletin* 86, no. 1 (January 2000): 23. <http://www.federalreserve.gov/pubs/oss/oss2/98/bull0100.pdf>.

Kerr, Michael E. and Murray Bowen. *Family Evaluation.* New York: W. W. Norton and Company, 1988.

Kluger, Jeffrey and Alice Park. "The Quest For a Superkid." *Time,* 30 April 2001, 50–55.

Knowles, Elizabeth, ed. *The Oxford Dictionary of Quotations,* 5th ed. New York : Oxford University Press, 1999.

Kraus, Richard. *Leisure in a Changing America,* 2nd edition. Boston: Allyn and Bacon, 2000.

Kubey, Robert and Mihaly Csikszentmihalyi. "Television Addiction Is No Mere Metaphor. *Scientific American,* vol. 286, no. 2 (February 2002): 74–80.

Langer, Ellen. *Mindfulness.* New York: Perseus, 1990.

Lasch, Christopher. *Haven in a Heartless World: The Family Besieged.* New York: W. W. Norton and Company, 1977.

Lerner, Richard M. *Adolescence.* New Jersey: Prentice Hall, 2002.

———. *Concepts and Theories of Human Development,* 3rd edition. New Jersey: Lawrence Erlbaum Associates, 2002.

Lewit, Eugene M. and Linda Schuurmann Baker. "Child Indicators: Homeless Families and Children." *The Future of Children: Financing Child Care* 6, no. 2 (summer/fall 1996): 146. <http://www.futureofchildren.org/usr_doc/vol6no2ART7.pdf>.

Line, William. "The Nature of Human Nature," *Emphatic Parenting,* vol. 3, no. 1 (winter 1980): 16–21.

Lucy-Allen, Dale and Jennifer Sydel. "Revitalizing the Community Through Neighborhood and Institutional Partnerships," in *Serving Children and Families Through Community-Univesity Partnerships: Success Stories,* Thomas R. Chibucos and Richard M. Lerner, eds. Boston: Kluwer Academic Publishers, 1999.

MacLean, Paul D. *The Triune Brain in Evolution.* New York: Plenum, 1990.

Maslow, Abraham. *Toward a Psychology of Being.* New York: Van Nostrand Reinhold, [1982] 1968.

McCubbin, Hamilton I., Elizabeth A. Thompson, Anne I. Thompson, and Jo A. Futtrell, eds. *The Dynamics of Resilient Families.* Thousand Oaks, California: Sage Publications, 1999.

McCubbin, Hamilton I., Elizabeth A. Thompson, Anne I. Thompson, and Julie E. Fromer, eds. *Stress, Coping, and Health in Families.* Thousand Oaks, California: Sage Publications, 1998.

McLanahan, Sara and Gary Sandefur. *Growing Up with a Single Parent.* Cambridge, Massachusetts: Harvard University Press, 1994.

Miller, Kim S. and Daniel J. Whittaker. "Predictors of Mother-Adolescent Discussions About Condoms: Implications for Providers Who Serve Youth." *Pediatrics* 108, no. 2 (August 2001): e28.

Minow, Martha. *Making All the Difference: Inclusion, Exclusion and American Law.* Ithaca, NY: Cornell University Press, 1990.

———. "Redefining Families: Who's In and Who's Out?" *University of Colorado Law Review* 62, no. 2 (1991): 269–85.

Minow, Martha, ed. *Family Matters: Readings on Family Lives and the Law.* New York: The New Press, 1999.

Mintz, Steven and Susan Kellogg. *Domestic Revolutions: A Social History of the American Family.* New York: The Free Press, 1988.

Mishel, Lawrence, Jared Bernstein, and John Schmitt. *State of Working America, 2000–2001, An Economic Policy Institute Book.* Washington, D.C.: Economic Policy Institute, 2001.

Murphy, Cullen. "Hello, Darkness: Dealing With Yet Another Deficit." *Atlantic Monthly.* March 1996. <http://www.theatlantic.com/issues/96mar/darkness/darkness.htm>.

National Alliance for Caregiving. "Caregiving in the U.S.: Findings from a National Survey." 1997. <http://www.caregiving.org/content/reports/finalreport.pdf>.

National Campaign to Prevent Teen Pregnancy. "Talking Back: Ten Things Teens Want Parents to Know About Teen Pregnancy." April 1999. <http://www.teenpregnancy.org/resources/reading/tips/talk_back.asp>.

National Center for Early Development and Learning. "Quality in Child Care Centers." *Early Childhood Research and Policy Briefs* 1, no. 1 (summer 1997): 1. <http://www.fpg.unc.edu/~ncedl/PDFs/brief11.pdf>.

National Center for Fathering. *Father of the Year Essay Contest.* "What My Father Means to Me." 1994.

National Council on Aging. "American Perceptions of Aging in the 21st Century": 6. 2002. <http://www.ncoa.org/study_aging.pdf>.

National Council of Jewish Women. "Opening a New Window on Child Care: A Report on the Status of Child Care in the Nation Today." 1999. <http://www.ncjw.org/news/childcare/ NCJWfinal.pdf>.

National Institute on Alcohol Abuse and Alcoholism. "Alcoholism, Getting the Facts." <http://www.niaaa.nih.go>.

National Institute of Child Health and Human Development, National Institutes of Health. "The NICHD Study of Early Child Care." Ongoing study. <http://www.nichd.nih.gov/publications/ pubs/early_child_care.htm>.

National Institute of Mental Health. *Television and Behavior: Ten Years of Scientific Progress and Implications for the Eighties*. Washington, D.C.: U.S. Government Printing Office, 1982.

National Institute on Out-of-School Time. "Fact Sheet on School-Age Children's Out-of-School Time." March 2001. <http://www.wellesley.edu/WCW/CRW/SAC/factsheet.pdf>.

National Low Income Housing Coalition. "Out of Reach 2001: America's Growing Wage-Rent Disparity, 2001." <http://www.nlihc.org/oor2001, 2001>.

National Research Council and Institute of Medicine. *From Neurons to Neighborhoods: The Science of Early Childhood Development*. Committee on Integrating the Science of Early Childhood Development. Jack P. Shonkoff and Deborah A. Phillips, eds. Board on Children, Youth, and Families, Commission on Behavioral and Social Sciences and Education. Washington, D.C.: National Academy Press, 2000.

National Sleep Foundation. "2001 Sleep in America Poll." <http://www.sleepfoundation.org/publications/2001poll.html#3>.

Nestle, Marion. *Food Politics*. Berkeley, California: University of California Press, 2002.

Nickelodeon, Kaiser Family Foundation, and Children Now. Talking With Kids About Tough Issues: A National Survey of Parents and Kids. March 2001. <http://www.talkingwithkids.org/nickelodeon/summary.pdf>.

Oh, Hyun Joo. "An Exploration of the Influence of Household Poverty Spells on Mortality Risk." *Journal of Marriage and Family* 63, no. 1 (February 2001): 224–34.

O'Neill, Paul. "The State of Financial Literacy and Education in America." Testimony before the Senate Banking, Housing, and Urban Affairs Committee, 5 February 2002.

Oxley, Howard and Maitland MacFarlan. "Health Care Reform: Controlling Spending and Increasing Efficiency." *OECD Working Paper*, 15 December 1994. <http://www.oecd.org/pdf/M00001000/M00001088. pdf>.

Ozment, Steven. *When Fathers Ruled: Family Life in Reformation Europe*. Cambridge, Massachusetts: Harvard University Press, 1983.

Panksepp, Jaak. *Affective Neuroscience: The Foundations of Human and Animal Emotions*. New York: Oxford University Press, 1998.

Parsons, Talcott and Robert F. Bales. *Family, Socialization and Interaction Process*. Glencoe, Illinois: The Free Press, 1960.

Peck, M. Scott. *The Road Less Traveled*. New York: Touchstone Books, 1978.

Pennsylvania State University. Smeal College of Business Media Relations Office. "Materialistic Children Expect More During 'Season of Giving.'" 29 November 2001. <http://www.smeal.psu.edu/news/releases/dec01/children.html>.

Perry, Bruce Duncan. "The Importance of Pleasure in Play." *Scholastic*. <http://teacher.scholastic.com/professional/bruceperry/pleasure.htm>.

Pew Internet and American Life Project. "Wired Seniors: A Fervent Few, Inspired by Family Ties." September 9, 2001. <http://www.pewinternet.org/reports/pdfs/PIP_Wired_Seniors_Report.pdf>.

Philipson, Ilene. "Married to the Job." *San Francisco Chronicle*, 30 January 2002, 21.

Phillips, Deborah, ed. National Academy of Sciences. Institute of Medicine. *Child Care for Low Income Families: Summary of Two Workshops*. Washington, D.C.: National Academy Press, 1995. <http://www.nap.edu/readingroom/books/childcare/>.

Pipher, Mary. *Another Country: Navigating the Emotional Terrain of Our Elders*. New York: Riverhead Books, 1999.

———. *The Shelter of Each Other*. New York: G.P. Putnam's Sons, 1996.

Pittman, Karen J. "Community, Youth, Development: Three Goals in Search of Connection." *New Designs for Youth Development* 12, no. 1 (winter 1996): 4–8.

Popenoe, David. *Disturbing the Nest*. New York: Aldine de Gruyter, 1988.

Postman, Neil. *Amusing Ourselves to Death: Public Discourse in the Age of Show Business*. New York: Penguin Books, 1985.

Putnam, Robert D. *Bowling Alone: The Collapse and Revival of American Community*. New York: Simon and Schuster, 2000.

Quale, G. Robina. *A History of Marriage Systems*. New York: Greenwood Press, 1988.

Quinn, William H. "The Family Solutions Program: A Collaboration of the University of Georgia and the Athens/Clarke County Juvenile Court," in *Serving Children and Families Through Community-University Partnerships: Success Stories*, Thomas R. Chibucos and Richard M. Lerner, eds. Boston: Kluwer Academic Publishers, 1999.

Rauscher, Frances H., Gordon L. Shaw, Linda J. Levine, Katherine N. Ky, and Eric L. Wright. "Music and Spatial Task Performance: A Causal Relationship." Paper presented at the American Psychological Association 102nd Annual Convention, Los Angeles, California, 12–16 August 1994.

Reeves, Terri D. "Reinventing the Family Reunion." *St. Petersburg Times*, 31 July 2001.

Regensburger, Linda. *The American Family: Reflecting a Changing Nation*. Detroit: Gale Group, 2001.

Remafedi, Gary. "Sexual Orientation and Youth Suicide." *Journal of the American Medical Association* 282, no. 13 (October 6, 1999): 1291–92.

Resnick, Michael D. et. al. "Protecting Adolescents from Harm: Findings From the National Longitudinal Study on Adolescent Health." *Journal of the American Medical Association* 278, no. 10 (10 September 1997): 823–32.

Rowe, John and Robert Kahn. *Successful Aging*. New York: Pantheon Books, 1998.

Rutter Michael. "Resilience in the Face of Adversity: Protective Factors and Resistance to Psychiatric Disorder." *British Journal of Psychiatry* 147, no. 6 (December 1985): 598–611.

Savin-Williams, Ritch. *"Mom, Dad. I'm Gay." How Families Negotiate Coming Out*. Washington, D.C.: American Psychological Association, 2001.

Scarf, Maggie. "Intimate Partners." *Atlantic Monthly*, vol. 258, no. 5 (November 1986): 45–58. <http://www.theatlantic.com/issues/86nov/scarf.htm>.

Scarlett, George. "Co-playing: Teachers as Models for Friendship," in *Connecting: Friendship in the Lives of Young Children and Their Teachers*, Dennie Palmer Wolf, ed. Redmond, Washington: Exchange Press, 1986.

———. "Not Just Fooling Around: Supporting Your Child's Play," in *Proactive Parenting: Guiding Your Child From Two to Six*. New York: The Berkley Publishing Group, forthcoming.

Schaffer, Allyson. "Girls and Alcohol: Closing the Gender Gap." *The National Clearinghouse for Alcohol and Drug Information*. 17 April 2002. <http://www.health.org/newsroom/rep/188.htm>.

Schor, Juliet B. *The Overspent American: Why We Want What We Don't Need*. New York: Harper Perennial, 1998.

Schorr, Lisbeth B. *Common Purpose: Strengthening Families and Neighborhoods to Rebuild America*. New York: Anchor Books, Doubleday, 1997.

Schulman, Karen. "The High Cost of Child Care Puts Quality Care Out of Reach for Many Families." *Children's Defense Fund Issue Brief*, 2000. <http://www.childrensdefense.org/pdf/highcost.pdf>.

Schwartz, Pepper. *Love Between Equals: How Peer Marriage Really Works*. New York: Free Press, 1995.

Schweinhart, Lawrence J. and David P. Weikart. "High/Scope Perry Preschool Program Effects at Age Twenty-seven." In *Social Programs That Work*, Jonathan Crane, ed. New York: Russell Sage Foundation, 1998: 148–61.

Seccombe, Karen. "Families in Poverty in the 1990s: Trends, Causes, Consequences, and Lessons Learned." *Journal of Marriage and Family* 62, no. 4 (November 2000): 1103.

Shellenbarger, Sue. "Parents See Benefits for After Work, Too." *Wall Street Journal*, 15 August 2000, B1.

Shelton, Phyllis. *Long Term Care: Your Financial Planning Guide*. New York: Kensington Books, 2001.

Shirk, Martha, Neil G. Bennett, and J. Lawrence Aber. *Lives on the Line: American Families and the Struggle to Make Ends Meet.* Boulder, Colorado: Westview Press, 1999.

Small, Meredith F. *Our Babies, Ourselves: How Biology and Culture Shaped the Way We Parent.* New York: Doubleday, 1998.

Smith, Adam. *An Inquiry into the Nature and Causes of the Wealth of Nations.* Fifth edition of 1789, Edwin Cannan, ed. New York: Modern Library, 1937.

Smith, Wes. *Hope Meadows: Real-Life Stories of Healing and Caring from an Inspiring Community.* New York: Berkley Books, 2001.

Spanier, Graham. "Bequeathing Family Continuity." *Journal of Marriage and the Family* 51 (February 1989): 3–13.

Spitz, Rene A., with W. Godfrey Cobliner. *The First Year of Life: A Psychoanalytic Study of Normal and Deviant Development of Object Relations.* New York: International Universities Press, Inc., 1965.

Spock, Benjamin. *The Pocket Book of Baby and Child Care.* Illus. by Dorothea Fox. 5th ed. New York: Pocket Books, 1947.

Squatrigia, Chuck. "Questions on Corporate Crime Cop." *San Francisco Chronicle,* 13 July 2002, A13.

Staten, Michael E. et al. "The Impact of Credit Counseling on Subsequent Borrower Usage and Payment Behavior." *Credit Research Center Monograph,* no. 36 (March 2002). <http://www.nfcc.org/mo/commark/news/counseling_study032102.pdf>.

Steele, Kenneth M., Karen E. Bass, and Melissa D. Crook. "The Mystery of the Mozart Effect: Failure to Replicate." *Psychological Science,* vol. 10, no. 4 (July 1999): 366–69.

Steiner, Peter. "On the Internet, No One Knows You're a Dog." *New Yorker,* vol. 69, no. 20 (5 July 1993): 61, illus.

Sutton-Smith, Brian. "Does Play Prepare the Future?" in *Toys, Play, and Child Development,* Jeffrey H. Goldstein, ed. Cambridge: Cambridge University Press, 1995.

Tannen, Deborah. *I Only Say This Because I Love You: How the Way We Talk Can Make or Break Family Relationships Throughout Our Lives.* New York: Random House, 2001.

Tanner, James M. "Menarche, Secular Trend in Age of," in Richard M. Lerner et al., eds. *Encyclopedia of Adolescence,* vol. 2 (New York: Garland Publishing, 1991): 637–41.

Taylor Humphrey. "Harris Poll on Child Care." Harris Poll #5. 28 January 1998. <http://www.harrisinteractive.com/harris_poll/index.asp?PID=200>.

———. "Reading, TV, Spending Time with Family, Gardening and Fishing Top List of Favorite Leisure-Time Activities." Harris Poll #38. 8 August 2001. <http://www.harrisinteractive.com/harris_poll/index.asp?PID249>.

Terr, Lenore. *Beyond Love and Work: Why Adults Need to Play*. New York: Scribner, 1999.

Twitchell, James B. *Lead Us Into Temptation: The Triumph of American Materialism*. New York: Columbia University Press, 1999.

U.S. Department of Commerce. Census Bureau. "Living Arrangements of Children Under Eighteen Years Old: 1960 to Present." 29 June 2001. <http://www.census.gov/population/socdemo/hh-fam/tabCH-1.txt>.

———. Families, by Presence of Own Children Under Eighteen: 1950 to Present." 29 June 2001. <http://www.census.gov/population/socdemo/hh-fam/tabFM-1.txt>.

———. "Family Status of Persons Under 14 Years Old by Age and Color, By Presence and Marital Status of Parents, for the United States, By Type of Residence, and for the South: 1960": Washington, D.C.: U.S. Government Printing Office, 1960.

———. "Grandchildren Living in the Home of Their Grandparents: 1970 to Present." 29 June 2001. <http://www.census.gov/population/socdemo/hh-fam/tabCH-7.txt>.

U.S. Department of Commerce. U.S. Census Bureau. "State Estimates of Child Care Establishments: 1977–1997." By Grace O'Neill and Martin O'Connell. August 2001. <http://www.census.gov/population/www/documentation/twps0055.html>. Working Paper Series No. 55.

———. *Statistical Abstract of the United States 1995*. Washington, D.C.: U.S. Government Printing Office, 1996.

———. *Statistical Abstract of the United States 2000*. Washington, D.C.: U.S.Government Printing Office, 2001.

———. The 65 Years and Over Population: 2000. <http://www.census.gov/prod/2001pubs/c2kbr01-10.pdf>. 2001.

U.S. General Accounting Office. *Child Care Subsidies Increase Likelihood That Low-Income Mothers Will Work*, GAO/HEHS-95-20. Washington, D.C.: U.S. Government Printing Office, 1994.

U.S. Department of Agriculture and U.S. Department of Housing and Urban Development. *What Works! In the Empowerment Zones and Enterprise Communities*. 1999.

U.S. Department of Education. National Center for Education Statistics. "Child Care and Early Education Program Participation of Infants, Toddlers, and Preschoolers." October 1996. <http://nces.ed.gov/pubs/95824.html>.

———. *Digest of Education Statistics 2000*, 2001. <http://nces.ed.gov/pubs2001/digest/tables/PDF/table248.pdf>.

———. "Fathers' and Mothers' Involvement in Their Children's Schools by Family Type and Resident Status." May 2001. <http://nces.ed.gov/pubs2001/2001032.pdf>.

U.S. Department of Health and Human Services. *Informal Caregiving: Compassion in Action.* June1998. <http://aspe.hhs.gov/daltcp/reports/carebro2.pdf>.

————. "The Surgeon General's Call to Action to Prevent and Decrease Overweight and Obesity, 2001." <http://www.surgeongeneral.gov/topics/obesity/calltoaction/CalltoAction.pdf>.

U.S. Department of Health and Human Services. "2002 Poverty Guidelines," *Federal Register,* vol. 67, no. 31 (14 February 2002): 6931–33.

U.S. Department of Health and Human Services. Centers for Medicare and Medicaid Services. *National Health Care Expenditures Projections Tables.* <http://www.cms.hhs.gov/statistics/nhe/projections-2000/>.

————. National Center for Health Statistics. Advanced Data, USDHHS, No. 205, 30 September 1991: 1.

————. "Advance Report of Final Divorce Statistics." *Monthly Vital Statistics Report* 39, no. 12(S2) (21 May 1991): 1. <http://www.cdc.gov/nchs/data/mvsr/supp/ mv39_12s2.pdf>.

————. "Advance Report of Final Divorce Statistics, 1989 and 1990." *Monthly Vital Statistics Report* 43, no. 9(S) (22 March 1995): 9. <http://www.cdc.gov/nchs/data/mvsr/supp/mv43_09s.pdf>.

————. "Births, Marriages, Divorces, and Deaths: Provisional Data for January–December 2000," *National Vital Statistics Report* 49, no. 6 (22 August 2001): 1. <http://www.cdc.gov/nchs/data/nvsr/nvsr49/nvsr49_06.pdf>.

————. *Health, United States, 2001.* Hyattsville, Maryland: National Center for Health Statistics, 2002. <http://www.cdc.gov/nchs/products/pubs/pubd/hus/hus.htm>.

————. "Nonmarital Childbearing in the United States, 1940–99." *National Vital Statistics Report* 48, no. 16 (18 October 2000): 17.

————. National Clearinghouse for Alcohol and Drug Information. "Children of Alcoholics: Important Facts." <http://www.health.org/nongovpubs/coafacts>.

————. Substance Abuse and Mental Health Services Administration. A Guide for Caring Adults Working with Young People Experiencing Addiction in the Family. <http://www.samhsa.gov/centers/csat/content/intermediaries>.

————. Substance Abuse and Mental Health Services Administration, Center for Mental Health Services, and National Institutes of Health, National Institute of Mental Health. *Mental Health: A Report From the Surgeon General.* Rockville, Maryland: U.S. Department of Health and Human Services, 1999. <http://www.surgeongeneral.gov/library/mental health/home.html>.

U.S. Department of Housing and Urban Development. "The State of the Cities 2000: Megaforces Shaping the Future of the Nation's Cities."

June 2000. <http://www.hud.gov/library/bookshelf18/pressrel/socrpt. pdf>.

U.S. Department of Justice. Office of Juvenile Justice and Delinquency Programs. "Juvenile Justice and Victims: 1999 National Report." <http://www.ncjrs.org/html/ojjdp/nationalreport99/chapter3.pdf>.

U.S. Department of Labor. Advisory Council on Employee Welfare and Pension Benefit Plans. "Report, Findings, and Recommendations of the Working Group on Long-Term Care." November 14, 2000. <http://www.dol.gov/pwba/adcoun/report2.htm>.

———. Bureau of Labor Statistics. *Report on the American Workforce 2001.* Washington, D.C.: U.S. Government Printing Office, 2001. <http://www. bls.gov/opub/rtaw/rtawhome.htm>.

———."Occupational Employment Statistics." <http://www.bls.gov/oes/ home.htm#tables>.

U.S. Federal Reserve. Statistical Release. "Consumer Credit." 8 July 2002. <http://www.federalreserve.gov/releases/g19/hist/cc_hist_sa.html>.

U.S. Senate Committee on Banking, Housing, and Urban Affairs. *A Financial Education and Literacy Primer.* Report prepared by the majority staff. 107th Cong., 2d sess. 2002.

Vuchinich, Samuel. *Problem Solving in Families.* Thousand Oaks, California: Sage Publications, 1999.

Wachhorst, Wyn. *Thomas Alva Edison: An American Myth.* Cambridge, Massachusetts: MIT Press, 1981.

Wallerstein, Judith S. and Sandra Blakeslee. *The Good Marriage: How and Why Love Lasts.* New York: Warner Books, 1995.

———. *Second Chances: Men, Women, and Children a Decade After Divorce.* New York: Ticknor and Fields, 1989.

Wallerstein, Judith S., Julia M. Lewis, and Sandra Blakeslee. *The Unexpected Legacy of Divorce: A 25 Year Landmark Study.* New York: Hyperion, 2000.

Walsh, Froma. *Strengthening Family Resilience.* New York: The Guilford Press, 1998.

Werner, Emmy E. "Risk, Resilience, and Recovery: Perspectives from the Kauai Longitudinal Study." *Development and Psychopathology* 5 (1993): 503–15.

White, Marsha and Steve Dorman. "Confronting Information Overload." *Journal of School Health* 70, no. 4 (April 2000): 160–61.

Whitehead, Barbara Dafoe and David Popenoe. "Who Wants to Marry a Soul Mate? New Survey Findings on Young Adults' Attitudes about Love and Marriage." *The State of Our Unions: The Social Health of Marriage in America,* 2001. <http://marriage.rutgers.edu/TEXTSOOU2001.htm>.

Wilder Research Center. "Filling the Gaps in Welfare Reform: The Minnesota Welfare-to-Work Partnerships Initiative." August 2001. <http://www.wilder.org/research/reports/pdf/mcknightreport8-01.pdf>.

Williams, Joan. *Unbending Gender: Why Family and Work Conflict and What to do About It*. Oxford: Oxford University Press, 2000.

Woodard, Emory H. IV and Natalia Gridina. "Media in the Home 2000: The Fifth Annual Survey of Parents and Children." 26 June 2000. <http://www.appcpenn.org/mediainhome/survey/survey7.pdf>

Working Women Department, AFL-CIO. "Working Women Say . . ." (2000). <http://www.aflcio.org/women/survey1.htm.>

Young, Lisa R. and Marion Nestle. "The Contribution of Expanding Portion Sized to the U.S. Obesity Epidemic." *American Journal of Public Health* 92, no. 2 (February 2002): 246–49.

Acknowledgments

We want to express first of all our profound gratitude to the families who allowed us to tell their stories in this book. Their willingness to speak so openly was motivated in large part by their hope—which we share—that this book will contribute to a better understanding of what family is all about: how the many changes in our society and culture have affected family, how families can succeed in this new environment, and how our nation can improve their chances for success. The more time we spent with each family, the more our respect for their dedication to one another grew. Each one taught us a great deal, and we thank them from the bottom of our hearts: the Corteses, the Crumptons, the Fadleys, the Hancocks, the Hendersons, the Hoyts, the Letke-Alexanders, the Logans, the Lys, the Nalleys, the Philpotts, the Reddemans, the Robinsons, the Simons-Jacksons, the Strongs, the Wageners, the Wallaces, and Lily Yeh and "The Village."

We are extremely grateful to the talented research team that helped us find and organize the voluminous quantity of information that has been written by scholars on virtually every aspect of the American family. For the better part of two years we have spent so much time working with them that we feel almost like—dare we say?—a family. Before thanking them individually, however, we would like to especially thank their families and loved ones for the support and understanding that made their extraordinary work possible.

Audrey Choi, who assembled and led the research staff, deserves the highest praise for her unwavering perseverance, her creativity, and her dedication throughout this effort. Due to her able leadership, our small staff quickly became an efficient and productive team. She consistently displayed a keen sense of good judgment on a wide range of issues, and we appreciate the ideas and insights she shared during this project. We are equally grateful for her organizational skills, intellectual collaboration, and devotion to the project. We believe, as does everyone who has worked with her, that her future has no limits.

Dan Taylor was unfailingly reliable, hardworking, and entrepreneurial in identifying and evaluating new research and scholarship. He was expert at locating the leading thinkers in virtually every field of inquiry relevant to the study of the family, and tracking key developments and findings. In this project, as in his service in the White House, Dan has been a loyal and invaluable member of our team.

Terry Lumish is a talented researcher, skilled at finding whatever facts we needed, interpreting them, and sorting through them for the ones that were precisely relevant. She was also our numbers expert, mining the bedrock census data along with numerous other data sets we used to trace how the American family has been transformed. We are grateful for her work.

Nathaniel Stankard, a gifted researcher, was a true lifesaver at a critical moment in the final stages of completing the book. He quickly became indispensable. We also want to thank our trusted and hardworking intern, Yinne Yu, whose assistance and team spirit helped us complete the book. Special thanks to Dwayne Kemp, who kept morale high with the best lunches we ever had at any workplace and with his support in so many other ways. Patricia Anderson's volunteer work was also much appreciated.

We would also like to thank the individuals outside the book office who were particularly helpful in our research. Nancy Hoit was invaluable throughout, and we thank her for her friendship and many years of stewardship of the Family Re-Union. Richard Lerner, one of several colleagues in studying families, went far above and beyond what any friend could expect. We thank him for his sage counsel and for sharing the benefit of his encyclopedic knowledge.

We are tremendously grateful to the friends and experts who read our manuscript and gave us the benefit of their expertise and wisdom: Larry Aber, David Beier, Elizabeth Birch, Jim and Dodie Brady, William Dement, Jacquie Lawing Ebert, Marti Erickson, John Kenneth Galbraith, Tom Gegax, John Gottman, Janice Griffin, Neal Halfon, Donald Hernandez, Arlie Hochschild, Reed Hundt, Elaine Kamarck, Peter Knight, Jim Kohlmoos, Steven Ozment, Marty and Anne Peretz, Julian Potter, Robert Putnam, Hilary Rosen, Juliet Schor, Pepper Schwartz, Greg Simon, Graham Spanier, Gene Sperling, Jose Szapocznik, John Tyson, and Maris Vinovskis.

Numerous other experts assisted us in our effort to understand particular aspects of family and community issues. Among those we would like to thank are: Brigitte Berger, Penney Brooks, Chief Jim Bueermann, Frank Gilliam, Jette Halladay, Tamara Harevan, Mavis Hetherington, Larry Howard, Rose Kreider, Anne McGintis, Martha Minow, Steven Mintz, Sheila Peters, Robert Pinsky, Samina Quraeshi, Fred Rothbaum, George Scarlett, Dr. Edward Schor, John Sweeney, Deborah Tannen, Judith Wallerstein, and Edward Zigler.

Our research was made infinitely more productive because of the courtesy, skill, and professionalism of Joanne Jenkins, Charles Stanhope, and other members of the Library of Congress staff. We are grateful to all of them. And thanks to all the folks who run Google, a quantum advance in search technology that we used heavily.

In so many ways, this book is an outgrowth of our eleven years of hosting the Family Re-Union gatherings in Nashville. We would like to thank all the organizations, companies, and institutions that have supported the Family Re-Unions and in the process have given us a chance to learn more about family. They are: A. L. Mailman Foundation, Inc.; A T & T Foundation; Allina Foundation; Annenberg Institute; Annette & Irwin Eskind Family Foundation; Annie E. Casey Foundation; Arthur K. Watson Charitable Trust; Augusta Clarke Trust; Baptist Hospital, Inc.; Baptist Memorial Health Care Foundation; Barbara R. Jordan Trust; Baruch Family Fund; Benton Foundation; Charles and Marjorie Benton; Bernard van Leer Foundation; California Endowment; Carlisle Foundation; Charles Stewart Mott Foundation; Citibank; Citigroup Foundation; Columbia/HCA Healthcare Corporation; Danforth Foundation; David and Lucile Packard Foundation; Eli Lilly and Company; FHC Health Systems; First Hospital Corporation Private Foundation; Ford Foundation; Foundations; Inc.; GTE; Gruber Family Foundation; Guilford Mills; Inc.; Harlken Foundation; Harmon Foundation; Benjamin Heineman, Jr.; Hitachi Foundation; Hulda B. and Maurice L. Rothschild Foundation; Isaac & Carol Auerbach Family Foundation; Iscol Family Foundation; Jane & Richard Eskind & Family Foundation; Johnson City Medical Center; Julie & Peter Cummings Philanthropic Fund; Laura S. and Jonathan M. Tisch Foundation; Martha and Bronson Ingram Foundation; Nathan Cummings Foundation; Lucent Technologies Foundation; John D. and Catherine T. McArthur Foundation; Meharry Medical College; Metropolitan Nashville General Hospital; Minneapolis Foundation; Mountain States Health Alliance; New Balance Athletic Shoe; Inc.; New Kalman Sunshine Fund; Inc.; Olan Mills; Omiydar Foundation; PaineWebber Group; Inc.; Progressive Foundation; Richard & Hinda Rosenthal Foundation; Robert Green Stephen and Myrna Greenberg Philanthropic Fund of the Jewish Communal Fund; Robert Wood Johnson Foundation; Saint Thomas Health Services; Mr. and Mrs. Eugene Stetson III; TCF Financial Management;

Tennessee State University; Vanderbilt University & Medical Center; W. K. Kellogg Foundation; W. T. Grant Foundation; William J. and Dorothy K. O'Neill Foundation; Work/Family Directions; and Xerox Foundation.

We would like to thank as a group all of the faculty members who have been a part of the twenty-university consortium sponsoring Al's course, "Family Centered Community Building," especially Neal Halfon at UCLA, Faye Johnson at Middle Tennessee State University, Sheila Peters at Fisk University, and Larry Aber at Columbia University. And we owe special thanks to Jacquie Lawing Ebert and Lisa Berg for their roles in coordinating communication and joint work projects with the group.

We would also like to thank all the university student research interns from Fisk, MTSU, UCLA, Columbia, Vanderbilt, and Belmont who assisted in our wide-ranging exploration of issues of importance to the family. We especially thank Kevin Coyne, Shanavia Dansby, Andre Fresco, Tony Gross, Lemika Hays, Jorie Henrickson, Antisha Partee, Autumn Spanne, Rochelle Szuba, and Cara Vallier.

We are thankful to Lisa Brown and Lauren Field for their legal advice, and to Bob Jones and Debra Shaver for their accounting and bookkeeping help. We also want to thank Danny and Paul Abramson of Abramson Properties, our friendly landlords, and their staff: Kathi Lynch, Karan Hinton, and Dave Dewhirst. Special thanks to Cinzia Ramundo and Carlo Pascarella, whose La Piazza restaurant was fortunately just one floor below us, and to St. Elmo's Coffeehouse, whose beverages kept us going.

Our multitalented agent, Andrew Wylie, not only helped us place this project with the right publisher, but also gave us invaluable advice at every step in the process, and we thank him and his staff, especially Lisa Halliday.

And we are once again greatly indebted to our editor, John Sterling, for his extraordinary—indeed, we believe, unique—skill in shepherding the transformation of an idea into a manuscript and then into a book. We say "again" because each of us had the privilege of working with John previously—a history that greatly simplified what we had been told by others would be the difficult challenge of being coauthors. Instead, it was fun. John believed in this book from the start, and it certainly would never have become a reality without him. We also want to express particular gratitude to Jennifer Barth, who contributed her outstanding editing skills, especially in the critical early stages. We want to thank as well Maggie Richards, Elizabeth Shreve, Kenn Russell, Marcy Beller, and Ruth Kaplan. And special thanks to Mindy Werner.

Finally, although there are no words that can ever express the love and thanks to God we feel for our family, we thank them for their help and patience and active collaboration in making this book possible.

Index

Entries in *italics* refer to photographs.

About the Authors

AL GORE is the former Vice President of the United States and the author of the *New York Times* bestseller *Earth in the Balance*. During twenty-five years of public service, he has made the family a priority by working for new solutions that address the needs of families and communities. He is now a professor at both Fisk University and Middle Tennessee State University, where he teaches "Family Centered Community Building."

TIPPER GORE is an advocate for mental health awareness and served as an Advisor to the President on Mental Health Policy from 1993 to 2001. She worked as a photojournalist for *The Tennessean* and published a collection of her photographs, *Picture This*, in 1996. Her first book, *Raising PG Kids in an X-Rated Society*, addressed the challenges families faced in the new media environment and was published in 1987.

For the past eleven years, the Gores have organized an annual two-day forum called Family Re-Union. They have four children and two grandchildren and live in Nashville, Tennessee.